D0562326

RISK AND RATIONALITY

RISK AND RATIONALITY

Philosophical Foundations for Populist Reforms

K. S. SHRADER-FRECHETTE

UNIVERSITY OF CALIFORNIA PRESS
BERKELEY   LOS ANGELES   OXFORD

Ledl
Circ
T
174.5
S
482
1991

University of California Press
Berkeley and Los Angeles, California

University of California Press, Ltd.
Oxford, England

© 1991 by
The Regents of the University of California

Library of Congress Cataloging-in-Publication Data

Shrader-Frechette, K. S., 1944–
    Risk and rationality : philosophical foundations for populist
reforms / Kristin Shrader-Frechette.
        p.   cm.
    Includes bibliographical references and index.
    ISBN 0-520-07287-1. — ISBN 0-520-07289-8 (pbk.)
    1. Risk assessment.   2. Risk—Social aspects.   I. Title
T174.5.S482   1991
363.1—dc20   91-3294
                                                  CIP

Printed in the United States of America
9 8 7 6 5 4 3 2 1

The paper used in this publication meets the minimum requirements of
American National Standard for Information Sciences—Permanence of Paper
for Printed Library Materials, ANSI Z39.48-1984. ∞

727848

For Marie

Contents

Acknowledgments

Much of the work in this volume originated as a result of research supported by the National Science Foundation under Grant SES82–05112 from the Program in History and Philosophy of Science and the Division of Policy Research and Analysis. Any opinions expressed in this book, however, are mine and do not necessarily reflect the views of the National Science Foundation.

Several of the chapters are better than they might have been, thanks to the lively exchanges provided by speaking invitations at a number of universities. During two series of invited lectures at the University of California, Berkeley (the first in March 1987 and the second in March 1988), I presented earlier versions of seven of the twelve chapters. I am grateful to the Energy and Resources Group (ERG) at Berkeley (especially John Harte, John Holdren, and Robert Sawyer) for providing the opportunity for these lecture series. Much of the material in the book has also been improved as a result of invited lectures presented at the AAAS meetings in Los Angeles; Baker University; Battelle Laboratories in Seattle; the Universities of British Columbia, Colorado, Guelph (Ontario), New Hampshire, North Carolina, and Notre Dame; as well as Oberlin College; Virginia Polytechnic and State University; Western Behavioral Sciences Institute in La Jolla; and Williams College. Earlier versions of parts of Chapters Five, Seven, and Eight were published, respectively, in *IEEE Spectrum, Energy Policy Studies*, and *Ethics*.

Since this volume includes philosophy of science, applied ethics, and policy analysis, it relies on insights from a variety of disciplines important to environmental risk assessment. Although my main debt is to philosophers, I am also grateful to a number of colleagues from law, engineering, mathematics, epidemiology, and sociology, as well as philosophy; the following persons have criticized oral presentations or earlier drafts of one or more of the chapters: Robert Almeder, Robert Bartlett, Robert Baum, Mike Bayles, Ed Byrne, Stan Carpenter, Paul Durbin, Tom Field, Ron Giere, Don Hatcher, R. M. Hare, Rachelle Hollander, Jim Humber, Paul Humphreys, Deborah Mayo, Alex Michalos, Carl Mitcham, Elizabeth Peele, Joe Pitt, Steve Rayner, Martin Schniederman, Tom Settle, Steve Unger, and Jeff Witmer. Whatever errors remain are my responsibility.

Dan Wigley, Ken Wilkinson, Glenn McClister, and Mike Kelly have done excellent work as research and editorial assistants for this book. I look forward to their continuing work in philosophy and to seeing publications of their own some day. I am also grateful to the excellent referees and editors of the University of California Press, especially Ernest Callenbach, Mark Jacobs, and Dorothy Conway. Thanks also to the University of South Florida for giving me a distinguished professorship that enabled me to spend much of my time in research.

My greatest debt is to my husband, Maurice, the brightest and most loving critic of my work, and to our children, Eric and Danielle. They make everything worthwhile.

University of South Florida   K. S. S.-F.
Tampa, Florida
May 1990

Part One

Introduction

Chapter One

Risk and Rationality

Guerrilla action and political unrest are not limited to places like El Salvador, Nicaragua, or Angola. In Michigan, for example, local residents put nails and tacks on their highways to prevent the state from burying cattle contaminated by polybrominated biphenyls. In New Jersey, citizens took public officials hostage when they were excluded from decisionmaking regarding a hazardous waste facility in their neighborhood. And in Illinois, townspeople halted the operation of a landfill by digging trenches across its access roads.[1]

Citizen protests such as these have resulted, in part, from the perceived failure of government and industry to protect the health and safety of the people. Acts of civil disobedience, in turn, have also helped to mobilize public awareness of a variety of environmental risks. For example, 75 percent of residents recently surveyed in Santa Clara County, California, charged that their water was "unsafe to drink" after they discovered chemical contamination in three local public wells.[2] More generally, a recent poll sponsored by the Council on Environmental Quality and funded by Resources for the Future found that only 10 to 12 percent of the U.S. population would voluntarily live a mile or less from a nuclear power plant or hazardous waste facility.[3] As a result, some communities are trying to discourage the establishment of treatment or storage facilities for chemical wastes; they are charging up to $100,000 for permit application fees.[4]

Hazardous waste facilities are not the only environmental risks repeatedly rejected by the public. In Delaware, Shell Oil was forced to leave the state in order to find a refinery site. And Alumax abandoned Oregon after a ten-year controversy over the siting of an aluminum-smelting plant. Likewise, Dow Chemical Company gave up its proposed petrochemical-complex site on the Sacramento River in California, after spending $4.5 million in a futile attempt to gain the required approvals. In fact, in the last ten years, approximately 50 percent of attempted sitings of oil refineries have failed because of public opposition. Likewise, no large metropolitan airport has been sited in the United States since the Dallas–Fort Worth facility was built in the early 1960s.[5] In a similar vein, there have been no new U.S. commercial orders for nuclear plants since 1974.[6] Although the government predicted in 1973 that the United States would have one thousand commercial reactors by the year 2000, citizen opposition and rising costs make it unlikely that the country will have even two hundred of the plants.[7]

Aversion to Risks: Public Paranoia or Technological Oppression?

Industry spokespersons attribute the blocking of oil refineries, nuclear reactors, and toxic waste dumps to public ignorance and mass paranoia. They charge that misguided and irrational citizens have successfully delayed so many technological facilities, driving up their costs, that wise investors now avoid them.[8]

Pete Seeger, however, has another story. He and the members of the Clamshell Alliance, as well as many other environmental and consumer activists, would claim that, just as the people created the moral victories won by the civil rights movements and the Vietnam protests, so also the people have successfully challenged potential technological oppressors. In their view, just as the people rejected a war fought without their free, informed consent, they also are rejecting public environmental risks likewise imposed on them without their free, informed consent. For them, to delay or stop construction of risky industrial facilities is a great moral triumph for populist democracy.

Industry sympathizers do not agree. They claim that laypersons' aversion to societal risks stems not so much from any real or apparent danger, such as toxic waste contamination, but from group attitudes that are anti-industry, antigovernment, and antiscience. They charge that the paranoid, neo-Luddite baby boomers who now dominate the environmental movement cut their political teeth during the Vietnam-era protests and then went on to become Yuppie lawyers, professors, and social workers. Holding their earlier political beliefs, they have merely transferred their activism from military to environmental issues. Thus, Pete Seeger now sings about "nukes," not "Nam." And Seeger's hair has turned gray, while the baby boomers long ago cut theirs, probably for an important job interview.[9]

Who is right? Is public aversion to societal risks caused by mass

paranoia and ignorance of science? Or by yet another form of oppression inflicted by "big industry," "big technology," and "big government"? Not surprisingly, I shall argue that the correct answer lies
between these two extremes. Despite a regrettable and widespread ignorance of science, nevertheless environmentalism is not merely the
product of an irrational "construct." Despite rampant technological
illiteracy, irrationality is not the sole explanation of typical public aversion to involuntarily imposed societal risks. Likewise, it cannot account
for widespread distrust of technologies having the potential to cause
catastrophic accidents and increased cancers.

The main purpose of this volume is to sketch a middle path between
the industrial charges of scientific illiteracy and the populist charges
of technological oppression. In so doing, I shall argue for an alternative
approach to contemporary, *societally imposed* risks. My focus is not on
personally chosen risks, like diet drinks or oral contraceptives, since each
of us is able to avoid such hazards. If my analysis is correct, then we
need a new "paradigm," a new account of when the acceptance of public
hazards is rational. We also need to recognize that laypersons are often
more rational, in their evaluation of societal risks, than either experts
or governments appear to have recognized.

The Rise of Risk Assessment and Evaluation

As Chapter Four will explain in greater detail, government and industry
experts perform most risk or hazard assessments. Their analyses include three main stages: (1) *identification* of some public or societal
hazard; (2) *estimation* of the level and extent of potential harm associated
with it; and (3) *evaluation* of the acceptability of the danger, relative to
other hazards.[10] (Most of the discussion in this volume will focus on
the third stage, *risk evaluation*.) Once assessors have completed these
three assessment tasks, policymakers then determine the best way to
accomplish *risk management* of a particular public threat—for example,
through regulation, prohibition, or taxation.

As a specific tool for societal decisionmaking, risk or hazard analysis
is relatively new. Although Mesopotamian priests, before the time of
Christ, regularly evaluated the impacts of proposed technological projects, risk assessment as a "developing science" did not arise until the
late 1960s and the early 1970s.[11] Public concern about the human and
environmental risks of thousands of technologies arose in part because
of tragedies like Love Canal and because of works like Rachel Carson's
Silent Spring.[12] Another important milestone in raising environmental
consciousness was the Club of Rome's famous 1972 report, *Limits to*

Growth. It predicted global human, economic, and environmental catastrophe in the twenty-first century unless we were able to stop exponential increases in pollution, resource depletion, population, and production.[13]

Widespread worries about impending environmental catastrophe and a rapidly increasing cancer rate were evident as early as 1969, as evidenced by the passage of the U.S. National Environmental Policy Act (NEPA), "the Magna Carta of environmental protection."[14] NEPA required, among other things, that all federal agencies prepare an environmental impact statement (EIS) every time they considered a proposal for federal actions significantly affecting the quality of the environment.

In addition to the passage of NEPA, much risk-analysis effort also arose as a direct consequence of the creation of new federal agencies, such as the Occupational Safety and Health Administration (OSHA). Pressured by growing public concern about environmental risks, and faced with approximately 100,000 occupation-induced fatalities per year,[15] the United States created OSHA in 1970. Many of the first hazard assessments—for example, regarding asbestos—were done under the direction of OSHA or other federal regulatory agencies, such as the Food and Drug Administration (FDA) and the Nuclear Regulatory Commission (NRC).

One of the main difficulties with risk assessments done in the 1970s and 1980s, however, was that there were inadequate standards for the practice of this new set of techniques. As a consequence, some hazards, such as carcinogens, were being monitored and regulated very stringently, whereas others, equally dangerous, were evaluated more leniently. To help address these methodological inconsistencies and regulatory difficulties, in 1982 the U.S. Congress passed the Risk Analysis Research and Demonstration Act (RARADA). This bill established a program, under the coordination of the Office of Science and Technology Policy, to help perfect the use of hazard assessment by federal agencies concerned with regulatory decisions related to the protection of human life, health, and the environment.[16] Numerous risk assessors, prior to the RARADA, bemoaned the fact that government safety regulations for the automobile industry, for example, presupposed an expenditure of $30,000 for the life of each automobile passenger saved, whereas analogous government regulations for the steel industry presupposed an expenditure of $5 million for the life of each steelworker saved.[17]

Despite the passage of the RARADA, however, quantitative risk assessment is still practiced in somewhat divergent ways; for example, the monetized "value of life" presupposed by government regulations (and used at the third, or *evaluation*, stage of assessment) varies dramatically from one federal agency to another.[18] This value, in turn, has a great effect on the acceptability judgments associated with various risks, particularly if the evaluation is accomplished in a benefit-cost framework. Even for the same hazard, risk analyses often do not agree, in part because there are many ways to evaluate harms at the third stage of assessment. There are many ways to answer the question "How much risk (in a given area) is socially, politically, economically, and ethically acceptable?" Hazard evaluations often contradict one another, not only because scientists frequently dispute the relevant facts but also because policymakers and the public disagree about what responses to risk are rational. Some persons claim that only *technical experts* are capable of making rational judgments about risk acceptability, whereas others assert that only potential victims, usually *laypeople*, are in a position to be truly rational about evaluation of possible hazards.

"Rationality" in Risk Evaluation and Philosophy of Science

'Rational', however, is a highly normative term. Controversies about the "rationality" of various evaluations of risk are no easier to settle than analogous debates in science. Conflicts among philosophers of science (about what methodological rules, if any, guarantee the rationality of science) generate alternative accounts of scientific explanation, as well as disputes over which scientific theory is correct. Likewise, conflicts among risk assessors (about what methodological rules, if any, guarantee the rationality of responses to hazards) generate both alternative accounts of acceptable harm and disputes over whose risk-evaluation theory is correct.

In the debate over the rationality of science, philosophers and scientists are arrayed on a spectrum extending from pluralist or relativist views to logical-empiricist positions. At the left end of the spectrum, the pluralist end, are epistemological anarchist Paul Feyerabend and others who believe that there is no scientific method, that "anything goes," and that "no system of [scientific] rules and standards is ever safe."[19] At the other end of the spectrum are logical empiricists, such as Israel Scheffler and Rudolf Carnap, who believe that there are at least some universal and fixed criteria for theory choice and that these criteria guarantee the rationality of science.[20] Somewhere in the middle, between the relativists and the logical empiricists, are the so-called naturalists, such as Dudley Shapere, Larry Laudan, and Ronald Giere. They maintain that theory evaluation can be rational even though there are no absolute rules for science, applicable in every situation.[21]

The challenge, for any philosopher of science who holds some sort of middle position (between the relativists and the logical empiricists), is to show precisely how theory choice or theory evaluation can be rational, even though there are no universal, absolute rules of scientific method that apply to every situation. Perhaps the dominant issue in contemporary philosophy of science is whether, and if so how, one can successfully develop and defend some sort of naturalistic middle position, as Larry Laudan, Ronald Giere, and Thomas Kuhn, for example, have tried to do.[22]

An analogous problem faces the hazard evaluator trying to articulate a middle position. In the debate over what methodological norms, if any, guarantee the rationality of risk evaluation, analysts are arrayed on a spectrum extending from the relativists to the naive positivists. At the left end of the spectrum are the cultural relativists,[23] such as anthropologist Mary Douglas and political scientist Aaron Wildavsky. They believe that "risks are social constructs," that "any form of life can be justified. . . . no one is to say that any one is better or worse,"[24] that there is "no correct description of the right behavior [regarding risks],"[25] and therefore that the third stage of risk assessment, risk evaluation, is wholly relative.[26] At the other, naive-positivist, end of the spectrum are engineers such as Chauncey Starr and Christopher Whipple. They maintain that risk evaluation is objective in the sense that *different* risks may be evaluated according to the *same* rule—for example, a rule stipulating that risks below a certain level of probability are insignificant.[27] They also claim that risk assessment, at least at the stage of calculating probabilities associated with harms and estimating their effects, is completely objective, neutral, and value free.[28] In their view, the objectivity of risk identification and estimation guarantees the rationality of specific evaluations of various hazards.

The challenge, for any risk evaluator who holds some sort of middle position (between the cultural relativists and the naive positivists), is to show how risk evaluation (the third stage of assessment) can be rational and objective, even though there are no completely value-free rules applicable to every risk-evaluation situation. My purpose in this volume is (1) to articulate why and how both the cultural relativists and the naive positivists err in their general accounts of risk evaluation; (2) to explain the misconceptions in a number of specific risk-evaluation strategies allegedly deemed "rational"; and (3) to argue for a "middle position" on the methodological spectrum of views about how to guarantee the rationality of risk evaluation. I call this middle position "scientific proceduralism," and I defend it by means of arguments drawn from analogous debates over naturalism in contemporary philosophy of science.

Outline of the Chapters:
Risk Evaluation Is Both Scientific and Democratic

In Chapter Two, "Science against the People," I introduce the problem of conflict over rational evaluations of risk. Specifically, I show how the cultural relativists and the naive positivists have wrongly dismissed lay evaluations of risk as irrational. The bulk of this chapter focuses on faulty epistemological assumptions underlying relativist and naive-positivist arguments about risk evaluation.

After defusing these arguments against "the people," in Chapter Three ("Rejecting Reductionist Risk Evaluation") I analyze in greater detail the two most basic risk frameworks out of which such antipopulist arguments arise. I show that both of these frameworks, naive positivism and cultural relativism, err in being reductionistic. The cultural relativists attempt to reduce risk to a *sociological* construct, underestimating or dismissing its *scientific* components. The naive positivists attempt to reduce risk to a purely *scientific* reality, underestimating or dismissing its *ethical* components. I argue that the sociological reductionists err in *overemphasizing* the role of values in risk evaluation, whereas the scientific reductionists err in *underemphasizing* the role of ethical values and democratic procedure in risk evaluation.

Because locating the flaws in accounts of rational risk evaluation comes down to clarifying the appropriate role of *values* at the third stage of hazard assessment, Chapters Four and Five attempt to provide a general overview of the various evaluative assumptions that are integral to all three stages of risk analysis. Chapter Four ("Objectivity and Values in Risk Evaluation") shows that—despite the presence of cognitive or methodological value judgments, even in pure science—science itself is *objective* in several important senses. After outlining the value judgments that arise in the three stages of risk assessment (risk identification, risk estimation, and risk evaluation), the chapter presents a case study from the field of energy studies. The case study shows how alternative value judgments at the first two stages of assessment can lead to radically different policy conclusions (third stage) regarding hazard acceptability.

Chapter Five ("Five Dilemmas of Risk Evaluation") shows how epistemic value judgments arise in the more scientific stages of risk assessment (viz., risk identification and estimation). It sketches some analogous difficulties arising at the third, or risk-evaluation, stage. It argues not only that methodological value judgments are unavoidable in risk evaluation, but also that the judgments often pose both methodological and ethical dilemmas, problems for which there are no zerocost solutions. Chapters in the last section of the volume (Part Three) argue that these five dilemmas raise troubling ethical questions and thus provide a basis for improving hazard evaluation.

Whereas the first part of the book (Chapters One through Five) provides an overview of risk analysis and evaluation and a discussion of the flaws in the two most *general* accounts of hazard evaluation, Part Two of the book (Chapters Six through Ten) addresses more *specific* difficulties in risk evaluation. Each chapter in Part Two evaluates a questionable methodological strategy common in various methods of risk evaluation.

Chapter Six, "Perceived Risk and the Expert-Judgment Strategy," argues that risk assessors' tendencies to distinguish "perceived risk" from "actual risk" are partially misguided. Typically, they claim that only "actual risk" (usually defined by experts as an average annual probability of fatality) is objective, whereas "perceived risk" (based merely on the feelings and opinions of laypersons) is subjective. I argue that both "perceived risk" and "actual risk" are partially subjective, since both involve value judgments. Further, I suggest that the evaluation stage of risk assessment will be more successful if analysts do not overemphasize the distinction between perceived and actual risk. Instead, they should focus on mediating ethical conflicts between experts and laypeople over risk evaluation.

Continuing in a similar vein, Chapter Seven also identifies a problematic strategy associated with the attempt to define risk in a largely quantitative way. This chapter, "Democracy and the Probabilistic Strategy," attacks two common methodological assumptions about risk evaluation. One is that risk abatement ought to be directed at the hazards to which persons are most averse. The other is that risk aversion ought to be evaluated as directly proportional to the probability of fatality associated with a particular hazard. After arguing against this probabilistic strategy, I show that other, nonprobabilistic criteria for risk evaluation (equity of risk distribution, for example) are equally plausible, in part because accurate knowledge of probabilities is sometimes difficult to obtain. If one employs these other criteria, I argue, one can conclude that technical experts should not be the only persons chosen to evaluate risks and therefore dictate which societal hazards are acceptable. Control of risk *evaluation* needs to become more democratic.

Chapter Eight, "Uncertainty and the Utilitarian Strategy," argues that, in many risk evaluations, it is more reasonable to pursue a "maximin" strategy, as most laypersons request, rather than the utilitarian (or Bayesian) strategy used by most experts. The main argument of this chapter is that, in situations of uncertainty, Bayesian accounts of risk evaluation are often unable to provide for considerations of equity and democratic process.

Chapter Nine, "Uncertainty and the Producer Strategy," addresses another problematic method of risk evaluation, one closely related to Bayesianism. The chapter asks whether, in a situation of uncertainty, one ought to implement a technology that is environmentally unsafe but not recognized as such (thereby running a "consumer risk") or fail to implement a technology that is environmentally safe but not recognized to be so (a "producer risk"). In cases of doubt, on whose side ought one to err? Chapter Nine argues that there are scientific, ethical, and legal grounds for minimizing consumer risk and maximizing producer risk, especially in cases of uncertainty.

Just as experts tend to overemphasize producer risk and underemphasize consumer risk, they also tend to discount hazards that are spatially or temporally distant. Because of this "discounting" tendency, risk assessors in developed countries often ignore the hazards their nation imposes on those in underdeveloped areas. I call this tendency the "isolationist strategy." Chapter Ten, "Third-World Risks and the Isolationist Strategy," argues that this risk-evaluation strategy is unethical.

Discussion of the isolationist strategy in Chapter Ten marks the end of the second part of the volume. Although this second section criticizes several of the problematic risk-evaluation methods (such as the probabilistic strategy, the Bayesian strategy, and the isolationist strategy) employed both by contemporary hazard assessors and by moral philosophers, it provides neither a technical nor an exhaustive account of all the questionable risk-evaluation methodologies.[29] Instead, its purpose is both to provide an overview of representative risk-evaluation errors (the strategies criticized in Part Two) and to cast doubt on the thesis that expert assessment dictates the only risk evaluations that are 'rational'. Instead, rational risk evaluation and behavior may be more widely defined than has been supposed. And if so, there are grounds for doubting experts' claims that lay responses to, and evaluations of, societal risks are irrational.

Together, the chapters in the first and second sections of the volume provide an overview of much of what is wrong with contemporary hazard assessment and with allegedly rational risk evaluation. The purpose of the third section is to sketch some solutions to the problems outlined in the two earlier parts of the book. Chapter Eleven, "Risk Evaluation: Methodological Reforms," makes a number of specific suggestions in this regard. It begins by offering an alternative risk-evaluation paradigm, "scientific proceduralism." According to this paradigm, risk evaluation is *procedural* in that it ought to be guided by democratic processes and ethical principles. It is *scientific* or "objective" in at least three senses: (1) It can be the subject of rational debate and criticism. (2) It is partially dependent on probabilities that can be affected by empirical events. (3) It can be criticized in terms of how well it serves the scientific end or goal of *explaining* and *predicting* hazardous events and persons' responses to them.

After arguing that risk evaluation is largely objective, because it is based in part on *probabilities*, and because it is assessed on the basis of its *explanatory and predictive power*, I also argue that risk evaluation ought to be defined in terms of social and ethical values. Explaining how risk evaluation can be both objective and evaluative, Chapter Eleven outlines a number of specific suggestions for methodological improvements in hazard evaluation—for example, the use of ethically weighted risk-cost-benefit analysis (RCBA) and the ranking of experts' risk opinions on the basis of their past successful predictions. The chapter also substantiates the claim that hazard assessment—although burdened both with reductionist definitions of risk (Chapter Three) and with a number of biased methodological strategies (Chapters Six through Ten)—is *objective* in important ways. Hence, it makes sense to continue to use quantified risk analysis (QRA). That is, although *in practice* problems of risk evaluation have led to poor policy, *in principle* they are capable of being solved by means of improved risk-evaluation methods and more participatory styles of hazard management.

Having considered the methodological solutions to some of the difficulties with QRA and risk *evaluation*, I conclude by addressing certain procedural and institutional reforms needed to make risk *management* more rational. Chapter Twelve, "Risk Management: Procedural Reforms," argues that, consistent with a more naturalized view of all knowledge, we must place less emphasis on whose hazard evaluations are correct or incorrect and instead focus on negotiating workable risk-management principles and practices. In addition, we ought to make use of several insights from medical ethics, such as requiring free, informed consent prior to imposing risks; guaranteeing legal rights to due process and compensation for all unavoidable risks and harms; and applying the theory of "market share liability," as in the celebrated DES case.

These chapters come nowhere close, of course, to providing a complete explanation of what makes a risk evaluation rational. This account does not pretend to be complete, in part because the problems of risk evaluation are too numerous to be treated in a single, nontechnical volume, and in part because I attempted (as far as possible) to avoid repeating analyses given in my earlier works.[30] These chapters will have accomplished their modest aim if they enable us to be more critical of existing attempts to define "risk evaluation" in highly stipulative and question-begging ways. They will have taken us in the right direction if they teach us to be suspicious whenever someone gratuitously attributes motives and causes to those allegedly exhibiting "irrational" risk evaluations. They will have helped us if they encourage us to consider alternative models of rationality and to remember that chronic errors in risk-evaluation heuristics are not limited to laypeople alone.[31] This being so, determining when a risk evaluation is rational is as much the prerogative of the people as of the experts. Science need not co-opt democracy.

Chapter Two

Science against the People

Claiming that they were a source of syphilis infection, the U.S. Navy removed doorknobs from a number of battleships during World War I.[1] Like many members of the nonscientific public, even the military shared in the "hysteria" over venereal infection during the first two decades of this century. Although the fear of doorknobs was misplaced, worries about venereal disease were not completely irrational. As late as 1910, about 25 percent of all blind persons in the United States had lost their sight through venereal insontium, blindness of the newborn.[2] Today, instead of venereal disease, AIDS is perhaps the greater object of public fear and ignorance. Florida legislators tried (unsuccessfully) to have students with AIDS kept out of the classroom,[3] and hospital workers in North Carolina, fearing contamination, put a living AIDS victim in a body bag reserved for corpses.[4]

Given such behavior, it is not surprising that scientists have often accused nonscientists of irrational fears concerning public health and safety. Recently, for example, the U.S. Department of Energy awarded $85,000 to a Washington psychiatrist to help "counter the public's 'irrational fear' about nuclear power." Robert L. DuPont, a former director of the National Institute on Drug Abuse, received the funds for a study described as "an attempt to demonstrate that opponents of nuclear power are mentally ill." DuPont says that he will study unhealthy fear, a phobia that is a denial of reality.[5]

Citizens who fear public-health or environmental hazards, however, would probably claim that their concerns are both realistic and justified. After all, AIDS cases are currently doubling every six months.[6] And with respect to nuclear power, December 1989 government reports indicate that the cancer risk from radiation is three to four times higher than previously thought.[7] Environmentalists also continue to point out that a Chernobyl type of accident could happen in the United States.

14

The U.S. government itself concluded that a catastrophic core melt could wipe out an area the size of Pennsylvania and kill 145,000 people.[8] According to many citizens, if such accidents were as unlikely as industry and government claim, then nuclear utilities would not need the Price-Anderson Act; this U.S. law limits the liability of reactor operators to $640 million—less than 1 percent of all total possible losses and far below the estimated cleanup for either Three Mile Island or Chernobyl. Since industry maintains that it does need the liability limit, in order to protect itself against bankruptcy, environmentalists conclude that catastrophic accidents must be likely.[9] And if such accidents are likely, then opponents of nuclear power are not necessarily mentally ill or irrationally fearful.[10]

Consumer activists maintain that there are indeed real environmental hazards, and that people are often reasonable in fearing them. These activists are wary, for example, of many current pesticides. They note that, according to a National Academy of Sciences report, 60 percent (by weight) of all herbicides used in the United States can cause tumors in animals, as can 90 percent (by volume) of all fungicides and 30 percent (by volume) of all insecticides.[11] Environmentalists also point out that rational people are likewise afraid of hazards such as depletion of ozone, the shield protecting life on earth from the sun's harmful ultraviolet radiation.[12]

Attacks on the Public's Aversion to Risk

At least three groups of persons maintain that citizens' worries about environmental risks, from carcinogenic pesticides to loss of global ozone, are typically biased or irrational: (1) industry spokespersons, (2) risk assessors, and (3) a small group of contemporary, antipopulist social scientists. All three have attacked the environmental fears of laypeople. Industry spokesperson Edith Efron, for example, maintains that both citizens and scientists have been corrupted by ideology. She says that the ideology takes the form of attempting to incriminate industry in the name of "cancer prevention." The politics of citizens, she says, derive from "warring attitudes toward the American industrial system." In Efron's view, most persons who fear environmental hazards (such as alleged carcinogens and nuclear power) are irrational because their concern is dictated not by the facts about risk but by their paranoid and primitive "fantasies" about "industrial mass murder."[13]

Risk assessors, often experts in the employ of industries responsible for the hazardous technologies they are paid to evaluate, constitute a second class of persons critical of alleged citizen "irrationality." Norman

Rasmussen and Christopher Whipple, for example, each authors of famous risk analyses, have accused the public of "inconsistency" in its attitudes toward hazards.[14] In their view, people who travel by automobile and, at the same time, oppose commercial nuclear fission are inconsistent, because they accept a large risk but reject an allegedly smaller one. Other hazard assessors claim that, if laypeople understood the relevant mathematics involved in calculating risk probabilities, they would no longer have "pathologic fear" of contemporary technologies like atomic energy. In other words, risk assessors claim that there are few rational reasons for fearing existing environmental threats, and that public concern is primarily a matter either of irrationality or of ignorance.[15]

A minority group of contemporary, antipopulist social scientists constitutes the third main camp of persons who are critical of lay evaluations of technological and environmental risks. Perhaps the most famous members of this group are anthropologist Mary Douglas and political scientist Aaron Wildavsky. Although their individual views are somewhat different, they are coauthors of a best-selling book, *Risk and Culture*.[16] In his *Searching for Safety* and in the coauthored *Risk and Culture*, Wildavsky argues, just as Weinberg does, that Americans are biased, witch-hunting opponents of technology. He and Douglas claim that laypersons ("sectarians" not at the center of industrial or governmental power) are dominated by "superstitions" about environmental risks and by fundamentalist desires for unrealistic environmental "purity." Like Hoyle, Fremlin, Weinberg, Thompson, and other critics, they allege that these contemporary "superstitions" and "biases" of contemporary environmentalists are no different in kind from those of pre-scientific, primitive people.[17]

Admitting that they have a "bias toward the center,"[18] Wildavsky, Douglas, and others (such as Efron and Thompson) claim that "America is a border country," a nation whose citizens, in general, are "sectarians" who reject the technological and environmental risks imposed by those at the economic and political "center" of the nation.[19] They identify Americans, in general, as environmentalists and sectists. Hence, when they attack U.S. *environmentalists and sectarians*, they are attacking the U.S. lay *public* as a whole.

Numerous industry spokespersons, engineers, hazard assessors, and natural and social scientists tend to use at least five basic arguments to attack the societal risk evaluations of laypersons: (1) Laypeople, the "border" citizens, are anti-industry and antigovernment and are obsessed with environmental impurity. (2) Laypeople are removed from centers of influence and power, and therefore attack the risks chosen by those who are at the "center." (3) Laypeople are unreasonably averse to risks because they fear things that are unlikely to occur, and they are unwilling to learn from their mistakes. (4) Laypeople are irrationally averse to risks because they do not realize that life is getting safer. (5) Laypeople have unrealistic expectations about safety and make excessive demands on the market and on hierarchies of power.[20]

Not all those with antipopulist risk views are consistently antisectarian.[21] Douglas, for example, is not antisectarian in some of her other works.[22] However, in *Risk and Culture*, Douglas and Wildavsky specifically admit that they are biased in favor of centrists (nonsectarians; those with market and hierarchical views); Wildavsky makes the same admission in his *Searching for Safety*.[23] Apart from whether Thompson, Wildavsky, or Douglas, for example, gives an *antisectarian* account of risk *aversion*, it is clear that many other risk writers do so (for example, Maxey, Cohen and Lee, Whipple, Weinberg, Rothschild, Hoyle, Efron, and Fremlin). Hence, the five arguments, apart from their specifics, represent paradigmatic attacks on lay evaluations of societal risk. Because they are representative, it is important to assess them.[24]

Is the Public Anti-Industry?

Antipopulist risk writers argue that the environmental movement (and therefore the public) is antiscience, antitechnology, and anti-industry. Their evidence for this claim is that environmentalists (such as Epstein) link cancer to the profit motive; Samuels attributes it to industrial "cannibalism," and Ralph Nader calls it "corporate cancer."[25] Others claim that public concern about societal and technological risk is largely evidence of a recurrent "cultural bias" manifested in "criticism of industry." They maintain, for example, that—just as members of the Lele tribe of Zaire face highly probable risks of leprosy and ulcers, but irrationally choose to focus on the much less likely hazard of being struck by lightning—contemporary Americans face highly probable harm from fires and from leisure-time sunburn but focus instead on technology-created risks, such as those from pesticides. According to these antipopulist risk writers, "hazards are selected for public concern according to the strength and direction of social criticism," especially criticism of industry, not according to their inherent danger. Weinberg, for example, says that environmental "hypochondriacs" engage in irrational "witch hunts" against industry.[26]

According to these antipopulist writers, U.S. public aversion to asbestos hazards is a good example of a risk response motivated by sectarian, antitechnology sentiment. Environmentalists, however, maintain that, with the expected deaths of 400,000 asbestos workers in the United States, they have good grounds for their aversion to asbestos.[27] Criticizing "the danger establishment," the antipopulist authors respond that hazards such as asbestos poisoning are seen as "fearsome" merely because laypersons (sectarian environmentalists) in the United States "choose to be panic-struck about dangers from technology, rather than from threats to the economy or education. . . . they [environmentalists] serve their own moral purposes by focusing on dangers emanating from large organizations [asbestos manufacturers] rather than on dangers arising from inadequate investment, blundering foreign policy, or undereducation. . . . [Environmentalists are] set against technology and institutions . . . [and are in] permanent opposition [to] government."[28]

Claiming that environmentalists respond to any level of risk in the same way that a member of a highly sectarian religious group would view any sort of "guilt" or moral "impurity," antipopulist writers say that "sectarian" fear of pollution is extreme. They allege that such fear is based on "ideology" and the need to "blame" industry for "impurity," for a "secular version of original sin."[29] They point out that "an internal social problem about guilt and innocence is stated in the pollution belief," and that there is "not much difference between modern times and ages past" in this regard.[30] Just as the Hima people believe that women's being near the cattle causes the animals to die, and just as medievalists believed that witches caused misfortune, so also, the antipopulists claim, contemporary persons believe that industry causes people to die through pollution. "Impurities in the physical world or chemical carcinogens in the body are directly traced to immoral forms of economic and political power."[31]

How plausible is the argument that aversion to environmental hazards arises because of an anti-industry and antigovernment risk-selection bias and because of an obsession with environmental purity? The attack is problematic for a number of reasons, the most basic of which is that the attackers are attempting to argue for a particular *cause* of risk aversion. As Hume pointed out long ago, however, it is virtually impossible to establish knowledge of causality of any kind.[32] Moreover, even if they were able to show that some sort of anti-industry social sentiment *caused* environmentalism, establishing these origins of environmental beliefs would not be sufficient to show that the attitudes were not *justified*. Freud made a similar mistake, the genetic fallacy, in assuming that arguing for the psychological origins of belief in a divine being was alone sufficient to discredit religion.[33]

In attributing risk aversion to misguided environmental purity, the argument also ignores the origins of much risk aversion in "centrist," "hierarchical" (i.e., governmental) values. Rather than being antigovernment, many U.S. environmentalists invoke government-sanctioned values to justify their positions. For example, when Allied Chemical Company in Virginia polluted the James River with the pesticide Kepone, environmentalists did not appeal to antigovernment sentiment. Instead, they used the government and the law to further their environmental concerns. They invoked strong centrist values of due process under law.[34] Environmentalists are also often angry not because they are anti-industry but because hazards threaten a constitutional "right to know"—a right that is at the heart of centrist values. Likewise (to return to a case mentioned earlier in this chapter), one of the most basic reasons why persons are so averse to commercial fission technology is that they see it as a threat to the very civil liberties that are championed and protected by centrist institutions such as government.[35]

If antipopulist risk writers are correct in asserting that environmentalists are anti-industry and antigovernment, however, then their own logic requires them to say something highly implausible: that environmental opposition to the Kepone spill or to nuclear fission, on constitutional grounds, is merely an example of antigovernment, anti-industry sentiment. Far from being antigovernment, many environmentalists may want to use government (or co-opt it) to serve their ends. Moreover, even if anti-industry feelings were correlated with environmentalism, it would be difficult to tell which was the cause and which was the effect.

The allegation of environmentalists' anti-industry bias also errs in ignoring reasonable human desires for preservation. In the wake of the Chernobyl, Three Mile Island, Bhopal, Love Canal, and *Challenger* disasters, one need not be anti-industry or antigovernment to be averse to the risks posed by certain technologies. Those who claim that the public's risk evaluations are motivated by anti-industry bias ignore other causes of risk aversion, just as they ignore U.S. environmentalists' support of the solar, biomass, and recycling *industries*.[36]

They also cannot substantiate their charges about the alleged anti-industry causes of lay aversion to many technological risks. They say that the aversion is "ideological," "political," and the product of biased choices that are "never made directly."[37] However, the claim that environmentalists *directly* choose to be members of a sectarian, anti-industry, antigovernment group, and therefore *indirectly* choose to minimize technological risks, seems highly questionable. What is to count as an indirect choice? What is the evidence for it?[38] Why couldn't persons choose to be members of a given group, but neither indirectly nor directly choose all of the values associated with the group? Likewise, why couldn't persons choose certain values or positions associated with a group, but never directly choose membership in the group?

Such questions suggest that the antipopulist writers are vulnerable to some of the same objections that Popper leveled against vague, nonempirical theories in the history of science.[39] Because such theories made no precise predictions, and could be interpreted as consistent with almost any evidence, they were nonfalsifiable and nonempirical. To the extent that those who attack risk evaluations of the public appeal to "indirect" reasons (as Popper argued that Freud, Marx, and astrologers do), their arguments are vague, nonfalsifiable, and nonempirical. Hence, they are unable to sustain the claim that anti-industry, antigovernment bias causes public aversion to societal risks.

Are Environmentalists Distrustful?

Other risk writers allege that those averse to environmental risks, in addition to being anti-industry and antigovernment, are remote from power and influence. Thompson says that they are "ineffectuals" instead of "entrepreneurs." According to this argument, U.S. environmentalists distrust those at the "center" of economic power and political influence, and therefore reject any risks imposed by these "capitalists."[40]

The most basic problem with this argument is that it reduces all causes of risk aversion to social structures. Such reductionism, however, is difficult to support. For example, if the psychometric studies of Fischhoff, Slovic, and others are correct, then risk aversion is highly correlated with personal preferences, such as the desire to avoid catastrophic consequences. Fischhoff and his associates have also argued that ethical beliefs (such as a commitment to equity of risk distribution or a belief in the necessity of obtaining free, informed consent from potential victims before imposing risk on them) are highly correlated with risk aversion.[41] If they are correct, then (contrary to this argument) risk choices are multifaceted and determined in large part by both one's *philosophy* and one's personal *psychology*. Moreover, there is some evidence that risk aversion is dictated in part by physiological and biochemical factors not correlated with social structures. Risk takers, for example, exhibit lower levels of monoamine oxidase, an enzyme that normally breaks down certain neurotransmitters related to emotion and cognition.[42] These findings suggest that the sociological reductionism inherent in this argument is suspect. Perhaps some persons reduce all causes of risk behavior to *social structures* because they are *social scientists*.

If so, they illustrate Mark Twain's observation: If one's only tool is a hammer, then all problems look like nails.

This sociological reductionism is also questionable because it identifies U.S. environmentalists as egalitarian sectarians, removed from the sources of power and influence. Even some sociological data contradict this identification, since environmentalists tend to be white, middle-aged, middle-class professionals—not young, blue-collar workers, or blacks.[43] White, middle-aged, middle-class professionals hardly seem distant from power and influence. Indeed, they constitute groups like the Natural Resources Defense Council, groups whose influence has stopped nuclear power plants, saved snail darters, and protected wetlands.[44]

Other environmentalists likewise do not seem removed from power and influence and therefore averse to technological risks. The late Orville Kelly was founder of the cancer support group "Make Today Count." Hardly a typical, powerless "outsider," he had been U.S. Navy Commander of Eniwetok Atoll. During his command, in the 1950s, he was within five miles of ground zero during twenty-three nuclear weapons tests. Like approximately 500,000 other American soldiers, many marched to within 300 yards of ground zero immediately after atomic tests, he was exposed to high levels of fallout. Like all these other servicemen, he was at a high risk for the radiation-induced cancers leukemia and myeloma. Arguing for benefits for his wife and four children, Kelly claimed that the leukemia that eventually killed him (during middle age) was caused by the fallout. The government denied benefits to him and to all but ten of the hundreds of thousands of servicemen overexposed to radiation. Instead, Kelly's supervisors claimed that his allegations about the cause of his leukemia were evidence of "psychiatric disorders."[45]

If the antipopulists are correct, then Kelly's risk aversion was caused by his powerlessness and lack of influence. But Kelly, as a naval commander, was not powerless or lacking in influence. Moreover, his risk aversion was arguably caused by the leukemia that killed him, not merely (if at all) by his desire to attack a centrist government institution. He had a flawless service record with many commendations. Indeed, he was an important part of a centrist institution, the United States Navy.

To the Kelly case, the antipopulist risk writers would likely respond that *individual* counterexamples (like Kelly) do not negate their *social* hypothesis, a hypothesis that is generally or statistically true.[46] To establish statistical truth, however, they would need to provide statistical data to support their point. This they have not done.

Are Laypersons Fearful and Ignorant?

Those who attack the risk evaluations of the public also provide no data to support their claim that laypersons (environmentalists) give "blind acceptance" to charges of environmental risk, because they are fearful and "almost totally ignorant of science." Even the National Research Council accuses the public of "misunderstanding" societal risks, yet provides no evidence for this charge.[47] Many antipopulist risk writers claim that laypersons are unreasonably averse to risk, fear things that are unlikely to occur, and do not realize that life is getting safer.[48] They argue that uncertainty ought not to inhibit societal or technological risk taking,[49] since taking risks is an opportunity that teaches us how to learn from our mistakes.[50]

In maintaining that it is not reasonable to be averse to a particular risk when one is uncertain about its probability and consequences, the antipopulists ignore the fact that most reasonable people accept a serious risk only when they have fairly reliable knowledge about its probability and alternatives to it.[51] Hence, in the face of uncertainty about a potentially catastrophic environmental hazard, laypersons could be acting reasonably when they take a conservative position on risk imposition.[52] Moreover, to claim that laypersons ought to take risks, since they provide opportunities to learn from mistakes, begs the question because it presupposes that the dangers are not serious.[53] But this is the very point at issue: whether the risks are serious, and whether a reasonable person ought to take them.

Do Laypersons Forget That Life Is Getting Safer?

Many risk authors also accuse laypersons of ignoring the fact that life is getting safer. They claim, for instance, that the cancer rate is not going up, even though alleged pollution is increasing. They attack numerous government studies on carcinogenicity, fail to provide any alternative data of their own, and then call the government evidence on carcinogenicity "ephemeral."[54] Likewise, in response to government claims that nickel, chromium, and nitrites are carcinogens, some antipopulist risk writers respond that they are "essential nutrients for human growth."[55] They conclude that only irrational persons would fear DDT (since its carcinogenicity has not been established) or high levels of chromium exposure (since some amount is essential for growth). They also say that "there is no unequivocal body of evidence that life is (or is becoming) less safe; on the contrary, such tentative evidence as there is leads in the opposite direction—life is growing longer not shorter; health is better not worse." Therefore, they conclude, environmentalists' aversion to public risks must be caused by their biased sectarianism and not by increasing hazards.[56]

This attack on environmentalists is an example of what Quine called a "what else" argument.[57] It is of the form: "Increasing risk cannot explain increasing risk aversion among the public; *what else* could explain it but the sectarian tendencies of environmental groups?" But a number of things besides alleged environmentalist sectarianism could explain increasing risk aversion. Some laypersons might, for example, be unwilling to consent to the risk because they regard its distribution as unacceptable. In this case, one might not care whether overall safety was greater but instead might ask: "Safer *for whom?*" "Safer in *which respects?*" If a person's *own life* were less safe, particularly because of industry irresponsibility, that person might be averse to industry-imposed risks, even though the overall safety of the public was increasing.[58]

Another possible explanatory factor might be that life could easily be even safer, or that the benefits associated with taking a particular risk are minimal. Even if our lives are getting longer and safer, reasonable persons might become more averse to environmental hazards if they believe that their current risk burden, albeit small in magnitude, is not worth the benefits generated. In fact, Fischhoff and his colleagues have demonstrated that scientists and nonscientists share roughly the same opinions about nuclear reactor safety but disagree sharply on whether the alleged benefits of atomic energy are worth the risks.[59] Antipopulist risk writers therefore may err in presupposing that the *magnitude* of hazard is the only factor that can explain public risk aversion.[60]

Is the Public Unrealistic?

If other factors can explain rational risk behavior, then perhaps antipopulist risk analyses fail because of the narrow way in which they define rational risk evaluation and environmentalists' views. This same narrowness is also exemplified in another argument against the public: "it is best to recognize that sectarians [laypersons or environmentalists, as opposed to proponents of markets or political hierarchies] can never be satisfied. If extensive effort were devoted to reducing risk, sectarians would not feel they had won what they wanted. [They believe that] there can never be enough [safety]."[61] "They [the public] do not tolerate rational limits on their knowledge."[62]

The most obvious problem with this argument is that there is no evidence to support it; it appears to be a mere ad hominem attack. And if there is no supporting evidence, how can one define or discover the characteristics that are allegedly associated with each of the three societal groups? For Thompson, these groups are sectists, entrepreneurs, and autonomists. For Douglas and Wildavsky, they are members of environmentalist sects (the public), market proponents, and advocates of political hierarchies. Why are U.S. laypersons and environmentalists, per se, said not to be satisfied with their victories? Why are market persons not charged with being "never satisfied"? The prototypical capitalist seeking profits appears to be as much the sort of person who would never be satisfied, who would always want bigger profits and more successful products. Moreover, even if members of one or another group were correctly said to have the characteristic of "not being satisfied," how can Efron, Thompson, Maxey, Wildavsky, and others say that this is a quality associated with *social structures* rather than with individual psychology? Perhaps such extreme dissatisfaction is a result of individual, rather than group, characteristics. None of these questions is answered by any of the risk assessors or industrial exponents who attack the public. This lack of answers is puzzling, given their expressed aims. These aims are "understanding . . . technological risk," giving "an overview of this environmental movement," and examining "the foundations of each set of arguments . . . for or against the center, . . . market or hierarchy."[63] Because they do not answer key questions and because they do not *empirically substantiate* their claims, they run the risk of providing, not "explanation," as they assert, but mere "ideology."[64] This is especially unfortunate, since they themselves attribute ideology to the public.

Another difficulty is that the allegation (that environmentalists are never satisfied, and therefore their risk demands are not reasonable) begs the question. To say that people who are "never satisfied" are not reasonable presupposes that they *ought* to be satisfied. And to presuppose that they ought to be satisfied, in a particular case of risk reduction, assumes that the danger in that situation is acceptable. But to presuppose that the hazard is acceptable is to beg the very question at issue.

Moreover, apart from the circularity, there are grounds for believing that reasonable people ought not be satisfied, in some cases, even when great improvements in risk reduction have been made. Consider the case of oil development on the Outer Continental Shelf (OCS) of the United States. Even though the technology for containing oil spills has improved, risk assessments for oil spills typically do not include damages to the public or funds necessary to handle liability claims. Instead, the costs of oil spills are defined only as the value of the product lost and the cleanup cost, *not* as damage to the public or the environment.[65] Since these latter data are not included, the distributive effects of oil-spill risks, on everyone from fishermen to motel owners, are ignored. Offshore operators are not required to demonstrate financial responsibility, and there is no current law requiring compensation to the public whenever there are damages that the cleanup cannot prevent.[66]

Given such ways of managing and evaluating offshore oil risks, and given that no offshore spill has ever been cleaned up and contained on site,[67] why should the public be satisfied with only limited improvements in reducing oil spills? Likewise, why should the public be satisfied with improvements in commercial nuclear fission technology, as the antipopulist arguments suggest? Consider the Price-Anderson Act, mentioned in the first section of this chapter. The act limits the liability of nuclear plant owners. Under this law, as amended, citizens are denied their due-process rights to sue for more than approximately 1 percent of their total losses, in the event of a catastrophic nuclear accident.[68] Now suppose Congress doubles the current liability limit ($640 million). A reasonable person could still claim that she was not satisfied and that more protection was needed; she could argue that doubling the liability limit would mean that less than 2 percent of total losses were covered, given current government estimates about the possible damages from a catastrophic nuclear accident. But then suppose Congress responded by quadrupling the liability limit, making it $2.6 billion. A reasonable person could still claim that she was not satisfied, since quadrupling the liability limit would nevertheless result in coverage for less than 4 percent of total possible losses in a worst-case accident. But suppose Congress responded a third time to this demand for protection and made the liability limit ten times its current level, raising it to $6.4 billion. A reasonable person still could respond that she was not satisfied, since less than 10 percent of total possible losses would be covered. If one has a legal right (e.g., a due-process right) to full coverage of losses, whether from oil spills, or nuclear power, or hazardous waste, then a reasonable person need not be satisfied with any concession short of recognizing this right.

The allegations of Efron, Wildavsky, Maxey, Rothschild, and others—that U.S. environmentalists are dissatisfied and therefore unreasonable—are analogous to that of a racist counseling a black in the 1940s: "Look, you're not being reasonable in demanding more equality [just as environmentalists demand more protection from risk]; after all, things have been steadily improving since slavery was abolished." A reasonable black could maintain that everyone ought to be accorded equal rights and therefore that *any* improvement short of full equality was not enough. Analogously, even if it is true that environmentalists are "never satisfied" with the level of safety, no one ought to *assume* that this dissatisfaction is irrational. One also needs to show that people have no grounds for being dissatisfied.[69]

The Need for a New Theory of Rationality

If the preceding analysis of arguments (for the bias and irrationality of lay responses to societal risk) is correct, then many risk assessors, industry spokespersons, and natural and social scientists have built their view of "rational" risk evaluation on a questionable foundation. Without significant evidence, they have attributed motives to environmentalists who are averse to risk. They have confused *causes* of behavior with *correlations*; they have defined 'rational' and 'environmentalist' in highly stipulative, question-begging ways.

If such arguments against lay views of environmental risk are wrong, then we may need a new theory of rationality.[70] We also may need new criteria for rational risk evaluation. After showing (in the next chapter) how risk experts subscribe to outmoded positivistic or relativistic notions of rationality, I shall sketch a new account of *rational risk evaluation*. Its main policy goal will be to enfranchise the very people who are most likely to be victimized by environmental hazards.

Chapter Three

Rejecting Reductionist Risk Evaluation

The Case for Redefining "Rationality"

Echoing the famous description in *A Tale of Two Cities*, many people would describe our own era as both the best of times and the worst of times. We are sending humans into space, creating new life through biotechnology, and bombarding ever smaller subatomic particles into their elementary components. We have been less adept at securing world peace, feeding the starving, and protecting the environment. Some persons might even say, despite our medical advances, that we have not been wholly successful even in saving lives. In 1982, the National Cancer Institute warned that one in every three Americans would die of cancer. Cancer already takes more American lives, each year, than were lost during all of World War II, the Korean War, and the Vietnam War combined; it is responsible for eight times as many annual deaths as automobiles.[1]

Apart from the magnitude of such statistics, at least three facts about cancer deaths are significant. For one thing, many epidemiologists claim that about one-third of the fatalities are correlated with cigarette smoking. Also, the deaths are occurring among the young, not merely among typical elderly victims; cancer is the leading cause of death for all U.S. children between the ages of one and ten and for all women between the ages of thirty and forty. It is second only to accidents as the leading cause of death for all Americans under the age of thirty-five. Cancer rates for all age groups have been increasing in the last three decades. Most important, the U.S. Office of Technology Assessment claims that up to 90 percent of all cancers are "environmentally induced" and hence "preventable."[2]

If hundreds of thousands of cancer deaths are preventable, why aren't they stopped? Part of the answer has to do with human ignorance of the hazards we create. Most people are probably unaware, for example, that the United States annually generates one ton of hazardous wastes for every man, woman, and child; that 90 percent of the 80,000 known contaminated sites for toxic wastes threaten groundwater; and that cancer rates near such dumps are typically 50 percent above average. Similarly, most American mothers probably don't know that their breast milk is so contaminated with toxins that it could not be sold in supermarkets.[3] Likewise, most people probably don't know that legal emissions of only four radioactive isotopes from the U.S. commercial nuclear program during the next hundred years will cause over 30,000 deaths[4] even if there is no catastrophic reactor accident, which alone could cause 145,000 fatalities.[5]

If people are unaware of risks close to home, risks carried by their own bodies and in the groundwater they drink, they are likely even less cognizant of hazards farther from home: 25,000 people are killed *daily*, worldwide, by water contamination and shortage.[6] In Africa alone (where 47 percent of the land is too dry for agriculture and where one million babies are born every three weeks), a million and a half persons have died of famine since 1950.[7] Sixty percent of the world's humans are cutting fuelwood faster than it can be replenished, and in countries like India 88 percent of the forestland has been lost since 1950. As a consequence, 28 percent of the ice-free surface of the earth is faced with desertification, drought, and famine.[8] In fact, the Sudan Desert has recently been extending southward at a rate of three miles per year.[9] Coping with the risks of desertification and famine, however, has increased the pressure to maximize farm yields, in part through use of chemicals. But such chemicals bring their own hazards. The World Health Organization (WHO) estimates that pesticides cause 50,000 deaths annually, many resulting because one-third of all U.S. pesticide exports, although banned in this country as unsafe, are marketed and used legally throughout the third world.[10]

As this catalogue of risks indicates, famine, firewood shortages, and pesticides are all interrelated. They are interrelated because virtually every *benefit*, from food and firewood to railroads and electricity, is bought at some environmental and human *cost*, such as pesticide risks. Perhaps we tolerate many of these hazards, from pesticides to deforestation to cancer fatalities, because we subscribe to a particular philosophy about the *rationality* of risk acceptance and risk trade-off.

In this chapter, I argue that at least two of the major positions regarding societal risk evaluation and acceptance are highly questionable, those of the *cultural relativists* and the *naive positivists*.[11] Proponents of both positions err, in part, because they are reductionistic and because they view the hazard evaluations of citizens who are risk averse as either biased or irrational. After showing why both views of risk evaluation are built on highly doubtful epistemological presuppositions, I argue in favor of a middle position, which I call "scientific proceduralism." This Popperian account is based on the notion that objectivity in hazard evaluation (stage three of assessment) is tied to at least three things: (1) the ability of risk evaluations to withstand criticism by scientists and laypeople who are affected by the hazards; (2) the ability of risk evaluations to change, as new facts about probabilities are discovered; and (3) the ability of risk evaluations to explain and predict both risks and human responses to them. Because of point 1, the position is sympathetic toward many populist attitudes about involuntary and public hazards. Because of points 2 and 3, the position is sympathetic to the scientific need for objectivity in risk evaluation.[12] Although scientific proceduralism is not the only reasonable view of risk evaluation, I argue that it is at least a rational one. I also argue that rational behavior should not be defined purely in terms of the evaluations of either the cultural relativists or the naive positivists. Most important, risk experts should not "write off" the common person.

Since hazard evaluation is dominated by these two questionable positions (cultural relativism and naive positivism), it is reasonable to ask whether criticizing them threatens the value of quantified risk assessment (QRA). Indeed, many of those allegedly speaking "for the people" are opposed to objective scientific and analytic methods of assessing environmental dangers. I am not. In Chapter Eleven, I shall argue that, although QRA is subject to various shortcomings and biases, it can and ought to be improved and used in policymaking; although it is in practice flawed, it is in principle necessary to rational, objective, democratic risk assessment.[13]

Three Philosophies about Risk Evaluation: Cultural Relativism, Naive Positivism, and Scientific Proceduralism

Contemporary controversy over rational evaluation of risks is, at the core, a conflict over values. Cultural relativists such as Douglas and Wildavsky, authors of the best-selling *Risk and Culture*, overemphasize value judgments in hazard evaluation (stage three of assessment). They claim that "risk is a collective construct."[14] I shall argue that, in so doing, they erroneously reduce the third stage of hazard analysis (risk evaluation) to anthropology or sociology, and they ignore its objective, scientific component. Naive positivists, such as Starr, Whipple, Hafele, Okrent, Jones-Lee, Morgan, and Rothschild, make the opposite mistake. They attempt to avoid value judgments in evaluating societal risks. In assuming that there are often value-free, mathematical criteria that are sufficient for evaluating risks, they presuppose that all risks can be objectively measured, independent of even methodological value judgments.[15] I show that, by virtue of their position, they attribute a misguided (that is, wholly value-free) notion of *objectivity* to risk assessment.[16]

The naive positivists are wrong, as this chapter will argue, because risk estimates are not completely objective (in the sense of being wholly value free)—as is evidenced by the U.S. National Academy of Sciences' statement that most risk assessments are performed in situations of probabilistic *uncertainty*.[17] As witness to this uncertainty, the current technological landscape is littered with the bodies of victims of various hazards. From Chernobyl to Bhopal, there are victims of risks that experts allegedly measured objectively, catastrophes that were not supposed to happen. They include radwaste dumps whose contents were "objectively" and definitively said to not be able to migrate[18] and toxic chemicals that were "objectively" claimed not to cause harm to humans.[19]

But even though risk evaluation is not wholly objective, neither is it *merely* evaluative nor only a construct.[20] Constructs don't kill people; faulty reactors, improperly stored toxics, and poor risk evaluations do. At least some hazards are real, and many of these are measurable. Hence, the cultural relativists are wrong in overemphasizing value judgments in risk assessment and evaluation. Risk evaluations assess real hazards, not just constructs.

In my view of risk evaluation, then, it is false to say that hazard assessments can be wholly value free (as many naive positivists claim), and it is equally false to assert (as many cultural relativists do) that any evaluation of risk can be justified.[21] That is, some risk evaluations are more warranted, more objective, than others, although none is wholly value free. Later in the chapter, I shall specify some of the criteria for democratically reaching more objective risk evaluations. For now, let's investigate the position of the cultural relativists, and then that of the naive positivists, to see where they go wrong. This will provide a basis for defining a middle path between them, a new account of risk evaluation.

Cultural Relativism

Cultural relativists begin from an astute (although not original) insight. They recognize that risk estimation is not wholly objective (value free), and they criticize assessors for their repeated error in assuming that lay estimates of risk are mere "perceptions" whereas expert analyses are "objective."[22] Clearly, the cultural relativists are to be commended for discussing this error, since both experts and the public have risk "perceptions," and no one has privileged access to the truth about risk acceptability *merely because* she is an engineer rather than a housewife. Even though the preponderance of technical errors made in estimating hazards obviously lies with laypeople, not experts, the cultural relativists are correct in affirming that engineers and housewives both employ value judgments, especially in evaluating risk acceptability.

Cultural relativists err, however, in assuming that, because everybody can be wrong at some time, everybody is wrong all the time. They say that any judgment or risk evaluation is merely a social construct. Some of these relativists reserve their harshest criticisms for the U.S. public. They claim that "risks are social constructs,"[23] but they single out U.S. environmentalist or sectarian laypersons (as opposed to technical experts) as having particularly biased constructs.[24]

Of course, as I argued in the previous chapter, if cultural relativists believe that "no one is to say that one [risk judgment] is better or worse" than another,[25] they are obviously inconsistent. It is inconsistent to affirm both that all risk evaluations are equally plausible and that environmentalists' risk positions are more questionable than those of the "centrists" (persons whose value systems, in their scheme, derive from the market or from hierarchical organizations).[26] The last chapter outlined allegations against the risk evaluations of U.S. laypersons. This chapter examines why cultural relativism, especially in the area of risk evaluation, is wrong. Among other things, cultural relativism contributes to a proindustry bias toward risks, a bias that disenfranchises the lay public and supports the status quo.

Risk relativists tend to employ five arguments (all variants of themes advanced by writers such as Sumner, Engels, Rothschild, and Herskovits[27]): (1) Increased knowledge and additional reasoning about risks do not make people more rational about hazards.[28] (2) Risk assessments are like judgments in aesthetics.[29] (3) "Any form of life," including risk behavior and attitudes, "can be justified," since all people—including experts who disagree about hazard analysis—are biased in their perceptions of danger.[30] (4) Modern persons are no different from "primitives" (Douglas and Wildavsky's term) in that social structures dictate their views on, and responses to, alleged hazards.[31] (5) More specifically, environmentalists' views on risk are a result of their "sectarian problems."[32] Let's examine each of these arguments.

Does Knowledge Dispel Relativism?

In arguing that additional knowledge and reasoning about risk do not make the public more rational about hazards, the risk relativists state explicitly that "objective knowledge about technology in general is not going to take us very far." They claim that "each method [of risk evaluation] is biased," and because "better measurement opens more possibilities, more research brings more ignorance to the light of day"; hence, when one is "thinking about how to choose between risks, subjective values must take priority." They conclude that risk evaluation is done "according to personal ideology."[33]

The main presupposition of this relativistic argument is that, because there are always things that we don't know, any research, measurement, and increased information about risk is not valuable. This is a version of the "all-or-nothing argument": Because I can't know everything about something, any knowledge about it has purely subjective or ideological value, or is worth nothing. Such "all-or-nothing" arguments presuppose that only *perfection* in a certain area (whether in making risk judgments, playing the piano, or parenting) is valuable, and that imperfect accomplishments have only subjective value. Clearly, these presuppositions are wrong, and for several reasons. The value of many activities lies in the *process* of accomplishing them, rather than in their *outcome* (e.g., mastering some skill). Moreover, we can make correct and noncontroversial judgments about better and worse instances of a thing (such as parenting), even in the absence of a perfect example (a perfect parent).

The argument also errs because it fails to take account of the many ways in which (even imperfect) knowledge has radically changed our risk judgments. Back in the 1950s, most people were ignorant, for example, of the hazards of ionizing radiation. As a result, shoe stores typically determined correct fit, in part, by taking X rays of their customers' feet inside new shoes. Several decades later, we have come to recognize, through epidemiological studies, that ionizing radiation is harmful, and this knowledge has eliminated its earlier uses in shoe stores. Likewise, scientific knowledge about the hazards of lead has caused us to avoid use of lead pipes, leaded gasoline, and paint containing lead. Similarly, when Arnstein published his classic study of lung cancer deaths due to radon daughter exposure among underground miners, he reported that lung cancer mortality was 40 percent. That estimate of mortality is still accepted by experts as valid, and it resulted in occupational guidelines for radon exposure.[34] Hence, knowledge directly affected both the evaluation and the management of the radon risk.

Is Risk Evaluation Purely Aesthetic?

Another faulty argument for the relativism of risk evaluations also discounts the role of knowledge and reason in evaluating hazards. Some relativists reduce risk evaluations to "ideology." Others claim that risk evaluations are like judgments in aesthetics: "public perception of risk and its acceptable levels are collective constructs . . . like language and . . . aesthetic judgment . . . [P]erceptions of right and truth depend on cultural categories created along with the social relations they are used for defending . . . there is no reasoning with tastes and preferences."[35]

This argument also has the "all-or-nothing" form. Its major presupposition is that, because our assessments of hazards and our evaluations of "right and truth" are laden with cultural values, "there is no reasoning" about them, and they are mere social constructs. This "construct" presupposition is erroneous because, even if something is merely a social construct, we can often still reason about it. We "socially construct" promises and contracts, for example, and our constructing them makes them real, as well as morally binding. Once we "socially construct" a promise or contract, following it is not merely a matter of taste or aesthetics; it is a matter of moral obligation. Likewise, even if risk evaluations (as contained in the Delaney Amendment, for example) were purely social constructs of civil law, those constructs would become real and obligatory, precisely because they are also civil law (and therefore part of an implicit contract). The dictates of aesthetics are not real and obligatory in this sense. Moreover, one can admit that risk judgments are not perfect and yet claim that it is possible to reason about them. Courts, for example, although they do not operate perfectly, often reason about value-laden risk judgments in the area of liability, and some court briefs and verdicts are arguably better or worse than others.

Although we obviously speak of civil rights and legal obligations in terms of our own categorizations of the world, such categories do not render our judgments completely relative (that is, arbitrary) in any but a trivial sense. Civil rights and legal obligations are *real*; they are not mind-dependent constructs, as Ross, Hare, Brandt, Taylor, and Ladd have argued.[36] Even though people conceptualize, interpret, or categorize *differently*, they do not necessarily do so in a wholly *relativistic* or arbitrary fashion.[37]

Another problem with claims that risk evaluations are "like aesthetic judgments," about which "there is no reasoning,"[38] is that there are strong disanalogies between aesthetic and risk-related judgments. Aesthetic judgments rarely have life-and-death consequences, but a wrong judgment about a technological risk could cause many people to die. Moreover, one can often "check" or substantiate one's evaluation of risk probabilities, although there is no similar way to check one's aesthetic judgments, since facts have less relevance to them. Therefore, relativists err in claiming that risk evaluations are as subjective as aesthetic judgments.

Can Any Risk Evaluation Be Justified?

Risk relativists believe that, because everyone has some bias, and because "any form of life [including risk behavior and attitudes] can be justified," there are no objective risk evaluations: "The center takes one view of risk, the border takes another. Is there any judgment possible between their views? Any form of life can be justified . . . no one is to say that one is better or worse."[39]

Not surprisingly, this argument fails for many of the same reasons as the previous one. It ignores the fact that risk evaluations can be more or less in keeping with morally binding laws or civil rights, or more or less in keeping with good scientific judgments or confirmed accident frequencies. For example, when the National Toxicology Program showed that di-2-ethylhexyl phthalate (DEHP), a plasticizer used in polyvinyl chloride, caused liver cancer in rats and mice, these findings enabled policymakers to argue, correctly, that not all evaluations of the DEHP risk could be justified. As a consequence, manufacturers of plastic tubing used in blood transfusions and makers of children's PVC toys, pacifiers, and teethers could no longer justify their manufacturing goods composed of 40 percent DEHP.[40]

Moreover, if there were "no correct description of the right behavior [for example, regarding risk],"[41] because any risk attitude could be justified, several problematic consequences would follow; ignorant, fearful people who attempt to avoid all risks of any kind would be no less rational in their risk decisions than well-informed persons who attempt only to avoid all unnecessary risks. But this conclusion is obviously false. Some risk evaluations or behaviors are more rational than others, because some activities are more dangerous than others. Even classical economists recognize this fact. They have argued that there ought to be a compensating wage differential (CWD); that is, the riskier the job, the higher the pay, all things being equal.[42] Moreover, if the risk relativists were correct, then insurance companies and actuaries would go out of business; they do not, so there must be better and worse evaluations of risk.

Most important, if cultural relativists were right in their contention that all risk evaluations are equally correct, then unscrupulous persons could, for example, avoid the cost of pollution controls by claiming that their own evaluation of the relevant risks was just as correct as any other evaluation. They could then simply impose environmental threats on innocent members of the public, under the guise that any risk evaluation is justifiable.[43] In such a case, it also would be impossible to regulate technology and industry in any rational way. One could merely charge that, since all hazard evaluations (and consequent regulations) were justifiable, none were. One could not morally justify the imposition of sanctions on those who violated safety laws, even violations that resulted in losses of lives.

A specific problem with the Douglas-Wildavsky version of the relativistic claim is that it is inconsistent. They affirm that there is no correct description of risk behavior; yet, at the same time, they admit that they have a "bias toward the center."[44] If there is no correct view of risk behavior, and if any position can be justified, then being biased toward only one of those accounts is neither reasonable nor consistent. Apart from their admission of bias, Douglas and Wildavsky have other difficulties with consistency. Within two pages of affirming their thesis of relativism ("no one is to say that one [position on risk] is better or worse"),[45] they assert that "there is nothing relativistic in this exercise" (their theory as articulated in *Risk and Culture*). Their basis for denying the relativism in their account is that they have merely described "with impartial care the deducible consequences of preferring one form of social organization over others."[46] However, when one claims that any risk position can be justified, and that none is better than another, as Douglas and Wildavsky do, then one is not making an "impartial," *first-order, descriptive* claim. One is making a *second-order, normative* assertion about evaluating risk positions. Douglas and Wildavsky err here because they seem to confuse both first- and second-order claims as well as descriptive and normative assertions.[47]

Are All Risk Evaluators Biased?

Cultural relativists also run into a consistency problem when they claim (1) that they are merely describing social reality and (2) that all actors in that social reality are biased. To claim that some or all persons (or evaluations) are biased is an *inference* or *value judgment* about events, not a description of events. For example, Thompson claims that his goal is "global understanding," and Douglas and Wildavsky assert that they are merely describing the consequences of various social positions (on risk) "with impartial care." Yet, following Herskovits and other relativists, they claim that "Everyone, expert and layman alike, is biased. No one has a social theory above the battle. . . . Thus the difference diminishes between modern mankind and its predecessors."[48] They attempt to substantiate this claim about bias with a string of anthropological examples concerning pollution fears from other cultures. They conjecture that contemporary aversion to environmental contaminants, with its blame of industry, is like fear of "pollution" in "primitive" cultures, where powerless individuals blame powerful persons and institutions for some impurity. They maintain that the inhabitants of the South African Transvaal, for example, fear drought and believe that their queen's anger causes it.[49]

After providing examples of how "primitives" irrationally "blame" those in power for environmental hazards, risk relativists conclude that "many pollution fears are associated with sex," that "ideas about pollution are not sufficiently explained by the physical dangers," and that contemporary laypersons, "hypochondriacs" regarding industrial risk, engage in "witch hunts" like those of medievalists.[50]

The main problem with such arguments is that, despite their proponents' assertions that they are merely describing consequences of various risk positions "with impartial care," their allegations (about sex, witches, and so on) are hardly mere descriptions. Instead, they attribute intentions to persons, even though intentions are not observable. They also postulate (unobserved, inferred) causes for American environmentalists' risk aversion, causes that go beyond environmentalists' desires to avoid technological hazards. Consequently, they are in a precarious position when they claim to be merely "describing" situations, even though persons whose behavior is so "described" would dispute the accuracy of the description (as "antiscientific," "hysterical," "ideological"). At the least, such writers may have fallen victim to the ethnocentrism condemned by cultural relativists and ethnographers.[51]

Another problem with the relativists' claim that risk aversion is a form of primitive superstition is that, although more primitive people have only a modest scientific understanding of risks and their causes, contemporary American laypersons typically have quite sophisticated technical knowledge about the etiology of various hazards. Hence, there is little reason to suppose that everyone's beliefs about pollution have the same source, or that people in two widely divergent groups are even explaining the *same thing*.

Just as differences in levels of scientific understanding among cultures undercut relativists' allegations of similar motives for pollution beliefs, so also variations in political organization undercut their claims that social life dictates one's response to risk. Specifically, they claim that "the selection of risk is a matter of social organization," or "group formation."[52] But the types of social organization dictating the same risk aversion and the same condemnation of environmental "impurity" are quite diverse. How could politically hierarchical, superstitious tribes' fear of pollution have the same causes as risk aversion among more (politically) egalitarian, scientifically sophisticated persons? It is difficult to believe that people in democratic societies enjoying great civil liberties have the same need to engage in "blaming the impure" as do more primitive, culturally deprived peoples in autocratic and discriminatory societies.

Apart from whether primitive and more technologically sophisticated people are alike in their hazard aversion and pollution beliefs, the relativistic argument is problematic because of the claim that risk attitudes are determined solely by sociology or "social organization."[53] As was noted in Chapter One, Fischhoff, Slovic, and other psychometric researchers suggest that many risk judgments may be a function both of personal psychology and of ethical beliefs—for example, about the equity of risk distribution[54] or about the severity of consequences.[55] If this assumption is correct, then the hazards themselves, not the characteristics of the social group responding to probable harm, are the key determinants of attitudes toward risk aversion.

Moreover, if this sociological reductionism were true, cultural relativists would be unable to explain a number of facts. One such anomaly is how members of the *same* social group (market, hierarchy, or sect) have *divergent* views about risk, or how those who share the same views about hazards can be members of different social groups. For example, Efron says that environmentalists are risk averse because they are antiscientific; yet she admits that many scientists are environmentalists.[56] Also, as the previous chapter revealed, Douglas and Wildavsky allege that environmentalists belong to sectarian, not hierarchical, groups; yet they admit that the Sierra Club is hierarchical in organization.[57] Likewise, Douglas and Wildavsky erroneously claim that environmentalists tend to be group oriented and democratic.[58] Yet numerous environmentalists in the Teddy Roosevelt tradition appear not to be shaped by any "social organization." Indeed, they are "loners," rugged individualists, entrepreneurial, and oriented toward survival activities in the wilderness.[59] By reducing all attitudes about hazards to *social* determinants, risk relativists forget that disagreement about ethics, psychology, and risk-assessment *methods* (for example, Bayesianism) also influences hazard evaluations.[60] Hence, it is questionable whether cultural relativists are right in claiming that social structures determine the risk evaluations of each of us.

Are Risk Evaluations Sectarian?

A central part of the relativists' claim is that persons' attitudes toward hazards are a result of their "problems" as members of particular groups. They characterize sectarian groups as pessimistic, anti-institutional, egalitarian, prone to believing conspiracy theories, and eager to find enemies and impurities to condemn.[61] Hence, the relativists allege, these group-induced sectarian characteristics explain why environmentalists criticize industrial pollution.[62]

Like other relativistic arguments, this one also invokes hidden causes of risk aversion and attributes questionable intentions and motives to environmentalists, both without substantiation. However, since up to 90 percent of cancers in the United States are environmentally induced and hence theoretically preventable,[63] there are often *real reasons* for risk aversion. In the absence of evidence supporting their claims, cultural relativists appear to have begged the question of the social determinants of risk aversion. They also appear to have invoked an ad hominem argument against environmentalists, who are alleged to have "problems" because of their allegedly socially determined sectarian views. Cultural relativists need to establish that environmentalists are more risk averse than the facts about hazards dictate; they also need to show that this aversion is caused by environmentalists' group-induced pessimism, paranoia, and anti-institutional sentiments. It will not do for cultural relativists to say, following Maxey and Cohen, merely that "life is growing longer not shorter, health is better not worse," and therefore that citizens have no right to complain or to be averse to technological risks.[64]

In reducing the reasonableness of risk aversion to the question of whether or not life is getting safer, cultural relativists have again ignored the ethical, psychological, and scientific issues that make risk acceptability more than a matter of mere quantity of safety. They appeal to alleged "facts" about hazards—namely, that life is getting safer—when they wish to discredit environmentalists' aversion to risk. Yet they repeatedly deny the existence of any such "facts" about hazards and claim that "risk is a collective construct,"[65] that it is *immeasurable*,[66] that it is determined by social structures, and that no hazard judgment is better or worse than another.[67] If their sociological reductionism and relativism are correct, however, then they are inconsistent in making the risk judgment that life is getting safer. Likewise, if their complaints about citizens' ignoring the "facts" are correct, then they are incorrect in their claims about sociological relativism and reductionism. As Sumner realized,[68] relativism is inconsistent with ethnocentrism.

Naive Positivism

Interestingly, in reducing all risk determinants to social structures, cultural relativists share a common error, reductionism, with the naive positivists.[69] Just as the cultural relativists attempt to reduce risk evaluations to *sociological* constructs, ignoring their objective, scientific content, the naive positivists attempt to reduce them to *scientific* rules, minimizing their ethical content.[70] The cultural relativists *overemphasize* values in risk evaluation and assessment, whereas the naive positivists *underemphasize* them. Other positivists, such as Hempel, maintain a defensible, objective, empiricist approach without espousing this reductionism.[71] Let's see why the naive positivists' account of risk objectivity goes awry.

The Principle of Neutrality

The naive positivists have adopted what amounts to a "principle of complete neutrality." That is, they believe that risk estimates can completely exclude normative (ethical and methodological) components. This belief is based on several assumptions. One such assumption is that the first two stages of hazard assessment can be wholly objective and value free.[72] Another assumption is that any foray into applied ethics or methodological criticism represents a lapse into advocacy and subjectivity. Representative statements of some such "principle of neutrality," central to the naive positivists' account of risk assessment, have been given by the National Academy of Engineering; the U.S. Office of Technology Assessment (OTA); and a variety of scholars and risk assessors, such as Starr and Whipple.[73] The OTA, for example, says that assessments must be "free from advocacy or ideological bias" and must be "objective."[74] Dorothy Nelkin claims that no scholar has any grounds for talking about "the rights and wrongs of policy choice," but should "understand . . . interpret . . . draw a coherent picture of what is going on."[75] Some scholars have even said that different persons, coming from alternative vantage points, ought to "come to the same conclusion" in their risk judgments.[76]

The principle of complete neutrality represents a noble aim and an important effort to keep both science and policy evenhanded and empirically relevant, rather than prejudiced, biased, and superstitious; nevertheless, the principle is open to question. It is clearly wrong if it is construed to mean that science and risk estimation can and ought to be wholly value free. (To their credit, cultural relativists generally recognize that such value freedom is unattainable.) Part of the reason why the naive positivists subscribe to the principle is that they have failed to distinguish among different types of values. Some of these values can be avoided, but others unavoidably occur in science and in risk judgments. In Longino's classification, they can be divided into three types: bias values, contextual values, and constitutive values—a classification (she admits) that is nether mutually exclusive nor exhaustive.[77]

Bias values occur in risk judgments whenever those making the judgments deliberately misinterpret or omit data, so as to serve their own purposes. These types of values obviously can be avoided in risk assessment and in science generally. Hence, the naive positivists' view is correct insofar as it stipulates that bias values can and ought to be kept out of science and risk assessment.

Contextual values are more difficult to avoid. Risk assessors subscribe to particular contextual values whenever they include personal, social, cultural, or philosophical emphases in their judgments. For example, assessors might employ contextual (philosophical) values if financial constraints force them to use existing probabilistic data in assessing a given risk, rather than to conduct their own (new) studies on a particular accident frequency. Although in principle it might be possible to avoid contextual values, in practice it would be almost impossible to do so, either in science or in risk assessment. For example, as Longino points out, industrial microbiology, as practiced by small firms of biochemists, has been heavily influenced by cultural and financial (contextual) values, such as the profit motive.[78] Likewise, risk evaluations of oral contraceptives, heavily influenced by the contextual value of checking population growth, have overemphasized the benefits of the contraceptives and underestimated the risks.[79] One reason why contextual values have played such a large role in many areas of scientific activity and risk assessment is that any research is hampered by some type of incomplete information. Because of this gap, contextual values often determine scientific procedures.

Constitutive or methodological values are even more difficult to avoid in both science and risk assessment than are contextual and bias values. Indeed, it is impossible to avoid them, since scientists and risk assessors make constitutive value judgments whenever they follow one methodological rule rather than another. Even collecting data requires use of constitutive value judgments because one must make evaluative assumptions about what data to collect and what to ignore, how to interpret the data, and how to avoid erroneous interpretations. Constitutive value judgments are required, even in pure science, because perception does not provide us with pure facts; knowledge, beliefs, values, and theories we already hold play a key part in determining what we perceive. The high-energy physicist, for example, does not count all the marks on his cloud-chamber photographs as observations of pions, but only those streaks that his *theories* indicate are pions. Even in the allegedly clear case where observational "facts" contradict a particular theoretical account, a researcher need not reject the theory (laden with values); she could instead reject the "facts" and hold on to the theory. Earlier in this century, for example, when beta decay was observed, it was not taken as a counterinstance to the theory of conservation of energy and momentum; rather, the value-laden conservation theory was accepted, and beta decay was treated, not as a hard-and-fast "fact," but as a "problem" that scientists needed to solve. All this suggests that methodological values unavoidably structure experiments, determine the meaning of observations,[80] and influence both science and risk assessment.

Not all methodological values are created equal, however, and while the naive positivists reject some of them, they accept others. Therefore, to see precisely where and why the naive positivists' account of risk judgments goes wrong, we need to clarify methodological value judgments.

Within such value judgments, McMullin and Scriven distinguish *evaluating* from *valuing*. We can make a largely *factual* judgment and (1) *evaluate* the extent to which a particular thing possesses a characteristic value (e.g., a theory about risk assessment possesses explanatory or predictive power). Or we can make a largely *subjective* judgment and (2) *value* an alleged property (e.g., assess the extent to which a characteristic, such as simplicity, is really a value for a scientific theory or a theory about risk aversion).[81] Like Hempel's "instrumental value judgments" and Scriven's "value-performance claims," what McMullin calls "evaluating" judgments assert that, if a specified value or goal is to be obtained, then a certain action is good. *Evaluating* judgments assess *instrumental goods*. For example, if the value of predictive power is to be obtained, then one ought to develop and test all relevant implications of the theory. Like Hempel's "categorical judgments" and Scriven's "real-value claims," what McMullin calls "valuing" judgments state that a certain goal is prima facie good, independent of particular circumstances.[82]

McMullin, Scriven, and other post-positivists accept both instrumental and categorical value judgments in science.[83] Hempel and the naive positivists, along with a number of risk assessors (such as Starr, Okrent, Rothschild, and Morgan), believe that categorical value judgments have no place in science and science-related activities such as risk estimation. Their complaint against categorical value judgments is that, because they cannot be confirmed empirically, they are subjective.[84]

In assuming that empirical confirmability is value free in science and in risk estimation (the second state of hazard assessment), and thereby excluding categorical judgments of value, naive positivists such as Carnap, Reichenbach, Starr, Okrent, Rothschild, and Morgan appear to err. Aristotle claimed that wise persons realize the reliability characteristic of different kinds of judgments, and therefore demand only the assurance that is appropriate to the particular type of investigation. For example, judgments about present observations are typically more reliable than judgments about events long past. The naive positivists demand an inappropriate level of assurance because their requirement of value-free empirical confirmability would allow neither pure scientists (if there is such a thing) nor risk assessors to decide on criteria for choosing a theory, gathering and interpreting data, or rejecting hypotheses, since such judgments could not be empirically confirmed in a value-free way. (And they could not be empirically confirmed in this way because each of them relies on at least one categorical judgment of value—for example, an assumption about the prima facie importance of some criterion for theory or hypothesis choice.) Yet, as examples such as beta decay and pion "observation" (cited earlier) indicate, scientists do make judgments about weighting criteria for evaluation of theories, observations, and hypotheses, and they do so all the time. Scientific practice does not confirm the naive positivists' notion of the role of value-free confirmability in science and in risk assessment. The positivists are right in their contention that epidemiological studies can be used to confirm risk estimates and to test their predictive power; they are wrong when they claim that confirmation and predictive testing (in science or risk assessment) are devoid of methodological value judgments.[85]

Moreover, if judgments about empirical confirmation were completely independent of methodological value judgments, then science as we know it would come to a halt. Scientists could never make judgments about theory choice, since such choices rely in part on categorical judgments of value. The same must hold true for hazard analysis, as a policy-related activity, since it is even more value laden than science is. Hence, if the naive positivists are correct in requiring that the empirical confirmation of all judgments be value free, then they have brought science and risk assessment to a halt. Moreover, if risk estimation (stage two of assessment) were as value free as many assessors have claimed,[86] then it would never progress, because purely value-free theories could never improve, and, therefore, impotent hypotheses used to estimate risks would never be discarded. But risk estimation does progress, and impotent theories often are discarded. Scientific revolutions occur, even in hazard analysis. Hence, it is obvious that, although empirical confirmation ought to drive good science, no judgments in science are empirically confirmed independent of value judgments. Indeed, they *cannot* be, if science and risk assessment are to continue to include methodological value judgments.

Perhaps many risk assessors and scientists have erroneously believed that it is possible to make value-free, confirmed judgments, about either risks or science, because they subscribe to an extreme form of the fact-value dichotomy, a famous tenet of naive positivism.[87] This is the belief that facts and values are completely separable, and that there are facts that include no value judgments. Applied to hazard assessment, this claim is that risk analysis ought to consist of *factual* and neutral risk estimates, although the policy decisions made as a consequence of them may be *evaluative*.[88]

It is, of course, important to try to keep bias and contextual values out of science.[89] For a number of reasons, however, it is doubtful that there can be a complete dichotomy between facts and values. For one thing, belief in the dichotomy is incompatible with formulation of any scientific theory or analysis to explain causal connections among phenomena, since such formulation requires one to make epistemic value judgments, including categorical value judgments. Also, presenting alternative accounts of one's methodological options, at any stage of science, can never be a purely descriptive or *factual* enterprise; one has to use *evaluative* criteria to select which options to present, and these normative criteria are outside the scope of allowable inquiry.[90] Finally, to subscribe to the fact-value dichotomy is to hold the belief that there can be pure facts and presuppositionless research. As the earlier discussion of bias, contextual, and constitutive values indicates, there is no presuppositionless research.

Admittedly, the traditional positivist motivation behind belief in the fact-value dichotomy is a noble and important one. It is noble because value-free observations, if they existed, would guarantee the objectivity of one's research. As we shall show later, however, value-free observations are not the only guardians of objectivity. Values threaten objectivity only if they *alone* determine the facts. A great many philosophers of science (myself included) maintain that both our values and the action of the external world on our senses are responsible for our perceptions, observations, and facts.[91] Even though facts are value laden, we still may have a sufficient reason for accepting one theory over another. Conceptual and logical reasons also ground theory choice and hence objectivity. One theory may have more explanatory or predictive power, or unify more facts, for example.

Quark theory provides a dramatic example of this point. Isolated quarks are in principle unobservable; yet there are numerous good reasons (simplicity, external consistency, explanatory power) for accepting quark theory. Hence, the value ladenness of facts (whether in science or in risk assessment) implies cultural relativism *only if* one accepts the positivists' presupposition that observation of value-free data, *alone*, provides reasons for accepting one theory rather than another. Because there are other good reasons for theory acceptance, one need not accept this presupposition. Since both the naive positivists and the cultural relativists accept this erroneous presupposition, both groups misunderstand the epistemological grounds for theory acceptance, whether in science or in risk assessment.

The Case against Neutrality

Admittedly, although complete freedom from value judgments cannot be achieved, it ought to be a *goal* or ideal of science and risk assessment. Naive positivists are correct to claim that, even if we can't make presuppositionless risk estimates, we ought to try to avoid bias values and contextual values.[92] There are good grounds for arguing, however, that risk evaluations ought not to be wholly neutral, in the sense of avoiding advocacy or criticism of particular positions on risk. For one thing, to avoid normative criticism in risk evaluation (third stage of assessment) is to assume that one ought never to analyze or criticize the constitutive, contextual, or cognitive values embedded in the data or methodology underlying a particular risk evaluation. But if such values cannot be avoided, to refrain from criticizing them is merely to endorse a risk evaluation that sanctions status quo values, regardless of the errors to which they might lead. Moreover, those who believe that objectivity requires one to refrain from criticizing questionable value judgments are inconsistent. They are implicitly arguing for sanctioning status quo values, because they do not criticize them, even as they explicitly claim to avoid normative work.

Moreover, a risk evaluator who always avoids normative criticism may actually, in many instances, fail to serve *authentic* objectivity. Consider the case in which largely political reasons for accepting a particular risk estimate were widely publicized by a special-interest group. For example, suppose that the owners of nuclear utilities used implausible assumptions in order to argue that future energy demand would be so high that it could not possibly be met by any energy source except breeder reactors. Because some assumptions about electricity usage are more reasonable (e.g., cost-induced elasticity of energy demand) than others (e.g., increasing energy demand, regardless of price), *authentic neutrality* would not be served if the risk evaluator presented all such assumptions in an equally plausible way. The most *objective* thing to do, in the presence of questionable methodological assumptions or constitutive values, is to be *critical* of them and not to remain neutral.

Admittedly, a problem arises when one erroneously criticizes a risk judgment, in the name of objectivity. One opens the door for extremism and ideology, both practiced in the name of risk assessment and science. To this danger, however, there is only one important reply: All activity of any kind would cease if a necessary precondition for it were that one never erred by engaging in it. Moreover, the antidote for moralistic excesses and absolutistic pronouncements is not to prohibit criticism but to ensure criticism of criticism, to provide a hazard-evaluation framework in which alternative risk judgments can be developed, compared, and criticized.[93]

By avoiding, at least at times, the ideal of complete neutrality in making risk evaluations, and by engaging in ethical and methodological criticisms, we contribute to better risk policy. To accept the ideal of complete neutrality in hazard evaluation is to ignore the reality that risk evaluations affect public policy, and that public policy is made in a political environment.[94] Policy is not made by some hypothetical decisionmaker pursuing the public interest; it is made by interaction among a plurality of partisans.[95] This being so, pursuing the ideal of complete neutrality in risk evaluation would limit both the quality and the quantity of these interactions necessary for creating public policy. Moreover, those who pursue the ideal of complete neutrality in hazard evaluation err because they are inconsistent.[96] They denounce all forms of ethical and methodological advocacy and criticism in risk evaluation, but they themselves are advocates for the naive positivists' presupposition that risk evaluators ought to be purely neutral. The real issue is not whether evaluators ought to speak normatively or critically, since values and assumptions unavoidably structure science and hazard analysis. The real issue is whether an evaluation is normative in a way that is misleading, incomplete, question begging, or implausible.

Finally, dangerous consequences would follow if one accepted the naive positivists' presupposition of the ideal of complete neutrality in risk evaluations. If one accepted the naive positivists' claims that only facts are neutral and objective, there would be no nonrelative grounds for deciding questions of value, questions that are nonfactual. If one believed that all value judgments were relative, then this belief could lead one to remain silent while great risks or great abuses were showered on innocent people.[97] Another consequence of sanctioning the naive positivists' view of neutrality, even in risk evaluation, is that it could lead one to accept the status quo and therefore racism, sexism, or violations of civil liberties. When Albert Einstein condemned Hitler's violations of civil liberties in 1933, the Prussian Academy of Sciences denounced Einstein for not remaining neutral. Yet, by their denunciation, the academy's members supported the status quo—namely, violations of civil liberties.[98] Analogously, if—under the guise of being neutral—one never makes normative evaluations about which risks are acceptable, this silence about alleged errors, evils, or misrepresentations will help legitimate whatever risk policy is currently being followed. Camus made the same point: "We are guilty of treason in the eyes of history if we do not denounce what deserves to be denounced. The conspiracy of silence is our condemnation in the eyes of those who come after us."[99] Abraham Lincoln said something similar: "Silence makes men cowards."[100]

Subscribing to the naive positivists' ideal of complete neutrality, even in risk evaluation, might also blind one to the real sources of controversy over risk acceptability. If one subscribes to this ideal and therefore emphasizes the factual side of risk estimates, there is little chance that the real (evaluative) sources of controversy over risk acceptance will be recognized, and therefore little chance that the policy debates they fuel will be fully rational.[101]

A Path between Naive Positivism and Cultural Relativism

If public policy about risk is to address the real sources of lay unrest and expert disagreement, that policy must be based on an accurate account of the reasons for the controversy. At least part of this unrest and disagreement, I have argued, is attributable to a misunderstanding about the role of values in hazard assessment. I have argued that hazard assessment can be objective and testable,[102] but not wholly value free. Cultural relativists, but not "soft relativists,"[103] *overemphasize* values and reduce all risk evaluations to mere sociological constructs, devoid of objective science. Naive positivists *underemphasize* values and attempt to reduce all risk evaluations to algorithms of allegedly pure science.[104] They ignore the ethical part of risk evaluation. A more plausible account of scientific rationality and objectivity is, I believe, one that falls midway between the views of the cultural relativists and those of the naive positivists. In this view, which I call "scientific proceduralism," the rationality appropriate to risk analysis is best defined by three propositions: (1) that, as Hempel asserts, there is at least one general, universal criterion for theory or paradigm choice in both science and risk assessment: explanatory power as tested by prediction; (2) that most of the remaining criteria for theory choice, although evaluated and interpreted on the basis of how well they serve explanatory power as tested by prediction, are situation specific or determined largely by practice (i.e., naturalistic); and (3) that we can best guarantee "scientific objectivity," as I define it, by testing the predictive and explanatory power of our risk theories and by subjecting risk evaluations to intelligent debate, criticism, and amendment by the scientific community and laypeople likely to be affected by the risk.[105]

Since I won't have time to defend all three propositions, I'll rely in part on the arguments of McMullin and Hempel for claim 1, that there is at least one general, universal criterion for theory choice in science and risk assessment—viz., explanatory power as tested by prediction.[106] To see how this general criterion might operate, one need only recall some of the arguments made earlier in the volume. For example, I claimed that the theory of risk behavior adopted by risk relativists such as Douglas and Wildavsky fails in *explanatory power* because it relies on social determinants of risk aversion and does not provide an account of hazard aversion arising from personal and psychological variables.[107] Likewise, the *predictive power* of their theory is flawed, as was already argued, since the Sierra Club is politically quite representative of the entire population.[108]

To understand how explanatory power as tested by prediction can function as a universal criterion or goal for theory choice in science and in hazard analysis,[109] however, we have to understand why scientific objectivity does not require value-free empirical confirmability. It is not reasonable to require value-free, empirical confirmability of all risk evaluations because such confirmability is not the only test of objectivity, either in science or anywhere else, and because essential methodological value judgments (in science) cannot be confirmed. Rather, we often call a judgment "objective," even in science, if it is not obviously biased or subjective. Objectivity, in this sense, is not tied to value-free empirical confirmability but, rather, is linked to avoiding *bias* values, to giving evenhanded representation of the situation. What I call "scientific objectivity" (and I say "scientific" not because the objectivity is unique to science, but simply because it is characteristic of science and related activities, such as making risk evaluations) is closely related to this sense of objectivity as evenhandedness.

Presumably, one could be blamed for failure to be objective, in the sense of not being evenhanded, if one were biased in a particular methodological value judgment about risk—for example, if one drew a conclusion about risk acceptability after deliberately misrepresenting some of the data on probability of the hazard. Since we do often blame people for not being objective—that is, for not being fair or even-handed—it is clear either that objectivity in this sense must be attainable or that one can be more or less objective, contrary to what the cultural relativists believe.

But how might one guarantee scientific objectivity in the sense of avoiding bias values and providing evenhanded representation of the situation?[110] Perhaps the best way to contribute to rationality and objectivity is to check the predictive and explanatory power of our hazard evaluations and to subject them to review by scientists and by laypersons likely to be affected by them. The assessments then might be said to possess "scientific objectivity," in some minimal sense, after they have been subjected to tests of predictive and explanatory power (see note 66), and to criticism, debate, and amendment. In this account, scientific *rationality* is served by a risk assessor working individually, pursuing a goal of explanatory power tested in part by prediction.[111] Scientific *objectivity*, however, can only be guaranteed both by predictive and explanatory power and by scientists and affected laypersons working together to criticize and amend proposed accounts of risk acceptability.[112]

It seems reasonable to define "scientific objectivity" in terms of criticism, as well as predictive and explanatory power, especially because such criticism need not be wholly subjective. When I make an epistemic value judgment about two accident probabilities, or about the acceptability of a particular risk, for example, I am not talking merely autobiographically and subjectively. I am talking about characteristics of possible, public, *external* events that are capable of being known and understood by other people. Moreover, the skills associated with making these judgments are a function of training, education, experience, and intelligence. Therefore, objectivity does not necessarily require one to have an algorithm guaranteeing the correctness of risk judgments. An algorithm is not necessary, in part because empirical factors (such as observed accident consequences or actual accident frequencies) could change the likelihood that our risk judgments are correct; hence, such judgments cannot be purely subjective. (That is why their predictive power can be tested.[113])

Finally, to make empirical confirmability alone (instead of predictive and explanatory power, for example) a necessary condition for the objectivity of all risk judgments would be to ignore the way that reasonable people behave. Reasonable people accumulate observations and inferences until the probability of their judgments is so great that they do not doubt them. They make assumptions when their evidence supports them; they do not rely exclusively on value-free empirical confirmation. Only if one were engaged in a search for objectivity that came close to avoiding all error would it seem reasonable to complain about well-supported risk evaluations that met the procedural criteria (predictive, explanatory power, surviving criticism) for scientific objectivity just outlined.[114] Since even science has never claimed such an unrealistic notion of objectivity (that came close to infallibility), it does not seem reasonable to demand more than the previous three criteria as standards for "objective" risk judgments.[115] My new sense of "scientific objectivity" also seems plausible because it relies, in part, on the social and critical character of science and science-related activities (like risk assessment). As Karl Popper,[116] William James, Ludwig Wittgenstein, and John Wisdom realized, the naive positivists make too strict a demand on scientific objectivity by requiring value-free confirmability, alone, in all evaluative situations.

The cultural relativists also make too strict demands by presupposing that "objective" risk estimates must be wholly value free and therefore infallible and universal.[117] They believe that, because every risk evaluation is value laden and because both experts and laypeople disagree about hazards, no risk evaluations can be said to be objective. Because of the lack of consensus on risk evaluation, they claim that none is certain, that any of them can be said to be justified, and that one is as good as another.[118] Although they are correct in recognizing the incompleteness of the naive positivists' model of rationality, the cultural relativists go too far in leaping to the premature conclusion that, because the naive positivists' criterion of value-free empirical confirmability fails, therefore risk evaluations are purely relative.[119]

A New Account of Objectivity

In searching for a certainty that appears to transcend the possibility of error, and in presupposing that objectivity requires infallibility and universality,[120] risk relativists assume that, since there is no perfect judgment, all risk evaluations are equally imperfect. Yet neither from the fact that all judgments have been falsified historically, nor from the fact that it is impossible for any judgment to escape falsification, would it follow that all risk evaluations are equally unreliable.[121] Historical falsifications of judgments provide only necessary, not sufficient, conditions for the claim that there are no objective risk evaluations. Both scientific inference and legal inference establish that something is prima facie true, that it is reasonably probable, or that there is a presumption in its favor, not that it is infallibly true. Hence, there is no reason to assume that risk evaluations need be more than prima facie true if they are said to be objective.[122] Moreover, great differences in scientific and policy-related behavior are compatible with "objective" risk judgments. Disagreements over how to analyze or evaluate a given hazard do not mean either that there are no rules of risk assessment or that any rule is as good as another. Rather, those who deny the existence of universal rules or values in science and risk assessment appear to do so because they fail to distinguish three different questions: (1) Are there *general principles* (for example, "Postulate risk probabilities that are consistent with observed accident frequencies" or "Postulate risk acceptability as proportional to the degree of public consent to the societal danger") that account for the rationality of hazard evaluation? (2) Are there *particular procedures*, or instantiations of the general principles (for example, "Accident frequencies should be observed for a period of at least five years before one concludes that they are consistent with postulated risk probabilities"), that account for the rationality of risk evaluations? (3) Does a particular risk evaluation, *in fact*, always illustrate either the general principles or the specific procedures? (For example, did the authors of WASH-1400 observe accident frequencies for a period of at least five reactor-years before postulating the annual probability of a core melt, per reactor-year?)

Cultural relativists appear to assume that, if one answers questions 2 and 3 in the negative, then the answer to question 1, the question before us, is also negative. This is false. Debate about question 2 doesn't jeopardize the rationality and nonrelativism of risk judgments, so long as we can agree on question 1. In fact, debate over question 2 must presuppose rationality in the sense of question 1, or the discussion would be futile.[123]

Insights from Moral Philosophy

Another way to argue that risk evaluations can be rational and objective, because we can often agree on general principles (above), is to incorporate some insights from moral philosophy. As both natural-law philosophers and contemporary analysts such as Hare recognize, there is a hierarchy of methodological rules and value judgments, with different degrees of certainty at different levels of generality in the hierarchy. In science, risk assessment, and ethics, the most general rules are the most certain and the most universal—for example, "Postulate risk probabilities that are consistent with observed accident frequencies" or "Do good and avoid evil." The least general rules or value judgments are the least certain and the least universal.[124]

In moral philosophy as well as in science and risk evaluation, one must make a number of value judgments, especially at the lower levels of universality and generality, in order to interpret and to apply the rules from the most universal and most general level. Even though there is no algorithm for these methodological value judgments, that does not mean that practice-based ethical, scientific, or risk-assessment judgments are purely relative. Some are better than others; that is, they are better *means* to the *end* or goal of explanatory and predictive power.

The risk relativists miss both these points because they focus on *infallibility* (in the scientific assessments reached by means of methodological rules and epistemic value judgments), rather than on prima facie truth, or on what I have called "scientific objectivity." This particular sense of objectivity relies on a number of insights of Popper, Wisdom, and Wittgenstein.[125] It anchors objectivity with actions and practices, as well as with explanatory and predictive power; it does not define objectivity in terms of an impossible, perhaps question-begging, notion of justification. This account secures objectivity, in part, by means of the criticisms made by the scientific and lay community likely to be affected by risk evaluations. It presupposes that rationality and objectivity, in their final stages, require an appeal to particular cases of risk evaluation as similar to other cases believed to be correct (just as legal reasoning requires). This account does not presuppose an appeal to *specific* rules, applicable to all risk situations, although the *general* rules of testing predictive and explanatory power are always applicable.[126] A *naturalistic* appeal to cases and to general methodological values, rather than to specific rules, is central to this account. This naturalistic appeal is necessary (1) because we need to avoid an infinite regress when justifying risk judgments; (2) because decisions about rules cannot ultimately rest on rules; and (3) because specific criteria would be too dogmatic, in all cases, to take account of counterinstances and the peculiarities of particular risk evaluations.

Conclusion

More generally, if relativistic arguments requiring that all *objective* risk evaluations be based on universal and stable rules were correct, and if these arguments were extended to other areas of epistemology and policy, then they would invalidate most of our knowledge claims.[127] Rather than admit that most of our knowledge claims are invalid, it seems more reasonable to say that the naive positivists and the cultural relativists have conceived of "objective" risk evaluations in partially unrealistic ways. Moreover, both groups of reductionists have confused *general principles* of risk-evaluation methods with *specific procedures*. I have argued that a more realistic way to conceive of rational risk assessment is in terms of "scientific proceduralism."

In subsequent chapters of this volume, I shall show how the failure to define rational risk evaluation in terms of "scientific proceduralism" leads both to flawed policy and to disenfranchising members of the public likely to be victims of societal risk. Later, in Chapter Eleven, I shall show how my proposals for reforming risk evaluation and management meet the criteria for scientific rationality and objectivity outlined in this chapter; I shall also answer several prominent objections to scientific proceduralism. These objections fail, in large part, because they miss the basic insight of Israel Scheffler: scientific "objectivity requires simply the possibility of intelligible debate over the merits of rival paradigms."[128]

Chapter Four

Objectivity and Values in Risk Evaluation

Why We Need a Procedural Account of Rationality

In 1988, the U.S. Department of Energy (DOE) applied for state permits to begin testing at Yucca Mountain, Nevada, the only candidate for the nation's first high-level nuclear waste dump. In winter 1990, Nevada's governor said that he would never issue the permits, even though the Justice Department has brought suit over the state's failure to comply. Nevada has argued that Yucca Mountain is full of fractured rock that could allow contaminated water to migrate. DOE says the site is safe.[1]

If previous experience at other U.S. hazardous waste sites is representative, the people of Nevada have cause for concern. In 1962, for example, geologists calculated the risks associated with a proposed site for shallow land burial of transuranics and low-level radioactive wastes. Scientists from industry and academia praised the (Maxey Flats) Kentucky location and calculated that, if plutonium were buried there, it would take 24,000 years to migrate one-half inch. They said that "the possibility of subsurface migration offsite is nonexistent."[2] They were confident about their predictions because experts typically have argued that, "in the main, epidemiology studies have not shown that these [hazardous waste] sites produce adverse health effects in humans who live near them."[3] Yet, only ten years after the facility was opened, plutonium and other radionuclides were discovered two miles off site.[4] The geological predictions were wrong by *six orders of magnitude*.

Although the Kentucky facility has been closed, it remains a problem. The site contains more plutonium (in curies) than any other commercial repository in the world,[5] and scientists have been unable to halt the radwaste migration. The half-life of plutonium 239 is 24,390 years, and less than a millionth of a gram is sufficient to cause lung cancer.[6]

Not surprisingly, journalists have called the Kentucky site the world's "worst nuclear dump," a "fountain of death."[7]

One of the many questions raised by this case is whether the faulty hydrogeological predictions at the Maxey Flats radwaste site were highly atypical. If they were, then perhaps Nevadans have little to fear. If they were not, then Yucca Mountain may also be a cause for concern. Are science, in general, and risk assessment, in particular, more reliable than these erroneous migration predictions suggest?

Probably not. Experts reveal that uncertainties of six orders of magnitude are "not unusual" in risk assessment.[8] Likewise, a famous study on the siting of LNG (liquefied natural gas) terminals in four countries showed that widely varying risk estimates for the same event are pervasive; in Oxnard, California, for instance, reputable hazard assessments (of citizens' average annual chance of dying in a liquefied natural gas accident) differed by three orders of magnitude.[9] Likewise, current U.S. government predictions for the likelihood of a Three Mile Island type of accident differ by two orders of magnitude.[10] Other cases are much the same; they suggest that scientific predictions and risk estimates are laden with methodological value judgments and enormous uncertainties.[11]

To claim that science is laden with value judgments, however, is to challenge the whole edifice of epistemology in the West. Science is the paradigm of all knowledge.[12] If it contains value judgments, then we must radically rework the ideal of scientific objectivity. As Rudner put it, "the slightly juvenile conception of the coldblooded, emotionless, impersonal, passive scientist mirroring the world perfectly in the highly polished lenses of his steel rimmed glasses—this stereotype—is no longer, if it ever was, adequate."[13]

As noted in Chapter Three, we need to build a new account of rationality and objectivity. This account (scientific proceduralism) falls midway between the positions of the naive positivists and the cultural relativists. Neither of them, as the last chapter showed, gives an adequate account of scientific rationality and objectivity. The naive positivists underemphasize the value judgments in science, whereas the cultural relativists overemphasize them. Both the naive positivists and the cultural relativists erroneously claim that citizen aversion to societal risks is biased. Calling people "biased" or "irrational" in their risk evaluations, however, presupposes that they are making illegitimate value judgments about acceptable risk. To determine the correctness of the "irrational" label, one must know something about *which value judgments* are legitimate and which ones (if any) are compatible with scientific rationality and objectivity. By further clarifying the nature of value judgments used in science, hazard assessment, and risk evaluation, I shall be able to present a new account of which risks are rational to accept. I begin by outlining the "standard view" of risk assessment. Next I argue that this "standard view" is wrong; it ignores the characteristic, epistemic values central to doing even pure science. Finally, I outline some typical value judgments essential to methods used at each of the three stages of risk analysis, closing with a familiar example of a highly value-laden hazard assessment, Inhaber's energy study.

The "Standard Account" of Risk Assessment

Many practitioners of risk or hazard assessment or analysis, as was mentioned in Chapter One, divide it into three stages: *risk identification, risk estimation,* and *risk evaluation.*[14] Most of the discussion in this volume focuses on the third stage, risk evaluation. At the first stage, one identifies a particular threat to human health and safety—for instance, vinyl chloride. At the second stage, scientists such as epidemiologists or environmental engineers estimate the risk of death or injury associated with particular levels of exposure to that hazard. At the third stage, scientists such as economists and health physicists, as well as psychologists and policymakers, evaluate what level of exposure to the risk, if any, is acceptable to society. After these three tasks of hazard analysis are completed, regulators and lawmakers begin the process of *risk management,* ensuring that the actual risk exposure conforms to the standards of acceptability already determined by assessors.

Proponents of the "standard account" of risk assessment, naive positivists such as Starr, Whipple, Maxey, Cohen, Lee, and Okrent, maintain that the expert methods employed in the first two stages of assessment (risk identification and risk estimation) are completely objective, neutral, and value free. They say that the somewhat subjective methods employed in the third stage (risk evaluation) can be made more objective and neutral merely by improving the analytic techniques used by experts to evaluate risks.[15] Risk assessment, in their view, is a largely scientific discipline, to be perfected along hypothetical-deductive lines.[16] They are on the quest for algorithms that will give them power to predict and assess risks in a wholly neutral way, much as Einstein and David Bohm hoped for deterministic, predictive power for quantum mechanics.[17]

Critics of the standard account argue, however, that risk analysis—especially its third stage, risk evaluation—ought to be accomplished both through hypothetical-deductive testing and through democratic give-and-take involving citizens. It cannot depend solely on an expert-controlled analytic or scientific methodology.[18] If these critics are correct, then risk evaluation is not merely a scientific investigation but also a political procedure to be negotiated among experts and the public. Many assessors ignore the *procedural* aspects of hazard evaluation, calling merely for "scientifically verifiable models with testable hypotheses" and urging fellow assessors to improve risk assessment so that it earns "more respect in the scientific community."[19]

Risk Evaluation, Like Science, Is Evaluative

Although they reveal good intentions and a healthy empiricism, such pleas are in part misguided. Confirmation and acceptance by the technical community are clearly *goals* for wholly scientific enterprises. These goals, however, are never fully realized, especially in risk evaluation. Although the first two stages of hazard analysis are largely scientific, they nevertheless rely on a number of methodological or epistemic value judgments.[20] Moreover, the third stage of hazard assessment requires comparing a given risk to a great many other ones, in order to determine whether it is tolerable to society. This means that the judgment of acceptability is a function not only of predictive and explanatory power but also of the kinds of comparisons used. Hazards may be compared on the basis of their probability, their consequences, their benefits, their equity of risk distribution, their voluntariness, the level of consent given to them, and so on. Obviously, these comparative notions are not subject to empirical confirmation, even though risk analysis is touted as a "developing science."[21]

This comparative side of risk evaluation, however, is one of its strengths. It provides opportunities for promoting *efficiency* by maximizing the benefits of government expenditures for health and safety. It also promotes *equity* and *consistency* in allocation of funds among safety programs. As one thinker put it, risk assessment enables us to ask important questions, such as "why OSHA intends, in a set of proposed regulations on coke-oven emissions, to protect the lives of steelworkers at $5 million each, while a national Pap-smear screening program that would save women's lives at less than $100,000 each has gone unfunded."[22]

Perhaps the greatest liability of comparative, quantified risk assessment, especially risk evaluation, however, is that it attempts to reduce qualitatively diverse risks to mere mathematical probabilities and numbers of fatalities. Critics of hazard analysis also charge that it threatens to remove health and safety from democratic social control and to place it solely in the hands of experts. Apart from whether opponents of risk analysis are correct in their allegations about its political liabilities, the third, or evaluative, stage of hazard assessment is the most controversial precisely because it involves quantitative comparisons of diverse risks. Because of such comparisons, risk evaluation is *both* objective or scientific (in the three senses discussed in the previous chapter) *and* procedural in focusing on the normative goals of efficiency and equity.

Several reasons why risk analysis, and especially risk evaluation, are value laden have been pointed out in the previous chapter.[23] Assessors must make value judgments about which data to collect; how to simplify myriad facts into a workable model; how to extrapolate because of unknowns; how to choose statistical tests to be used; how to select sample size; determine criteria for NOEL (no-observed-effect level);[24] decide where the burden of proof goes, which power function to use, what size of test to run, and which exposure-response model to employ.[25] All these methodological value judgments in hazard identification and estimation suggest that, even though it is objective in the three senses already discussed, risk assessment is also value laden.

To claim that science and risk assessment are value laden, however, is to challenge naive-positivist orthodoxy, as the previous chapter argued.[26] Although most philosophers of science realize that science may be described in terms of some sort of Kuhnian revolution, few seem to understand that this recognition of scientific revolution was caused by a new awareness of the role played by *value judgments* in scientific work. The reason why many philosophers continue to follow the naive-positivist, Carnapian view of the nature of science (as free from values) is likely that, although they correctly believe that emotive values have no place in science, they erroneously associate values only with emotion and feeling.[27]

Admittedly, science should not include emotive values. As the previous chapter argued, however, values can be cognitive and not just emotive. Consequently, one can argue that there are methodological value judgments in science,[28] and that they substantively affect scientific conclusions.[29] The case of physicist Wolfgang Pauli's postulation of the neutrino illustrates this point. Pauli emphasized the value of *internal consistency* with conservation principles and therefore postulated the existence of the neutrino before it was observed. Other physicists of his time emphasized a different value—*external consistency* with principles demanding empirical proof—and therefore rejected the neutrino.[30]

In response to these claims about values, some positivistically oriented persons would likely argue that, although science does rest on nonverifiable "postulates," it does not involve values per se.[31] The problem with this sort of response, however, is that the "postulates" (e.g., Keynes's postulate that economics can obtain legitimate conclusions by ignoring all human desires except the desire for wealth) involved in science are matters of controversy among experts. Therefore, someone could come up with different "postulates" or "values" and defend them on different grounds. This means that science is not more objective by virtue of employing "postulates" rather than "values." Both labels are threats to naive accounts of objectivity.[32]

Value Judgments in the Three Stages of Risk Assessment

One of the most important threats to naive accounts of objectivity in risk analysis is the postulate or value judgment that one ought to define risk as a compound measure of the probability and magnitude of adverse effect. This measure is often expressed as the "average annual probability of fatality." It presupposes that one is justified in interpreting "risk" in terms of fatalities alone and ignoring injuries; financial losses; carcinogenic, mutagenic, and teratogenic effects; and political and philosophical harms, such as threats to due-process rights. Various emissions standards for industrial pollutants, for example, threaten due-process rights because it is virtually impossible to tell which pollutant is responsible for an injury. It is therefore almost impossible to collect damages for particular harms caused by industrial air pollutants, even though air pollution in the eastern United States poses nearly as great a danger of death as smoking a pack of cigarettes each day. The standard account of risk, however, ignores such dangers because of its narrow, highly evaluative definition of risk.[33] Indeed, each of the three stages of hazard assessment (risk identification, risk estimation, and risk evaluation) involves numerous evaluative judgments.[34]

It is difficult, first, to *identify* risks because each of the five commonly used methods of carcinogen identification, for example, has serious defects whose presence requires the assessor to make epistemic and pragmatic value judgments. For instance, the use of case clusters (looking for adverse effects to appear in a particular place) is helpful only when specific hazards cause unique diseases and only when the population at risk is known in some detail. Since often it is not known whether these conditions are satisfied, especially in cases involving new risks, assessors must evaluate the situation as best they can.

Comparison of compounds on the basis of structural toxicology, a second method of risk identification, likewise is problematic. It reveals only that a potential toxin, for example, has the same structure as a carcinogen. Yet, in using this method, assessors typically assume that this similarity of structure is sufficient to determine that a substance is a positive carcinogen. Use of mutagenicity assays also relies on a normative judgment, that most chemical carcinogens are mutagens. But mutagenicity assays are rarely sufficient to support the conclusion that a particular mutagen is also carcinogenic. Long-term animal bioassays likewise depend on an epistemic value judgment, that particular results from animal experiments are applicable to humans.

Another class of risk-identification methods, biostatistical epidemiological studies, employs more sophisticated case clusters that aim to show an association between an agent and a disease. The obvious deficiencies with this method are that it is often difficult to accumulate the relevant evidence, particularly if exposure is at low dosage or if the effects are delayed, as in cancers with latency periods of up to forty years. In the absence of complete data and long years of testing, assessors are forced to interpret and to extrapolate from the information that they do have, and hence to make both pragmatic and epistemic judgments. Moreover, most substances are not even tested with epidemiological methods; apart from other sources of hazards, roughly 60,000 chemicals are used annually in various manufacturing processes, and at least 1,000 new ones are added each year. A new toxic chemical is introduced into U.S. industry every twenty minutes.[35] Deciding which chemicals to test, when not all can be tested, is perhaps one of the greatest pragmatic value judgments in risk identification. Yet without biostatistical epidemiological testing, it is unlikely that hazardous chemicals will be removed from the market. Only a few pesticides commonly used in the United States, for instance, have received biological epidemiological testing, even though a recent U.S. National Academy of Sciences study reports that 60 percent of all herbicides and 90 percent of all fungicides used in the United States can cause cancer in animals.[36]

At the second stage of risk assessment, risk estimation, one is concerned primarily with determining a dose-response relationship for a particular hazard, the population at risk, and the dose it receives from the hazard. Determining a dose-response curve is important in order to set exposure limits and to trace causal pathways back from a harm (for example, cancer incidence in a population) to its origin in a hazard such as radiation. Dose-response methods are conceptually problematic because risk assessors do not have open to them the obvious standard techniques of justification. They cannot expose a series of populations to a dose of some carcinogen and then count the cancer fatalities in each population. Instead, assessors must make many value judgments about the validity of extrapolation from high to low doses, from animals to humans, and from one group of humans to another.

The problems associated with such extrapolation are well known. For example, health physicists often must try to estimate a dose-response curve for low-level radiation exposure when they are given data points only for higher-level exposures. Environmentalists, industry representatives, and members of health physics associations have extrapolated, respectively, to a dose-response curve for radiation that is typically logarithmic or supralinear; quadratic, linear-quadratic, or linear with a large threshold; and linear with no threshold. On the basis of their differing value judgments about the low-dose end of the curve, they have concluded, respectively, that low-level radiation is very dangerous, not very dangerous, and moderately dangerous. To give some idea of the differences in the estimates produced when the several models for radiation dose-response curves are used, consider the excess incidence of cancers predicted, other than leukemia and multiple myeloma. For a 10-rad exposure, the quadratic model predicts 560 excess cancers per million persons exposed, whereas the linear-quadratic predicts 4,732 excess cases, and the linear model predicts 10,630 excess cancers. Thus, there is a twentyfold difference between the quadratic and the linear models! More surprisingly, there is an eighty-six-fold difference between the predictions of the quadratic and the supralinear models. However, the National Academy of Sciences' (NAS) Committee on Biological Effects of Ionizing Radiation claims that there is no reason to prefer one model over the other at low doses. The committee therefore seems to suggest that one value judgment about which curve to use is not always more objective than another.[37]

Estimating the population at risk and the dose received is just as problematic as determining the dose-response curve, because estimators must assume that their theories provide a reasonable measure of exposure; that the exposure is related in some clear way to the administered dose; that the absorbed dose is a specific function of the administered dose; that phenotypic variation in populations does not inordinately affect the dose received; that the critical organ dose is related precisely to the absorbed dose; and that the effect is a particular function of the critical organ dose. Because actual measurements of particular doses of a chemical, for example, cannot be made in all situations, a mathematical model of assumed exposure must be used, and assessors must make an epistemic judgment as to its suitability. Sometimes these judgments differ radically; toxicologists, for example, typically view the notion of a safe threshold dose as controversial, whereas engineers, who equate dispersal with dilution, tend to assume some threshold below which a substance is no longer harmful. Neither group, however, typically addresses synergistic effects,[38] even though seemingly unimportant pathways of exposure can assume great significance—owing, for example, to biomagnification or food-chain effects.

Moreover, it is rare that a substance is uniformly distributed across pathways and time. Numerous studies have shown that the target dose, pathway, and persistence of a toxic chemical, for example, are difficult to predict, as was illustrated by the 1976 accident in Seveso, Italy; a toxic cloud of TCDD, including dioxin, was released over 5,000 people.[39] Similar difficulties plagued epidemiologists tracing the distribution of radiation after the Chernobyl nuclear accident on 25 April 1986. Maps showing the areas of greatest radionuclide deposition look like Rorschach drawings; the distribution did not follow a predictable pattern based on prevailing wind direction and the rotation of the earth. Instead, numerous factors, such as rainfall patterns and the height of the radioactive plume, affected the highly irregular spread of radiation following the accident.[40] Moreover, even if pathways of various toxins could be determined exactly, phenotypic variations among populations would mean that one person could be two hundred times more sensitive to a chemical than another, even when both received equal doses.[41] Given such situations, the assessor is forced to make a number of interpretative, value-laden risk-estimation judgments.

Highly evaluative judgments also are made at the third stage of hazard assessment, risk evaluation. At this stage, analysts typically determine whether a risk is acceptable to society. They employ at least four different methods: risk-cost-benefit analysis (RCBA), revealed preferences, expressed preferences, and natural standards. RCBA is widely used and consists simply of converting the risks, costs, and benefits associated with a particular project to monetary terms and then aggregating each of them, in order to determine whether the risks and costs outweigh the benefits.[42] In using RCBA, assessors are forced to make a number of highly evaluative judgments—for instance, that monetary-term parameters can adequately represent the real cost or benefit of a thing or that the *magnitude* of risks, costs, and benefits is more important than their *distribution*.[43]

The second method of risk evaluation, *revealed preferences*, consists of making inductive inferences about acceptable risk on the basis of the levels of risk that existed in the past.[44] The most worrisome value judgment in this method is that past societal risk levels reveal desirable risk levels for the present. This assumption requires one to judge that, where risk is concerned, the present ought to be like the past, and that hazards accepted in the past *ought* to have been accepted. Both of these highly evaluative judgments may be questionable, either because past levels of risk may be indefensible (for example, they may have been imposed on unwilling victims), or because our ethical obligations regarding present risk may be greater than those of our ancestors regarding past risk.

The third method of risk evaluation, *expressed preferences*, consists of using psychometric surveys to determine the acceptability of particular hazards.[45] It is built on the questionable assumption that the preferences people express via instruments such as surveys provide reliable indicators of acceptable risks. Obviously, however, preferences are not always authentic indicators of welfare: some persons have irrational fears, and others are too ignorant to realize a serious danger. This method also requires assessors to make a number of evaluative judgments whenever they encounter inconsistencies in survey preferences or whenever the responses fail to correspond with actual behavior regarding environmental hazards.

The fourth method of risk evaluation, *natural standards*, uses geological and biological criteria to determine hazard levels current during the evolution of the species.[46] Like the method of revealed preferences, this method is based on the assumption that, if a particular level of risk was present in the past, then that same level is acceptable at present. Such an assumption seems unwarranted, however, especially if the risk can be avoided, or especially if no overarching benefits arise from allowing the risk to remain high. Moreover, since the method is based on a "natural standard" for each different hazard, it totally fails to take account of synergistic or cumulative effects. These effects could be many orders of magnitude greater than the actual "standard level" of exposure.

All the assumptions, extrapolations, and inferences built into each of the methods in the three stages of hazard assessment arise in large part because nearly every situation of risk identification, estimation, or evaluation is factually incomplete and imprecise, and therefore empirically underdetermined. Because it is empirically underdetermined, risk assessors are forced to make some methodological value judgments, so as to interpret the data available to them. At root, these assumptions and inferences often reduce to the problem of getting a grip on causality. This is difficult, since causes are not seen; they are inferred on the basis of their effects. Cancers, for example, don't wear tags saying that they were caused by their subject's smoking, or by use of oral contraceptives, or by diet drinks, or by the subject's breathing the emissions of the chemical plant next door. Moreover, we know statistically how much of one agent causes cancer in *general*, but we can never determine whether a substance caused a *particular* cancer. We can only *infer* what caused a certain cancer.

Classic examples of the difficulty of establishing *causality* of harm, given a certain *probability* of risk, occur throughout industry and government. Industry analyses of Monsanto and Dow workers, all exposed to chemical accidents and all victims of chloracne for a mean time of twenty-six years afterward, claimed that those exposed had "no heightened mortality." Likewise, a study of GI victims of Agent Orange, thirteen years after exposure, concluded that there were "no unusual findings attributable to the herbicide." The government drew similar conclusions when U.S. servicemen were exposed to above-ground nuclear weapons tests in the western United States and in the South Pacific. Many of them were within five miles of ground zero for as many as twenty-three separate explosions, or were marched to within three hundred yards of ground zero immediately after detonation. Yet, of the half million soldiers so exposed during the 1950s and 1960s, only ten have won benefits when they or their survivors claimed that their cancers were *caused* by the fallout. Like risk victims everywhere, they were able to show a statistically significant increase in certain types of injuries or deaths, a *correlation* between increased dose and increased response, but no *cause* of particular cancers. Without proof of causality, they could claim no benefits. In the absence of proof and complete data, they were forced, like risk assessors everywhere, to rely on value judgments, on inference, extrapolation, and simplification.[47]

Inhaber's Risk Assessment

One famous example of a highly evaluative, highly controversial hazard analysis is that of Herbert Inhaber. Commissioned by the Canadian Atomic Energy Control Board and summarized in *Science*, his study estimated the dangers from alternative energy technologies. It concluded that the risk from conventional energy systems, such as nuclear or coal power, is less than that from nonconventional systems, such as solar or wind energy. It also concluded that noncatastrophic risks, such as those from solar power, are greater than catastrophic risks, such as those from nuclear power.[48]

How did Inhaber arrive at his surprising conclusions? He made some highly questionable evaluative assumptions. In *estimating* the risk posed by particular energy technologies, he assumed, for example, that all electricity was of utility-grid quality (i.e., able to be fed into a power grid).[49] As a result, he ignored the low-risk benefits of solar space heating and hot-water heating, neither of which can be fed into a power grid. Indeed, he ignored the wide variety of low-temperature forms of solar energy, which could supply 40 percent of all U.S. energy needs at competitive prices and at little risk.[50]

Another highly evaluative assumption central to Inhaber's risk estimates was that all nonconventional energy technologies have coal backups.[51] As a result, for example, in the case of solar thermal electric, 89 percent of the risk that he attributed to it comes not from the solar (involving mainly risk from construction of components) but from the coal backup, which he classified as a solar risk! Moreover, Inhaber assumed that nuclear fission requires no backup, even though these plants have a downtime of 33 percent per year for checkups, refueling, and repairs.[52]

In the area of *risk evaluation*, Inhaber's assumptions are just as questionable. When he aggregated and compared all lost workdays, for all energy technologies, he ignored the fact that lost workdays are more or less severe, depending on the nature of the accident causing them and whether or not they are sequential. In Inhaber's scheme, a lost workday due to cancer or the acute effects of radiation sickness is no different from a lost workday due to a sprained ankle.[53] Yet obviously the cancer could result in premature death, and the radiation exposure could result in mutagenic effects on one's children. Neither is comparable to a sprained ankle.

Inhaber made a similar questionable assumption in evaluating the severity of risks. Unlike other hazard assessors, he totally ignored the distinction between catastrophic and noncatastrophic risks. He assumed that there is no difference between 1,000 construction workers who fall off a roof and die, in separate accidents, and 1,000 workers who die because of a catastrophic accident in a nuclear fuel fabrication plant.[54] Numerous risk assessors, however, typically make a distinction between catastrophic and noncatastrophic accidents. They suggest, for example, that because of increased societal disruption, n lives lost in a single catastrophic accident should be assessed as a loss of n^2 lives.[55] Whether or not this n^2 interpretation is a reasonable one, the point is that Inhaber made numerous evaluative assumptions, such as that the distinction between catastrophic and noncatastrophic accidents could be ignored. In so doing, he passed off his results as purely objective hazard assessment. Instead, were one to trace Inhaber's methods, step by step, it would be clear that virtually every assumption he made in estimating and evaluating alternative risks had the effect of increasing his alleged nonconventional risks and decreasing his alleged conventional risks.[56]

Even if persons such as Inhaber avoided their questionable means of aggregating and estimating risks, values would unavoidably enter the hazard-evaluation process. This is because value judgments are often the only ways to resolve some ethical dilemmas facing risk assessors, especially at the third or risk-evaluation stage. The next chapter will survey some of the dilemmas besetting risk evaluation, showing that they reflect the need for a new account of rational risk acceptance.

Chapter Five

Five Dilemmas
of Risk Evaluation

Why We Need a New Framework
for Rational Risk Evaluation

By late 1987, 25 percent of all Ugandans tested positive for AIDS (acquired immune deficiency syndrome), "slim disease," as it is called there. Since those affected are both heterosexual and homosexual, officials fear that this new retrovirus will wipe out an entire generation of central Africans, from Zaire to Kenya. Indeed, even if the AIDS epidemic does not enter the Asian population, the World Health Organization (WHO) expects one hundred million people, worldwide, to be infected by 1991. If AIDS does travel to Asian countries, then the WHO says that one hundred million "is an excessively conservative figure."[1]

Even though cases of AIDS in the United States increased from approximately 500 in 1982 to about 40,000 in 1987, managing the disease in the West is not as traumatic as in developing nations. In Uganda and other African countries, there are (for most people) no doctors, no medicine, no suitable hospital facilities, and no one to care for the children of victims. Apart from treatment, the cost of the AIDS test, alone, is more than total annual per capita health expenditures, about a dollar, in Uganda. Consequently, doctors or clinicians diagnosing AIDS in Africa face a dilemma. Ought they to tell the patients about their disease, in the name of honesty, even though nothing can be done (at least in central Africa) to alleviate their condition? Or, to counter "the secondary epidemic" of fear, ought they to lie to AIDS victims about their ailment, on the grounds that the truth would only worsen their mental, and perhaps their physical, state?[2]

Similar, although less poignant, dilemmas face those who manage other medical, environmental, and technological hazards. U.S. regulators, for example, have discovered that they face a typical risk dilemma in the meat-cutting industry. The Occupational Safety and Health Administration (OSHA) *reduced meat cutters' risks of accident* by requiring construction of guard rails around the cutting machinery. Once they installed the protective equipment, however, officials realized that the unsanitary rails *increased consumers' risks from infected meat*.[3]

Risk management generates pressing dilemmas, in part, because of two characteristics of risk situations: competing opportunity costs and incompatible risk-displacement options. Regarding opportunity costs, if one spends research dollars to help reduce the risk of heart disease, for example, then one has lost the opportunity to use those same funds to reduce cancer hazards, and vice versa. Incompatible risk-displacement options arise because risk can never be removed; it can only be transferred or displaced. One might reduce meat cutters' risk, but only by increasing meat consumers' risk, and vice versa. Or, by lying about the nature of AIDS patients' ailments, a medical doctor might reduce their traumas, but only by increasing the risk to the victims' future sexual partners.

Fully rational people, whether medical personnel in central Africa or OSHA regulators in the United States, often are caught in risk situations for which there are no desirable solutions. Although the situations do not pose logical difficulties, they are dilemmas in the sense that all the options for managing risks lead to unwanted consequences. Often these dilemmas arise at the third, or risk-evaluation, stage of analysis. Discussing five dilemmas of risk evaluation, this chapter shows that several philosophical problems, revealed by these dilemmas, require us to reform risk evaluation and to redefine "rational" risk acceptance. Later in the volume, in Chapters Eleven and Twelve, I shall outline these reforms and redefinitions.

The Fact-Value Dilemma

The first problem, the fact-value dilemma, arises because of the methods used at the third (or risk-evaluation) stage of risk analysis. Recall, from the last chapter, that four methods dominate this stage of assessment: risk-cost-benefit analysis (RCBA), expressed preferences, revealed preferences, and natural standards. None of these four methods of risk evaluation employs any explicitly ethical criteria, even though each of them (as the previous chapter argued) is laden with evaluative assumptions. Therein lies the dilemma: Ought or ought not assessors to employ risk-evaluation criteria that are overtly normative? For example, should they avoid explicitly ethical analyses and instead use (largely factual) risk-cost-benefit analysis? Or should they insert explicit norms into risk-cost-benefit analysis? Such norms might require, for example, that, regardless of the benefit-cost ratio, all persons ought to be guaranteed equal protection from all risks above a certain threshold.

At the heart of the fact-value dilemma is the assumption that methods of risk evaluation must be either primarily factual and scientific (and accomplished by experts) or predominantly ethical and political (and accomplished by democratic procedures). If they are not mainly scientific (and accomplished by experts), then the evaluation is open to the charge of being subjective and arbitrary. If they are not primarily ethical and political (and accomplished by democratic procedures), then the analysis is open to the charge of ignoring citizens' rights to self-determination and representation.

Admittedly, risk evaluators strive to make their analyses as factual, objective, and scientific as possible, on the grounds that such evaluations will be rational and persuasive tools of public policy.[4] Yet, if they are truly factual and scientific, risk evaluations ought to be done only by experts, not by laypersons. But if they are accomplished only by experts, their conclusions probably will not be wholly acceptable to the public. This is because—especially at the third stage of hazard assessment—citizens wish to make their own judgments about how safe is safe enough. There have been too many Chernobyls, Love Canals, Three Mile Islands, Bhopals, and Utah weapons tests for citizens to allow their judgments of acceptable risk to be preempted completely by experts. As one environmental activist put it, deciding to accept a risk "is an entirely human judgment that has nothing to do with whether you're a farmer or an engineer or a mathematician."[5] The fact-value dilemma is that risk evaluation cannot be both wholly factual/scientific and wholly sanctioned via democratic procedures.[6]

The Standardization Dilemma

A second difficulty, the standardization dilemma, raises similar problems. This dilemma arises because, in the name of consistency and avoidance of arbitrariness, many analysts argue that assessment procedures and risk-evaluation theories ought to be standardized.[7] For example, one ought to use similar risk-estimation models to evaluate substances and exposure levels that are relevantly similar. Yet, when procedures, models, and theories of risk evaluation are standardized, the assessor is unable to take into account persons' claims about special or unique needs, circumstances, and merits.

Proponents of standardization have often made an equity argument. They argue, for example, that hazard assessors employing risk-cost-benefit analysis (at the third stage of risk analysis) ought to make the marginal cost of saving lives, across opportunities, the same.[8] In other words, they maintain that risk evaluation ought to embody the principle that the same amount of government funds be spent, per life saved, in different risk situations. One could argue that politically powerful persons (e.g., middle-aged, overweight, white, male congressmen who typically die of heart disease) should not be able to have great amounts of risk-abatement and research monies spent to protect them from heart disease, while politically powerless persons (e.g., blacks dying of sickle-cell anemia) have fewer funds spent to protect them from anemia.

The obvious problem with this standardization proposal is that, if the same amount of money were spent to save lives, regardless of different risk situations, then assessors could violate (at least intuitive) standards of rationality. For example, suppose proponents of standardization argued that the same number of taxpayer dollars, per life saved, ought to be spent to protect citizen victims of dam failures as to protect the public from commercial nuclear accidents. Opponents of standardization might object that, since death from radiation is more unknown and more feared than death because of dam failure, more money ought to be spent to protect potential victims of nuclear accidents.

More generally, opponents of standardization could question the equity argument on a number of epistemological and ethical grounds. They might claim that standardization forces one to assume (1) that sameness of *expenditures* guarantees sameness of *protection*; (2) that *sameness* of protection guarantees *equality* of protection; or (3) that all discrimination (all deviation from standardization or consistency of treatment) is ethically indefensible and that there are never any *morally relevant* grounds for discrimination. Finally, they might claim (4) that standardization ignores the fact that different persons have different claims of merit, need, incentive, and compensation, any of which might be grounds for "special," rather than "standard," treatment.[9] For example, public figures might claim that they *need* better-than-standard risk protection; or they might argue that they bring about *societal benefits* and therefore ought to have above-average help. For these and other reasons, Ronald Dworkin has observed that there are no ethical grounds for claiming that everyone ought to receive the *same treatment*. Instead, he argues, there is an ethical basis only for asserting that everyone ought to have the *same concern or respect* in the political decision about how to allocate goods (and risk-abatement monies). Not only would it be impossible to accord the same treatment to everyone, even if it were desirable, but there are also strong reasons, some given in points 1–4 above, for doubting that sameness of treatment is desirable.[10]

Because of the constraints posed by the standardization dilemma, evaluators must make a value judgment. They must choose between efficiency and equity, between standardization and ethical analysis.[11]

The Contributors Dilemma

A third difficulty faced by risk evaluators is how to assess numerous small hazards. I call this problem the "contributors dilemma." It consists of the fact that citizens are subject to many small hazards, each of which is allegedly acceptable; yet together such exposures are clearly unacceptable. For example, each of the many carcinogens to which we are exposed—such as asbestos, vinyl chloride, and radiation—is alleged to be acceptable because it is below the threshold at which some statistically significant increase in harm occurs. Yet, statistically speaking, 25 to 33 percent of us are going to die from cancers, 90 percent of which are environmentally induced and hence preventable.[12] Many of the cancers are caused by the aggregation of numerous exposures to carcinogens, none of which is alone alleged to be harmful.

The contributors dilemma forces assessors both to assume (in the case of aggregate risks) and not to assume (in the case of individual risks) that the whole risk faced by an individual is greater than the sum of the parts of that risk. Risk evaluators who condone subthreshold hazards, but who condemn the deaths caused by the aggregate of these subthreshold harms, are something like the bandits who eat the tribesmen's lunches in the famous story of Oxford philosopher Jonathan Glover:

Suppose a village contains 100 unarmed tribesmen eating their lunch. 100 hungry armed bandits descend on the village and each bandit at gun-point takes one tribesman's lunch and eats it. The bandits then go off, each one having done a discriminable amount of harm to a single tribesman. Next week, the bandits are tempted to do the same thing again, but are troubled by newfound doubts about the morality of such a raid. Their doubts are put to rest by one of their number [a government risk assessor?]. . . . They then raid the village, tie up the tribesmen, and look at their lunches. As expected, each bowl of food contains 100 baked beans. . . . Instead of each bandit eating a single plateful as last week, each [of the 100 bandits] takes one bean from each [of the 100] plate[s]. They leave after eating all the beans, pleased to have done no harm, as each has done no more than sub-threshold harm to each person.[13]

The obvious question raised by this example is how risk assessors can say both that subthreshold exposures are harmless, as the data indicate, and yet that the additivity, or contribution, of these doses causes great harm. If they claim that subthreshold risks are *unacceptable,* then they face the undesirable consequence that government must regulate such risks, an extraordinarily difficult and expensive task, since attaining zero risk is impossible. If they claim that subthreshold risks are *acceptable,* then they must admit that, although it is immoral to murder fellow citizens, it is moral to allow them to be killed by carcinogens, little by little, much as the bandits stole the tribesmen's lunches, bean by bean.

The *De Minimis* Dilemma

The *de minimis* dilemma, named after a *Science* editorial about *de minimis,* or negligible, risk, poses many of the same problems as the contributors dilemma.[14] It is based on the fact that society must declare some threshold, below which a hazard is judged to be negligible. Often this *de minimis* level for a given risk is set at what would cause less than a 10^{-6} increase in one's average annual probability of fatality.[15]

The reasoning behind setting such a level is that a zero-risk society is impossible, and some standard needs to be set, especially in order to determine pollution-control expenditures. Choosing the 10^{-6} standard also appears reasonable, both because society must attempt to reduce larger risks first and because 10^{-6} is the natural-hazards death rate.[16] The dilemma arises because no *de minimis* standard is able to provide equal protection from harm to all citizens. On the one hand, if one rejects the *de minimis* standard, then pollution-control requirements would be difficult to determine. On the other hand, if one accepts the *de minimis* standard, then citizen protection would be based on some *average* annual probability of fatality, not on equal protection for all.

Although this 10^{-6} threshold seems acceptable, on the average, it is not necessarily acceptable to each individual. Most civil rights, for example, are accorded not on the basis of the *average* needs of persons but on the basis of *individual* characteristics. We do not accord constitutionally guaranteed civil rights to public education, for example, on the basis of average characteristics of students. If we did, then retarded children or gifted children would have rights only to education for children at the average level. Instead, we say that guaranteeing "equal" rights to education means according "comparable education," given one's aptitudes and needs.

If civil rights to education are accorded on the basis of individual, not average, characteristics, why are civil rights to equal protection from risks not accorded on the basis of individual, rather than average, characteristics? Why is a 10^{-6} average threshold accepted for everyone, without compensation, when adopting it poses risks higher than 10^{-6} for the elderly, for children, for persons with previous exposures to carcinogens, for those with allergies, for persons who must lead sedentary lives, and for the poor? Blacks, for example, face higher risks from air pollution than do whites, because "average" exposure standards cover up the fact that blacks live in neighborhoods with greater air pollution, while whites live in those with less, even though the average, citywide, exposure is the same.[17] The *de minimis* dilemma forces us to choose between *average* and *equal* protection, between efficiency and ethics.

The Consent Dilemma

Another evaluative dilemma arises from the recognition that imposition of certain risks is legitimate only after consent is obtained from the affected parties. The dilemma occurs because those who are genuinely able to give legitimate consent are precisely those who likely will never do so, whereas those who allegedly have given consent are those who are probably unable to do so. Perhaps the best example of the consent dilemma occurs in the workplace. Here there is an alleged compensating wage differential, noted by both economists and risk assessors. According to the theory behind the differential, the riskier the occupation, the higher the wage required to compensate the worker for bearing the risk, all things being equal.[18] Moreover, imposition of these higher workplace hazards apparently is legitimate only after the worker consents, with knowledge of the risks involved, to perform the work for the agreed-upon wage.

The consent dilemma appears as soon as one considers who is most likely to give legitimate informed consent to a workplace hazard. It is a person who is well educated and possesses a reasonable understanding of the risk, especially its long-term and probabilistic effects. It is a person who is not forced, under dire financial constraints, to take a job that he knows is likely to harm him. Sociological data reveal that, as education and income rise, persons are less willing to take risky jobs, and that those who do so are primarily those who are poorly educated or financially strapped.[19]

Consider, for example, those who bear the risks of coal mining in Appalachia. (Appalachia includes much of the states of Kentucky, West Virginia, Virginia, Tennessee, North Carolina, and South Carolina.) It is common knowledge that poorer workers are typically employed in the most risky jobs,[20] and that residents of Appalachia generally have no alternative to working in the mines unless they want to move out of the region. This is because the Appalachian economy is not diversified; because there is no job training for a variety of positions; and because absentee corporations, which control 80 percent of all Appalachian land and mineral rights, also control the only jobs. The situation is one of monopsony, where owners of most of the land also control most of the employment.[21] Even if all Appalachian coal miners were generously compensated, and even if they all had perfect information about the dangers of their jobs, very likely the situation of monopsony would prevent their making a wholly voluntary choice to work in the mines. They would essentially have the choice between a risky job and no job at all, unless they wanted to leave their homes. Hence, it is problematic to claim that, in exchange for the higher wages, they have genuinely given free consent to the high-risk mining jobs.

Analogous questions about free, informed consent could be raised in other situations involving environmental hazards. Consider, for example, the type of community most likely to accept a particularly dirty, dangerous factory or a controversial toxic waste dump. It would, very likely, be a town where people needed the jobs, or the tax benefits of the facility, or where levels of education about the relevant dangers of the facility were less known than in other places.[22] In other words, the communities least able to give free, informed consent to a risk are typically those that allegedly consent.

Risk evaluators who face the consent dilemma may have something to learn from medical experimenters who face analogous constraints. They taught us, long ago, that prisoners who are promised early release in exchange for being subjects in risky medical experimentation very likely are unable to give free, informed consent to the risk.[23] This is because the prison situation provides a highly coercive context that could jeopardize inmates' free, informed consent. Analogous reasoning has led to the prohibition of medical experimentation, not only on prisoners but also on medical and psychiatric patients, on recipients of welfare, and on those who have not given free, informed consent, as in the celebrated Tuskegee syphilis study, which has been called both racist and "ethically unjustified."[24] Following these examples from medical ethics, one could argue that a workplace where high wages are paid to economically desperate workers who take hazardous jobs provides a highly coercive context that could jeopardize their alleged free, informed consent. As one labor representative (at government hearings to set occupational exposure standards for lead) put it: "We just cannot expect a group of employees to be put on a sacrificial table because we happen to need lead and because it is a vital metal and we cannot do without it."[25]

If we cannot sacrifice workers, then risk evaluators are faced with a value judgment. They must either deny the traditional doctrine of free, informed consent, or they must provide extra compensation to persons who are otherwise unlikely to consent to societal and occupational risks. Either choice involves a value judgment that is itself not risk free.

Where We Go from Here

How might one avoid these five dilemmas? More generally, how might one avoid the unfairness, inequity, or loss of freedom following from various value judgments made as part of risk evaluation? Before moving to some proposed solutions for the dilemmas outlined in this chapter, we must be clear on the precise nature of the difficulties we face. Bound up with each of the five dilemmas are a whole host of biases that cause risk assessors to employ faulty methodological strategies in analyzing and evaluating risks. In the next five chapters, we shall examine some of these problematic strategies. Once that is accomplished, we shall have a clearer idea of the ways in which we need to redefine "rational" risk acceptance and to reform risk evaluation and management.

Part Two

Problematic Risk-Evaluation Strategies

Chapter Six

Perceived Risk and the Expert-Judgment Strategy

The Case for a Negotiated Account of Risk and Rationality

Until recently, the study of risk behavior—what some have called "motivated irrationality"—has suffered from a lack of attention by any single group of researchers. Brain scientists at the National Institute of Mental Health recently sought to remedy this deficiency. They gave evidence that those who voluntarily increase their individual (not societal) risk—rock climbers and hang gliders, for example—have lower levels of the brain enzyme monoamine oxidase. They also have lower levels of a brain chemical called DBH and higher levels of gonadal hormones.[1]

One problem with attributing risk taking simply to biochemical factors, however, is that many people delight in taking certain kinds of risks but detest others. American visitors to China, for example, are appalled at the high percentage of Chinese men who smoke, while most Chinese are surprised at Americans' chronic overconsumption of alcohol, especially when it is associated with half of the fatal automobile accidents in the country and with many types of violence.[2] How do we explain such phenomena? Perhaps everyone employs subjective criteria for rational risk behavior. Or perhaps the criteria are not subjective but are so complex that they are impossible to formulate.

If the arguments in the last five chapters have been correct, then at least one fact about responses to societal hazards is certain: they are highly *value laden*, often in ways that discount lay views of risk, and often in ways that disenfranchise the very persons likely to be risk victims. Now that we have analyzed the value judgments in hazard assessment, and especially in risk evaluation, we are ready to examine some of the more specific techniques and methods used to define acceptable risk. Fundamental to many risk techniques and methods is what I call the "expert-judgment strategy."

The Expert-Judgment Strategy

Assessors who subscribe to the "expert-judgment strategy" assume that one always can make a legitimate distinction between "actual risk" calculated by experts and so-called "perceived risk" postulated by laypersons.[3] They assume that experts grasp real, not perceived, risk, but that the public is able only to know perceived risk.

To understand more precisely what is meant by the expert-judgment strategy, recall that one of the most fundamental sources of divergence, in technology-related risk assessments, is whether evaluation of specific hazards is in part a function of a real, probabilistically described risk or wholly a product of the societal processes by which information concerning the danger is exchanged. More succinctly put, do people fear nuclear power, for example, because they assume that it is an inherently dangerous technology or because they are victims of a sensational media campaign that has played on ignorance and paranoia about technology?[4]

The expert-judgment strategy consists of the belief either that risk can be reduced to some characteristic of a technology, determined only by experts, or that it is possible for experts alone to distinguish "actual risk," as a property of a technology, from so-called "perceived risk" postulated by laypersons. Once they make the distinction between perceived and real risk, many assessors assume that the perceived risks of laypeople cause most controversy over technology.[5] As a consequence, they ask how to mitigate the impact of risk *perceptions* (which they assume to be erroneous), rather than how to mitigate the impact of *risk* itself. They assume that public relations, "risk communication," is their only problem.[6]

The expert-judgment strategy can also occur when assessors presuppose that a technological risk is defined purely in terms of *physical impacts.* For example, if researchers speak of the "social amplification of risk" as a process whereby hazards produce social impacts (e.g., fear) that exceed their health and safety effects,[7] then they appear to presuppose that the risk itself is purely physical and measurable by experts. On the contrary, however, it is arguable that *social impacts* (such as increased trauma or decreased civil liberties) are part of the risk itself.

Some researchers who fall victim to the expert-judgment strategy also speak, for example, of "perception-caused impacts."[8] But there are no impacts that are purely perception induced unless one has uncontroversial measures of hazards (versus perceptions of hazards) and uncontroversial measures of risk impacts (versus impacts of risk perceptions). We have wholly exact measures for neither. What we have, instead, is a quantitative, "expert" definition of *risk*, as opposed to a qualitative, allegedly subjective notion of lay *risk perception*. Those who fall victim to the expert-judgment strategy typically assume that risk can be defined purely probabilistically, as an average annual probability of fatality.[9] They likewise assume that anyone (for instance, a layperson concerned about consent, equity, and the like) who does not subscribe to this purely probabilistic definition has an erroneous *risk perception*, rather than an accurate, alternative conception of *risk*. But one cannot stipulatively define one type of risk (that of laypeople) merely as a misperception of another type of risk (that of experts) unless one can distinguish precisely and completely between the risks and perceptions of them.

All Risks Are Perceived, Although They Are Not Wholly Relative

One can distinguish between risks and risk perceptions only if one is able to establish that a perception about a risk (and not the risk itself) *caused* a particular impact. Yet this is virtually impossible to do, since behavior has multiple causes; sometimes neither a researcher nor the actor knows what those causes are. In particular, it is not enough to establish correlations between particular impacts (such as an aversion to a particular danger) and specific risk perceptions, because this would not show that the perceptions *caused* the alleged effects. For example, there might be a correlation between catastrophic risks and the impact of high risk aversion. Yet this correlation might be accidental. Instead, the real cause of high risk aversion might be the lack of control over the hazard, not its catastrophic nature. If so, then it may be difficult to distinguish between impacts of risks and impacts of risk perceptions.

To understand why this distinction is problematic, consider another example. Suppose a person becomes an antinuclear activist because he believes that a commercial reactor accident might occur, and because nuclear liability is limited to approximately 1 percent of the total possible losses in the event of a catastrophe.[10] The problematic question raised by this case is whether the impact, the person's activism, is caused by the *real risk* (the risk of not being compensated fully) or by the *perceived risk* (the perception that he will not be compensated fully).

If one argues that the *risk* causes the activism, then to mitigate this impact, the threat of noncompensation ought to be removed and the

Price-Anderson Act (which limits nuclear liability) ought to be repealed. If one argues that erroneous *risk perceptions* (that noncompensation is likely) cause the activism, then mitigating the impact requires removing these allegedly erroneous perceptions. But one can do this only by guaranteeing full compensation, should an accident occur, and hence only by repealing the Price-Anderson Act. Therefore, whether risk or risk perception causes an impact (lay aversion or activism), strategies for mitigating the impact are often the same. But this case suggests that it is often difficult to determine whether risks or risk perceptions *cause* a particular impact; whether one can distinguish between *strategies* for mitigating impacts of risks, versus risk perceptions; and therefore whether one can distinguish *impacts* of risks, versus perceived risks. These difficulties raise the question of whether one can differentiate hazards from perceptions of them.

Our inability to distinguish risks from risk perceptions does not, however, force us into the *cultural relativism* that we criticized in Chapter Three. Even though all risks are perceived, many of them are also real. The *risk* of death, for instance, is real. But it is also, in part, a probability, and such probabilities can rarely be known with certainty. *Until* death becomes a certainty, the *risk* of death is purely perceived, theoretical, or estimated. Indeed, the occurrence of death, in a particular case, reveals how accurate our perceptions or estimates of the risk of death were. More generally, although the risk that some X will occur is real, the exact degree and nature of this risk are not, in principle, confirmable until X actually occurs. Prior to this occurrence, risk perceptions can be judged as more or less accurate only on the basis of nonempirical and theoretical criteria such as explanatory power, simplicity, or internal coherence. Nevertheless, risk perceptions are often *real* and *objective*, at least in the sense that empirical evidence (e.g., accident frequency) is relevant to them and is capable of providing grounds for amending them. All risks (the probability p that some X will occur), then, are both *perceived* and *real*. Their exact nature and magnitude become more fully *knowable*, however, insofar as more instances of X occur. The relativists (discussed earlier) erred in believing that, because all risks are *perceived*, all risks are therefore *relative*. (Later in the volume, I shall provide a number of more specific criteria for securing the objectivity and rationality of hazard evaluation.)

Now that we have sketched at least a partial basis for showing how one might argue that this account is not completely relativistic, let's examine why actual risk is not typically distinguishable from perceived risk. One reason is that risk *probabilities* often do not reflect risk *frequencies*. This is in part because there are numerous difficulties of hazard estimation that do not admit of analytic, probabilistic resolution by experts. Often the risk problem is not well enough understood to allow accurate predictions, as the use of techniques like fault-free analysis shows. Hence, experts are forced to rely on subjective or perceived risk probabilities, instead of on actual empirical accident frequencies established over a long period of trial. Even if assessors based their notions of *probability* on actual, empirical, accident *frequency*, this move would not always deliver their estimates of risk from the charge of being "perceived." Since there are reliable frequencies only for events that have had a long recorded history, use of historical accident/hazard data for new technologies likely results in underestimating the danger, because certain events may not have occurred between the inception of a technology and the end of the period for which the risk information is compiled. Moreover, low accident frequency does not prove low accident probability. Only when the period of observing accident frequency approaches infinity would the two, frequency and probability, converge.

Another reason why one cannot distinguish actual from perceived risk, in any wholly accurate way, is that actual risk estimates are always very *rough* and *imprecise*, as the first two sections of Chapter Four indicated. The estimates typically vary from two to six orders of magnitude. Such imprecision is unavoidable, whether the estimates are based on probabilistic calculations or on actual experience. On the one hand, if they are based on probabilities, then assessors are forced to employ a number of value-laden theoretical assumptions and mathematical models. On the other hand, if the risk estimates are based on actual experience, or accident frequency, they are likewise "perceived," because probability does not equal frequency, as has already been argued. Moreover, even actual frequencies do not provide a precise measure of a particular risk, because this number is always formulated as an *average*, and such averages, by definition, do not take particular, perhaps site-specific, deviations into account.

Also, some of the most important aspects of hazards, whether real or perceived, are *not amenable to quantification*. (What experts call) "actual" risk estimates are based on the presupposition that risk is measured by probability and consequences, and that both can be quantified. Yet most laypeople would probably claim that what makes a thing most hazardous are factors that are not susceptible to quantification, factors such as a risk's being imposed without consent, or being unknown, or posing a threat to civil liberties.[11]

Distinguishing *risks* from *risk perceptions* is likewise impossible because both are *theoretical concepts* and hence not amenable to precise empirical

prediction or confirmation. If risks were empirically confirmed or determined, they would be certain, and hence not risks. In general, "risk"
is defined in terms of expected-utility theory and hence is a theoretical
concept carrying with it all the baggage of this specific decision theory.[12]
In particular applications, "risk" is always defined on the basis of a
whole host of theoretical assumptions, many of which are often controversial. For example, a number of incompatible "cancer models"
(dose-response models), each with attendant assumptions, have been
used to estimate the incidence of tumors in populations exposed to
formaldehyde. In 1987, the U.S. Environmental Protection Agency
(EPA) called formaldehyde a "probable human carcinogen." The EPA
said that those exposed to formaldehyde-treated pressed wood could
face a cancer risk, over ten years, of 2 in 10,000. Experts at the Harvard
School of Public Health, however, criticized the EPA risk assessment
as premature and said that the true formaldehyde risk was uncertain.
Other experts, including scientists at the American Cancer Society and
the Consumer Product Safety Commission, argued that the EPA
models were incorrect, but in the opposite direction. They said that
the EPA findings underestimated the cancer risk. The formaldehyde
case—as well as those of ethylene dibromide (EDB), dioxin, and methylene chloride—illustrates that, even as late as the 1980s, particular accounts of risk have been highly controversial and theory laden.[13] But
if all risk is defined in accordance with the categories of a particular
scientific or modeling *theory*, then there is no actual hazard apart from
some particular theoretical account of it. Hence, there is no uncontroversial way to distinguish "actual" from "perceived" risk.

Moreover, because risk perceptions often affect risk probabilities,
and vice versa, it is frequently impossible to distinguish hazards from
perceptions of them. This phenomenon is well known to social scientists
as part of the "self-fulfilling prophecy." For example, if I perceive my
chances of getting cancer to be high, then my perceptions can exac-
erbate stress and therefore increase the probability that I actually do
develop cancer. Hence, there is often no clear distinction between actual
and perceived risk.

There are also a number of reasons for arguing that the distinction
between actual and perceived risk cannot be based on the alleged *objectivity* of *expert* estimates, as opposed to the alleged *subjectivity* of *lay*
risk estimates. Admittedly, laypersons typically overestimate the severity of many technological hazards.[14] However, even if it could be established that the public exaggerates the accident probabilities associated with some technology, such as liquefied natural gas (LNG), this
fact alone would be a necessary, but not a sufficient, condition for
establishing the thesis that laypersons erroneously overestimate risks.

Their risk perceptions could be said to be erroneously high only if they were *based solely on* incorrect accident probabilities. These perceptions might also be based, for instance, on the potentially catastrophic consequences of an accident, or on the fact that such consequences are involuntarily imposed.

Also, apart from whether probabilities alone explain risk judgments, there is reason to believe that, at least in some areas, expert estimates of probabilities are not necessarily superior to those of laypeople. In their classic studies of the heuristic judgmental strategies that often lead to error in probability estimates, Kahneman, Tversky, and Oskamp concluded that experts, whenever they have merely statistical data, are just as prone as laypeople to judgmental error regarding probabilities. Experts are particularly susceptible, for example, to the fallacy known as representativeness, the gratuitous assumption that a particular sample is similar in relevant respects to its parent population and that it represents the salient features of the process by which it was generated. Kahneman and Tversky showed not only that experts are just as prone to this probabilistic bias as laypeople but also that, even after the error is explained to the experts, the bias cannot be "unlearned."[15]

Another common judgmental error of mathematically trained professionals is overconfidence. Experts' trust in their probability estimates is typically a function of how much information they have gathered, rather than a function of its accuracy or its predictive success. Since everyone, even those highly trained in probability and statistics, must make simplifying assumptions in estimating probabilities, and since experts are just as prone as laypeople to these judgmental errors, there is little reason to believe that experts are always able to calculate actual or *real* risk, while laypeople are merely able only to construct perceived or *subjective* risk.[16]

Another difficulty is that those who attempt to distinguish "actual risk" and "perceived risk" are wrong to assume that the latter is merely an erroneous understanding of the former.[17] They are wrong because there is no universal definition of risk underlying the two concepts. For one thing, experts disagree on whether (and when) to employ concepts such as "individual risk," "relative risk," "population risk," and "absolute risk."[18] Moreover, as was already suggested, the term 'risk' in "actual risk" and "perceived risk" has neither the same referent nor the same meaning. What Hafele, Okrent, Jones-Lee, Morgan, and others (see Chapter Three) call "actual risk" is the probability of a particular hazard's occurring, times the magnitude of its consequences. What they call "perceived risk," alleging that it is an incorrect view of actual risk, however, is not merely (an incorrect) *perception* of probability times consequences. Rather, most laypeople would claim that (what typical risk assessors call) "perceived risk" includes *more* than mere probability. Hence, when laypeople say that something is a "high risk," they do not necessarily mean only that it has a high probability of causing death. (See the next chapter for more discussion of this point.) And if so, then "actual risk" is not mere probability times fatality, and "perceived risks" are not merely perceptions of probability times fatality.

In sum, there is no distinction between perceived risks and actual risks because there are no risks except perceived risks. If there were hazards that were not perceived, then we would not know them. That we do know them, in some sense, proves that even real risks are perceived and that even real risks must be known via categories and perceptions. This is related to the earlier point that all risks are, *in part*, theoretical constructs, not completely empirical, not wholly capable of confirmation.

If we did accept the distinction between *actual* and *perceived* risk, such acceptance could lead to undesirable *consequences*. One negative effect is that the distinction misidentifies the source of controversy over risk judgments and misattributes it to accurate, versus inaccurate, knowledge of probability times accident consequences. Hence, it provides policymakers with little insight on controversy over hazards, little basis for investigating the important ethical, methodological, and evaluative reasons for divergent risk judgments. Moreover, if policymakers assume that there is a distinction between perceived risk and real risk, then there is less reason for them to take account of lay views, since error could be said to have no rights. As a result, laypersons and other democratic decisionmakers might be disenfranchised.

But if accepting a sharp distinction between risk and risk perception is both politically dangerous and epistemologically confused, then what follows? It makes no sense to talk about risks versus perceived risks, as if experts had some magic window on reality. Instead, we must deal with all hazards as they are perceived, even though (as was just argued) they are not purely relative. We must focus on disputes over risk perceptions and attempt to ameliorate them and the controversy surrounding them.

The EPA: Negotiating Consent and Compensation

If we ought to deal with all risks as risk perceptions, then we might rely on what Liebow and Herborn call an "institutional memory" in order to learn how to use past conflicts as a basis for resolving current risk controversies.[19] One case is particularly instructive in this regard. It has been the nation's most celebrated, lengthiest, and perhaps most costly environmental controversy.

The conflict began in 1964 and pitted the Environmental Protection Agency (EPA) against five New York utility companies. It focused on the potential environmental impacts of Con Ed's proposed Cornwell Project, a pumped-storage facility to be built on a mountain overlooking the Hudson valley. Central to the debate was the impact of the facility's water withdrawals on the Hudson River's striped bass population. As several authors in *BioScience* put it:

The Hudson River controversy was a unique test of the ability of biologists to use their science to aid public decisionmakers in achieving an equitable solution to an important environmental problem. . . . After more than a decade of study and the expenditure of tens of millions of dollars, it was still not possible to draw definitive conclusions about the long-term effects of entrainment and impingement on fish populations in the Hudson River. We do not believe that this failure can be blamed on lack of effort, on the incompetence of the biologists involved, or on the use of the wrong model. We believe that it occurred because of insufficient understanding of underlying biological processes [even though,] . . . in the Hudson River controversy, the scientific issues were more clearly defined, and the research effort greater, than for any other major environmental dispute known to us.[20]

The settlement of the Hudson River case, negotiated between the EPA and the five companies, called for the utilities to deviate from the outage schedule, provided that the overall degree of mitigation of impacts was not reduced. The credit allowed for shutting down a specific generating unit during a given week was determined by the contribution of that unit to the conditional entrainment mortality rate for striped bass.

What scholars learned (from tens of millions of dollars of research spent on biological processes that were impossible to define in the Hudson River case) is that science, even science regarding risk perception and behavior, is often at an impasse. In the Hudson River case, a resolution was reached only after all affected parties decided *not* to try to define particular impacts and ascertain their causes. Likewise, I suspect that the controversy over risk and risk perception will not be resolved until people stop trying to distinguish perceived risk from real risk. Aristotle astutely noted that the wise person recognizes the degree of certainty appropriate to particular types of inquiries and does not seek a level of certainty inappropriate to the specific kind of investigation. If Aristotle's insight is applicable to the question of hazard evaluation and management, then perhaps assessors ought to stop the interminable haggling over who is correct, the experts or the public. Instead, perhaps we and they, the experts, ought to shift our focus, in part, from the *scientific* to the *ethical* dimension. We ought to attempt to formulate a *procedural* or *negotiated* solution as a means of solving the problem of defining, evaluating, and managing risks.

But how does one negotiate among persons so as to resolve some of their conflicts about acceptable risk? Elizabeth Peelle, sociologist at Oak Ridge Laboratories, has argued that creating a citizens' task force to specify mitigation, compensation, and incentive measures for hazardous technologies could help resolve controversies over risk. In Tennessee, for example, such task forces have already succeeded in negotiating consent to hazardous facilities. The "net local balance" of the DOE's (Department of Energy's) proposal to site a monitored retrievable storage (MRS) facility in the state changed from negative to positive after a citizens' task force was organized.[21] What the Tennessee experience suggests, and what Chapters Eleven and Twelve of this volume argue in more detail, is that there are both pragmatic and ethical grounds for rejecting the expert-judgment strategy. Instead, we ought to focus on negotiating citizen consent and compensation, regardless of how a risk is perceived or defined.

Guaranteeing Consent and Compensation

No matter how experts define a hazard, its imposition is ethically justifiable only if the persons affected by it have given free, informed consent and are compensated for the danger they face. As was suggested earlier, the obvious analogue for hazard evaluation and management is medical ethics; a physician is ethically justified in imposing a possibly nontherapeutic risk on patients only after they or their representatives have given free, informed consent. Even if the patients are not experts and have faulty risk perceptions, the doctor cannot make the consent decision for them.[22]

The *pragmatic* justification for recognizing the ethical requirements of free, informed consent, and then negotiating regarding compensating persons for consenting to higher risks, is that such recognition defuses opposition about the level of the risk imposed, the justification for it, and alternative perceptions of it. That is, the necessity of providing a "risk package" (including compensation and risk-mitigation agreements), to which potential victims will give consent, drives both proponents and opponents to work toward a negotiated agreement. Admittedly, opponents of taking a particular technological risk may view this negotiated consent as a way to co-opt them, and proponents of the technology may see negotiation as an expensive way to buy agreement. Nevertheless, negotiation is necessary for reform of risk evaluation and management.[23] Not to negotiate is to be forced either into curtailing technological progress or into a situation in which someone other than all those affected makes risk evaluations and decides risk policies.

Moreover, the compensation negotiated must be commensurate with the potential victims' perception of the hazard, not merely with an expert's judgment. The ethical justification for requiring compensation includes both the due-process and the equal-protection provisions of our ethical and legal traditions. Equal protection requires, at a minimum, that when society sanctions placing some persons at higher risks than others, those disadvantaged deserve compensation, particularly if the risk is associated with benefits received by others not bearing the risk.[24] The pragmatic grounds for compensation are closely related to contemporary and neoclassical economic theory. As later chapters will spell out, contemporary benefit-cost analysis presupposes that, if a transaction is to be economically efficient, the gainers will compensate the losers. The compensation rule simply moves the concept of "money changing hands" from the level of economic theory to that of practical dispute resolution. Also, compensation for those facing special technology-related hazards is consistent with current market mechanisms for compensating those who bear risks—for example, those endangered by noise because they live near airports. Risk compensation for those living near a waste facility, for example, is also consistent with the economic theory of the compensating wage differential. According to that theory, imposition of a higher workplace risk is justified, in part, if those bearing the additional risk give free, informed consent to it, and if they receive higher wages proportional to the hazards they face.[25]

Admittedly, all the ethical and social costs associated with risks (such as those from hazardous waste facilities) may not be compensable.[26] If they are, then compensation is pragmatically desirable because it addresses equity problems and is likely to help eliminate opposition to the facilities and resolve conflict.[27] If the risks are not compensable, then society must decide whether they are avoidable or are, instead, "necessary risks."[28] If they are avoidable, society can forgo the benefits obtained through such hazards. If the risks are not avoidable and not compensable, then society must develop an equitable scheme for distributing the risk; at least part of such an equitable scheme is likely to involve some form of compensation, since society sanctions the equitable imposition of unavoidable harm.[29]

Removing Liability Limits

Along with compensating those affected by technological risks, there are also ethical and pragmatic grounds for not limiting liability in the event of a catastrophic technological accident. As was mentioned earlier, the energy controversy has been fueled by the Price-Anderson Act. This law limits the liability of nuclear power plant owners to $640 million, even though property damages alone, typically only about one-fourth of total accident costs, could go as high as $17 billion for a catastrophic fission accident.[30] Even Chernobyl, not a worst-case accident, will cost more than $10 billion to clean up.[31]

Such damage figures suggest that, apart from the due-process and equal-protection arguments, there are strong pragmatic grounds for risk managers to rid all risk policy of the "insurance asymmetry." This asymmetry consists of the fact that, although laypeople can be insured against plane crashes, surgeon malpractice, and a whole host of technology-related dangers, societally imposed risks (such as nuclear fission) are often uninsurable. If public officials expect laypeople to believe them when they say that something is safe, then they ought to *act as if* it were safe, and provide full liability. After all, there would be no danger in guaranteeing full coverage if, indeed, the likelihood of a catastrophe were quite small. Only if such probabilities are not low, reasons the public, is there a basis for the government not to require full liability for all societally imposed risks.[32] Moreover, if proponents of risky technologies are interested in winning acceptance for their point of view, then they ought to leave no obvious targets, such as liability limits, for their opponents to attack. Otherwise, public controversy over safety will never cease.

Conclusion

If any single lesson can be learned from the arguments of this chapter, it is that experts do not always know best—particularly if the problem at issue, distinguishing risks from risk perceptions, is not wholly amenable to theoretical resolution. Like successful adjudication of the Hudson River controversy, adjudicating conflicts over hazard evaluation often requires that we supplement the *theoretical* task of *defining* the risk problem in some purely *scientific* way. Instead, we need also to focus on the *practical* task of *negotiating* its resolution in a *procedural* way.

Chapter Seven

Democracy and the Probabilistic Strategy

The Case for a Populist Account of Risk and Rationality

From the fourteenth through the sixteenth centuries, courts executed over a million "witches." According to risk assessor Alvin Weinberg, witch hunts subsided only after the Inquisitor of Spain convened a group of savants who proclaimed that there was no proof that "witches" caused misfortunes. Our current "environmental hypochondria," says Weinberg, is like the hysteria that drove witch hunts, and only savants realize that there is no proof that "environmental insult" causes "real health problems." Weinberg concludes that risk assessors need a new Inquisitor who is able to bring the public to its "senses."[1]

Like Weinberg, many scientists, risk analysts, and government policymakers have not dealt kindly with the public's distrust of high technologies and industrial toxins. A well-known energy spokesperson has condemned laypersons and environmentalists as victims of "pathological fear" and "near-clinical paranoia."[2] Others have said that laypersons would not fear certain scientific and industrial activities if they only understood that catastrophic accidents are extremely unlikely.[3] As the previous chapter argued, many risk assessors subscribe to the expert-judgment strategy, perhaps in part because they see themselves as the experts, the Inquisitors, who ought to bring ignorant and fearful laypersons to their senses.

Many risk assessors believe that laypersons will "come to their senses," in evaluating environmental risks, if they can learn to base their risk aversion on accident probabilities calculated by experts, rather than on their feelings. In other words, many assessors subscribe to the "probabilistic strategy."

The Probabilistic Strategy

The probabilistic strategy is the belief that, for any rational and informed person, there is a linear relationship between a risk, defined as an actual probability of fatality (associated with a particular technological activity), and the value of avoiding the risk posed by that technology.[4] Following this strategy, many hazard assessors "explain" a societal aversion to certain low-probability technological risks by alleging that the public does not know the accident probabilities in question. These assessors maintain that, given knowledge of the actual likelihood of death, rational persons always are more averse to high-probability risks than to low-probability ones.

In thus subscribing to the probabilistic strategy, risk analysts likely err, in part, because the restriction of risk to "probability of fatality" is highly questionable. There are obviously many other cost burdens (for example, "decreasing the GNP by a given amount") whose probability also determines the value of avoiding a given risk. Another problem is that the value of avoiding a given risk often depends on whether there are benefits to be gained from it, or whether it is distributed equitably.[5] In fact, if Fischhoff and other assessors who employ psychometric surveys are correct, then risk acceptability is more closely correlated with equity than with any other factor.[6]

Catastrophic potential and the fact that low-probability/high-consequence situations are often the product of societally imposed (as opposed to privately chosen) risks may also explain risk aversion. There is evidence that the psychological trauma (feelings of impotence, depression, rage) associated with the imposition of a *public* hazard is greater than that associated with the choice of a *private* risk of the same probability. One author even suggests that widespread despair and an increasing suicide rate may be attributable to the hazards and fatalities caused by "industrial cannibalism."[7] If so, then there may be good reason why society's risk aversion is not proportional to the probability of fatality. Moreover, although according to utility theory, a high-probability/low-consequence event (10,000 accidents, each killing one person) and a low-probability/high-consequence situation (one accident killing 10,000 persons) may have the same expected value, reasonable persons are typically more averse to the low-probability/high-consequence situation. One explanation may be that the high-consequence events, such as catastrophic global warming, are often more difficult to quantify.[8]

If it is true that a risk's importance is measured not only by its probability, but also by other factors, then it makes sense for people to value the same level of safety differently in different settings. Although this valuing may be economically inefficient, it is neither inconsistent nor irrational. Why, then, do risk assessors believe that societal aversion to allegedly low-probability risks is a consequence of false beliefs about the relevant probabilities?

Probabilities Are Not the Problem

To support their claims, many assessors maintain that laypersons view low-probability nuclear accidents as quite likely. Starr and Whipple, for example (citing research by Otway; Lawless; and Fischhoff, Slovic, and Lichtenstein), argue that "the bulk of disagreement" over nuclear power is over different beliefs about accident probabilities. Likewise, Cohen criticizes the public as being "uninformed" about the real risk probability from hazardous waste and obsessed with regulating risks that are "trivial."[9] Starr points out that "society has not learned to place . . . hypothetical man-made events [like nuclear catastrophes]" in the same perspective that it places natural catastrophes such as earthquakes.[10] Generalizing on the basis of the controversy over nuclear power, he criticizes public concern with "imaginary large catastrophes."[11] Finally, Cohen, Starr, and Whipple suggest that conflicts over technology arise "because of intuitive estimates of unreasonably high risk," and because the public is "emotional" in its risk evaluations.[12] This chapter will show that all these claims are questionable.

Starr and Whipple assert that Otway substantiates their claim about the public's misperception of nuclear accident probability.[13] But Otway's studies show that, in his view, the real controversy is over *values* and over incompatible views of the *benefits* attributed to nuclear power, not over different beliefs about accident probabilities. For example, Otway says that "in general the con [nuclear power] group . . . assign high importance to the risk items while the pro group view benefit-related attributes as most important."[14] Otway also claims that, although both pro and con groups "strongly believe that nuclear power is in the hands of big government or business, . . . the pro group evaluates this attribute positively, the con group evaluates it negatively."[15] In fact, Otway says explicitly that his research confirms the existence of only three statistically significant differences between pronuclear and antinuclear persons, all of which concern "the benefits of nuclear power." The pro group, Otway says, "strongly believed" that nuclear power offers three benefits: an essential good for society, economical energy, and a higher quality of life. On these three points, "the con groups tended to be uncertain to somewhat negative."[16] Regarding probabilistic evaluation of nuclear power, Otway explicitly states: "There were no significant differences between the [pronuclear and antinuclear] groups on the *eb* [evaluation-belief] scores of any items related to risk."[17] This conclusion appears to be a flat contradiction of the claim that Otway's research supports the probabilistic strategy.

Lawless's work does not seem to support it either. In fact, Lawless never mentions that misperceived probabilities cause disagreements over environmental risk. He argues instead that conflict over technology is greatest where proof of harm is *uncertain*, not where there is incorrect public perception of *certain* hazards.[18]

In the recent controversy over methylene chloride (dichloromethane, DCM), for example, the dispute was clearly a function of *uncertainty* in scientific knowledge, not a result of incorrect public perception of *certain* knowledge. DCM is a multipurpose solvent used in paint stripping, metal cleaning, foam blowing, electronics, chemical processing, and in certain aerosol propellant mixtures. Because of its many applications, citizens are exposed to DCM in the workplace, through use of consumer products, and from emissions to ambient air. In 1987, the U.S. Environmental Protection Agency listed DCM as a probable human carcinogen, although industry groups disagreed. The EPA cited the fact that DCM was carcinogenic in mice (although not in hamsters and rats), whereas industry cited the fact that the two studies of humans exposed to DCM in the workplace showed no significant increase in cancer deaths.[19]

At the heart of the controversy over DCM between industry and environmentalists is the fact that industry tended to use pharmacokinetic models. These permitted the calculation of internal doses of DCM through integrated information on administered dose, the physiological structure of the species involved, and the biochemical properties of DCM. As a result, industry (e.g., Dow Chemical) predicted an average annual probability of fatality, for lifetime exposure to DCM, of 3.7×10^{-8}. (This risk is below the level of those typically regulated by government.) Other scientists, however, predicted the same risk as 4.1×10^{-6} for lifetime exposure to DCM. (Two orders of magnitude higher, this latter risk is at the level typically requiring government regulation.) Assessors obtained the higher risk figure by means of more conventional (than the pharmacokinetic) models. These involved linear extrapolation of external DCM dose and an interspecies factor based on body surface area.[20]

Although numerous other risk cases exemplify the same point, the DCM controversy shows clearly that the dispute was not caused because the public incorrectly perceived the real, or probabilistic, risk. Indeed, even now (in the early 1990s), the "real" level of risk is unknown (and cannot be calculated) because the carcinogenic mechanism, in the animals in which it has occurred, is unknown, according to the EPA.[21] Hence, scientific uncertainty, not faulty public knowledge, appears to be driving the conflict.

Lawless also argues that the nuclear controversy, in particular, has been caused not only by scientific uncertainty, but also by the lack of credibility of federal regulators and by apparent government failure to consider environmental values. He notes, in general, that disputes over risk arose (in more than 50 percent of the cases studied) because technologies were allowed to grow, despite evidence that they were beset with problems, and because they were used irresponsibly.[22] All this suggests that laypersons' risk aversion may be reasonable, rather than merely a product of their erroneous risk perceptions.

As with the Otway and Lawless studies, there is little clear evidence— contrary to the claims of Starr, Whipple, and others—that the work of Fischhoff and his associates supports the thesis that environmental controversy arises because of lay misperception of risk probabilities. Their research with the League of Women Voters indicates that the commercial nuclear risk, for example, was not perceived as worth the benefits accruing from it.[23] A number of risk assessors, however, appear to dismiss the importance of the question of whether the nuclear benefit is worth the risk.[24] Since these same assessors claim that risks and benefits are not evaluated independently, however, it is not clear how they can be so sure that the debate over nuclear safety is primarily over probabilities, rather than whether the benefit is worth the risk.

Fischhoff and his colleagues specifically note that, in their surveys, the public (students and members of the League of Women Voters) judged nuclear power to have "the *lowest* fatality estimate" for the thirty activities studied, but the "*highest* perceived risk."[25] As a consequence, they conclude, "we can reject the idea that lay people wanted to equate risk with annual fatalities, but were inaccurate in doing so. Apparently, laypeople incorporate other considerations besides annual fatalities into their concept of risk."[26]

According to the Fischhoff study, the key consideration influencing judgments of high risk was not perceptions of high accident probability but the fact that certain technologies represent an unfamiliar (as opposed to a common) risk; an inequitably (as opposed to equitably) distributed risk; and a hazard with severe consequences in the unlikely event that an accident were to occur.[27] In fact, the assessors found that perceived risk could be predicted almost completely accurately solely on the basis of the single variable "severity of consequences," even though the probability of those consequences' occurring was quite small and was perceived as quite small.[28] If this is true, then the suggestion that environmental controversy is fueled primarily by incorrect *probability* estimates of laypersons is less helpful than the suggestion that, for high-magnitude events, it is the possible *consequences* that are important to societal evaluation. Several authors have proposed that n lives lost simultaneously in a catastrophic accident should be assessed as a loss of n^2 lives. They argue that the risk-conversion factor for catastrophic accidents should be exponential.[29]

Admittedly, the studies by Fischhoff and others show only that, contrary to the assertions of other assessors, controversy over hazardous technologies very likely arises because of the value placed on consequences, not because of overestimated risk probabilities. The studies do not show that consequences ought to be valued in this way. Moreover, the Atomic Energy Comission (AEC), the Nuclear Regulatory Commission (NRC), and the courts generally have not attributed much importance to consequences. Courts "have consistently taken the position that probabilities are determinative of risk, regardless of potential consequences."[30] Nuclear risk assessments have also consistently adopted the newer nuisance rule that probabilities alone determine risk, probably because of society's interest in technological development. Historically, the rule has owed its inspiration to the reluctance of the nineteenth-century courts to allow the traditionally restrictive law of nuisance to hinder economic progress.[31]

There are, however, a number of reasons for arguing that, in certain cases, risk consequences are more important than the accident probabilities. For one thing, greater social disruption arises from one massive accident than from a number of single-fatality accidents, even though the same number of people may be killed. The law of torts also recognizes the heightened importance of high-consequence events, apart from their probability of occurrence. In fact, for the rule of strict liability, risk is based almost totally on grave potential consequences, regardless of the associated probability.[32] Part of the justification for this judicial emphasis on accident consequences is apparently the fact that the parties involved in litigation over catastrophic accidents—the injured persons and those liable for the injury—are not equal in bargaining power.[33] The representative of some technological or industrial interest usually has more clout than the person damaged by it. Moreover, as Chapter Twelve will argue in more detail, a person is more deserving of compensation according to strict liability when she is victimized by an impact that she did not voluntarily accept or help to create. For all these reasons, societal risk evaluation of potentially catastrophic technologies ought to focus on the accident consequences as well as on their probabilities.

This point is clear if one considers a rational response to the invitation to play Russian Roulette. Suppose the probability that a bullet is in a chamber when the trigger is pulled is 1 in 17,000—the same likelihood, per reactor-year, as a nuclear core melt. Even with such a small probability, a person could still be rational in her refusal to play the game. She could even maintain that the probability in question is irrelevant. Any probability of fatality might be too high if the benefits deriving from taking the risk were not great enough. And if so, then probabilities might not be as important, in environmental risk evaluation, as proponents of the probabilistic strategy suggest. As one expert expressed it, current debate over whether a given technology has a particular risk probability is a spurious issue. "Risk assessors tend to choose methods and data that support the position to which they are already committed."[34] If so, then debate over environmental risks is likely to be over many factors other than probability.

Probabilities Are Often Uncertain

The claim that probabilities are central to risk evaluation, and that "the bulk of disagreement" over environmental hazards has been caused by "intuitive estimates of unreasonably high risk," also errs in ignoring reasonable disagreement over risk probabilities. Risk assessment has been repeatedly criticized as an "arcane expert process" that is over-dependent on probability estimates of assessors.[35] Many risk assessors appear to believe that it is "perfectly valid to base public policy on expert estimates and data," but that, once a risk expert has spoken, any disagreement is unreasonable and intuitive.[36] Such a notion is doubly questionable.

It is in part implausible because it presupposes a far more objective picture of probabilistic risk data than is now available. Even the authors of the most complete hazard analysis ever accomplished, WASH-1400, cautioned that their probability estimates were deficient, unprovable, possibly incomplete, assumption laden, and saddled with "an appreciable uncertainty." They said that "the present state of knowledge probably will not permit a complete analysis of low-probability accidents in nuclear plants with the precision that would be desirable."[37] More generally and more recently, risk assessors have pointed out that "uncertainties of six orders of magnitude are not unusual" in any probabilistic risk analysis.[38] In the face of such caveats, alleged certitude about which risk probabilities are correct, and which are incorrect, may be doubtful. As this chapter has noted, often the scientific mechanisms causing a hazard are unknown, as in the case of methylene chloride.[39] And, as the previous chapter also argued, *accident probability* often cannot be determined on the basis of observed *accident frequency*.[40] On the one hand, very low values of an accident probability per LNG trip, or per reactor-year, for example, are consistent with an assumed record of zero accidents in 800 voyages, or zero core melts in 17,000 reactor-years. On the other hand, an annual accident probability as high as 1 in 100 or 1 in 200 would still be consistent with the current LNG accident-frequency record, just as a yearly probability as high as 1 in 2,000 would be consistent with the existing record for nuclear accidents. Even though an accident record may be consistent with very low risk-probability values, this frequency alone "does not prove that the values are low."[41]

Proponents of the probabilistic strategy also err, in emphasizing risk probabilities, because they are unable to account for the reasonable controversy—among Nobel Prize winners, the American Physical Society, the Environmental Protection Agency, the Nuclear Regulatory Commission, and the American Nuclear Society—over various risk probabilities.[42] Reputable assessors affirm that many of the most serious environmental risks, such as global warming from burning of fossil fuels, are "highly resistant to quantification."[43] Moreover, for a number of reasons, nuclear probabilities, for example, are especially resistant to accurate estimation. Compound events, sequential component failures, sabotage or human error, and weapons proliferation are not amenable to quantification.[44] Rasmussen computed the probability of having a Three Mile Island type of accident as anywhere from 1 in 250 to 1 in 25,000 reactor-years.[45] All this suggests that certain accidents are not really "impossible," because many low probabilities are not believable. For example, the probability for a royal flush is 1 in 464,000. Yet, in a card game the probability is actually much higher, since the probability of cheating is likely to be as high as 1 in 10,000. Likewise, although the probability of a given environmental or technological accident may be only very slight, the higher probability of sabotage or terrorism is likely to increase this number by several orders of magnitude. Real risks, then, are likely to include so-called "outrageous events" or "rogue events," which are difficult to handle in probabilistic risk assessment.[46] Indeed, human error causes a majority of most industrial, marine, and transportation accidents.[47]

In claiming that the public overestimates many risk probabilities, such as those for nuclear accidents, many assessors assume that, in some of the most controversial, untested, and potentially catastrophic areas of technology, it is possible to judge clearly when a risk probability is accurate and when it is not. This is an appeal to authority, an appeal that (given the history of science) simply does not hold up.

Risk assessors' emphasis on the importance of probability estimates is especially vulnerable because the characteristics that, according to various experts, influence judgments of perceived and acceptable risks are highly intercorrelated; involuntary hazards, for example, "tend also to be inequitable and catastrophic."[48] Therefore, as noted in Chapter Six, it is especially difficult to determine whether society's expressed concern about involuntary risks, for example, is merely an artifact of the high correlations between involuntariness and other undesirable risk characteristics. There are numerous allegedly causal explanations, all consistent with the same "observed" phenomena. Kasper makes an analogous observation:

Even the best of epidemiological studies is confounded by the myriad explanations for low-level neurobehavioral effects; the same effects attributed to lead may be caused by exposure to low levels of many other trace metals, and indeed by exposure to the pace and stress of urban life itself. The result is that careful studies yield not proof but only suggestions.[49]

Or, as Cox and Ricci put it, "multiple models, having quite different implications at low doses, may all adequately 'fit' the observed dose-response data."[50]

Precisely because their hypothesis about misperceived probabilities is consistent with other explanations, proponents of the probabilistic strategy are not warranted in singling out the public's alleged misperceived probabilities as the *cause* of its high aversion to societal risks. Rather, as the previous chapter argued, the distinction between expert/objective and lay/subjective determination of environmental risks will not hold up. Because of problems of actual risk *calculation* (prior to any alleged evaluation), many hazard estimates are merely the intuitive *guesses* of individuals. Authors of a recent study conducted at the Stanford Research Institute admitted, for example, that analytic techniques could not handle probability estimates for certain human-caused events. They concluded: "We must rely on expert judgment, quantified, using subjective probabilities."[51] Likewise, the loss of the astronauts in the *Challenger* disaster, as well as the death of three astronauts on the ground at Cape Kennedy, demonstrated that even the best systems-analytic approaches cannot anticipate every possibility. In fact, one of the most famous nuclear risk probabilities, widely touted as "objective," is highly value laden. This is the reactor-year probability of a core melt in a nuclear plant, 1 in 17,000. As defended in WASH-1400, this probability is notoriously laden with value judgments about the effectiveness of evacuation in the face of catastrophe, the probability of weather stability, and the Gaussian Plume rise of radioactivity.[52] The problem, however, is *not* that such "objective" probabilities (as given by experts) are value laden but that they are apparently not recognized as such by proponents of the probabilistic strategy.

Lessons Learned from Experts' Claims about Societal Risks

The tendency of proponents of the probabilistic strategy to overemphasize the importance of risk probabilities and to condemn the public's alleged "misperceptions" of societal risks reveals an important flaw in contemporary environmental risk analysis. Assessors presume that, if there is a public preference for a risk whose probability of fatality is statistically higher than that of an alternative, then this preference is a result of misperceived probabilities, not a legitimate value system.[53] Their failure to recognize the value components of allegedly objective probability estimates goes hand in hand with assessors' tendencies to define *ethical* and *political* issues as merely *technical* ones, as the naive positivists are prone to do.[54] They assume, incorrectly, that agreement about technical matters is sufficient for resolving normative disputes.

Apparently, they make this assumption because they are afraid of damaging "the scientific pretenses of their work."[55] As a consequence, their emphasis on the importance of abstract, "objective" science helps both to disguise the often exploitative way in which technology is used and to condone a passive acceptance of the status quo. It allows assessors to dismiss as irrational or unscientific (as Okrent, Starr, Whipple, Maxey, Cohen, Lee, and others have done) any attempts to challenge our contemporary ethical or political values.[56] But, as Dickson has argued, "the use of supposedly objective models of . . . social behavior serves to legitimate the imposition of social policy," because the real risk concerns of laypersons can then be dismissed as subjective.[57] As one critic puts it, this is "like playing Monopoly with the Mafia: they always start the game owning Boardwalk."[58]

Conclusion

Because experts often define risk only in terms of probability of fatality, and consequently neglect ethical and political concerns, they fail to attack an essential problem of risk evaluation: how to make the decision process more *democratic*. Later chapters will suggest ways to democratize risk evaluation and management. As Thomas Jefferson warned, the only safe locus of societal power is in the people: "I know of no safe depositor of the ultimate powers of the society but the people themselves; and if we think them not enlightened enough to exercise their control with a wholesome discretion, the remedy is not to take it from them, but to inform their discretion."[59]

Chapter Eight

Uncertainty and the Utilitarian Strategy

The Case for a "Maximin" Account of Risk and Rationality

A recent U.S. National Academy of Sciences study pointed out that the estimates of increase in bladder cancer, caused by consuming normal amounts of saccharin over seventy years, differed by seven orders of magnitude. Despite these uncertainties, U.S. officials have sanctioned the use of saccharin, justifying their decision on the basis of a liberal risk assessment. As a result of a very conservative risk analysis, however, they banned cyclamates. If the two risk-assessment methodologies were consistent, experts have argued, cyclamates could easily have been shown to present a lower relative risk than saccharin. In Canada, for example, cyclamates are permitted, and saccharin is banned, making Canadian regulations in this area exactly the reverse of those in the United States.[1]

As the saccharin-cyclamates controversy illustrates, risk evaluations may be uncertain, not only because of the wide range of predicted hazard values, but also because of inconsistent risk models and rules of evaluation. This chapter will assess several of the prominent rules for evaluating risks. To see how alternative rules can generate different risk-management decisions for the same hazard, consider the following case.

The probability of a core melt for U.S. reactors is about 1 in 4 during their lifetime.[2] Risk assessments conducted by both the Ford Foundation–Mitre Corporation and the Union of Concerned Scientists (UCS) *agree* on the probability and consequence estimates associated with the risk from commercial nuclear fission, but they *disagree* in their recommendations regarding the advisability of using atomic energy to generate electricity. The UCS risk analysis decided against use of the technology; the Ford-Mitre study advised in favor of it.[3]

How could hazard assessments and evaluations that agree on the probability and consequences associated with a particular technological accident reach contradictory conclusions about the advisability of using the technology? In many such cases, including that of the UCS–Ford-Mitre controversy, the reason is that the two studies used quite different methodological rules at the third (risk-evaluation) stage of assessment. The Ford-Mitre research was based on the widely accepted Bayesian decision criterion that it is rational to choose the action with the best expected value or utility, where "expected value" or "expected utility" is defined as the weighted sum of all possible consequences of the action, and where the weights are given by the probability associated with each consequence. The UCS recommendation followed the maximin decision rule that it is rational to choose the action that avoids the worst possible consequence of all options.[4]

To know whether a particular policy analysis provides the best recommendation for rational behavior regarding risk, we obviously need to know under what circumstances a particular decision rule is to be preferred. Ought we to be technocratic liberals and choose a Bayesian rule? Or ought we to be cautious conservatives and follow a maximin strategy?[5] The "prevailing opinion" among scholars, according to John Harsanyi, is to use the Bayesian rule,[6] even in conditions of uncertainty.[7]

In this chapter, I argue that the prevailing Bayesian or utilitarian rules are often wrong. Like the expert-judgment strategy and the probabilistic strategy (Chapters Six and Seven), the Bayesian strategy dismisses the views of ordinary people as conservative, pessimistic, and irrational (rather than liberal, optimistic, and rational).[8] This chapter argues that there are compelling reasons for rejecting the Bayesian or utilitarian strategy under uncertainty, and that it is often more rational to prefer the maximin strategy.

Harsanyi versus Rawls: Expected Utility versus Maximin

Perhaps the most famous contemporary debate over which decision rules ought to be followed in situations of risk and uncertainty is that between Harvard philosopher John Rawls and Berkeley economist John Harsanyi. Following the utilitarian strategy, Harsanyi takes the Bayesian position that we ought to employ expected-utility maximization as the decision rule in situations of uncertainty, certainty, and risk.[9] Typical conditions of *uncertainty* occur when we have partial or total ignorance about whether a choice will result in a given outcome with a specific probability; for example, if we use nuclear power to generate electricity, we have partial ignorance about whether that choice will result in the probability that at least 150,000 people will die in a core-melt accident. Under conditions of *certainty*, we know that a choice will result in a given outcome; for example, if we use nuclear power to generate electricity, we are certain to have the outcome of radwaste to manage. Choices between bets on fair coins are classical examples of decisions under *risk*, since we can say that we know, with a specific probability, whether a choice will result in a given outcome. (Let's call the Bayesian sense of risk, involving specific, known probabilities, "risk$_B$" and the sense of risk, often involving uncertainty, with which hazard assessors deal, simply "risk.")

Most technology-related decisionmaking probably takes place in situations of uncertainty. We rarely have complete, accurate knowledge of all the probabilities associated with various outcomes of taking technological risks (e.g., from hazards such as pesticides, liquefied natural gas facilities, and toxic wastes), since very risky technologies are often new. The U.S. National Academy of Sciences confirmed, in a 1983 report, that the basic problems of risk assessment stem from the "uncertainty of the scientific knowledge of the health hazards addressed."[10] This statement suggests that many of the difficulties facing risk evaluation concern uncertainty, not "risk$_B$." If that is so, then one of the most important questions in the Harsanyi-Rawls expected-utility–maximin debate is what decision rule to follow under the conditions of uncertainty that characterize various technologies.

Harsanyi believes that, under conditions of uncertainty, we should maximize expected utility, where the expected utility of an act for a two-state problem is

$$u_1 p + u_2 (1 - p) \, ,$$

where u_1 and u_2 are outcome utilities, where p is the probability of S_1 and $(1 - p)$ is the probability of S_2, and where p represents the decisionmaker's own subjective probability estimate.[11] More generally, members of the dominant Bayesian school claim that expected-utility maximization is the appropriate decision rule under uncertainty.[12] They claim that we should value outcomes, or societies, in terms of the average amounts of utility (subjective determinations of welfare) realized in them.[13]

Proponents of maximin maintain that one ought to maximize the minimum—that is, avoid the policy having the worst possible consequences.[14] Many of them, including Rawls, take the maximin principle as equivalent to the *difference principle*. According to a simplified version of this principle, one society is better than another if the worst-off members of the former do better than the worst-off in the latter.[15] As previously noted, the obvious problem is that often the maximin and the Bayesian/utilitarian principles recommend different actions. Consider an easy case:

Imagine two societies. The first consists of 1,000 people, with 100 being workers (workers who are exposed to numerous occupational risks) and the rest being free to do whatever they wish. We can assume that, because of technology, the workers are easily able to provide for the needs of the rest of society. Also assume that the workers are miserable and unhappy, in part because of the work and in part because of the great risks that they face. Likewise, assume that the rest of society is quite happy, in part because they are free not to work and in part because they face none of the great occupational risks faced by the 100 workers. (This means, of course, that the compassion of the 900 nonworkers does not induce them to feel sorry for the workers and to feel guilty for having a better life. Hence we must assume that the nonworkers' happiness is not disturbed by any feeling of responsibility for the workers.) We must assume that the nonworkers have been able to convince themselves that each of the workers and their children were given good educations and equal opportunity. Likewise we must assume that the nonworkers believe that the workers were able to compete for the positions of nonworkers, and that, since the workers did not try hard enough, and work diligently enough to better themselves, therefore they deserve their state. With all these (perhaps implausible) assumptions in mind, let us suppose that, using a utility scale of 1 to 100, the workers each receive 1 unit of utility, whereas the others in society each receive 90 units. . . . Thus the average utility in this first society is 81.1

Now consider a second society, similar to the first, but in which, under some reasonable rotation scheme, everyone takes a turn at being a worker. In this society everyone has a utility of 35 units. Bayesian utilitarians would count the first society as more just and rational, whereas proponents of maximin and the difference principle would count the second society as more just and rational.[16]

Although this simplistic example is meant merely to illustrate how proponents of Bayesian utilitarianism and maximin would sanction different social decisions, its specific assumptions make maximin (in this case) appear the more reasonable position. Often, however, the reverse is true. There are other instances, especially situations of risk$_B$ or certainty, in which the Bayesian position is obviously superior. In this chapter, we shall attempt to determine the better decision rule for cases of *societal* hazard decision under *uncertainty* (not personal hazard decisions under uncertainty or risk$_B$), since environmental hazards are often typified by uncertainty.[17] A reasonable way to determine whether the Bayesian/utilitarian or maximin position is superior is to examine carefully the best contemporary defenses, respectively, of these evaluation rules. The best defenses are probably provided by Harsanyi, an act utilitarian who defends a Bayesian version of utilitarianism,[18] and Rawls, a contractarian.

Harsanyi's Arguments

Harsanyi's main arguments in favor of the Bayesian/utilitarian, and against the maximin, strategy under uncertainty are as follows: (1) Those who do not follow the Bayesian/utilitarian strategy make irrational decisions because they *ignore probabilities*. (2) Failure to follow this strategy leads to irrational and impractical consequences. (3) This failure also leads to unacceptable moral consequences. (4) Using the Bayesian/utilitarian strategy, with the equiprobability assumption, is desirable because it allows one to assign equal a priori probability to everyone's interests.

Do Non-Bayesians Ignore Probabilities?

Choosing the maximin stategy, claims Harsanyi, is wrong because "it is extremely irrational to make your behavior wholly dependent on some highly unlikely unfavorable contingencies, regardless of how little probability you are willing to assign to them."[19] To substantiate his argument, Harsanyi gives an example of maximin decisionmaking and alleges that it leads to paradoxes. The example is this. Suppose you live in New York City and are offered two jobs, in different cities, at the same time. The New York City job is tedious and badly paid; the Chicago job is interesting and well paid. However, to take the Chicago job, which begins immediately, you have to take a plane, and the plane travel has a small, positive, associated probability of fatality. If you were to follow the maximin principle, says Harsanyi, you would accept the New York job. The situation can be represented, he claims, on the following table:

	If the Chicago plane crashes	*If the Chicago plane does not crash*
If you choose New York job	You have a poor job but will be alive.	You have a poor job but will be alive.
If you choose Chicago job	You will die.	You have a good job and will not die.

In the example, Harsanyi assumes that your chances of dying in the near future from reasons other than a plane crash are zero. Hence, he concludes that, because maximin directs choosing so as to avoid the worst possibility, it forces one to ignore both the low probability of the plane crash and the desirability of the Chicago job and instead to choose the New York job. However, Harsanyi claims that a rational person, using the expected-utility criterion, would choose the Chicago job for those very two reasons—namely, its desirability and the low probability of a plane crash on the way to Chicago.

How successful is Harsanyi's first argument in employing the counterexample of the New York and Chicago jobs? For one thing, the example is highly counterintuitive; it is hard to believe that the greatest risk comes from dying in a plane crash, since hazard assessors have repeatedly confirmed that the average annual probability of fatality associated with many other activities—driving an automobile, for example—is greater, by an order of magnitude, than that associated with airplane accidents.[20] Harsanyi has stipulated, contrary to fact, that the worst case would be dying in a plane crash. Therefore, his stipulation, not use of the maximin rule, could be the source of much of what is paradoxical about the example.

Even if the example in this first argument were plausible, it would prove nothing about the undesirability of using maximin in situations of *societal* risk under uncertainty—for example, in deciding whether to open a liquefied natural gas facility. Harsanyi makes the questionable assumption, in using this example, that the situation of uncertainty regarding *one* individual's death, caused by that person's decision to fly to Chicago, is the same as a situation of uncertainty regarding *many* individuals' deaths, caused by a societal decision to employ a hazardous technology.

Objecting to Harsanyi's example, John Rawls claimed that the example failed because it was of a small-scale, rather than a large-scale, situation.[21] My claim is similar but more specific: Situations of individual risk are *voluntarily chosen*, whereas situations of societal risk typically are *involuntarily imposed*; hence, they are not analogous. Therefore, to convince us that *societal* decisions in situations of uncertainty are best made by following a Bayesian/utilitarian rule, Harsanyi cannot merely provide an example of an *individual* decision. Harsanyi, however, disagrees. Answering Rawls's objection, he says: "though my counterexamples do refer to small-scale situations, it is very easy to adapt them to large-scale situations since they have intrinsically nothing to do with scale, whether large or small. . . . [It is a] strange doctrine that scale is a fundamental variable in moral philosophy."[22]

There are several reasons why Harsanyi is wrong in this claim. In the *individual* case, one has the right to use expected utility so as to make efficient, economical decisions regarding *oneself*. In the *societal* case, one does not always have the right to use expected utility so as to make efficient, economical decisions regarding *others* in society, since maximizing utility or even average utility might violate rights or duties. On the individual level, the question is whether the individual's definition of 'risk' is *theoretically* justifiable. On the societal level, the question is whether a group of people's definition of 'risk' is *democratically* justifiable.

Rational societal decisionmaking requires an ethical rule that takes account of the fairness of the allocational *process* (for instance, whether potential victims exercise free, informed consent to the risk), not merely the *outcomes*.[23] And if so, then (as Diamond and others have argued) there are strong reasons to doubt what Sen calls "the strong independence axiom" (and what Harsanyi calls the "sure-thing principle" or the "dominance principle").[24] According to this axiom, if one strategy yields a better *outcome* than another does under some conditions, and if it never yields a worse outcome under any conditions, then decisionmakers always ought to choose the first strategy over the second.[25] But if there are grounds for doubting the sure-thing principle, because it ignores ethical process and focuses only on outcomes, then one ought to doubt Bayesian utilitarianism. This is because the sure-thing principle is one of the three main rationality axioms underlying the Bayesian approach.[26]

If the sure-thing principle fails to provide a full account of rational behavior, especially in the societal case, there are even stronger grounds for questioning Bayesian utilitarianism in situations of decisionmaking under *uncertainty*. Democratic process is probably more important in cases where probabilities are unknown than in those where they are certain, since it would be more difficult to ensure informed consent in the former cases. This, in turn, suggests that the individual case has to do more with a *substantive* concept of rationality, whereas the societal case has to do more with a *procedural* or "process" concept of rationality.[27] That is, the societal case must take account of conflicting points of view, as well as various ethical and legal obligations, such as those involving free, informed consent and due process.

For example, I may have an obligation to help ensure that all persons receive equal protection under the law, even if a majority of persons are unaware of their rights to equal protection, and even if their personal utility functions take no account of these unknown rights. In other words, if I make a decision regarding my own risk, I can ask "How safe is rational enough?" and I can be termed "irrational" if I have a fear of flying. But if I make a decision regarding risks to others in society, I do not have the right to ask, where their interests are concerned, "How safe is rational enough?" In the societal case, I must ask, because I am bound by moral obligation to others, "How safe is free enough?" or "How safe is fair enough?" or "How safe is voluntary enough?"[28]

Another problem with Harsanyi's first argument is that he begs the very question he sets out to prove—namely, that it "is extremely ir-rational to make your behavior [taking the job in New York] wholly dependent on some highly unlikely unfavorable contingencies [the Chi-cago plane crash], regardless of how little probability you are willing to assign to them"; by Harsanyi's own admission, he is attempting to prove that maximin ought not to be used in situations of risk under *uncertainty*.[29] Yet, if the worst consequence, death in a plane crash, is, *by his own definition*, "highly unlikely," then this consequence has a stipu-lated low probability.[30] The situation is not one of uncertainty but one of risk$_B$. Harsanyi's example has proved nothing about rational deci-sions under *uncertainty*. A related problem with Harsanyi's account is that he claims that people behave *as if* they maximized utility. In situa-tions of uncertainty, this claim begs the question because it cannot be demonstrated; we do not know the relevant probabilities.

Even as a strategy for rational decisions under risk$_B$, it is not clear that Harsanyi's principles would always be successful. He claims that reasonable people do not forgo great benefits in order to avoid a small probability of harm. However, it appears equally plausible to argue that many rational people do not wish to gamble, especially if their lives are at stake.[31] Moreover, in instances where they might justifiably gamble (with something other than their lives), it is not clear that humans are Bayesian utilitarians at all. Their risk aversion does not necessarily seem to be a linear function of probability.[32]

Many risk assessors—Bruce Ames, for instance—assume that risk aversion ought to be a linear function of probability, and they criticize laypersons for being more averse to industrial chemicals than to natural toxins (such as the mold in foods) that have a higher probability of causing injury or death. Invoking the concept of "relative risk," they fault laypersons for their "chemophobia," for greater aversion to lower-probability risks than to higher ones.[33] As the last two chapters have argued, however, probability is neither the only nor the most important factor determining risk aversion. And if it is not, then we have grounds for doubting both the Bayesian/utilitarian strategy and the probabilistic strategy (discussed in the last chapter). Likewise, as has been mentioned in earlier chapters, Kahneman and Tversky may be right that the Bayes-ian model does not always capture the essential determinants of the judgment process.[34] If subjective probabilities are frequently prone to error, then (contrary to Harsanyi's first argument) rational people might well avoid them.

Harsanyi's first argument is also problematic because it is built on the supposition that "it is extremely irrational to make your behavior wholly dependent on some highly unlikely unfavorable contingencies regardless of how little probability you are willing to assign to them."[35] What Harsanyi is saying is that it is irrational to base decisions on *consequences* and to ignore either a small or an uncertain probability associated with them. However, suppose that one has the choice between buying organically grown vegetables and those treated with pesticides, and that the price difference between the two is very small. Also suppose that the probability of getting cancer from the vegetables treated with pesticide is "highly unlikely," to use Harsanyi's own words. It is not irrational to avoid this cancer risk, even if it is small, particularly if one can do so at no great cost. Similarly, it is not irrational to avoid a possibly catastrophic risk, such as nuclear winter, even if it were small. In assuming that a low probability, alone, is a sufficient condition for ignoring a risk, Harsanyi has fallen victim to the probabilistic strategy criticized in the last chapter.

Is Maximin Irrational?

Harsanyi defends himself, in part, by claiming that, although the two different decision principles (Bayesian and maximin) often result in the same policies, whenever they differ, it is "always the maximin principle that is found to suggest unreasonable consequences."[36] One way to refute this argument is to give an example in which the two decision strategies dictate different actions, but in which the maximin action is clearly superior.

Consider the following (fictitious) example. Suppose that the night-shift foreman has discovered a leak in one of the large toxic-gas canisters at the local Union Carbide plant in West Virginia. Because of past instructions, he must immediately notify both the plant's safety engineer (who will bring a four-man crew with him to try to repair the leak within a half hour) and the president of the company. However, the foreman is still faced with a problematic choice: to notify the local sheriff of the situation, so that he can begin evacuation of the town surrounding the plant, or not to notify him. If he notifies the sheriff, as is required both by the *Code of Federal Regulations* and by the agreement Union Carbide signed with the town, when it leased the land to the company, then no townspeople will die as a result of the leak.

However, he and five other employees (the safety engineer and his crew) will lose their jobs as a result of the adverse publicity, especially after the Bhopal accident, if they cannot fix the leak within a half hour. Moreover, there are no other jobs available, since this is a depressed area, and even the coal companies cannot hire additional people. If the foreman does not notify the sheriff, and if the safety crew can repair the leak during the first half hour of their work, then he and the members of the five-person safety crew will each receive a $25,000 bonus from the company, not (of course) for disobeying the law, but for avoiding mass panic and adverse publicity. However, if the foreman does not notify the sheriff, and if the safety crew cannot repair the leak during the first half hour of their work, then the ten persons living closest to the plant (all residents of a nursing home for the aged) will die after a half hour's exposure to the fumes; all six of the employees will lose their jobs; and the foreman will have to notify the sheriff anyway.

The foreman uses expected utility to make his decision and employs the following table, consisting of two acts (notifying or not notifying the sheriff) and two states (fixing or not fixing the leak in thirty minutes). Since he is in a state of ignorance, the foreman uses the principle of insufficient reason,[37] or what Harsanyi calls "the equiprobability assumption,"[38] to assign equal probabilities (0.5) to both possible states. Thinking about all four possible outcomes, the foreman assigns a value or utility (u) to each of the outcomes. He decides not to notify the sheriff, since the expected utility for this act is higher $((0.5)(38) + (0.5)(-16) = 11)$ than the expected utility $((0.5)(16) + (0.5)(4) = 10)$ for notifying him. The safety engineer agrees with the foreman that the worst outcome is that in which both the jobs and the lives are lost, but he uses the *maximin* procedure and decides that they ought to notify the sheriff, so as to be sure to avoid this worst outcome.

In the example, the Bayesian/utilitarian and maximin strategies dictate different actions, and the maximin recommendation is arguably superior, for at least three reasons: (1) The *Code of Federal Regulations* establishes an obligation to notify the sheriff. (2) The lease contract that Union Carbide made with the town establishes an obligation to notify the sheriff. (3) The ten endangered persons have a right to know the risk facing them. The nursing home residents face the worst consequence of anyone, death (the crew and foreman have gas masks). Hence, their right (and the rights of their guardians, if any) to know is more important than the foreman's desire to avoid frightening people and to obtain a bonus. Indeed, their consent may be one of the

	If crew fixes leak in thirty minutes	*If crew doesn't fix leak in thirty minutes*
If I notify the sheriff now (10*u*)	Ten lives and six jobs are safe. (16*u*)	Six people lose jobs but ten townspeople are safe. (4*u*)
If I fail to notify the sheriff now (11*u*)	Ten lives and six jobs are safe; six men get bonus; people suffer no fear. (38*u*)	Ten lives and six jobs are lost. (−16*u*)

most important factors in deciding how to deal with this situation.[39] But if the maximin recommendation is superior, then this case provides a counterexample to Harsanyi's (and Arrow's) claim that, whenever the recommendations of the two strategies differ, it is "always the maximin principle that is found to suggest unreasonable consequences."[40]

It might be objected, at this point, that the counterexample violates Harsanyi's criteria for moral value judgments.[41] According to the objector, the foreman's decision is wrong, not because he used Bayesian/utilitarian principles, but because he computed the utilities in a self-interested way. Hence, the example may not show that Bayesianism or utilitarianism leads to wrong consequences, but only that self-interest leads to them.

In response, the foreman could plausibly claim, either that it is right to impose some risks on society, or that he was not acting in self-interest in assigning the utilities he did to the act of not informing the sheriff immediately. He could claim that he was trying to avoid mass panic (a frequently used defense) and needlessly troubling people.[42] Also, the foreman could complain that the Bayesian/utilitarian strategy is difficult to use, since it requires agents in situations of uncertainty to rank the lives of members of various societies on a common interval scale. It requires interpersonal comparisons of utility—something very difficult to make, as we shall argue shortly. Therefore, the foreman need not consciously have acted out of self-interest; he may merely have been unable to rank the lives of other people on a common interval scale, particularly if those being ranked were elderly and sick, and the foreman would rather be dead than elderly and sick.[43]

Does Maximin Lead to Unethical Consequences?

In the Bayesian/utilitarian scheme, warning the elderly and sick makes sense only if it would benefit society and if they deserve it. But this brings us to Harsanyi's third claim. Maximin would lead to unacceptable *moral* consequences: benefiting the least-well-off individuals, even when they do not deserve it, and even when doing so will not help society. To establish this point, Harsanyi gives two examples.[44]

In the first example, there are two patients critically ill with pneumonia, but there is only enough antibiotic to treat one of them, one of whom has terminal cancer. Harsanyi says that Bayesians would give the antibiotic to the patient who did not have cancer, whereas maximin strategists would give it to the cancer patient, since he is the worse off. In the second example, there are two citizens, one severely retarded and the other with superior mathematical ability. The problem is whether to use society's surplus money to help educate the mathematician or provide remedial training for the retarded person. The Bayesian utilitarian would spend the surplus money on the mathematician, says Harsanyi, whereas the maximin strategist would spend it on the retarded person, since he is the less well off.

Let us grant, for purposes of argument, that Harsanyi is right on two counts in these examples: on what decisions the respective strategists would make, and on the fact that the Bayesian utilitarian makes the more reasonable decision in each of these two cases. Even if we grant these two points to Harsanyi, however, he has still not established that the Bayesian/utilitarian strategy provides a superior basis for *societal* decisionmaking under *uncertainty*.

In the first (pneumonia) case, the risk is of fatality, but one knows, with *certainty*, that the cancer victim is soon to die, since Harsanyi defines his state as "terminal." In the second case, the risk is of improving the lot of two persons, one retarded and one gifted mathematically. However, Harsanyi tells us that spending money to train the latter "could achieve only trivial improvements in *B*'s condition," whereas spending the same funds to train *A* in mathematics would be quite successful, because of *A*'s interest and ability. Hence, one is not in a state of uncertainty about the probability of success in spending the monies for education in the two cases. Consequently, both examples show that there are cases, decisionmaking under risk$_B$, in which Bayesianism/utilitarianism dictates reasonable strategies. But that point is not at issue. Hence, Harsanyi has not argued for using Bayesian/utilitarian rules under *uncertainty*.

A second problem with these examples is that Harsanyi defines the retarded person as "less well off," and therefore deserving of funds for remedial education under the maximin strategy. However, being "less well off" is not merely a matter of intelligence. It is also a matter of financial well-being and of having equal political and social opportunity. If society has given equal consideration to the needs and interests of both the mathematician and the retarded person, if the retarded person is happy and incapable of being made better off, regardless of what society spends on him, then it is not clear that he is less well off than the mathematician. If the mathematician could be made better off through greater societal expenditures, then he may be less well off than the retarded person, who has reached his potential and is as happy as he is capable of being.

Admittedly, Harsanyi speaks of the retarded person as having "greater need" of the resources.[45] But if he cannot be bettered by any greater expenditure, does he really have a need? Presumably, one only has a need for that which is capable of bettering him in some way. Being well off is also a matter of having one's needs met to a degree comparable to that of others, perhaps others with differing abilities. It is not merely a matter of intelligence, money, or any other single factor. Consequently, Harsanyi's example may not provide even a case of Bayesian/utilitarian superiority in decisionmaking under $risk_B$.[46]

Does the Utilitarian Strategy Treat Persons Equally?

Having given general, Bayesian/utilitarian justifications for his position, Harsanyi provides a final argument that is non-Bayesian. This non-Bayesian defense focuses on what Harsanyi calls "the equiprobability assumption."[47] Decisionmakers ought to subscribe to this assumption, says Harsanyi, because doing so enables them to treat all individuals' a priori interests as equal.[48] That is, regardless of the social system chosen, one "would have the same probability, $1/n$, of taking the place of the best-off individual, or the second-best-off individual, etc., up to the worst-off individual." If everyone has an equal chance of being better off or worse off, Harsanyi claims that the rational person would always make the risk decision yielding the highest "average utility level."[49]

Although some scholars have alleged that Bayes makes use of the equiprobability assumption, most experts claim that his argument is free of this assumption.[50] Bayesian or not, the assumption is central to Harsanyi's defense of utilitarian decisionmaking and hence bears some examination.

A variant of the so-called "principle of insufficient reason," the equiprobability assumption was first formulated by the seventeenth-century mathematician Jacob Bernoulli. It says that, if there is no evidence indicating that one event from an exhaustive set of mutually exclusive events is more likely to occur than another, then the events should be judged equally probable.[51]

The most basic difficulty with the equiprobability assumption is that, if there is no justification for assigning a set of probabilities, because one is in a situation of uncertainty, then there is no justification for assuming that the states are equally probable.[52] Moreover, to assume, in a situation of uncertainty, that states are equally probable is to revert to reliance on a very subjective notion of probability. As Amos Tversky and Daniel Kahneman have argued persuasively, it is often irrational to rely on subjective probabilities,[53] since they are often the result of judgmental errors.[54] There are other difficulties as well. First of all, to assign the states equal probabilities is to contradict the stipulation that the situation is one of uncertainty.[55] In addition, it is often impossible to specify a list of possible states that are mutually exclusive and exhaustive;[56] therefore, different ways of defining states could conceivably result in different decision results, different accounts of how best to maximize average utility.[57]

The equiprobability assumption is also ethically questionable because it does not enable one to assign equal a priori weight to every individual's interests, as Harsanyi claims. It merely *postulates* that, in a situation of uncertainty and in different social systems or states of affairs, every individual has the *same probability* of being the best-off individual, or the second-best-off individual, and so on. In reality, however, different states of affairs are rarely equally probable. To assume that they are, when one is in a situation of uncertainty, is problematic in part because equally probable states often affect different individuals' interests unequally.

Using *averages* also affects individuals unequally. Therefore, even if one granted that it is rational to maximize expected utility in individual decisions, it would not necessarily be rational to choose the average of the expected utilities of different persons. Such a procedure would not maximize *my* expected utility, but only the average of the expected utilities of members of society.[58] Thus, the concepts of "average utility" and "equiprobability" could hide the very problems that most need addressing, the problems of discrimination and inequality. For example, assigning the occurrence of a nuclear core melt an equal probability with the nonoccurrence obviously does not treat people's a priori interests equally. If the core-melt probability is actually higher than

0.5, then the original assignment treats the interests of the consumers of nuclear power with less equality than those of its producers. And if the core-melt probability is actually lower than 0.5, then the original assignment treats the interests of the producers of nuclear power with less equality than those of its consumers.

Moreover, even though the equiprobability assumption assigns every individual the *same* probability (in every state of affairs) of being the best off, second best off, and so on, this does not guarantee that every individual's interests receive *equal* weight. Because Bayesian utilitarianism focuses on expected utility and *average* utility, it dictates that decisions be made on the basis of highest average utility. This rule guarantees that the minority, with less-than-average utility, can receive a disproportionate risk burden. In such cases, one would not be treating the interests of each person in the minority as equal to those of each person in the majority. In at least one important sense, therefore, Harsanyi does not treat people the same, as he claims to do through his equiprobability assumption.[59]

In confusing equiprobability with equity, Harsanyi assumes that what is *average* is what is *equitable*. Obviously it is not, as was illustrated in a recent assessment of the cancer risk posed by emissions from a municipal waste-combustion facility.[60] The study concluded that for dioxin, polychlorinated biphenyls, arsenic, beryllium, and chromium, the maximum individual lifetime cancer risk varied across three orders of magnitude. Since phenotypic variation can cause more than a 200-fold difference in sensitivity to toxins among individuals,[61] these figures alone are enough to show that one individual could easily bear a risk that was five orders of magnitude greater than that of another person, even though they shared the same average risk. In such a case, averaging the uncertainty and the differences in sensitivity would not mean that all persons were treated equitably.

Moreover, even if the equiprobability assumption did guarantee that everyone were treated the same, such treatment also would not be equitable. Genuinely equal treatment requires that we treat people differently, so as to take account of different degrees of merit, need, rights to compensation or reparation, and the like. Treating people the same, in a situation where existing relationships of economic and political power are already established, merely reinforces those relationships, apart from whether they are ethically defensible. Treating people the same, as most persons wish to do in situations of uncertainty, also ignores the fact that duties and obligations almost always require that people's interests *not* be treated the same. For example, suppose that Mr. *X* builds a pesticide-manufacturing plant in Houston. Also suppose that Mr. *Y*, who lives next door, has demonstrably damaging health effects from the emissions of the pesticide facilitv. To say that Mr. *X*'s and Mr. *Y*'s interests in stopping the harmful emissions ought to be given the same weight is to skew the relevant ethical obligations. It would give license to anyone wishing to put others at risk for his own financial gain.[62] Hence, there are rarely grounds for treating persons' interests the *same*, since they are almost always structured by preexisting obligations that determine whose interests ought to have more weight. Equity of treatment can be achieved only after ethical analysis, not after an appeal to treating everyone the same, in the name of the equiprobability assumption.

A third difficulty with this assumption is that it could lead to disaster whenever the higher/highest actual probability is associated with a catastrophe. Consider the following case:

	If reactor operators are careless	*If reactor operators are careful*
If we continue to use commercial nuclear plants (25)	More than 100,000 could die in an accident. (-200)	We have a potentially good source of electricity. (250)
If we discontinue use of commercial nuclear plants (20)	We will have a financial loss but no commercial nuclear disaster. (10)	We will have a financial loss but no commercial/ research disaster. (30)

As this example shows, the decision to use or discontinue nuclear power is one made under uncertainty. If the state having catastrophically bad consequences (that of reactor operators being careless) has the higher actual probability (0.6), then the equiprobability assumption and the expected-utility rule yield a disastrous decision: to continue to use commercial nuclear reactors, since the expected utility of this option is $(0.5)(-200) + (0.5)(250) = 25$, whereas the utility of its alternative is only $(0.5)(10) + (0.5)(30) = 20$. However, if the real probability associated with reactor operators' being careless is 0.6, then the expected utility for continuing to use commercial fission is $(0.6)(-200) + (0.4)(250) = -20$. Likewise, if the real probability associated with their being careful is 0.4, then the expected utility for discontinuing use of nuclear power is $(0.6)(10) + (0.4)(30) = 18$. The example shows that use of the equiprobability assumption could have catastropic effects.

But if use of the equiprobability assumption could lead to devastating consequences, why do many decisionmakers defend it? One reason is that, as Luce and Raiffa point out, situations rarely involve complete uncertainty.[63] Because they do not, one often has some partial information concerning the true state. And if one does have partial information, then use of the equiprobability assumption, together with the Bayesian/utilitarian strategy, makes more sense than in the actual case of uncertainty. Another reason for using the principle of insufficient reason is that, according to Luce and Raiffa,[64] it satisfies all the axioms required in situations of partial uncertainty, while maximin satisfies all but one of the axioms. In response, however, it is important to point out that the Luce and Raiffa claims are applicable only to *individual* decisionmaking under uncertainty. Luce and Raiffa explicitly warned that they were not discussing the societal case. But if not, then their warning provides further evidence that there are strong disanalogies between "event" and "process" rationalities, and therefore that the case of *societal* decisionmaking is not amenable to Bayesian rationality and the equiprobability assumption.[65]

Rawls's Arguments

Admittedly, discovering difficulties with Harsanyi's arguments for Bayesian/utilitarian rules is not a sufficient condition for rejecting them. We also need to assess maximin, perhaps the best alternative rule for certain classes of cases under uncertainty. To assess this option, let's evaluate Rawls's analysis. His main arguments to support the maximin strategy in situations of uncertainty (his "original position") are as follows: (1) It would lead to giving the interests of the least advantaged the highest priority. (2) It would avoid using a utility function, designed for risk taking, in the area of morals, where it does not belong. (3) It would avoid the Bayesian/utilitarian use of interpersonal comparisons of utility in defining justice. More generally, (4) it would avoid making supererogatory actions a matter of duty, as do utilitarian theories. And (5) it would avoid the Bayesian/utilitarian dependence on uncertain predictions about the consequences of alternative policies.

Maximin Gives Priority to the Least Advantaged

Consider the first argument in favor of the maximin strategy: It would lead to a concept of justice based on Rawls's "difference principle," which evaluates every possible societal or policy arrangement in accordance with the interests of the least advantaged or worst-off persons.[66] The "first virtue" of social institutions, in Rawls's view, is justice or fairness. We could arrive at just or fair social institutions, he believes, if we were all rational individuals caring only about our own interests, and if we negotiated with each other (about the nature of these institutions) behind the "veil of ignorance"—that is, without knowledge of anyone's social or economic positions, special interests, talents, or abilities. Under these circumstances, Rawls claims that we would arrange society so that even the worst-off persons would not be seriously disadvantaged.[67] We would simply choose the risk distribution where the least well off are least disadvantaged.[68] Also, not knowing our own situation, Rawls argues that we would be more likely to mitigate the "arbitrariness of the natural lottery itself,"[69] the natural lottery according to which we receive talents, a beneficial family background, and so on.[70]

The main objection to this argument is that we ought not to use maximin (or what Rawls calls "the difference principle") because it might not increase the average utility of society, and increasing average utility is more important than helping a subset of persons. Therefore, goes the objection, in the situation of technological risk under uncertainty, one should not try to protect those who are most at risk, since such an action would take away resources from society. Instead, one ought to use a Bayesian/utilitarian strategy, to employ expected utility so as to maximize the average well-being of each member of the group.[71]

The main problem with this objection is that it could sanction using members of a minority who are most at risk so as to benefit the majority; that is, some persons could be used as means to the ends of other persons—an action condemned by most moral philosophers. Presumably, however, all persons ought to be treated as ends in their own right, not merely as a way to satisfy the desires of someone else, not merely as objects. Moreover, there are good grounds for believing that everyone ought to receive equal treatment, equal consideration of interests: (1) The comparison class is all humans, and all humans have the same capacity for a happy life.[72] (2) Free, informed, rational people would likely agree to principles of equal rights or equal protection.[73] (3) These principles provide the basic justifications for other important concepts of ethics and are presuppositions of all schemes involving consistency, justice, fairness, rights, and autonomy.[74] (4) Equality of rights is presupposed by the idea of law; "law itself embodies an ideal of equal treatment for persons similarly situated."[75]

If all members of society have an equal, prima facie right to life, and therefore to bodily security, as the most basic of human rights, then allowing one group of persons to be put at greater risk, without compensation and for no good reason, amounts to violating their rights to life and to bodily security. Indeed, if there were no obligation to equalize the burden of technological risk imposed on one segment of the population, for the benefit of another segment, there could be no authentic bodily security and no legal rights at all. The majority could simply do whatever they wished to any victimized minority. That is why John Rawls called his notion of justice "fairness," and why he spoke about maximin under the rubric of fairness.[76]

Admittedly, sanctioning *equal* treatment, in the name of fairness, does not mean guaranteeing the *same* treatment, as was already argued in this chapter and in Chapter Two.[77] Establishing the prima facie duty to treat persons equally, as far as possible, does require that we use maximin in situations of societal risk under uncertainty,[78] unless we have *relevant moral reasons* for treating people differently.[79]

Efficiency, however, does not appear to provide relevant moral grounds for discrimination, especially discrimination against the least well off, for several reasons. First, discrimination against persons, on grounds of efficiency, is something that would have to be justified for each and every situation in which it occurs. That is, to argue (as we just have) that a principle of equal rights and equal treatment under the law is desirable, but that there may be morally relevant grounds for discrimination, is to argue for a principle of prima facie political equality.[80] In this view, sameness of treatment of persons and communities need no justification, since it is presumed defensible; only unequal (different) treatment requires defense.[81] Therefore, the burden of proof is on the person who wishes to discriminate, who wishes not to give equal protection to some minority that is exposed to societal risk.

Since the burden of proof is on the discriminator and since, by definition, we are dealing with a situation of decisionmaking under uncertainty, it is difficult to believe that the discriminator (the person who does not want to use maximin) could argue that efficiency provides *morally relevant* grounds for discrimination.[82] The potential grounds justifying such discrimination (for example, empirical factors about merit, compensation, or efficiency) would be, by definition, unknown in a situation of uncertainty.

Efficiency also does not appear to serve any higher interest.[83] Admittedly, many risk assessors and policymakers claim that efficiency serves the interests of everyone; they say that "the economy needs" particular hazardous technologies.[84] They also claim that certain risk-abatement measures are not cost-effective and therefore are not beneficial to our national well-being.[85] However, if efficiency is to serve the overall interest of everyone, it must be "required for the promotion of equality in the long run"; any other interpretation of "serving the overall interest" would be open to the charge that it was built upon using humans as means to the ends of other persons, rather than treating them as ends in themselves.[86] We must therefore ask whether efficiency per se (for example, avoiding pollution controls and therefore equal distribution of risk) leads to the promotion of equality in the long run. The problem with answering this question in the affirmative, as Harsanyi would do, is that such an answer would contain a highly questionable *factual assumption*—namely, that promoting technology, without also seeking equal risk distribution, will lead to greater equality of treatment in the long run. This is false.

Historically, there is little basis for believing that efficiency will help promote a more equitable distribution of wealth, and therefore more political equality.[87] In the United States, for example, although there has been an absolute increase in the standard of living in the past thirty-five years, the relative shares of wealth held by various groups have not changed. The poorest 20 percent of persons still receive 5 percent of the wealth, while the richest 20 percent still hold 41 percent; the share of the middle three quintiles has remained just as constant.[88] These figures suggest that economic and technological growth, coupled with efficiency in the form of inequity of risk abatement, has not promoted economic equality. Because of the close relationship between wealth and the ability to utilize equal opportunities,[89] it is unlikely that such efficiency and economic expansion have promoted equal political treatment.[90] If anything, they have probably made inequities even wider.[91]

Technological expansion (achieved through economic efficiency and through failure to abate technological risks) also does not ordinarily help to create a more egalitarian society, because technology generally eliminates jobs; it does not create them.[92] In the United States, for example, the new jobs that have become available in the last thirty years have largely been in the service sector and not in manufacturing or in technology.[93] Consequently, it seems difficult to argue that efficiency and Bayesian/utilitarian risk strategies help to equalize opportunities.[94] If anything, the plight of the least advantaged, whether the poor or those who bear a heavier burden of technological risk, is exacerbated by technological progress because they must compete more frantically for scarcer jobs. Moreover, because a larger portion of the indigent are unemployable, progress makes little immediate impact on the problem of hard-core poverty.[95]

Technological progress, without a commitment to equal distribution of societal risks, likewise typically fails to remove distributive inequities because the poor usually bear the brunt of technological hazards. Most environmental policies, including risk policies, "distribute the costs of controls in a regressive pattern while providing disproportionate benefits for the educated and wealthy, who can better afford to indulge an acquired taste for environmental quality [and risk mitigation]."[96] This means that, for the poor, whatever risk abatement and environmental quality cannot be paid for cannot be had. A number of studies have shown that "those square miles populated by nonwhites and by all low socioeconomic groups were the areas of highest pollution levels."[97] In fact, various adverse environmental impacts, such as higher risk burdens, are visited disproportionately upon the poor, while the rich receive the bulk of the benefits.[98] All this suggests that Bayesian/utilitarian strategies, in allowing the poor (persons who are least advantaged economically and therefore most helpless politically) to be further burdened with disproportionate technological risks, are especially questionable. They harm those who already bear many of society's adverse impacts.[99] Hence, if one has a moral obligation to help those who are most helpless,[100] then Bayesian/utilitarian risk strategies are likely to be wrong. Moreover, it is questionable whether most utilitarians (as Harsanyi assumes) would defend the Bayesian commitment to average utilities, at the expense of the minority who must bear higher-than-average risk burdens. As Brandt points out, "most utilitarians think that inequalities of distribution tend to reduce the total welfare."[101]

In response to these equity-based arguments against Bayesian utilitarianism, and in favor of maximin, Harsanyi would likely respond that he is misunderstood. After all, when Sen raised equity objections against his position, Harsanyi argued that individual utility functions already reflected concern for social inequities and that imposing equity requirements on expected utilities would be "double counting."[102] Such a response does not seem to invalidate equity and distributional objections, however, because individual utility functions do not necessarily reflect concern for equity. These functions could provide, at best, only individual *preferences* for equity, not an *in-principle* guarantee that equity must be taken into account by all individuals.[103] Harsanyi also cannot guarantee that equity of distribution will be taken into account in his scheme because, by definition, his account is relativistic. It recognizes no standards except personal preferences and tastes.[104] In addition, Harsanyi's idealized utility functions specifically do not express distributional concerns. Different humanistic moral codes might make conflicting recommendations regarding social action. Yet, using his idealized utility function, Harsanyi would have no way of deciding among them.[105] Moreover, because he proves that social welfare must be a linear function of individual utilities,[106] Harsanyi must be maximizing personal consumption of socially produced goods. But if his welfare functions maximize consumption and are affected only by personal consumption, then they cannot possibly take account of equity, which is not a type of personal consumption.[107]

Harsanyi's problems with equity can be expressed in the form of a dilemma: If (A) social welfare is a linear function of individual utilities, then interpersonal comparability of utilities is possible. And if it is possible, then Harsanyi has a utilitarian social welfare function, as he claims. But if he has a utilitarian social welfare function, then he cannot possibly deal with equity, as he claims. Alternatively, if (B) social welfare is not a linear function of individual utilities, then interpersonal comparability of utilities is not possible, and Harsanyi has no utilitarian social welfare function. But if not, then he could theoretically deal with equity issues; but, because he has no vehicle for doing so, his account is conceptually incoherent. Hence, if (A), then Harsanyi's claim that he can deal with equity is false. But if (B), then his claim is conceptually incoherent within his system. In either case, Harsanyi appears unable to answer maximin objections based on equity.[108]

Maximin Avoids Utility Functions

Another argument of maximin proponents is that maximin would avoid using a von Neumann–Morgenstern utility function (designed for risk taking) in the area of morals, where it does not belong. This argument is that utility functions express the subjective importance that people *do attribute* to their needs and interests, not the importance that they *ought to attribute*; hence, there is no way to discriminate rationally or morally among alternative tastes or preferences.[109] For maximin proponents, equating *preferences* with *oughts* is problematic because people often prefer things (such as cigarettes or a particular marriage partner) that do not actually increase their welfare.[110] More generally, maximin proponents say that, if one's welfare is assumed to be identical with one's preferences, at least four undesirable consequences follow: (1) One ignores the *quality* of the preferences or choices[111] and is forced into moral relativism.[112] (2) One's choices appear inconsistent with the Bayesian/utilitarian assumption that tastes or preferences are stable, consistent, precise, exogenous, and relevant to outcomes.[113] (3) There is no distinction between needs and wants,[114] and none between *utility* or personal welfare and *morality* or moral principle.[115] (4) One must assume that *group* welfare is merely the aggregate of *individual* preferences, as is expressed by summing utilities and getting an average.[116] Opponents of Bayesian utilitarianism claim that public well-being is not simply the aggregate of individual preferences, because widespread egoism might serve each individual's personal welfare but might destroy the common good. Moreover, in a rapidly changing situation, where leaders must act on the basis of likely *future* events, public welfare clearly is not merely the aggregate of *present* individual preferences.[117]

Harsanyi's response to arguments such as these, that *utility* functions ought not be used to decide about *morality*, is that the argument is based on a misunderstanding. He claims that a utility function is not merely an indication of an individual's attitude toward risk (as he says many moral philosophers suppose); it is also an indication of how much utility or *subjective importance* the individual assigns to various goals.[118] For this reason, Harsanyi would argue, there is no necessary distinction between moral judgments and utility judgments.

But such a response ignores the fact that utility judgments are based on *preferences*, whereas moral judgments are based on *principles*. If there is a moral principle to treat equal beings equally, then that moral principle is binding, even if those victimized by nonadherence to the principle do not have a preference for being treated equally. Principles protect everyone, not merely those who have free, well-informed preferences.

Harsanyi's position is also problematic because of an apparent incoherence between his interpretations of the utility function and interpersonal comparisons of utility. Harsanyi wishes to make moral judgments on the basis of subjective utility functions, rather than on the basis of unchanging moral principles (such as the principle that equal justice should be granted to equal beings). For him, weighting the subjective importance attached to things is more important than guaranteeing adherence to moral principles, because people's preferences are *different*. But if people's preferences are different, then presumably even two people in similar circumstances, with a similar background, could have different preferences.[119] And if similar people do have different preferences, then it is questionable whether the utility functions/preferences of all persons are governed by the same psychological laws. If not, then interpersonal comparisons of utility are not possible, because each person's preferences and utility functions may operate according to different psychological laws. But this conclusion contradicts two of Harsanyi's claims: (1) that "preferences and utility functions of all human individuals are governed by the same basic psychological laws";[120] (2) that interpersonal utility comparisons are theoretically capable of being specified completely because they "have a completely specific theoretical meaning."[121]

If the reasoning in the previous arguments is correct, then Harsanyi cannot coherently claim *both* that preferences are needed as measures of welfare, because people's preferences/utility functions are *different*,[122] *and* that interpersonal comparisons of utility are possible because people's utility functions "are governed by the *same* basic psychological laws."[123]

In response to this argument, Harsanyi would likely claim that interpersonal comparisons of utility are possible and that we make them all the time. But why, then, should utility be based on purely subjective preferences, rather than also on ethical principles, such as those stated by Rawls?[124] Likewise, Harsanyi (and, indeed, any Bayesian utilitarian) may have a related problem, in *both* stipulating the existence of an ideal individual decisionmaker *and* maintaining that such a person has no individual utility function. In order to treat the problem of societal decisionmaking as an ideal individual decision, Harsanyi must eliminate differences among persons and define rational behavior as *average* expected utility, rather than in terms of any particular person's decisions. But eliminating differences among persons, so as to obtain an ideal individual decision, eliminates the individuality of the decisionmaker. Hence, Harsanyi cannot consistently claim both that his theory, like Rawls's, formulates the problem of the social contract in terms of an ideal individual decision and that his decisionmaker has no individual utility function.[125]

Maximin and Preference Orderings

Economists try to resolve these problems with interpersonal comparisons of utility by offering the notion of a rational preference ordering, rather than a Bayesian cardinal scale. Since maximin can use merely an ordinal scale, its proponents argue that it places far fewer burdens on the individual attempting to evaluate risk options and consequences. Such an individual, they say, would not have to make interpersonal comparisons of utility and hence would not have to estimate what utility level he would enjoy if placed in the objective physical, economic, and social conditions of another individual.[126] Such an estimate is difficult, because different persons' preferences do not have the same intensity, because stronger preferences are not always better preferences, and because feelings of different persons might not combine linearly.[127]

Admittedly, despite these difficulties with interpersonal comparisons of utility, presupposing an ordinal ranking (as do proponents of maximin) also causes problems. For example, one could only obtain such an ordering through direct responses or a questionnaire. Yet, if one were unclear about how to maximize her well-being, then the ordering would not be an indicator of authentic welfare, any more than a decision based on the interval utility scale would be,[128] and there is no system that would ever enable her to maximize her welfare. Although this problem is not unique to the maximin approach, the difficulties facing anyone determining ordinal utilities appear to be less than those associated with similar determinations on an interval scale,[129] for the reasons given earlier in this section. Hence, at least on this criterion, the maximin strategy may be superior to the Bayesian/utilitarian.

Maximin and Supererogation

Another potential problem with Bayesian (and any utilitarian) theories is that they appear to make supererogatory actions a matter of duty.[130] If Bayesians and utilitarians are correct, then one is always equally obliged to perform both normal duties and heroic actions, since the (Bayesian/utilitarian) criterion for any action is whether it maximizes average utility.[131] One might be obliged under Bayesianism/utilitarianism, for example, to give up one's own projects and desires in life, including those related to family and profession, and instead dedicate oneself sacrificially to helping third-world victims of environmental risks.[132] For particularly talented individuals, such a sacrifice of their lives seems likely to maximize average utility and hence to be required of them, on Bayesian grounds (assuming that average utility can be determined). This alleged obligation presents a problem, however, in the light of our ordinary understanding of fairness and what is right and wrong.[133]

Harsanyi disagrees. He claims that freedom from burdensome moral obligations, such as the duty to perform supererogatory actions, has high utility; therefore, one is not bound to maximize average utility if it imposes burdensome obligations.[134]

If Harsanyi's response is correct, then his system is not one of Bayesian utilitarianism, but one of Bayesian utilitarianism joined with some deontological principles or side constraints (such as "One ought not to burden individuals for the purpose of maximizing overall utility"). Harsanyi can escape the problem of supererogatory actions, but only at the price of having a theory that admits that maximizing utility sometimes imposes too great a burden.[135] An analogous problem arises in the case where duty conflicts with maximizing utility. Consider the following example. Suppose a father sees a building on fire. In one room of the building is his child, and in another room of the building are two other children. He has to decide whether to try to save his child or the other two children. He knows that he can only do one or the other, because the rooms are far apart, and the fire is progressing rapidly. Moreover, he believes that his chances of getting to the different rooms are the same. Parental duty dictates that he try to save his own child, whereas maximizing expected utility dictates that he try to save the two other children. A Bayesian utilitarian could not *consistently* argue that the father ought to save his child.[136]

Maximin and Calculating Consequences

A final potential problem with utilitarian theories such as Bayesianism is that they seem to be dependent on uncertain predictions about the results of alternative policies. As a consequence, two well-informed and well-intentioned Bayesians could each come to different conclusions about what is right or wrong, good or bad.[137] This problem is in part a result of the fact that many variables affect outcomes, and these variables are neither known nor predictable.[138] Bayesian/utilitarian decision strategies are therefore in trouble, since they rely on one's ability to predict consequences. It might be objected, of course, that the maximin strategy also relies on ability to predict consequences. By definition, although maximin is not concerned with probabilities, it must attempt to avoid the worst possible outcome.

To some degree, this objection is correct, although maximin may have less of a problem with predicting consequences than does the Bayesian/utilitarian strategy, and for several reasons. For one thing, it is often easier to tell which consequences will be the worst than it is to rank the interval-scale utility of each (as was already mentioned). Also, if the worst technological and environmental risks are typically imposed on the poor, it may be possible to look at the existing income distributions in order to assess who, in the future, is likely to be least advantaged and hence more likely to bear some of the highest risks. It may not be difficult to discover the worst outcomes.[139]

In response, Harsanyi admits that contractarian theories, such as Rawls's, "go a long way toward deciding our moral uncertainties in a fairly unambiguous manner," whereas Bayesian/utilitarian morality has a great many "uncertainties." Harsanyi claims, however, that this ambiguity is an advantage, since it enables Bayesian utilitarians to avoid "simple minded rigid mechanical rules" that do not do justice to the complexity of moral problems.[140] The difficulty with Harsanyi's response, however, is that the absence of second-order rules of priority in Bayesian utilitarianism (rules that Rawls, for example, does have) leaves Harsanyi open to a number of objections.[141] Because Harsanyi denies that his system has any second-order rules, and because he claims that every decision "must always depend on the balance of the advantages and disadvantages it is likely to yield,"[142] Harsanyi appears to be an *act* utilitarian and to face a number of objections associated with this position. For example, a Bayesian utilitarian could well conclude that the welfare of the majority could be served by secretly disenfranchising the minority.[143] Harsanyi admits as much himself. He says: "Who is the moral philosopher to lay down the law . . . that no amount of economic and social development, however large, can ever justify any curtailment of civil liberties."[144] This seems to be a classic statement of the position that everyone has his price, and that expediency can supersede duty.

Maximin and Practical/Prudential Considerations

These arguments about the merits of maximin and Bayesian/utilitarian strategies for decisions under uncertainty suggest several general reasons why the maximin principle might be superior in certain situations. For one thing, Bayesianism/utilitarianism might demand both too much and too little of agents. It might demand too much of them in committing them to supererogatory acts, as necessary for maximizing utility. It might demand too little of agents in committing them to maximizing average utility, even in instances when maximum average utility supports a tyranny of the majority against the minority. Furthermore, although the maximin position is also susceptible to its own types of difficulties (for example, it assumes that we can specify ordinal preferences), these problems often appear less troublesome, especially in situations of uncertainty, than those inherent in the Bayesian approach.[145]

There are also at least three practical arguments for preferring maximin. For one thing, the wording of the 1969 U.S. National Environmental Policy Act (NEPA) makes it clear that federal policymakers should ensure that *every individual* enjoys safe and healthy surroundings, not merely that government maximizes *average* safety or utility.[146] In requiring safety for "all Americans" and for "each person," NEPA clearly rejects the Bayesian/utilitarian notion that it is acceptable to deprive a minority of persons of their health or safety.

Common sense, as well as specific laws such as NEPA, likewise enjoin us to use maximin in situations of societal decisionmaking under uncertainty. One of the most commonsensical of notions is that bureaucracies are notoriously slow moving and inefficient. For this reason, bureaucracies ought not to be trusted, in the absence of specific requirements, to make reliable and timely decisions about life-and-death matters, especially worst-case situations. Perhaps those decisions should instead be governed by prima facie rules, such as "In cases of technological risk under uncertainty, especially cases of potentially catastrophic risk, follow maximin strategies."[147]

Pearl Harbor illustrates the inefficiency, irresponsibility, and inability of the bureaucracy to "handle the unexpected":

By December 7, Admiral Kimmel, the Pacific Fleet Commander, had received the following information: a warning from the Navy on November 27 about possible attacks, a report of a change in Japanese codes (evaluated as very unusual), reports of Japanese ships in Camranh Bay, orders to be alert for Japanese action in the Pacific, messages deciphered from Japan's most secure code ordering Japanese embassies to destroy secret papers, government authorization to destroy all American codes and secret papers in outlying islands, and personal warnings from Admiral Stark in Washington. Assuming honesty and competence, a[n] . . . analyst would be led to predict: (1) the fleet would be out of the harbor; (2) the island would be air patrolled; (3) the emergency warning center would be staffed; and (4) the Army would have been notified under the Joint Coastal Frontier Defense Plan. But each of these predictions would have proved incorrect.[148]

The example suggests that society ought to have procedures for implementing protections, such as the maximin rule, to guard against the inadequacies of bureaucracy. Society might also need a way to avoid the catastrophic consequences of human error. The case of commercial nuclear fission is a classic instance of the need to guard against the results of poor risk evaluations and operator error. "Nowhere are issues of perceived risk more salient or the stakes higher than in the controversy over nuclear power."[149] The Chernobyl accident occurred at least partly because assessors called the disaster "highly improbable" before it happened.[150] In a Bayesian/utilitarian scheme, highly improbable accidents are not a significant concern in decisionmaking. But in a maximin scheme, the fact that a worst-case nuclear core melt could kill 150,000 persons[151] would be a significant cause for concern. Had regulators implemented a maximin strategy, with appropriate procedures for ensuring it, then the Chernobyl accident might have been less likely.

If technological rulemaking created a "climate" of maximin, a climate in which decisionmakers aimed at avoiding worst cases, both they and society would likely be more aware of potential accident consequences, more aware of erroneous subjective probabilities, and more aware of human errors in risk assessment. In their classic works, as was already mentioned, Tversky and Kahneman showed that virtually everyone falls victim to a number of characteristic biases in the interpretation of statistical and probabilistic data. These biases are the result of following erroneous intuitions, and they often result in disastrous consequences. For example, as was mentioned earlier, people often follow an intuition called "representativeness," according to which they believe that various samples are similar to one another and to the population from which they are drawn. In subscribing to this bias, both experts and laypeople are insensitive to such matters as the prior probability of outcomes, sample size, the inability of sampling to obtain a good prediction and to correct itself, the inaccuracy of predictions based on redundant and correlated input variables, and regression toward the mean—despite the fact that training in elementary probability and statistics warns against all these errors.[152]

Both risk assessors and statistics experts also typically fall victim to a bias called "availability"[153] and to the "anchoring" bias.[154] These systematic and predictive errors of experts are significant because risk assessment is based on complex theoretical analyses that "include a large component of judgment. Someone, relying on educated intuition, must determine the structure of the problem, the consequences to be considered, and the importance of the various branches of the fault tree."[155] According to Kahneman and Tversky, "people do not follow the principles of probability theory in judging the likelihood of uncertain events,"[156] and "the same type of systematic errors . . . can be found in the intuitive judgments of sophisticated scientists." These findings indicate that risk assessment, especially Bayesian/utilitarian risk assessment, is likely to produce many erroneous analyses.[157] After all, the experts were wrong when they said that irradiating enlarged tonsils was harmless. They were wrong when they said the X-raying feet, to determine shoe size, was harmless. They were wrong when they said that irradiating women's breasts, to alleviate mastitis, was harmless.[158] And they were wrong when they said that witnessing A-bomb tests at close range was harmless.[159]

More specifically, psychometric researchers have concluded that risk experts typically overlook six common "pathways to disaster": (1) They fail to consider the ways in which human error can cause technical systems to fail, as at Three Mile Island. (2) They have too much confidence in current scientific knowledge, even though inadequate scientific knowledge caused such catastrophes as the 1976 collapse of the Teton Dam. (3) They fail to appreciate how technical systems, as a whole, function. For example, engineers were surprised when cargo-compartment decompression destroyed control systems in some air-planes. (4) Experts also do not take into account chronic, cumulative effects, as in the case of acid rain. (5) They fail to anticipate inadequate human responses to safety measures, such as the failure of Chernobyl officials to evacuate immediately. (6) They fail to anticipate "common-mode" failures simultaneously afflicting systems designed to be inde-pendent. A simple fire at Brown's Ferry, Alabama, for example, dam-aged all five emergency core-cooling systems for the reactor.[160] The fact that experts typically overlook these six "pathways to disaster" sug-gests that they are often unable to *model* risk situations correctly. As Kahneman and Tversky point out, however, "the usefulness of the normative Bayesian approach to the analysis and the modeling of sub-jective probability depends primarily . . . on whether the model cap-tures the essential determinants of the judgment process."[161] It is important, therefore, both to avoid the errors frequently made by ex-perts and to correct our risk models. By definition, we cannot avoid errors and correct models under uncertainty. Therefore, prudence dictates that we use conservative risk-evaluation rules, such as maximin.

Some Objections to Using Maximin

An important objection to using maximin is that it violates a rationality axiom. This objection loses some of its force if one recalls that Bayesian utilitarians have a similar problem. They ignore ethical and democratic *processes* and emphasize only *outcomes*. As was argued earlier, this em-phasis provides grounds for doubting the adequacy of the sure-thing principle (one of the three main rationality axioms underlying Bayes-ianism),[162] especially in cases of *societal* risk under *uncertainty*.

Another objection to maximin is that it appears to sanction an anti-progress, antiscience notion of risk assessment. To this claim, one could respond that use of Bayesian methods for evaluating societal risks un-der uncertainty has itself resulted in highly publicized scientific failures, such as the Chernobyl disaster. Such disasters, in turn, have thwarted nuclear progress. If the dependence of Bayesian/utilitarian rules on subjective decisionmakers has contributed to such catastrophes, then restricting the use of Bayesian rules to cases in which they are suc-cessful—namely, *individual* hazards under *uncertainty* and *risk*—is likely to promote respect for science, for technical progress, and for Bayesian methods.[163]

Utilitarians also complain that maximin approaches are more ex-pensive than Bayesian/utilitarian approaches to hazard assessment, since it costs more to protect society against worst-case, highly improbable hazards than against more probable lesser harms.[164] The obvious response to this objection, however, is that worst-case occurrences, such as Bhopal and DES liability, are extremely costly. Moreover, one knows that preventing worst cases is more costly only if one has the assurance that they are highly improbable, which, by definition, one cannot know in a case of *uncertainty*.

Apart from cost considerations, some experts also allege that maximin is not obviously the only *moral* choice under uncertainty. This objection, formulated by a statistician,[165] is that positive utility attaches to being moral. Hence, for example, the Union Carbide chemical spill could not be justified on Bayesian grounds under conditions of uncertainty. However, there is no in-principle duty under Bayesian utilitarianism to consider moral or legal obligations and prima facie rights. Hence, Bayesian utilitarianism permits, but does not guarantee, avoidance of situations like the Union Carbide chemical spill.

Chapter Nine

Uncertainty and the Producer Strategy

The Case for Minimizing Type-II Errors in Rational Risk Evaluation

In 1973, U.S. assessors established that the fungicide ethylene dibromide (EDB) is carcinogenic. Gathering epidemiological data and following the procedures required for regulation, however, took more than a decade. Meanwhile, EDB began showing up in bread, flour, and cereal products in such quantities that risk assessors predicted that, based on lifetime consumption, EDB would cause up to 200,000 cases of cancer per year in the United States. Immediately after the Environmental Protection Agency announced regulations limiting its presence in food, industry switched to using methyl bromide instead. The main benefit of the new chemical is that it is unregulated, although it is a very close chemical relative of EDB and almost certainly highly carcinogenic. Policymakers expect it to take another decade to develop regulations to cover methyl bromide. Meanwhile, it is being used in bread, flour, and cereal products.[1]

Apart from whether industry ought to have regulated itself and not begun use of methyl bromide after EDB was banned, this case raises another question. What is appropriate risk behavior when methyl bromide carcinogenicity is not absolutely certain? If the arguments presented in Chapter Eight are correct, then in situations of uncertainty, especially those involving potential catastrophes, policymakers ought to act so as to avoid the worst case. In this fungicide instance, the worst case is probably something like 200,000 annual cancers caused by the chemical. In order to avoid the "worst case," we might need to protect the public from high-consequence technological dangers that are less likely to occur than more ordinary, lower-consequence events. But—because it is more expensive to protect against improbable, worst-case accidents than against more likely ones—this higher level of protection typically leads to potential financial losses for industry and to the possibility that a certain technology will be rejected on grounds of safety.[2]

All this indicates that choosing a maximin strategy, in cases of uncertainty (see the previous chapter), typically minimizes public risk (to citizens) and maximizes industry risk (to those responsible for the dangerous technology). But this raises the question of whether, in a situation of uncertainty where we must do one or the other, we ought to minimize industry risk or public risk. This chapter argues that *rational* risk evaluation and management often requires us to minimize public risk.

Type-I (Industry) Risks and Type-II (Public) Risks

The concepts of industry and public risks are related to those of type-I and type-II statistical error. In a situation of uncertainty, errors of type I occur when one rejects a null hypothesis that is true; errors of type II occur when one fails to reject a null hypothesis that is false. Statistics dictates that we make assumptions about the size of each of these types of error that can be tolerated, and, on this basis, we choose a testing pattern for our hypothesis. This concept of *significance*, for example, is often defined in terms of a type-I risk of error of either 0.01 or 0.05, where there is not more than a 1 in 100 or a 5 in 100 chance of committing the error of rejecting a true hypothesis.

Determining significance, however, is not a sufficient basis for answering an important question. Given a situation of uncertainty, which is the more serious error, type I or type II? An analogous issue arises in law. Is the more serious error to acquit a guilty person or to convict an innocent person? In assessing technological impacts, ought one to minimize type-I risk, which Churchman terms the "Producer Risk," or ought one to minimize type-II risk, which he calls the "Consumer Risk"? (I also call the producer risk and the consumer risk, respectively, "industry risk" and "public risk.") That is, ought one to run the risk of rejecting a true null hypothesis, of not using a technology that is really acceptable and safe; or ought one to run the risk of not rejecting a false null hypothesis, of using a technology that is really unacceptable and unsafe? To decrease industry risk might hurt the public, and to decrease public risk might hurt industry.[3]

Why Risk Assessors Tend to Minimize Industry Risk

Just as most experts (risk assessors) probably tend to pursue the dominant Bayesian strategy, even in situations of uncertainty, they also probably tend to minimize producer or industry risk and to maximize consumer or public risk.[4] This tendency likely arises because preferences for type-II errors and for minimizing type-I risks appear more consistent with scientific practice. Hypothesis testing in science operates on the basis of limiting false positives (assertions of effects where none exists), or limiting incorrect rejections of the null hypothesis. In order to minimize type-I errors, scientists design studies to guard against the influence of all possible confounding variables, and they demand replication of study results before accepting them as supporting a particular hypothesis. They apply tests of statistical significance, which reject results whose probability of occurring by chance (whose p value) is greater than, for example, 5 percent. Moreover, it is difficult to see how the scientific enterprise could function without such rigorous reluctance to accept positive results. As Abraham Kaplan put it: "The scientist usually attaches a greater loss to accepting a falsehood than to failing to acknowledge a truth. As a result, there is a certain conservatism or inertia in the scientific enterprise, often rationalized as the healthy skepticism characteristic of the scientific temper."[5]

The preference for type-II errors (for consumer or public risks) and for minimizing type-I errors (industry risks) is also consistent with the standards of proof required in criminal cases, as opposed to cases in torts. Our law requires the jury in a criminal case to be sure beyond a reasonable doubt that a defendant is guilty before deciding against him; standards of proof in criminal cases thus also reveal a preference for type-II error, a preference for accepting the null hypothesis or innocence, a preference for the risk of acquitting a guilty person. In a case in torts, however, our law requires the jury to believe only that it is more probable than not that the defendant is guilty; standards of proof in civil cases thus reveal no preference for either type-I or type-II error.

As Judith Jarvis Thomson points out, "our society takes the view that in a criminal case, the society's potential mistake-loss is very much greater than the society's potential omission-loss."[6] Presumably, this difference in the standards for proof in civil and criminal law stems at least in part from the fact that the consequences to the defendant in the criminal case are more likely to lead to grave harms (such as death or life imprisonment) than are the consequences to society.[7] Moreover, the state needs to protect its moral legitimacy by minimizing type-I risks in criminal cases. If it fails to convict the guilty, the state commits wrong in a more passive (less reprehensible) sense than if it errs by convicting the innocent. For these reasons, if standards of proof in cases of industry (or type-I) risks were analogous to those in criminal cases, then this analogy might provide a good reason for minimizing industry, rather than public, risk. (As the next section of this chapter will argue, however, they are analogous neither to hypothesis testing in pure science nor to determination of guilt in criminal cases.)

Preferences for type-II error or public risk might also arise from the fact that many risk assessments and impact analyses are done by those who are closely associated with the technology being evaluated and who are therefore sympathetic to it and to those who implement it.[8] In such cases, assessors typically underestimate risk probabilities,[9] at least in part because it is difficult to identify all hazards, and because unidentified risks are usually assumed to be zero. Minimizing industry risk probably also arises because technical experts almost always use widely accepted Bayesian decision rules based on expected utility and subjective probabilities, rather than the maximin principle.[10] As a result, even when everyone agrees that the probability of a high-consequence impact is uncertain but low, using a Bayesian decision rule typically generates a choice in favor of the potentially catastrophic technology or environmental impact, whereas using a maximin principle likely produces a verdict against the technology or environmental impact.[11]

Why Analogies from Scientific Practice and Criminal Law Are Not Applicable

Contrary to most assessors, I shall argue that there are prima facie grounds for minimizing public, rather than industry, risk. Before doing so, however, I will attempt to explain why standards of proof in assessing technological and environmental risks under uncertainty are analogous neither to hypothesis testing in pure science nor to determination of guilt in criminal cases. If my explanation is correct, then neither science nor criminal law provides arguments for minimizing industry, over public, risk.

Researchers doing pure science apparently prefer to minimize type-I error and to risk type-II error (consumer or public risk) because it is a more conservative course, epistemologically speaking, than is risking type-I error (industry risk). It is more conservative in the sense that it avoids positing an effect (e.g., that a substance causes cancer above a given level). Instead, it presupposes that the null hypothesis is correct (e.g., that a substance causes no cancer above a given level). Hence, it is reasonable to claim that one ought to follow a model of "epistemological rationality," rationality concerned with maximizing truth and avoiding positive error, when one is engaged in pure science.

Societal decisionmaking under uncertainty, however, is arguably not analogous to decisionmaking in pure science. "Epistemological rationality" is an insufficient basis for making decisions about whether to minimize industry and public risks affecting the welfare of many people. This is because, as was argued in the previous chapter, judgments about societal welfare involve "cultural rationality," and hence an assessment of the democratic justifiability of the risk imposition. Individual risk cases, or cases of purely scientific decisionmaking, might involve a *substantive* concept of epistemological rationality; but cases involving societal risk decisions require a *procedural* concept of rationality, one able to take account of a process for recognizing ethical and legal obligations. When one moves from pure science to applied science affecting policy, the question of what is rational moves from epistemological considerations to both ethical and epistemological ones. Therefore, the fact that pure scientists minimize type-I errors provides no compelling reasons for arguing that societal decisionmakers ought to minimize type-I errors.

Likewise, the legal system provides no strong reasons for minimizing type-I errors. For one thing, civil law exhibits no preference for minimizing type-I errors. Although criminal law does reveal such a preference, it does not appear to be analogous to the societal situation of technological or environmental risk under uncertainty. In protecting the accused criminal, presupposing his innocence, and therefore minimizing type-I errors, the criminal law is protecting the most vulnerable person. Since an accused criminal is more vulnerable than his potential or alleged societal victims, harm to him is more serious than harm to society, in the event of a mistake. In a case of societal risk from technology, however, harm to the public is more serious than harm to industry. If decisionmakers err in assuming that a given technology is safe, then this type-II error could result in loss of life by members of the public. However, if decisionmakers err in assuming that a given technology is harmful and therefore err in rejecting it, then the main losses for industry are economic. Hence, if the aim of decisionmaking under risk is to avoid the more serious harms, this case is not analogous to that of the criminal being tried, since in the risk case the greatest threat is to the public, and in the criminal case the greatest threat is to the defendant.

Moreover, if Thomson is correct in claiming that criminal law shows a presupposition in favor of minimizing type-I error, industry risk, because alleged criminals are more vulnerable than are societal victims of criminals, then this reason also shows that the criminal case and the societal risk cases are disanalogous. The public is far more vulnerable than are industrial producers and users of risky technologies. The public is privy to less information about the alleged risks, and the public typically has fewer financial resources to use in avoiding the risks. Also, it is extremely difficult for victims of societal/industrial hazards (for example, people who have cancer) to exercise their due-process rights, since such an exercise requires that they prove causality in the case of a technological risk.[12] Hence, if the public is more vulnerable than industrial producers of risk, protecting the more vulnerable persons requires that one minimize public or type-II risks (rather than the type-I risks minimized by the criminal law).

The Prima Facie Case for Minimizing Public Risk

In arguing that there are prima facie grounds for reducing public (rather than industry) risk, I intend to show that, all things being equal, one ought to take this approach. Obviously, however, the decision to minimize either public or industry risk must be decided in part on a case-by-case basis (so that, for example, the particular benefits at stake are considered). Arguing that there are prima facie grounds for reducing public risk therefore amounts to arguing that the burden of proof (regarding risk acceptability) should be placed on the person wishing to reduce industry, rather than public, risk. If that person cannot provide evidence to the contrary, one ought to minimize public risk.

There are at least eight different reasons for holding that assessors' prima facie duty is to minimize the chance that an unsafe technology is implemented; that is, to minimize public risk. The first five arguments stress that the dangers faced by the public (rather than by industry) represent the *kind* of risk most deserving of reduction. The last three arguments focus on the public as the *locus* of decisionmaking regarding societal hazards, since laypeople typically argue for reducing public risk.

Arguments for Minimizing Public Risk as a Kind of Risk

Minimizing false positives, judgments that an unsafe technology is acceptable, is prima facie reasonable on ethical grounds. That is, it is more important to protect the public from harm than to provide, in some positive sense, for welfare, because protecting from harm seems to be a necessary condition for enjoying other freedoms.[13] Bentham, for instance, in discussing an important part of liberalism, cautioned, much as Nozick and others might, that "the care of providing for his enjoyments ought to be left almost entirely to each individual; the principal function of government being to protect him from sufferings."[14] In other words, Bentham established protection from harm as more basic than provision of enjoyments.

Admittedly, it is difficult to draw the line between providing benefits and protecting from harm, between positive and negative laws. Nevertheless, just as there is a basic distinction between *welfare* rights and *negative* rights,[15] there is an analogous relationship between welfare laws (that provide some good) and protective laws (that prohibit some infringement). Moral philosophers continue to honor distinctions similar to this one; indeed, they distinguish not only between welfare-enhancing laws and protective laws but also between closely related concepts, such as letting die versus killing, and between acts of *omission* and acts of *commission*.[16] Given such distinctions, it is arguably more important to protect from harm or to avoid committing wrong than it is to provide some good or to avoid some omission. It therefore seems more important to protect citizens from public hazards than to attempt to enhance their welfare by implementing a risky technology. Also, industrial producers, users, and implementers of technology, not the public, receive the bulk of benefits from it. Because they receive most of the benefits, they ought to bear most of the risks and costs.[17]

There are likewise prima facie grounds for limiting public, rather than industry, risk because the public typically needs more risk protection than does industry. The public usually has fewer financial resources and less information to deal with the societal hazards that affect it, and laypersons are often faced with bureaucratic denials of public danger. Their vulnerability in this regard is well established in a number of cases of environmental risk. When the toxic polybrominated biphenyl (PBB) was accidentally used in cattle feed in Michigan, for example, it was the most widespread, least reported, chemical disaster ever to happen in the Western world. There was strong evidence of contamination in September 1973, but detailed articles on the problem did not appear, even in the local papers, for two more years. Larger newspapers, such as the *Detroit Free Press* and the *Detroit News*, did not examine the crisis until four years after it was evident. The problem was ignored for this length of time because the local bureaucrats denied the claims made by the farmers. Typically, a reporter would interview the owner of a contaminated farm and then check with the Michigan Farm Bureau and the Michigan Department of Agriculture, both of which would claim that the farmer's allegations were false. Because of all this bureaucratic denial, industry indifference, and isolation of the afflicted, PBB led to the deaths of tens of thousands of farm animals and to the contamination of nine million people who ate contaminated meat.[18]

Likewise, in 1976, after repeated bureaucratic denials of risk, a poisonous cloud of dioxin escaped from a chemical plant at Seveso, Italy, contaminating an area of 18 million square meters, killing thousands of animals and causing numerous cases of disfiguring skin disease in children. A similar situation occurred in Japan, where the dangers of mercury poisoning were identified in 1940, deaths were reported in 1948, and the famous Minimata poisoning occurred in 1953. Because of industry indifference, however, it was not until the 1960s that public awareness of the problem caused officials to take action against mercury contamination. These and similar instances of whistle-swallowing (rather than whistle-blowing), in cases involving asbestos, biotechnology, and chemical dumps, suggest that new public risks very likely will also be ignored. Hence, there is reason to believe that the public, rather than industry, has a greater need for protection.[19]

Another reason for minimizing public risk, especially in cases of uncertainty, is that laypersons ought to be accorded legal rights to protection against industrial decisions that could threaten their health or physical security. These legal rights arise out of the consideration that everyone has both due-process rights and rights to bodily security.

The problem of protecting the consumer against the extended effects of industrial decisions typically addresses three general kinds of protection: prevention, transferral of loss, and retention of the risk. When citizens protect themselves against losses (resulting from the decisions of others) by maintaining enough assets to sustain damages caused by those decisions, they protect themselves by *retention* of the risk. When they use mechanisms like insurance and legal liability to transfer the risk or loss, they are protecting themselves by *transferral* of the majority of the loss to someone else—namely, the insurer or the liable party. The practical advantage of risk transfer over retention is that it does not require one to retain as many assets, idle and unproductive, as a way of guarding against damages. The moral advantage is that, if the harm itself is caused by another legal/moral "person," an industry, then that person—and not the individual harmed—is liable. And if the "person" causing the damage is liable, then there are practical grounds for using this moral responsibility as a basis for the individual or his insurer to remove the financial responsibility from the victim. Insurance is probably a better vehicle for risk transfer than is liability, since insurance (unlike liability) does not typically require the victim to use legal remedies to obtain protection or compensation.[20]

Prevention, of course, is the most thorough way for members of recipient populations to protect themselves against losses resulting from the decisions of others. By eliminating the sources of the risk, the potential victim has more to gain, practically speaking, than by using risk transfer or retention as means of protection. This is because prevention does not tie up any of the potential victim's assets. The moral grounds for prevention are that, in cases where those responsible or liable cannot redress the harm done to others by their faulty decisions, risk should be eliminated. When industrial decisionmakers cannot adequately compensate or insure their potential victims, surely these incompensable risks should not be imposed on those who fail to give free, informed consent to them.

Thomson describes "incompensable harms" as harms so serious that no amount of money could possibly compensate the victim. By this definition, death, at least, is an obviously "incompensable harm," since there is no way to compensate a dead person. As Thomson puts it, speaking of another case, "however fair and efficient the judicial system may be, . . . [those] who cause incompensable harms by their negligence cannot square accounts with their victims."[21] Clearly, anyone who imposes a significant risk of death on another, without free, informed consent, is imposing an incompensable, and therefore morally unjustifiable, harm. But how do we know when someone is imposing a significant risk of death on another, without free, informed consent?[22]

Although the boundary cases would be difficult to decide, potentially catastrophic technologies such as nuclear power do appear to impose a significant risk of death on another. As has been mentioned, even the government admits that a nuclear accident could kill 150,000 people, and that the core-melt probability, for all existing and planned U.S. commercial reactors, is 1 in 4 during their thirty-year lifetime. To the degree that this hazard is imposed on citizens without their free, informed consent, then to that extent is the risk both unjustified and incompensable. Moreover, as was also mentioned earlier, U.S. citizens are prohibited by law from obtaining full compensation from the negligent utility, in the event that there is a commercial nuclear catastrophe.[23]

Other cases of incompensable harm seem to arise most often in connection with potentially catastrophic, involuntarily imposed technologies whose risks are uncertain (for example, specific lethal pesticides or liquefied natural gas facilities). Precisely because these technologies are catastrophic, and have the potential for causing incompensable and involuntarily imposed harm, one might argue that the risks they impose are unjustifiable. This is all the more true if the probability of harm is uncertain, because the person imposing the risk is unable to know how grave a danger he is imposing. Moreover, as was argued in the previous chapter, harm can be imposed, or discrimination justified, only when it leads to greater good for all, including those most disadvantaged by it. If there is uncertainty about the level of the harm, then it would also be difficult (if not impossible) to prove that imposing such a risk would lead to greater good for all.

An Objection: Does Economic Well-Being Justify Minimizing Industry Risk?

In response to all these arguments for minimizing public (not industry) risk, it might be objected that assessors have a duty, for the good of the *economy* (which allegedly maximizes overall welfare), to minimize industry, not public, risk.[24] To defend this point, however, the objectors would have to show that their position does not amount to violating a basic ethical rule prohibiting the use of persons (the public) as means to the ends of other persons (industry and society as a whole). Both tort law and the Fifth and Fourteenth Amendments to the U.S. Constitution arguably presuppose this rule.[25] It would probably be quite difficult to show that minimizing industry risk, on grounds of economic efficiency, would not violate both this rule and the right to bodily security.[26]

Proponents of economic efficiency would also have to show that, contrary to what conflicting hazard assessments suggest, risk probabilities as calculated by experts provide a reliable basis from which to assess and pursue economic efficiency and societal welfare. If Kahneman, Tversky, and others are right, this point might be hard to prove, since there is strong evidence (as discussed in the previous chapter) that experts have as many heuristic biases in estimating probabilities as laypeople.[27] Therefore, especially since expert opinion on risk may err, we ought to minimize public risk so as to protect the public's right to security.

Obviously, no one is eager either to cripple technology or to set back the economy in order to minimize public risk. Many potentially catastrophic technologies, however, are in principle able to "set back" the economy. Nuclear technology, for example, has "set back" the economy in the sense that it could not have survived without protection from normal market mechanisms. If there were no government-guaranteed liability limit for catastrophic accidents involving commercial nuclear fission, then no major U.S. atomic interests would ever have gone into generation of electricity. Even the major pronuclear lobby, the Atomic Industrial Forum (AIF), admits this.[28] The upshot is that, although nuclear utilities have been relieved of the burden of competing in an open market, including the liability market, they nevertheless have the potential to cripple the economy with a dangerous accident that could (on the government's own estimates) wipe out an area the size of Pennsylvania. Because the industry risk is minimized, while the public risk from nuclear power is maximized, the liability limit could easily contribute to massive economic harm.[29]

Hazardous technologies could also "set back" the economy in the sense that many of the most dangerous industries (in the sense of high public risk and high public risk aversion) are also among the most capital intensive. Because they are so capital intensive, they threaten the flow of available money for other societal projects and hence jeopardize the economic well-being of society. This is particularly the case with nuclear technology.[30]

These argument sketches suggest that insistence on the operation of the free market (free from regulations to minimize public risk and free from liability limits to minimize industry risk) might be just as threatening to dangerous technologies as to members of the public who are risk averse. They also suggest that proponents of maximizing public risk and minimizing industry risk are inconsistent; often they wish to interfere with the market so as to *protect industry*, but they complain when risk regulation interferes with the same market in order to *protect the public*. Given this inconsistency, it is unclear why incompensable risks should be borne only by their victims (which seems to be the intention of the Price-Anderson Act), rather than also by their perpetrators.[31]

There are other problems, however, with the basic argument that one ought not to mandate high levels of public safety because this would hurt the economy or "progress." Such a line of reasoning sounds vaguely like several others: "We can't abolish slavery, because this would destroy the economy of the South." Or "We can't pass the ERA, because women won't stay home and take care of their children, and this would hurt the family." All these arguments pit important values, such as family and economic well-being, *against* moral values, such as citizen safety or abolishing racism and sexism. The arguments are troubling because they force us to choose between two goods. Thomson's response to such arguments—those that force us to choose between risking our life versus starving, for example—is simple. "It is morally indecent that anyone in a moderately well-off society should be faced with such a choice."[32]

Moreover, these three arguments—about technology, slavery, and women's rights—all propose using humans—whether citizens at risk from technology, or blacks who are victims of slavery, or women who are disadvantaged by sexism—as *means* to some economic or social *end*. But humans ought never be used as means to some end sought by other persons, especially not if all humans have equal rights and equal dignity. We do often have to weigh the interests of one group in society over those of another, and we do often discriminate. Yet the only grounds justifying discrimination, the failure to treat one person as equal to another, as Frankena has pointed out, is that the discrimination will work to the advantage of everyone, including those discriminated against. Any other attempt to justify discrimination fails because it would amount to sanctioning the use of some humans as means to the ends of other humans.[33]

Applied to technological risk assessment and type-I and type-II risks, this insight about justified discrimination suggests that a necessary condition for discriminating against members of the public who prefer conservative health and safety standards would be to prove that rejecting conservative standards would work to the advantage of everyone, including the public. In other words, the burden of proof is on the industry attempting to put the public at risk. And if the burden ought to be on industry, then this is grounds for minimizing public risk.

Arguments for Giving the Public the Power to Make Risk Decisions

In addition to the five reasons already given, there are also several arguments for minimizing public risk by means of giving potential victims the power to make risk decisions affecting them. For example, one could argue, on grounds of democratic process and procedural rationality, that there ought to be no imposition of risk without the free, informed consent of those who must bear it. This dictum holds true in medical experimentation, and it could easily be shown to have an analogue in risk management.[34] Likewise, there are strong *economic* grounds for minimizing public risk whenever this minimization is consistent with public preferences. Consumer sovereignty in matters of risk is not justified merely by reference to the alleged unseen hand controlling economic events, but by a revered economic and political principle: "No taxation without representation." Welfare economics, in particular, establishes the convenience and efficiency of consumer sovereignty, and citizens themselves, as Schelling notes, have safeguarded it by means of "arms, martyrdom, boycott, or some principles held to be self-evident. . . . [I]t includes the inalienable right of the consumer to make his own mistakes."[35]

Minimizing public risk, in the name of consumer or citizen self-determination, is also consistent with most ethical theories about situations in which paternalism is or is not justified. In his classic discussion of liberty, Mill makes clear that it is acceptable to override individual decisionmaking only to protect others or to keep someone from selling himself into slavery. Any other justification for a limitation on individual freedom, claims Mill, would amount to a dangerous infringement on individual autonomy.[36] But if Mill is correct,[37] then there are no paternalistic grounds for overriding the hesitancies of the public about accepting a particular technological risk. This is because, in arguments to minimize industry risk at the expense of the public, experts are arguing that citizens are overprotective of themselves. The assessors want to provide the public with less, not more, protection, and largely for the benefit of industry. Hence, their paternalism is suspect.

Consider, for example, what happened in 1987 when the U.S. Environmental Protection Agency (EPA) proposed new standards to protect the public (living near steel mills) from coke-oven emissions. One of the greatest hazards caused by the emissions was lung cancer, both among steelworkers and nearby residents. As soon as the EPA issued its proposed standards, risk assessors employed by the steel industry developed a hazard analysis critical of the EPA study. In defending less stringent emissions standards to protect public health, the industry assessors (working under a taxpayer-funded National Science Foundation grant) made a number of arguments, none of which was directed at protecting the public health and safety. The industry assessors criticized the EPA standards on grounds that they "would weaken the [steel] industry" and that "the cost to reduce exposure under the EPA standard is very high."[38]

The self-interested nature of the industry assessment of coke-oven emissions was even more apparent when the assessors argued that the EPA was "unjustified" in proposing regulations that could save one person in one thousand from cancer induced by emissions from the nearby steel mills. They wrote:

Even if the population were subjected to exposures that produced an increase in cancers equal to the upper bound risk calculated by the EPA, an increase of one cancer per 1000 residents over their lives, this represents only a 2 percent increase in the cancer rate. This rate is too small to detect using epidemiology. Is a 2 percent or smaller increase in the lung cancer rate for the most exposed population worth all the effort of an EPA regulation? . . . The EPA approach is an arbitrary one in the name of prudent public protection. . . . The EPA's proposed regulation seems unjustified.[39]

This reasoning of industry risk assessors appears seriously flawed. They assume that, in order to benefit steel manufacturers financially, it is acceptable to cause the death of one person in a thousand. Moreover, the government typically regulates all risks above the level of one fatality in one million.[40] This means that the industry risk assessors are trying to impose a steel-emissions risk on the public that is three orders of magnitude *greater* than those typically *prohibited*. Moreover, since government epidemiologists typically discover risks of one in one million, it is simply false for the two industry assessors to claim that the rate (one in one thousand) "is too small to detect using epidemiology." (See quotation above.) Finally, despite their admission that failure to adopt the new EPA standards could result in an increase of one cancer per thousand members of the public, the industry risk assessors never gave any ethical or political rationale for rejecting the standards. They ignored issues of consent, compensation, and equity, but justified the standards on the basis of industry's economic interest. Hence, as this example illustrates, those who wish to increase public risks often tend to make self-serving arguments.

At this point, industry might object that the public wants the benefits associated with technological hazards, and hence that those arguing for reducing public risk must bear the charge of behaving paternalistically toward those who do not want public risk minimized. There are at least two responses to this objection. For one thing, there is substantial social scientific and philosophical evidence that those bearing high levels of public risk have not given free, informed consent to imposition of the hazards.[41] Another response is that economists have long recognized that risk imposition represents a diminution in welfare for those who bear the hazards.[42] Since industry imposes risks on the public, industry ought to bear the burden of proof in justifying the imposition, particularly since the public typically has not given free, informed consent.

Minimizing public risk is also defensible because it might be less likely to lead to social and political unrest than minimizing industry risk. Although developing this point fully is not possible in this chapter, there might be pragmatic and political, as well as ethical and economic, grounds for following public preferences to minimize public risk. As many risk assessors have pointed out, effective hazard management requires the cooperation of many laypeople; otherwise, accidents, costly publicity, and civil disobedience may result. The long controversy over the Seabrook (New Hampshire) nuclear facility illustrates the need for such cooperation between industry and the public. Both industry and members of the public must agree to do without some things and to accept substitutes for others. They must vote sensibly, act reasonably, and engage in much give-and-take over regulations and standards. If they do not, then a hazardous technology could be crippled. Moreover, "even if the experts were much better judges of risk than laypeople, giving experts an exclusive franchise for hazard management would mean substituting short-term efficiency for the long-term effort needed to create an informed citizenry."[43]

Chapter Ten

Third-World Risks and the Isolationist Strategy

The Case for an Egalitarian Account of Rational Risk Management

Between 300,000 and 400,000 of the 1,000,000 current and former U.S. asbestos workers are expected to die of occupation-induced cancer. As a result, the U.S. Occupational Safety and Health Administration (OSHA) has issued new workplace standards, and manufacturers have developed cleaner technologies for processing asbestos. Rather than installing the safer technologies, however, many U.S. corporations are continuing to use the dirtier methods and moving their asbestos operations to other countries, notably Mexico. For example, Amatex, a Norristown, Pennsylvania, firm, closed its U.S. asbestos facilities and opened plants in Agua Prieta and Ciudad Juárez, Mexico, both just across the border. There are no Mexican regulations to protect workers from asbestos, dust levels in the Mexican plants are not monitored, and workers wear no respirators. Employees receive minimum wage and are told nothing about the hazards they face. Asbestos waste covers the factory floor and clings to the fence and the dirt road, behind the factories, where Mexican children walk to school.[1]

Asbestos processing is not the only hazardous technology typically transferred from the United States. Recently the Nedlog Technology Group, Inc., of Arvada, Colorado, offered the president of Sierra Leone up to $25 million to dump millions of tons of toxic chemical wastes in his west African nation. Each year U.S. companies offer nations in the Caribbean and in west Africa hundreds of dollars for every fifty-five-gallon barrel of toxic waste that can be dumped legally.[2] One of the greatest problems with transfer of hazardous technologies arises in connection with pesticides. Massive advertising campaigns by corporations such as Dow and Chevron have turned the third world into both a market and a dumping ground for dangerous chemicals, es-

146

pecially DDT. For example, Ortho (a division of Chevron and an arm of Standard Oil of California) in Costa Rica is the main importer of eight banned or heavily restricted U.S. pesticides: parathion, DDT, aldrin, dieldrin, heptachlor, chlordane, endrin, and benzene hexachloride (BHC). In Ecuador, Shell, Velsicol, Bayer, American Cyanamid, Hercules, and Monsanto are the main importers of pesticides banned in the United States. In Colombia, fourteen different corporations import virtually every U.S. pesticide banned since 1970.[3]

The consequences of third-world use of banned pesticides are not small. According to the U.S. General Accounting Office (GAO), 29 percent of all U.S. pesticide exports are products that are banned (20 percent) or not registered (9 percent) for use in the United States. The World Health Organization (WHO) estimates that there are approximately half a million cases of pesticide poisoning annually, with a death-to-poisoning ratio of one to ten. This means that about 49,000 persons, many in developing nations, die annually from pesticides. One person is poisoned by pesticides every minute in developing countries.[4]

The fundamental moral problem raised by each of these cases is whether corporations have an obligation to guarantee equal protection from risks across national boundaries. Or do they simply have an obligation to provide whatever protection is legally required in the country to which they export? Perhaps the dominant attitude toward transfers of hazardous technologies is that the ethics of risk evaluation in developed nations is isolated or separate from analogous moral requirements in developing countries. I call this view the "isolationist strategy." It sanctions corporate transfers of hazardous technologies to other countries, provided only that the risk imposition meets whatever conditions are imposed by the host nation. For third-world peoples, these conditions are typically minimal or nonexistent.

Advocates of the isolationist strategy characteristically reject risks close to them in space or time but sanction those that are distant from them. The object of this chapter is to provide some grounds for challenging the isolationist strategy, for questioning the view that we are not morally responsible for hazards that are spatially or temporally distant from us. In order to evaluate this strategy, I discuss four main arguments used to justify transfers of hazardous technologies to third-world countries. Next I show why all these arguments, except the last, can be defused easily. If my analysis is correct, then effective action to protect citizens of third-world nations may demand not only individualistic efforts but also coordinated political activity. Indeed, a rational risk response may require political activity that is nothing less than revolutionary.[5]

The Social-Progress Argument

Transfers of hazardous technologies often are defended on the grounds that one is not ethically bound to accept any principles of equal protection for all persons. Many utilitarian moral philosophers, especially act utilitarians, for example, are opposed to accepting principles of equal protection, whether within a nation or across nations.[6] For this reason, many act utilitarians would likely hold some variant of what I call the "social-progress argument." They would maintain that, although they do not wish to see third-world peoples killed or injured by asbestos, hazardous wastes, or banned pesticides, nevertheless adopting a principle of equal treatment or equal protection for all persons could jeopardize social progress. Act utilitarians, such as J. J. C. Smart, also typically believe that more human suffering is caused by following principles of equal treatment than by attempting to maximize the well-being of the majority. They believe there is no "right" to equal treatment and equal opportunity because, if there were, then economic and social improvements for the majority of the people would be delayed.[7]

Good act utilitarians, pursuing the social-progress argument, might point out, for example, that worker fatalities during the building of the U.S. transcontinental railroad reached a peak of approximately three per thousand per year.[8] Although this death rate is three orders of magnitude greater than the current, allegedly acceptable level of regulated risk in the United States, they might view it as a necessary evil.[9] It might be seen as the price paid to ensure a greater good—western expansion and consequent economic growth bringing an extraordinary level of prosperity to a majority of U.S. citizens. If failure to provide equal protection to these railway workers was a partial cause of widespread prosperity that otherwise would not have been possible, a number of act utilitarians would likely justify it.

The main problem with the social-progress argument, however, is its presupposition that there is no in-principle obligation to recognize individual rights, and that there are ethical grounds for sacrificing the welfare of significant numbers of human beings for the sake of the majority. This presupposition is questionable in part because it is inconsistent with individualistic, democratic, liberal traditions that are embodied, for example, in the U.S. Bill of Rights. The argument is also problematic because act utilitarians admit that, in their view, not every individual would be protected from capricious or expedient denials of justice.[10] This admission renders their argument problematic, for reasons outlined in Chapter Eight—namely, that discrimination is unjustified unless it works to the advantage of everyone, including those discriminated against.[11]

The Countervailing-Benefits Argument

Another argument for transfer of hazardous technologies to third-world nations is the "countervailing-benefits" argument. It amounts to the claim that, although it would normally be wrong to transfer technologies known to cause injury and death, recipients of risky technologies are better off than they would have been without them. Proponents of the countervailing-benefits argument admit that, although there are health costs, for example, to third-world asbestos workers or victims supplied with banned U.S. pesticides and toxic wastes, there are also benefits that are part of the same package. And the crucial point, in their view, is that the benefits outweigh the costs. The Mexican asbestos worker might not have a job if he did not work in substandard asbestos-production facilities, and the African village might have neither a local school nor clean water were it not for the revenues supplied by storing toxic wastes from the United States. The argument is that a bloody loaf of bread is sometimes better than no loaf at all, that a dangerous job is preferable to no job, and that food riddled with banned pesticides is better than no food at all.[12]

Perhaps the greatest presupposition of the countervailing-benefits argument is that any cost is allowable as long as the benefits are greater.[13] One could easily challenge this assumption by arguing that some costs are *preventable evils* that should never be allowed, even for countervailing benefits. One might argue that not everything "has its price." Since utilitarians would typically be the moral philosophers most likely to claim that "everything has its price," one could invalidate this claim by showing that not even all utilitarians support the counter-vailing-benefits argument. Mill, for example, would not support it.

Moral Grounds for Rejecting the
Countervailing-Benefits Argument

Although Bentham rejected the notion of moral rights that disallowed certain preventable evils, other utilitarians, such as Mill, challenged this rejection. Indeed, one can read Mill as holding that utilitarian principles require adherence to rules, even rules conferring rights, and that such rules exclude a case-by-case appeal to the general welfare.[14] After all, Mill does not apply the general-welfare standard to all cases of moral reasoning. In his classic essay *On Liberty*, he does not condone paternalistic intervention in order to serve the general welfare, but only to prevent harm to other people or to prevent persons from selling themselves into slavery.[15] This statement suggests that, in Mill's view, the observance of some such rule about paternalistic noninterference would best serve the general welfare. His principle of liberty therefore can be construed as a defense of a related right.[16]

A second reason why Mill might be interpreted as a rule utilitarian, with commitments to human rights, is that he specifically distinguishes between immorality and mere expediency.[17] Mill also points out that utilitarians have particular obligations to recognize moral rights:

The moral rules which forbid mankind to hurt one another (in which we must never forget to include wrongful interference with each other's freedom) are more vital to human well-being than any maxims, however important, which only point out the best mode of managing some department of human affairs.[18]

Mill explains that the primary object of moral rights is security, which he calls "the most vital of all interests," "the most indispensable of all necessaries, after physical nutrition," and "the very groundwork of our existence."[19] He affirms: "to have a right, then, is, I conceive, to have something which society ought to defend me in the possession of. If the objector goes on to ask, why it ought? I can give him no other reason than general utility."[20]

These passages suggest that according to Mill, persons have something like basic "rights" to security and "rights" not to have their liberty constrained, apart from the requirements of the general welfare. Mill believes that society ought to recognize these rights to security because such recognition also promotes the general welfare.[21] All this suggests, in turn, that classical utilitarian doctrine is not "a hunting license, allowing the infliction of whatever wounds one likes, provided only that one's pleasure in the infliction is greater than the victim's pain."[22] Rather, one is not allowed, under classical utilitarian doctrine, to threaten another's security. Were one allowed to do so, then maximization of net benefits could be said to justify the worst sort of barbarism or sadism.

There are also a number of nonutilitarian grounds for believing that all persons have equal, basic rights to security and, therefore, that no countervailing benefits can justify failure to recognize these rights. One of the strongest arguments for recognizing equal, transnational rights to security is that human interdependence, across national boundaries, creates transnational moral obligations to recognize basic human rights.

As Lichtenberg puts it, certain kinds of actions by some people are likely to affect other persons in a significant way, and no one can escape such effects by staking out new territory.[23] As the argument goes, since the *effects* of one's actions (for instance, burning fossil fuels and possibly causing the greenhouse effect) are not limited to those within one's country, therefore the constraints provided by the basic rights of those in one's nation are not the *only* constraints on one's actions.

Still other reasons can be given to support the contention that we should guarantee equal rights to all persons, regardless of their country or their generation:[24] (1) All persons possess the two essential powers of moral personality: a capacity for an effective sense of justice and the ability to form, amend, and pursue a conception of what is good.[25] (2) Individuals and national societies are not self-sufficient but exist within a scheme of social cooperation.[26] (3) The comparison class is all humans, and all humans have the same capacity for a happy life.[27] (4) Free, informed, rational people would agree to a social contract based on treating all humans equally.[28] (5) Equal treatment of all persons provides the basic justification of all schemes involving justice, fairness, rights, and autonomy.[29] (6) All law presupposes a social contract guaranteeing equal rights.[30] Therefore, without the recognition of basic human rights, it would be impossible for anyone to enjoy any particular right (such as a right to property) that is legally guaranteed. There also seem to be ethical, as well as prudential, duties to provide some standard of equal protection to those outside our national borders. For example, in Singer's scheme, reasonable and benevolent people should not forgo a chance to do great good for others simply because a trifling sacrifice would thereby be required. From this point of view, we may have duties to protect others from transfer of hazardous technologies, or from other environmental harms, whenever it is possible to do so without great sacrifice of comparable values on our part.[31]

But if there are potential grounds for recognizing either a right to security or a duty to protect others from threats to their security, then the countervailing-benefits argument could be wrong. It could be wrong in its attempt to justify violation of rights to security in exchange for a job or economic well-being. And if rights to security should not be violated, a critical question is whether transfer of hazardous technology threatens security. As Shue points out, the security of Mexican asbestos workers, for example, is threatened because (1) the technology does physical damage to their lives, limbs, and vitality, not just damage to their life-style; (2) it damages the workers in a life-threatening way; (3) it damages them in a way that is irreversible; (4) it does damage that is avoidably undetectable (because people in such a situation are likely to be poor and hence unlikely to have proper medical advice and examination); (5) it does damage that is avoidably unpredictable (because workers lack the technical information about the risk, even though their employers may have it); and (6) it induces serious damage having a high probability of occurrence.[32]

Practical Grounds for Rejecting
the Countervailing-Benefits Argument

Even if transfer of hazardous technologies to third-world nations were not questionable on the moral grounds that it jeopardized individuals' rights to bodily security, it might still be problematic for factual or practical reasons. The whole countervailing-benefits argument rests on a central factual assumption that transferring hazardous technology provides great benefits to those who receive it. Many persons argue, for example, that we need to export banned pesticides to third-world countries because they are cheaper than other forms of pest control and thus beneficial to developing countries. For them, the chemicals are a necessary evil, the price of averting famine. An executive of Velsicol Chemical Company, defending his company's sales of Phosvel after it was banned in the United States, said: "We see nothing wrong with helping the hungry world eat."[33]

The problem with such an argument is that it is built on doubtful factual premises—namely, that the "hungry world" will eat. But between 50 and 70 percent of pesticides used in underdeveloped countries are applied to crops destined for export. Although the poor and hungry labor in the fields and expose themselves to pesticides, they rarely are able to eat the crops on which they work. In Latin America, 70 percent of agricultural production (mainly coffee, cocoa, and cotton) is exported. Moreover, cotton is the crop to which most pesticides are applied.[34]

Even if third-world peoples do not benefit directly from the pesticide-ridden crops they grow, one might argue that they benefit *indirectly* from the foreign exchange earned. Even this assumption is questionable, however, since foreign-exchange monies are often not used to improve wages, housing, schools, and medical care for farm laborers. Instead, they are typically used for luxury consumer goods, urban industrialization, tourist facilities, and office buildings. Most of these goods, in turn, benefit the upper classes living in the cities.[35] Such use of foreign-exchange earnings benefits farm workers and pesticide users only if one is able to assume that "trickle-down" economic procedures improve the overall welfare of workers most subjected to the hazards of transported technology.

If the preceding analysis is correct, then the countervailing-benefits argument is questionable on both moral and practical grounds. The *practical* problem is that many of the benefits alleged to go to third-world peoples in exchange for hazardous technologies might be over-estimated. The *moral* problem is that the argument could lead to un-desirable consequences (e.g., justifying sadism), since it alleges that great benefits could justify any cost, however great. It also erroneously ignores classical emphases on rights to security. Hence, the counter-vailing-benefits argument is not likely to justify many transfers of risky technologies to developing nations.

The Consent Argument

Even if transferred risks do threaten individual security, one might argue that the recipients of the technology consented to them. More-over, goes the objection, unless we want to deny the autonomy of native peoples and their rights to make their own choices, we are bound to allow them to have the technology transfers that they request. Even if such transfers involve substandard asbestos processing or the import of pesticides banned in the United States, third-world peoples have a right to determine their own fate.[36] In a nutshell, this "consent argu-ment" is that corporations are not morally responsible for inflicting harm through technology transfer because the recipients agreed to it.

The plausibility of the consent argument rests in part on the classical economic theory of the compensating wage differential: when people accept risky jobs for higher pay, they implicitly consent to the hazards. As Adam Smith expressed it, "the whole of the advantages and dis-advantages of the different employments of labor" continually tend toward equality, because the wages vary according to the hardship of the occupation.[37] Analogously, proponents of the consent argument might claim that imposition of greater public health risks is acceptable because citizens voluntarily agree to trade some societal safety for greater public benefits, such as a stronger economy or a higher standard of living.

Clearly, the acceptability of the consent argument depends on whether recipients of technology transfer (such as Mexican asbestos company employees, Central American farm workers who use pesti-cides, and African workers in hazardous waste facilities) accepted these technological risks in situations of informed consent. That is, it depends on whether (1) the *workers* were informed of the severity and probability of harm, and, after being given this knowledge, they freely chose to work; and (2) the *governments* allowing imports of hazardous technologies, such as banned pesticides, also gave free, informed consent to the risks. But both the amount of *information* and the level of *freedom* likely to be present in cases of technology transfer to many third-world countries are open to question.

Just because a third-world worker, for example, holds a particular risky job, it cannot be assumed that that occupation is an expression of the worker's authentic preferences. Many people engage in certain work, not because they voluntarily and autonomously choose to do so, but because they have no alternatives. Moreover, in the absence of minimum standards for occupational safety, and without alternative opportunities for employment, one could hardly claim that the worker's occupation and its attendant risks were the result of autonomous or free choice.

Several years ago in the United Kingdom, for example, the government's Advisory Committee on the Safety of Pesticides (PAC) was locked in battle with the National Union of Agricultural and Allied Workers (NUAAW) over the spraying of 2,4,5-T by farm workers. The PAC asserted that the pesticide was safe when used properly. The NUAAW responded that worker consent, safety, and distribution of the pesticide were precisely the areas of concern. Its argument was that "the organizational realities of farm life often do not allow a farm worker to refuse to spray just because the climate is not correct, or because specified protective equipment is defective or nonexistent. Chemicals called 'adjuvants' that speed up the action of the main chemical are often added . . . and new spraying technologies designed to improve economic efficiency have had marked effects on exposures." In other words, the cultural reality of a low-paid, "dispensable" farm worker does not allow him to say that he is concerned about risks. Hence, such workers are not likely to give free, informed consent to the risks they incur.[38]

A similar example concerns the recent conflict over hormones fed to beef cattle. In 1985, a scientific committee of the European Commission said that certain "growth promoters" were safe if used (1) by means of earlobe injection, (2) with a specified dose threshold, and (3) in connection with a ninety-day waiting period before sale of the cattle. The Council of Ministers rejected the alleged safe use of the hormones on the grounds that such conditions of use are not enforceable in reality. Consequently, the public is unable to give *informed* consent to the beef hormone injection.[39]

Market constraints or greed often militate against the conditions necessary for free, informed consent. For example, after the 1985 Bhopal disaster, a French board of inquiry discovered numerous improprieties in the handling of the toxin methyl isocyanate (MIC) in France. MIC was imported through Marseilles and sent to a plant in Béziers. At the Marseilles docks, however, because of the economics of unloading operations (e.g., piece rates being paid to increase productivity), and the necessity to fill shifts productively, barrels of MIC were being thrown, lifted, and hauled as if they were bales of straw. The cultural and economic realities of the dock situation made *free, informed* consent (among workers and residents living near the docks) highly questionable.[40]

One reason why an occupation and its associated risks are not necessarily the result of a free decision is that job choices are often *not* made in the context of what John Rawls might call ethically desirable "background conditions." Such background conditions might include the operation of a free market, lack of coercion by employers, and the existence of alternative employment opportunities. If background conditions necessary for procedurally just, voluntary employment decisions are not met, an appeal to the theory of informed consent cannot justify exposing persons to workplace hazards imposed because of technology transfer.[41]

Consider a farm worker, for example, hired to apply pesticides in a third-world country. It is well known that such jobs are very risky and also that, as education and income rise, employees are far less likely to remain in hazardous occupations. Therefore, workers in high-risk jobs are likely to be both financially strapped and poorly educated. Moreover, the situations in which third-world peoples would be most in need of work are precisely those in which background conditions are likely to preclude genuine *free* consent to accepting those jobs. In Mexico, for example, the unemployment rate is typically 50 percent. This suggests that, in rural third-world countries likely to employ pesticides, for instance, there is probably no diversified economy that would provide a variety of alternative employment options. Hence, the situations in which one most needs to take risky work are precisely those in which *free* consent could not likely be given to the job.[42]

Indeed, for half the world's population, free, informed consent may not even be possible. About 800 million people, one-fifth of the humans on the planet, are deprived of all income, goods, and hope. They live primarily in India, Bangladesh, Pakistan, Indonesia, sub-Saharan Africa, the Middle East, Latin America, and the Caribbean. Another one-fifth to two-fifths of the world's people, above the one-fifth that Robert McNamara called the "absolute poor," are chronically malnourished.

Given pervasive disease, malnutrition, illiteracy, and squalor—not to mention few job alternatives and an economy likely not diversified—it is questionable whether, even with perfect information on the risks involved, employees could be said to freely choose to work with hazardous technology.[43]

Often consent is not likely to be truly *informed*, since the same third-world conditions that militate against free consent also militate against education. An isolated African or Latin American region where banned pesticides are used, for example, is unlikely to have an educated populace to help make citizens aware of pesticide danger. It is also unlikely to have a local chapter of the Sierra Club or of Ralph Nader's Public Interest Research Group or any other social institution that could help remedy the citizens' inability to give free, informed consent.

Moreover, even in some of the most developed countries of the world, such as the United States, where societal institutions are in place, free, informed consent is still rare. When the Binghamton (New York) state office building caught fire recently, it was highly questionable whether the accident victims gave free, informed consent to the risk of reentering the building. The fire spewed about 180 gallons of coolant containing polychlorinated biphenyls (PCBs), from the electrical transformers in the mechanical room, throughout the building. Later, despite the fact that the state office building's garage was contaminated with PCBs, officials opened the garage because of "the shortage of parking space in downtown Binghamton." It was opened only because officials withheld crucial information about testing the garage and about the toxicity of PCBs. The director of health for the state "intentionally concealed important information . . . to mollify public concern."[44] If even highly developed nations cannot guarantee free, informed consent to their citizens, it is questionable whether the consent argument is able to justify transfer of hazardous technologies to less developed countries.

The Reasonable-Possibility Argument

If the analysis thus far has been correct, all three arguments enlisted to support transfer of hazardous technologies face serious objections. Someone could still maintain, however, that such transfers are legitimate because it is impossible to prevent them. I call this the reasonable-possibility argument. It is based on the ethical maxim "*Ought* implies *can*"; if corporations *ought* to be required not to transfer banned technologies to third-world countries, then this requirement must be one that *can* be achieved. If it is not achievable, then it is not required.

The main reason for believing that it might not be possible for a corporation to introduce safer technology on its own, in the absence of mechanisms to control the behavior of competing firms, is that such an action could financially destroy a company. Moreover, goes the argument, governments (not individual corporations) are in the business of promoting and regulating worker and citizen safety. To expect a firm to introduce safer technology, and thus be undercut by other corporations with fewer moral qualms, is thus ethically questionable. It is to impose an unrealistic, heroic, and self-sacrificial burden on a corporation. And morality does not require heroism, only justice.[45] That is why Gewirth, for example, in his classic argument for the absolute right not to have cancer inflicted on one, argues that it is necessary for *the state* to regulate and enforce this right. One cannot expect voluntary compliance with strict environmental and technological standards.[46]

Attorney Richard Stewart likewise has recognized that strong federal regulation, rather than heroism, is necessary to restrain technology. Stewart points out that states cannot afford to impose more stringent environmental standards than their neighbors, unless they want to hurt their economy. Similarly, it could be argued that corporations cannot accept more stringent standards than other firms, unless they want to go out of business.[47]

A Possible Moral Response to the Reasonable-Possibility Argument

Despite the plausibility of the suggestions that morality cannot rest on heroism, many philosophers are likely to respond that it is both reasonable and possible—not heroic—to cease transfer of hazardous technologies. In subsequent paragraphs, I argue that this response is questionable. Henry Shue, for example, claims that corporations are morally bound to cease transfer of hazardous technologies because (1) no institution has the right to inflict harm, even to hold down production costs; and (2) underdeveloped countries, alone, cannot be expected to impose strict environmental and technological standards because they are competing with other countries for foreign investment.[48] Although Shue's first argument is correct, that one ought not inflict harm in order to hold down production costs, a critical problem is knowing how to define "infliction of harm." At what point does inflicting a higher *probability* of damage constitute infliction of harm?[49] Contrary to an assumption behind Shue's argument, we do inflict harm in the form of increased *probability* of risk, in order to hold down production costs in the United States. Our pollution-control regulations are specifically designed to trade a certain amount of safety for a given amount of production savings. The typical norm, adopted by the Environmental Protection Agency, a National Academy of Sciences panel, the Nuclear Regulatory Committee, and other government groups, is that safer technology is not required unless the risk to the public is greater than a one-in-a-million increase in the average annual probability of fatality. Moreover, allowable worker risk is typically ten times greater than that for the public, in part because permitting higher workplace risks is sometimes more cost-effective than prohibiting them.[50]

Many U.S. corporations often are merely required to keep environmental hazards "as low as is reasonably achievable," on the basis of a "favorable cost-benefit analysis." If it costs the licensee of a nuclear power plant, for example, more than $1,000 to avoid an additional person-rem of exposure to the public, then the licensee is not required to do so. If it costs less, then the licensee must aim at reducing maximum radiation exposure to the public to 0.0005 rem per person per year. Hence, according to current law, there is no (and indeed there cannot be an) absolute prohibition against harm (where "harm" includes increased probability of risk), in part because such a prohibition would be impossible to achieve in a technological society.[51] Therefore, Shue's first argument, as it stands, may sanction a morality (absolute prohibition of harm) that is impossible to fulfill.

Shue's second objection, that underdeveloped countries cannot be expected to impose strict environmental standards because they are competing with other nations for foreign investment, also makes a reasonable point, but it contains a flawed assumption: that because *countries* compete with one another for foreign technological-investment dollars, just as *corporations* compete with one another for profits, therefore nations have no more responsibility than do private industries to protect their citizens' health and safety by regulating technology. This assumption is flawed because it puts countries and corporations on the same level, so to speak, as far as protecting citizens is concerned. Putting them on the same level is problematic, because firms are concerned primarily with promoting *private* interests (maximizing shareholders' profits), whereas nations are obliged to promote the *public* welfare. Moreover, a strong case could be made for the claim that citizens, by virtue of their citizenship, share an explicit contract with their country. In exchange for citizens' paying taxes and remaining loyal, for example, the country performs many services, such as protecting the health and welfare of the public. Except in the employer-employee relationship, there is no comparably strong contract between a corporation and citizens in a given nation. Therefore, it could easily be argued that the greater responsibility for protecting public health and welfare belongs to the country, and not to the corporation that imports pesticides or agrees to manage toxic wastes. Moreover, at least in part, the nation appears to have the stronger obligation to protect citizens because corporations often fail to do so.

Consider the consequences that would follow if one were to accept Shue's notion that corporations have more responsibility to force use of safe technology than do host countries. Corporations that did not willingly accept this responsibility would be able to act with impunity, knowing that they, not government, had primary responsibility for citizen safety. And government would be powerless to "right" corporate wrongs, since it would have no mandate to protect citizens working in risky facilities. Indeed, one of the most common industry arguments against government regulation is that it is "not needed" and that corporations themselves can do the job. This is exactly the argument made by Henry Shue. Obviously, however, industry cannot police itself completely, as our earlier examples of risks suggest.[52] If it could, then it would have nothing to lose through government regulation. Because firms have something to lose, they oppose governmental regulation; therefore, such regulation must be needed.

A Practical Response to the Reasonable-Possibility Argument

If government regulation is typically needed to protect citizens and workers from environmental/technological hazards, and if industry alone cannot do the job, then it may be neither reasonable nor possible to expect corporations to cease transfer of banned technologies, especially if government does not require them to do so. Since "ought implies can," corporations are morally obliged to use safer technologies only if they can do so without heroic sacrifices. Moreover, even if it were reasonable to argue that firms are morally obliged to make heroic sacrifices, they are unlikely to do so, at least for long, because they will not survive. Hence, even if corporations are *morally* required to use safer technologies, they are not *likely* to do so if the safety threatens their competitive advantage. Apart from what is ethically desirable, one cannot realistically expect certain companies to cut their profits, in the name of safety, unless governments, corporate employees, and consumers force them to do so. We are therefore faced with an interesting practical problem, one quite different from the one with which we began: Do we have any ethical obligations, as consumers in developed nations, to force transfer only of the safest technologies? We consumers in developed countries may have the greatest power, and perhaps also the greatest obligation, to help solve the problems of transferring hazardous technologies.

Our Responsibility through Ability

We citizens in developed countries do seem to have a moral obligation to help prevent use of certain hazardous technologies in underdeveloped countries. This is a "responsibility through ability."[53] That is, since we have the ability to make a positive difference in such situations, therefore we are obliged to do so. (Later I shall discuss *how* one might make a positive difference.) Our duties to help defenseless persons arise in part from the fact that we and they are interdependent and not self-sufficient and hence share an implicit social contract. We are thus obligated to help other persons because we are able to do so and because they are human beings.[54]

The fact that we have no *explicit* social contract with members of other nations, as we have with citizens of our own country, need not significantly change our obligation. For example, if two people are facing almost certain death, either because of banned pesticides or because of their working in substandard asbestos-processing plants, why should we be bound to aid one victim, merely because he is a fellow citizen, and not bound at all to aid the other victim, simply because he is not a compatriot? Admittedly, fellow countrymen have prior claim to our loyalties, in large part because of an explicit social contract we share with them. But just because they have *prior* claims, they do not necessarily have *exclusive* claims to our loyalties. Surely what we all share as humans, with common conceptions of the good life and with our equality as members of the same species, is at least as important a foundation for our interpersonal duties as is common citizenship. Therefore, we have some obligation to aid third-world victims of the transfer of hazardous technologies.[55] Even the U.S. Agency for International Development (USAID) has been forced, in recent years, to perform environmental impact assessments for the technologies they transfer. USAID has implemented the U.S. National Environmental Policy Act (NEPA), so as to review, for example, its pesticide programs in other nations. These reviews have "resulted in significant changes in USAID's operations," particularly in the area of pest management. U.S. agencies evidently are beginning to recognize that recipients have rights to protection from the transfer of hazardous technologies.[56]

But how does one specify the limits on our duty to help citizens in other nations, because we are able to do so and because they are humans? One could exclaim, "Look, I have my own life to lead and my own children to raise. I ought to be free of the obligation to help third-world nations by promoting transfer of only the safest technologies."[57] As Fishkin formulates the objection, one is morally required to "prevent great harm" when one is able to do so and when the costs are minor. He says that this moral obligation breaks down, however, when it is applied to large numbers. Fishkin's reasoning is as follows: If one has only a modest number of occasions to help others, then the obligation to prevent great harm is not excessively burdensome and does not restrict one's freedom of action. This "minimal altruism," however, could have the *cumulative* effect of imposing great burdens and severely restricting one's choices. The result, says Fishkin, could be "breakdown," or "overload."[58]

Fishkin's objection is obviously correct in the sense that there is an upper bound to the cost that can be said to be required of persons striving to help those who need more physical security. Individuals clearly have a right to pursue their own commitments, apart from the sacrifices that appear to be demanded by impersonal global morality. Nevertheless, if one believes in a transnational social contract among all humans, then one ought not to forgo a chance to do great good for others in order to avoid a trifling sacrifice, as was already mentioned.[59] Likewise, a nation ought not to forgo a chance to do a great good for the people of other nations in order to avoid a trifling sacrifice for itself. (The obvious question here, of course, is whether the sacrifice is trifling. I shall address this issue in a moment.)

Another limit on our duty to help others is set by the fact that individual sacrifices are more burdensome and hence less of a moral imperative when they set us, either individually or as nations, at a disadvantage relative to others who have sacrificed less. For example, I have less of an obligation than do wealthier persons to share my goods with underprivileged persons if my doing so puts me at a disadvantage, relative to wealthier persons who have not shared as much of their goods as I have.

Henry Shue's distinction between the *scope* and *magnitude* of justice also provides some clues for an "upper bound" on my obligations to sacrifice for others.[60] With respect to *scope*, everyone on the planet may have rights and duties grounded in global justice, because we may all be said to share a social contract. Of course, the *magnitude* of the duties imposed on each of us is not the same. This is because there are a number of considerations which limit one's obligation to bring about social change. For example, my duties to others cannot be so great that fulfilling them jeopardizes my security and the security of those for whom I am personally responsible. This principle is obvious on the grounds of consistency.

A final constraint is that justice ought to require only what some normal, nonheroic persons can be convinced to do. If at least some persons (having healthy self-interest) do not freely assent to these demands, then it is questionable whether the proposed standards of justice are legitimate. It is questionable because one is only bound to do what it is possible to do. Moreover, one is not required to pay *any* price in order to achieve what is possible. Gains in security bought at the price of either bloody revolution or totalitarian enforcement are highly questionable, primarily because of the cost in lives and in civil liberties. "Sometimes an unbloody half loaf is better than a bloody loaf."[61]

What all these limits suggest is that it is impossible for citizens in developed countries to completely reject the duty of helping to ensure the safety of citizens in underdeveloped nations. Although one cannot be expected to help protect all peoples, one can (as Henry Shue puts it) protect "a few at a time until it becomes too heavy a burden."[62]

Our Responsibility through Complicity

We also have a "responsibility through complicity" to help third-world victims of technology transfer, because we have accepted lower inflation and lower prices for foreign-produced goods. These are two benefits bought, at least in part, at the price of health hazards for peoples in underdeveloped countries.[63] Therefore, we owe them a debt of compensation or reparation. Judith Lichtenberg formulates a similar argument:

Suppose we consider a relationship, R, between a developed country, D, and an underdeveloped one, U. It may be that both D and U are better off with R than without it (though, of course, we make the artificial assumption here that the state to which we compare R is just the absence of R, with nothing replacing it). But suppose that by any reasonable standard, D benefits much more than U, not just in the sense that D ends up absolutely better off but also that it is improved more incrementally as well. This accords with the claim that economic relations between rich and poor countries widen the gap between them even if those relations bring absolute gains for all. So D is benefitted more by U's participation than U is by D's. Here the principle of unequal benefit applies to show that D owes something to U by way of compensation, for D owes its advantageous position in part to U's participation.[64]

Lichtenberg's argument (that because D has benefited from U and is dependent on U, therefore D has obligations of compensation, and perhaps reparation, to help U) is similar to rebuttals to "lifeboat ethics." When Garrett Hardin proposed his famous "lifeboat ethics," he argued that members of developed nations had no obligations to help those in underdeveloped countries because such aid would only cause the populations in the third world to increase, making their progress even more difficult. He also said that persons in developed nations would have to reduce themselves to subsistence levels in order to make a difference in underdeveloped countries. Or, as one person put it, about *eight times* the annual GNP of the United States would be required in order to attain a five-to-one ratio of the income of developed to underdeveloped nations, and a three-to-one ratio of the income of developed and developing nations. In other words, only massive redistribution could make much of a difference. Finally, Hardin claimed that helping third-world persons would only cause greater harm, both to the environment and to members of future generations.[65]

Although there is no time here to analyze the "lifeboat ethics" just outlined, it is important to sketch some of the responses to it, simply because those responses might help clarify the argument for "responsibility based on complicity." One can ignore this argument only by making several erroneous assumptions also shared by proponents of lifeboat ethics. One such assumption is that developed countries are self-sufficient and do not need the help of underdeveloped nations. This assumption is false, as the oil crisis shows. Moreover, many of the wealthy countries were helped to prosperity because they bought resources cheaply from poor nations and then sold finished products back to them at a high cost.[66]

Other "lifeboat" objections to the complicity argument err because they ignore the fact that wealthy nations are using a disproportionate share of the planet's resources. This depletion of nonrenewable materials might be questioned both on the grounds that it violates the Lockean proviso to leave "as much and as good" for others, and on the grounds that third-world peoples deserve some compensation or reparation for having their opportunities (to use these resources) reduced. Consequently, first-world citizens may have some obligation to assist third-world peoples who are victimized by technology transfer.

Our Prudential Responsibilities

From a pragmatic point of view, we also have a moral and a prudential obligation to help prevent use of hazardous technologies in developing countries because many of the associated harms affect us in first-world nations. As one author put it, the question of transfer of hazardous technologies is not a question of "them versus us." Persons in both the developed and the underdeveloped world are victims of unsafe technology transfer. For example, crops containing pesticides are grown in third-world countries but actually feed the first world, but they endanger the poor and the hungry in both the first and the third world. As has been mentioned, up to 70 percent of the food crop in third-world nations is exported to developed countries.[67] Over 15 percent of the beans and 12 percent of the peppers imported from Mexico violate the Food and Drug Administration's pesticide-residue standards, and half of imported green coffee beans contain measurable levels of banned pesticides. The U.S. General Accounting Office estimates that 14 percent of all U.S. meat is now contaminated with illegal residues. The pesticide-residue problem has become so great that all beef imports from Mexico, Guatemala, and El Salvador have been halted. Moreover, government investigators found that half of all the imported food identified as pesticide contaminated was marketed without any penalty to the producers and without any warning to the consumers.[68]

What all these examples illustrate is that it is virtually impossible to protect even U.S. citizens from the hazardous effects of technology transfers to third-world countries. Apart from the direct hazards that return to U.S. consumers (e.g., on imported food), there is still the problem that global contamination eventually will increase because of hazards initially felt only in developing nations. There has been a significant increase in the concentration of lead in the successive snow layers from the Greenland ice cap and in seawater, for example.[69] Likewise, because of increasing levels of chlorofluorocarbons, there has been an increase in the size of the ozone hole over Antarctica.[70] As these two examples suggest, no spot on earth is ever wholly protected from the chemical or atmospheric hazards occurring elsewhere on the planet. Just as planetary interdependence at the political and economic level establishes a *moral* foundation for our duty to help those in underdeveloped nations, so also our ecological interdependence establishes a *prudential* basis for our obligation to help ourselves by helping them.

The Precise Nature of Citizen Obligations

But what is the nature of our precise responsibility to help third-world victims of transfer of hazardous technology? What are we obliged to do, and what do we have the ability to do? Although there is no space here for a comprehensive answer to these questions, the general response is clear. We have the ability to make it more costly for firms *not* to use, than to use, safe technology. We have the ability to make a corporation use safe technology for reasons of self-interest. As both the U.S. case of boycotting nonunion lettuce and the third-world case of boycotting Nestlé products revealed, well-organized Western consumers can send corporations a message via their pocketbooks. They can boycott the products of firms known to use unsafe technology abroad. They can ensure that corporations will find it less expensive, in the long run (because of lost sales), to use safe, rather than more hazardous, technology. U.S. citizens also could force U.S. export controls. For example, they could argue for abandoning the lax current policies and returning at least to the Carter administration's procedures.[71] Citizens likewise could force developed nations to admit that all countries have duties to protect the security of their citizens and to recognize rights to security. Citizens could lobby for stopping all forms of assistance to all governments that do not recognize their citizens' rights to security.[72]

Shue suggests a more specific citizen act: forcing abolition of the U.S. Overseas Private Investment Corporation (OPIC), an agency receiving congressional (public) funds to distribute to American firms locating abroad. OPIC has used taxpayers' money, for example, to help a U.S. company, Abex, build a substandard asbestos plant in Madras, India. OPIC has also used tax dollars to underwrite a U.S. corporation–owned substandard smelting complex in Africa. In addition to forcing the abolition, or at least tighter control, of OPIC, citizens could also help third-world victims of transfer of hazardous technology by urging the United States to differentially favor governments that are more supportive of strong, independent unions.[73] Another practical strategy for helping victims of hazardous technologies would be to urge the USAID to promote the most environmentally sustainable development projects. John Seiberling and Claudine Schneider, members of the U.S. House of Representatives, have already made this proposal, and their suggestions have been the focus of congressional efforts in this regard. Seiberling and Schneider also support efforts to press multilateral development banks to promote sound development projects.[74] Groups such as CARE, the World Bank, and the Church World Service can all be lobbied, successfully, to use lending and assistance guidelines that promote only the safest environmental and technological projects.[75]

Conclusion

This chapter has argued that we have an obligation to "make a difference," to make it difficult for nations and corporations to subject unwitting third-world peoples to transfers of hazardous technology. But the only clear way that we can "make a difference" is through coordinated political activity, not primarily through individual efforts. We need to put pressure on U.S. agencies such as OPIC. We need to recognize that we have a moral obligation to political activism.

Such recognition has been in short supply in recent years, especially in the United States. We no longer seem to believe that, as Plato argued, each of us is an essentially political animal, concerned with the affairs of the *polis* or state; or that, as Thucydides argued, all citizens ought to spend time concerning themselves with public affairs as well as with their own personal activities. As Thucydides reminded us, if we succumb to the belief that "someone else" will carry our political responsibilities for us, the common cause will imperceptibly decay.[76] We, as citizens and consumers, owe it to the common cause to help prevent many risks of technology transfer.

Part Three

New Directions
for Risk Evaluation

Chapter Eleven

Risk Evaluation

Methodological Reforms

A naturally occurring decay product of radium 226, radon 222 has an important impact on human health. Because it can leave the soil or rock in which it is present and enter the surrounding air or water, radon gas is ubiquitous. When it decays into a series of radioisotopes collectively referred to as "radon daughters," two of these daughters (polonium 218 and polonium 214) give off alpha particles. These alpha particles, when emitted in the lung, can cause lung cancer.[1]

Until recently, radon daughter exposure was associated with lung cancer in uranium miners. Now we know that radon daughters are present in the air of buildings, building materials, water, underlying soil, and utility natural gas. Although radon concentrations in American homes have not been systematically surveyed, available data show that some dwellings have concentrations greater than the control levels in underground mines.[2] This means, for example, that the lung cancer risk for lifetime exposure from age one is approximately 9.1×10^{-3}, assuming an average life span of seventy years, or 70 WLM.[3] This is a risk of lung cancer of nearly 1 in 100, as a result of lifetime radon exposure. Despite such risk figures, the present state of scientific knowledge does not allow one to specify the best values characterizing the dose in a home or mine; there are fundamental uncertainties surrounding the radon dosimetry factors.[4]

Risk assessment and evaluation are beset with typical uncertainties, similar to those in the radon case. Indeed, as was already mentioned, uncertainties of six orders of magnitude "are not unusual."[5] As a result of these uncertainties, hazard assessors often fall victim to a variety of methodological errors, such as the probabilistic strategy and the isolationist strategy. In this chapter and the next, I shall outline several proposals for avoiding some of the worst effects of these uncertainties and erroneous methodological strategies. This chapter will examine

169

several *methodological* suggestions designed to improve quantitative risk analysis, especially risk evaluation. The last chapter will outline some *regulatory* and *procedural* solutions for reforming hazard management. These suggestions should address many of the problems criticized earlier in the volume; they should fill out the new account of rational risk evaluation, scientific proceduralism, begun in Chapter Three.

Policymakers have attempted for some time to improve various methods of risk analysis and evaluation, but their proposed methodological reforms have been fraught with controversy—notably, the debate between the cultural relativists, who overemphasize values in hazard evaluation, and the naive positivists, who underemphasize them.[6] Decisionmakers and evaluators likewise disagree over how to resolve some of the more practical problems associated with risk management. At one end of the "solutions spectrum" are environmentalist policymakers, such as Howard Latin. They argue for uniform environmental standards, for prohibitions against agents suspected of causing harm (carcinogens, for example), and against economic incentives and benefit-cost techniques for reducing risk.[7] At the other end of the spectrum are industry-oriented policymakers, such as Bernard Cohen and Lester Lave. They argue for situation-specific environmental standards, for negotiation regarding agents suspected of causing harm, and in favor of economic incentives and benefit-cost techniques for reducing risk.[8]

In this and the next chapter, I shall continue to argue for a middle position, between the industry and the environmentalist solutions to the problems of hazard evaluation and risk management. Agreeing to some extent with the environmentalists, I have argued throughout this book that quantified risk assessment (QRA), risk evaluation, and risk-cost-benefit analysis (RCBA) are seriously flawed, in part because of questionable methodological strategies associated with them.[9] However, siding also with the industrial experts, I shall show (in this chapter) that, although QRA is in practice deficient, there are in-principle reasons for continuing to use it.

More specifically, this chapter argues for a number of *methodological* claims regarding risk evaluation: that we need to use QRA and RCBA; that RCBA could be significantly improved by means of ethical weighting techniques; that hazard evaluation ought to be accomplished by means of alternative analyses designed to take account of different methodological, ethical, and social assumptions; that expert opinions on risk estimates ought to be weighted on the basis of their past predictive successes; and that assessors generally ought to give up both the naive positivist and the cultural relativist views, as well as the environmentalist and the industry-oriented accounts of risk. Instead, the chapter argues that experts ought to adopt a middle position, scientific proceduralism, that emphasizes increasing the *analytic precision* of hazard assessment and the *democratic control* of environmental risks.

Admittedly, the conclusion of many persons who have followed my repeated criticisms of methodological strategies associated. with QRA and RCBA might be that we ought to discontinue use of both. Such a conclusion would follow, however, (1) only if the problems with QRA and RCBA were essential to the use of these quantitative and economic methods and (2) only if there were alternative, superior tools capable of achieving better risk analysis and management. Since I believe that both (1) and (2) are false, more modest and reformist conclusions follow from the criticisms leveled earlier in the book. The case for using QRA can probably be made most clearly by considering RCBA, a method described briefly in Chapter Four.[10] Since most of the methodological criticisms of QRA in this volume have been directed at the risk-evaluation stage, any plausible defense of the claim that we ought to continue to use QRA ought to focus on this third stage and on the most prominent tool of risk evaluation, RCBA. Moreover, since most people object to QRA because of its quantitative, reductionistic approach, their criticisms typically focus on RCBA. Let's examine RCBA, in order to see why, although these complaints are partially correct, they fail to show that policymakers ought to abandon either RCBA or QRA.

Why We Need QRA, despite Its Flaws: The Case for RCBA

Currently, nearly all U.S. regulatory agencies (with the exception only of the Occupational Health and Safety Administration) routinely use RCBA to help determine their policies. Although the National Environmental Policy Act (NEPA) of 1969 requires that RCBA be used to evaluate all proposed environment-related federal projects, opponents of this technique often view its practitioners as dehumanized numerators engaging in a kind of economic Philistinism.[11] Amory Lovins compares RCBA to the street lamp under which the proverbial drunkard searched for his wallet, not because he lost it there but because that was the only place he could see.[12] The most common objections to RCBA generally focus on four alleged problems: there is no accepted theory of rationality to undergird RCBA; the democratic process, as well as mathematical-economic techniques, ought to determine risk policy; RCBA ignores factors such as the equity of distribution and the incommensurability of various parameters; and its data base is inadequate.[13]

Rather than focus on each of these objections, I want to ask a more basic question: What arguments ought to be counted as decisive in the case for and against RCBA? Unless proponents and opponents of this technique agree on the criteria for resolving their disputes, no consensus on the methods for making public policy seems possible. Currently, much of the debate is at cross-purposes. Both opponents and proponents of this technique are arguing for theses which those who disagree with them do not regard as decisive on the issue of whether or not to use RCBA.

One argument used by opponents of RCBA appears to be both misguided and central to their objections. I would like to expose its flaws and to point out what alternative reasons might be decisive grounds for arguing for or against use of RCBA. This flawed argument is that, since RCBA is deficient in a number of serious ways, it should not be used routinely for societal decisionmaking regarding environmental projects. More descriptively oriented variants of this argument, such as those by Dreyfus, focus on the claim that RCBA cannot model all instances of "human situational understanding."[14] More normative variants, such as those by MacIntyre, maintain that RCBA exhibits some of the same defects as "classical utilitarianism."[15]

Two Main Attacks on RCBA

Although those who attack RCBA do not formulate their arguments in terms of explicit premises, they all appear to be employing a simple, four-step process. For the more normative philosophers, these steps are as follows:

1. RCBA has a utilitarian structure.
2. Utilitarianism exhibits serious defects.
3. Typical applications of RCBA—for example, in risk assessment and in environmental impact analysis—exhibit the same defects.
4. Just as utilitarianism should be rejected, so should the use of RCBA techniques.[16]

The more descriptive attacks on RCBA are similar:

1. RCBA is unable to model all cases of human situational understanding and decisions.

2. The inability to model all cases of human situational understanding and decisions is a serious defect.

3. Typical applications of RCBA—for example, in risk assessment and in environmental impact analysis—exhibit the same defect.

4. Just as faulty models of human situational understanding and decisions should be rejected, so should RCBA.

This four-step argument is significant, not only because persons such as Dreyfus, Gewirth, MacIntyre, and MacLean appear to be employing it, but also because it seems to reflect the thinking of many (if not most) philosophers who discuss RCBA and applied ethics. After taking a closer look at both variants of the argument, I shall attempt to establish two claims:

1. Even if all the premises of both versions of the argument were true, because the *inference* from them to the conclusion is not obviously *valid*, it is not clear that the conclusion (4) ought to be accepted.

2. Although the second and third premises of the normative variant of the argument are likely true, because the *first premise* is not obviously *true*, it is not clear that the conclusion (4) ought to be accepted.

Let's examine first the descriptive variants of the argument. Although its proponents would probably admit that RCBA is useful for some cases of individual decisionmaking (for example, for determining whether to repair one's old car or buy a new one), they claim that, in most instances, individuals do not use RCBA to do a "point count."[17] Dreyfus and Tribe maintain, instead, that they use intuition. Socolow and MacLean claim that they employ open discourse, argument, or debate.[18] In any case, all critics agree that any formal model such as RCBA is unable to capture what goes on when someone understands something or makes a decision. They maintain that such formal models fail in being too narrow and oversimplified.[19]

As Dreyfus put it, much policymaking is "beyond the pale of scientific decisionmaking." It requires "wisdom and judgment going beyond factual knowledge," just as chess playing and automobile driving require "expertise" and "human skill acquisition" not amenable to RCBA.[20] The expert performer, so the objection goes, plays chess or drives the automobile "without any conscious awareness of the process." Except during moments of breakdown, "he understands, acts, and learns from results," without going through any routine such as RCBA. Indeed, he not only *does* not go through any such routine; he *could* not. And he could not, according to critics of RCBA, because he is often unable to tell a cost from a benefit; much of the time, he doesn't know either the probability or the consequences of certain events.[21] Hence, goes the argument, because RCBA cannot model many cases of *individual* decisionmaking, it cannot model *societal* decisionmaking.[22]

More normative policymakers likewise reject use of RCBA for societal risk decisions, but their emphasis is on the claim that RCBA *should* not, rather than that it *cannot*, succeed. The gist of their objections to RCBA is that the technique forces one to assume that "everybody has his price." Lovins and MacLean are quick to point out that some things are priceless and hence not amenable to RCBA calculation.[23] Gewirth argues that certain rights cannot be costed and then traded for benefits. Critics of RCBA all argue that moral commitments, rights, and basic goods (such as the sacredness of life) are inviolable and incommensurable and hence cannot be bargained away for any benefits revealed in an RCBA.[24] In a nutshell, they allege that RCBA shares the same defects as classical utilitarianism; it cannot account for crucial values such as distributive justice.[25] Hence, they conclude, in a society where decisionmaking ought to be based on rights and justice, hazard analysis and management ought not to be based on RCBA.

Problems with the Main Inference of the Argument against RCBA

Even if all three premises of the argument against RCBA were true, its conclusion ought not to be accepted, since the relevant inference is not obviously valid. This inference is that RCBA should be rejected because it exhibits a number of serious deficiencies. The inference is questionable because proponents of RCBA are likely to admit, with their opponents, that RCBA has shortcomings. For its advocates, RCBA is one way of facilitating democratic decisionmaking, not a substitute for it. Hence, proponents of RCBA maintain that, although critics are correct in pointing out deficiencies in the method, these flaws alone do not constitute decisive reasons for abandoning it.

Proponents claim that the problems with RCBA are not the issue; the real issue is whether RCBA represents the least objectionable of all the methods used for policymaking. If so, it is not sufficient for an opponent of RCBA to find fault with the technique and then reject it. He must, in addition, show that there is a viable decisionmaking alternative that has fewer deficiencies than RCBA.

One reason why recognition of RCBA deficiencies is a *necessary*, but not a *sufficient*, condition for inferring that it ought not be used in policymaking is that RCBA provides at least some benefits to society. For example, it enables policymakers to cope with externalities. It is essential for providing estimates of social costs, so that prices can be set equal to marginal costs.[26] Government then can set standards to regulate output and to determine the optimum size of projects. If RCBA were rejected as a part of decisionmaking, then we would have to abandon not only techniques used for regulating externalities and achieving social benefits such as traffic control but also the means of ensuring competitive pricing.[27] Because of these assets of RCBA, those who attack it ought either to defend the claim that there is an alternative that is superior to RCBA or to refrain from the call to reject RCBA. Surprisingly, many of those who criticize RCBA, with the exception of perhaps Hare and Self, do not discuss what might constitute sufficient conditions for rejecting it. Instead, they merely point out deficiencies in the method.[28]

A second reason for denying that RCBA deficiencies are decisive grounds for abandoning the method is that (in many cases) acceptance of this inference would preclude *all* systematic forms of societal decisionmaking. In other words, if the descriptive variant of the argument proves anything at all, it proves far too much—namely, that the deficiencies rendering RCBA questionable likewise count against all systematic societal decision methods used in similar situations.

Consider first Dreyfus's charge that "the analytic decomposition of a decision problem into component probabilities, utilities, and tradeoffs" is misguided because true understanding of policymaking cannot be made *explicit*; decisionmakers, so the argument goes, "know how to do things, but not why they should be done that way."[29] MacIntyre says much the same thing: "Moral [and policy] arguments are in our culture generally unsettleable."[30] Other proponents of this descriptive argument claim, as was already noted,[31] that people can't tell what is a cost and what is a benefit of a particular technological proposal. Since we are unable to sort out costs from benefits, they claim, RCBA cannot lead to good policymaking.[32]

If all such claims were correct—that is, if policy disputes are generally unsettleable, and if costs cannot be distinguished from benefits—then the difficulties noted would undercut even any *non*quantitative risk methods, as well as any rational analysis of them. If Dreyfus and others are right about these difficulties, then criteria for policy would have to remain implicit and, by their very nature, could not be made explicit. As a result, no one could understand either decisionmaking or the criteria for its success. Moreover, any systematic, rational form of public policymaking—whether quantitative or nonquantitative, scientific, democratic, or legal—would be undercut. This is because any nonarbitrary form of decisionmaking requires specification of policy goals and criteria for its success. Any democratic form of decision-making requires, further, rendering these goals and criteria explicit, so that they can be recognized and evaluated by the body politic. There-fore, instead of condemning RCBA for reasons that would indict any systematic decision methodology, policymakers would do better to ar-gue for a particular risk-assessment method, on the grounds that it was superior to all known alternatives. Indeed, any other approach would amount to begging the question of whether the deficiencies of RCBA are *sufficient* grounds for rejecting it.

In begging this question, policy analysts fail to take account of the fact that *any* theory of decisionmaking, not just RCBA, leaves some residual unaccounted for by the theory. For Gewirth and MacLean, for example, the main theoretical residue of RCBA is that it allegedly can-not explain the overarching significance given to human rights and to the sacredness of life. However, any opponent of any theory is always able to charge that it cannot account for some important value. This is because any theory must employ simplifying assumptions that have a "residual" not accounted for by the theory of which they are a part. Hence, arguments focusing merely on the deficiencies of RCBA miss the point. The point is which residuals are more or less important, and which decision alternatives have the least deficiencies.

The more normative arguments against RCBA fail, for example, because often they merely rehash the old problems with utilitarianism, instead of recognizing that both utilitarian and deontological policy alternatives have theoretical residues. Coburn, for example, is one of the many who take this approach.[33] Yet, as Sen points out, Bentham and Rawls capture two different aspects of interpersonal welfare con-siderations. Both provide evaluations *necessary* for ethical judgments, but neither alone is *sufficient*. Utilitarians are unable to account for the theoretical residue of how to evaluate different *levels* of welfare, and Rawlsians are unable to account for the theoretical residue of how to evaluate *gains and losses* of welfare.[34] Hence, merely pointing out one or the other of these deficiencies misses the point.

In particular, Dreyfus's claim that one does not normally employ RCBA, to play chess or to drive an automobile, misses the point.[35] Likewise, MacLean's claim, that he does not use RCBA to value his antique Russian Samovar, misses the point. One reason why persons do not use the technique in such situations is that one's own experiences, values, and goals are unified, and hence provide a single, integrated basis from which to make *individual* decisions about valuing risks and actions. RCBA, however, has been proposed for *societal* decisionmaking precisely because the disparate members of society have no unifying experiences and goals that would provide an integrated basis from which to make decisions about how to spend funds or assess technological risks. Collective choices, exercised through government, require some analytic "logic" or method to reconcile and unify the diverse experiential bases of all the members of society. Hence, the fact that RCBA is not used by individuals, in playing chess or pricing samovars, does not count against the desirability of using RCBA in making societal decisions about risk. The two cases are fundamentally disanalogous.

Admittedly, there is no way to show in advance that RCBA, when refined and developed, will or will not enable us to account for some of our obviously correct normative or descriptive intuitions about choice. This being so, it seems inappropriate for proponents and opponents of RCBA to provide unqualified support, respectively, for acceptance or rejection of RCBA. Rather, they ought to aim at showing why one ought or ought not try to work toward an allegedly adequate RCBA theory.[36] Not to pursue this line of argumentation is merely to beg the question of what might constitute the soundest basis for policy.

Many critics of RCBA do not provide convincing grounds for rejecting it, because they underestimate the benefits of using an explicit, clearly defined decision technique, and they overestimate the possibility for rational policymaking when no analytic procedure such as RCBA is part of the process. A society pleading for policymaking based solely on Dreyfus's expertise, "intuition," and "wisdom," or on MacLean's "open discourse," rather than also based on RCBA or on any other analytic method, is like a starving man pleading that only steak will satisfy him. Since much current policy is arbitrary and based on purely political considerations, at least some use of any analytic method seems desirable.

One reason why *some* use of RCBA is better than *none* is that failure to use a well-defined system leaves one open to the charge of both methodological and substantive arbitrariness. At least in the sense that its component techniques and underlying value judgments are capable of being known and debated, use of an analytic decision procedure is rarely arbitrary in a methodological sense, although it may be controversial in a substantive sense. For example, a decision (based on RCBA) to use a particular technology for storing low-level radwastes may be *substantively* controversial in the sense, for instance, that different persons have opposed views on how much risk is acceptable. If the RCBA were done properly, however, its conclusion would not be *methodologically* arbitrary, in the sense that someone who examined all the calculated costs and benefits would be unable to tell *why* a particular policy were said to be more or less beneficial than another. A proper RCBA is not methodologically arbitrary, at least in the sense that its decision criteria, however faulty, are explicit; the bases for its conclusions, including the numbers assigned to particular values, are there for everyone to see and evaluate.

If someone were to use a nonanalytic decision procedure, such as "intuition" or "open discourse" (as suggested by many opponents of RCBA), then the resulting conclusions would likely be both methodologically arbitrary and substantively controversial. There would be no way to analyze and evaluate a particular intuitive decision; that is the whole point with something's being intuitive: it is *directly* apprehended. In this sense, a systematic technique (such as RCBA), even with known flaws, is less methodologically arbitrary than an intuitive approach, whose assets and liabilities cannot, in principle, be the object of some reasoning process.

The opponent of RCBA, however, is likely to believe that use of a seriously deficient analytic decision procedure, incorporated within the democratic process, is not necessarily preferable to using no decision procedure or to relying on the democratic process alone. He would likely argue that, in the absence of some decisionmaking system, people would be forced to confront the arbitrariness of their social choices. They would be forced to seek "wisdom" and intuitive "expertise" as the only possible bases for policymaking. In fact, this is exactly what Dreyfus has claimed, and what philosopher Holmes Rolston argued when he criticized an earlier version of these remarks. Rolston claims that using RCBA is like weighing hogs in Texas. Those doing the weighing put the hog in one pan of a large set of scales, put rocks in the other pan, one by one, to balance the weight of the hog, and then guess how much the rocks weigh. Rolston says that the Texans ought to guess the weight of the hog, just as policymakers ought to use intuition and discourse, through the democratic process, and not bother with RCBA.

Rolston's criticism of RCBA does not work, however, and for several reasons. He fails to distinguish the *method* of valuation from the precision with which any factor can be calculated by means of that method. If consistent methods, such as RCBA, yield imprecise results, these results are not arbitrary in a damaging sense, since the assumptions used in quantification and the value judgments underlying them are clear and consistent. Moreover, if one rejects RCBA and opts merely for the intuition and discourse of *normal democratic channels*, likely he forgets that the necessary conditions for participatory democracy are rarely met. As Care pointed out, these conditions include:

1. that all the participants be: noncoerced; rational; accepting of the terms of the procedure by which they seek agreement; disinterested; committed to community self-interestedness and to joint agreement; willing to accept only universal solutions; and possessed of equal and full information;

2. that the policy agreed to prescribe something which is both possible and non-risky, in the sense that parties are assured that it will be followed through; and finally

3. that the means used to gain agreement be ones in which all participants are able to register their considered opinion and ones in which all are allowed a voice.[37]

Once one considers these constraints, it becomes obvious that circumstances seldom permit the full satisfaction of these conditions for procedural moral acceptability. Consequently, it is unclear that democratic procedure *alone* will produce a more ethical policy than that achieved by democratic procedure together with RCBA. If anything, the moral acceptability of the democratic process seems to require use of analytic methods, since they are one way of being rational.[38]

Without some use of analytic methods of policymaking, back scratching, payoffs, bribes, and ignorance could just as well take over, except that these moves would be harder to detect than within a clear and systematic decisionmaking approach. Given no nonarbitrary decision procedure for identifying either intuitively correct or wise policies, we might do well to employ a policy technique which, however deficient, is clear, explicit, and systematic, and therefore amenable to democratic modification. Given no philosopher-king and no benevolent scientist-dictator, opponents of RCBA need to explain why they believe that society has the luxury of *not* opting for some analytic procedure such as RCBA as a part of democratic decisionmaking. At a minimum, they ought to explain why they believe RCBA is unlikely to aid policymakers in satisfying the conditions for procedural democracy, just as proponents of the technique ought to argue why they claim RCBA is likely to help decisionmakers meet those conditions. Otherwise, arguments about the adequacy of RCBA merely beg the question.[39]

In begging the question, such arguments fail to take account of many of the constraints on real-world decisionmaking. It often requires, for example, that one make a decision, even though it is not clear that the factors involved are commensurable or that one can adequately take account of rights. In rejecting RCBA, either because it fails to give a "true" description of all the situations of human choice or to take account of certain truths about ethics, its critics often forget that public policymakers are not like pure scientists; they do not have the luxury of seeking truth alone. There are other values, pragmatic ones, that also have to be considered, and this is where RCBA might play a role.

The pragmatic assets of an analytic scheme like RCBA are clear if one considers an example. Suppose citizens were debating whether to build a newer, larger airport in their city. Suppose, too, that an RCBA was completed for the project and that the benefits were said to outweigh the risks and costs of the project by $1 million per year, when nonmarket, qualitative costs were not taken into account. It would be very difficult for citizens to decide whether the risks and costs were offset by the benefits. But if one hypothetically assumed that fifty thousand families in the vicinity of the airport each suffered qualitative risks and costs of aircraft noise, traffic congestion, and increased loss of life worth $20 per year per family, then the decision would be easier to make. It would be much easier to ask whether it was worth $20 per family per year to be rid of the noise, congestion, and auto fatalities associated with a proposed airport, than it would be to ask whether the airport pros outweighed the cons, or what a wise or expert person would say about the situation.[40] Formulating the problem in terms of hypothetical monetary parameters, and using an analytic scheme to make a cardinal estimate of one's preferences, appears to make this particular problem of social choice and risk assessment more tractable. Moreover, one need not believe that the hypothetical dollars assigned to certain costs are "objective" in order to benefit from RCBA. RCBA preference ordering, including the assignment of numbers to these preferences, is merely a *useful device* for formulating the alternatives posed by problems of social choice.[41]

Despite all its difficulties related to the freedom of choice of the poor and the diminishing marginal utility of money, RCBA is useful in suggesting what individuals will "trade off" for safety or for amenities. Hence, it appears to yield some insights about preferences and about constraints on choice. It can't tell us about processes of valuation that guide these choices. Rather, the goal of RCBA is to provide relevant information about preferences—information that is useful for rational, democratic debate. Hence, any decisive argument against RCBA cannot merely fault the technique for its admitted inability to enlighten us about the values that guide our choices. RCBA is not a substitute for moral philosophy, merely one way to elucidate problems within it.

Problems with the Normative Attack on RCBA

But if the RCBA methods are not meant to prescribe various ethical *ends*, but only to illuminate their consequences and alternative *means* for achieving them, then how is it that MacIntyre and other opponents of risk assessment can allege that RCBA is a "normative form of argument" which "reproduces the argumentative forms of utilitarianism"?[42] RCBA is indeed utilitarian in that the optimal choice is always determined by some function of the utilities attached to the *consequences* of all the options considered. It is not obvious, however, that RCBA is *solely* consequentialist. For one thing, before one can apply RCBA strategies, one must first specify alternative courses of action open to the decisionmaker. Since one can consider only a finite set of options, the decisionmaker must make a *value judgment* that the eliminated alternatives would not be the best, if they were left in the calculation. But an infinite set of options cannot be reduced by means of a utilitarian value judgment, because it would presuppose knowing the utilities attached to the consequences of an infinity of options. It is impossible to know these utilities, both because they are infinite and because the only utilitarian grounds for reducing the options is to carry out the very calculations that cannot be accomplished until the options are reduced. Thus, any application of RCBA principles presupposes that one makes some value judgments that cannot be justified by utilitarian principles alone.[43] One might decide, for example, that any risky technologies likely to result in serious violations of rights ought to be eliminated from the set to be subjected to RCBA calculations. In this case, use of the allegedly utilitarian RCBA techniques would presuppose a deontological value judgment.

RCBA also includes many presuppositions that can be justified by utilitarian principles only if one engages in an infinite regress. Hence, these presuppositions must be justified by some nonutilitarian principles. Some of the presuppositions are that each option has morally relevant consequences; that there is a cardinal or ordinal scale in terms of which the consequences may by assigned some number; that a particular discount rate be used; and that certain values be assigned to given consequences. Moreover, these assignments could be made in such a way that RCBA was able to account for nonutilitarian considerations. For instance, one could always assign the value of negative infinity to consequences alleged to be the result of an action that violated some deontological principle(s).[44] Thus, if Gewirth, for example, wants to proscribe risk policy that results in cancer's being inflicted on people, then he can satisfy this allegedly nonutilitarian principle by assigning a value of negative infinity to this consequence.[45]

Suppes also supports the claim that using RCBA does not necessarily commit one to a utilitarian ethical theory. He argues that "the theory could in principle be adopted without change to a calculus of obligation and a theory of expected obligation." From the standpoint of moral philosophy, says Suppes, this material indifference means that RCBA has an incomplete theory of rationality. It is a formal calculus that can be interpreted in a variety of ways. One could conceivably interpret rights violations and inequities as RCBA costs; Dasgupta and Heal, for example, show that the social welfare function of RCBA can be interpreted according to at least three different moral frameworks: egalitarianism, intuitionism, and utilitarianism.[46]

If my arguments, as well as those of Suppes, Rosenberg, and others are correct, then RCBA is nonutilitarian in at least three senses: it presupposes prior, nonutilitarian value judgments; it provides for weighting the consequences of the options considered; and it allows one to count virtually any ethical consideration or consequence as a risk, cost, or benefit. This means that there are at least three grounds for arguing that the first premise of the normative argument against RCBA is untrue.

There also appear to be good reasons for continuing to use RCBA. (1) It responds to the need for a unified, *societal* (rather than *individual*) form of risk decisionmaking. (2) It is a way of clarifying and facilitating democratic decisionmaking. (3) It enables policymakers to compare diverse risks on the basis of probabilities and consequences, to cope with externalities, to provide social benefits, and to ensure competitive pricing. (4) RCBA contributes to rational policymaking, whereas rejecting it usually amounts to rejecting any systematic risk decisions, a stance that leaves room for arbitrary, dishonest, purely political, or irrational hazard assessment. Moreover, (5) since RCBA operates by means of explicit decision criteria, the bases for its conclusions are in principle amenable to debate and discussion by the public; they are not purely intuitive. (6) RCBA helps to make many virtually intractable risk decisions more intelligible. (7) It helps to clarify the values that guide our choices by forcing us to order our preferences. (8) It provides a way for us to spend societal resources on risk abatement so as to save the most lives for the fewest dollars. Finally, (9) RCBA provides a formal calculus that is in principle capable of being interpreted in terms of many value systems.

Improvement of RCBA by Ethical Weighting Techniques

Because RCBA is often misinterpreted in purely utilitarian ways, it typically fails to take account of egalitarian values, social obligations, and rights. One way to remedy these deficiencies would be to employ a weighting system for RCBA. Many of the dilemmas of risk evaluation, discussed in Chapter Five, could be ameliorated by a weighting scheme. For example, in cases where free, informed consent to risk imposition was in question (the "consent dilemma"), policymakers could assign a negative weight to those risks. In cases where dangers to hazard victims were likely to combine to some unacceptable level (the "contributors dilemma"), decisionmakers likewise could assign a negative weight to those risks. Ethically weighted RCBA could also be used to counteract some of the risk-analysis strategies criticized in Chapters Six through Ten. For example, if a potentially catastrophic technology imposed a greater risk on consumers, rather than on producers, then its costs could be weighted more negatively.

Admittedly, neither RCBA nor risk assessment can tell us what weights to impose; RCBA is a formal calculus amenable to the weights dictated by any ethical system. Its purpose is to help us clarify our ethical values as a society, not to dictate them. Hence, perhaps the best way to use RCBA would be to have different interest groups prepare alternative RCBAs, each with different ethical weights. The public or its representatives could then decide which weighting scheme best represented its values. I have argued elsewhere that RCBA ought to be weighted by various parameters, but that teams of analysts, including ethicists and members of various public-interest groups, ought to be responsible for devising alternative, ethically weighted RCBAs.[47] Once these were completed, normal democratic procedures could be used to choose the desired RCBA. Before I go into that proposal, however, it makes sense to explain why any ethical weighting at all appears desirable.

Because no necessary connection exists between Pareto optimality, the central concept of RCBA, and correct policy,[48] it would be helpful if there were some way to avoid the tendency to assume that RCBA alone reveals socially desirable policy. Alternative, ethically weighted RCBAs would enable persons to see that good policy is not only a matter of economic calculations but also a question of ethical analysis. If people follow Gresham's law and thus persist in their tendency to accord primacy to quantitative results, such as those of RCBA, then using ethically weighted RCBAs might keep them both from ignoring ethical parameters, which are not normally represented in a quantitative analysis, and from identifying *un*weighted RCBA results with a prescription for desirable social policy.

Ethically weighted RCBAs would also provide a more helpful framework for democratic decisionmaking. Policy analysis would be able to show how the chosen measures of social risks, costs, and benefits might respond to changed value assumptions.[49] Likewise, ethically weighted RCBAs might bring values into policy considerations at a very early stage of the process, rather than later, after the RCBA conclusions were completed. In this way, citizens might be able to exercise more *direct* control over the values to which policy gives *indirect* assent. Acceptance of the willingness-to-pay measure, for example, implies acceptance of the existing scheme of property rights and income distribution, since risks, costs, and benefits are calculated in terms of existing market prices and conditions.[50] To employ a system of alternative, ethically weighted RCBAs, among which policymakers and the public can decide, would be to assent to the theses (1) that existing RCBAs already contain ethical weights (which are probably unrecognized) and (2) that proponents of the ethics implicit in current analyses ought to be required to plead their cases, along with advocates of other ethical systems, in the public court of reason. Given that weighting is already done anyway, both because of the implicit presuppositions of economists who practice RCBA and because of the political process by means of which the public responds to RCBA, it makes sense to bring as much clarity, ethical precision, openness, and objectivity to it as possible, by explicitly weighting the RCBA parameters in a variety of ways.[51]

Another reason for using ethically weighted RCBAs is that it appears more desirable than alternatives such as the use of revealed preferences or the current market assignments for income distribution, risks, costs, and benefits.[52] Employing revealed preferences requires one to make a number of implausible assumptions, as Chapter Four argued.[53] These could be avoided if, instead of employing revealed preferences, one followed the practice of preparing a number of alternative, ethically weighted RCBAs. Following Mill's lead,[54] several economists have also proposed that RCBA can take account of the nonutilitarian distinction between *right* and *expediency* by using a system of weights.[55] Economists Allen Kneese, Shaul Ben-David, and William Schulze, for example, working under National Science Foundation funding, have developed a scheme for weighting risks, costs, and benefits by means of alternative ethical criteria.[56] They also suggest that each ethical system be represented by a general criterion rather than by a list of rules, such as the Ten Commandments.[57] They claim that the requirement that an ethical system be represented as a transitive criterion for individual or social behavior leaves at least four ethical systems (and probably more) for use in reweighting RCBA parameters: Benthamite utilitarianism, Rawlsian egalitarianism, Nietzschean elitism, and Paretian libertarianism. On their scheme, the Benthamite criterion is that one ought to maximize the sum of the cardinal utilities of all individuals in a society. The Rawlsian criterion is that one ought to try to maximize the utility of the individual with the minimum utility, so long as that individual remains worst off. According to the Nietzschean weighting scheme, one ought to maximize the utility of the individual who can attain the greatest utility. Finally, according to the Paretian criterion, say Kneese, Ben-David, and Schulze, one ought to act in such a way that no one is harmed and, if possible, that the welfare of some persons is improved.[58]

The merit of the ethical weighting criteria described by Kneese and his associates is that they could theoretically provide a unique sort of nonmarket information. For example, one could ask an individual how much he would be willing to pay for redistributing income to less fortunate members of society. The purpose of asking about such ethical beliefs, of course, would not be to provide a prescription for policy, but to allow the public and policymakers to see how different assumptions about the desirability of given distributions change the overall ratio of costs to benefits. They would be able to examine alternative, ethically weighted options, and not merely marginal costs or benefits across opportunities.

The work of Kneese and his associates illustrates dramatically that what is said to be feasible or unfeasible, in terms of RCBA, can change dramatically when different ethical weighting criteria are employed. Using case studies on helium storage, nuclear fission, and automobile-emission standards, they showed how alternative ethical weights can be used to generate contradictory RCBA conclusions. For example, when used with a Benthamite weighting criterion, RCBA reveals that using nuclear fission for generation of electricity is not feasible. When either the Paretian, Rawlsian, or Nietzschean criterion is used, however, nuclear power may be said to be feasible or unfeasible, depending on the value attributed to factors such as compensation for damages and the utility attributed to future generations.[59]

Admittedly, the weighting schemes outlined by Kneese and his colleagues have a number of limitations. Most notably, because they employ simple criteria, they fail to capture the complexity of ethical systems. They are allegedly unable, for example, to represent a priority ordering of different ethical claims within the same ethical system.[60] Since I have argued elsewhere that one can order the ethical claims of individuals and societies, and then use them to weight RCBA parameters, I shall not repeat those arguments here.[61] The main objection to them is that any sort of weighting scheme would be "at variance with the allocative principles by which the competitive economy is vindicated."[62]

However, government often makes policy decisions inconsistent with certain presuppositions underlying the competitive economy. Whenever government takes account of an externality such as pollution and imposes restrictive taxes or outright prohibitions, it is clearly making decisions inconsistent with particular presuppositions underlying a purely competitive economy. Indeed, if it did not, then grave harm, such as pollution-induced deaths, could occur. Also, it is well known that economists "correct" their (competitive) market parameters for risks, costs, and benefits.

Another classic objection to the use of any weighting scheme in RCBA is that weightings ought to be left to politicians and the democratic process and not taken over by economists.[63] On the contrary, although economists and ethicists might help to formulate lexicographic rules and to weight RCBA parameters in accordance with these rules,[64] they need only be responsible for helping to formulate a number of alternative, ethically weighted analyses. The public and policymakers would decide among the alternative RCBAs. Indeed, one reason why this proposed weighting scheme would not lend itself to control by experts, who have no business dictating policy in a democracy, is that it calls for preparation of alternative RCBAs, each with different ethical weights.[65] This amounts to employing an adversary means of policy analysis (see the next chapter).

Use of Alternative Risk Analyses and Evaluations

Weighting QRAs and RCBAs so as to reflect different methodological, ethical, and social preferences, however, is valuable only to the degree that one is able to see how alternative evaluative assumptions generate different risk-assessment conclusions. In other words, weighting schemes are valuable as *sensitivity analyses*. They make it possible to observe the effects of *different* assumptions on the *same* hazard assessment. Therefore, several risk analyses ought to be done for any single societal or environmental threat, and each of these analyses should contain different methodological assumptions.

One reason for mandating that several alternative hazard assessments be done is that successful decisionmaking depends in part on knowing all the relevant facts and seeing all sides of a given "story." It is more likely that all sides to a story will be revealed if different groups conduct hazard analyses.[66] Moreover, the public deserves a role in the *process* of determining rational risk choices, if the locus of public decisionmaking ought to be with the people, rather than merely with scientific experts. Public control and consumer consent can hardly be obtained if only one risk evaluation, controlled merely by scientific experts, is performed. Also, because all risks are both perceived and value laden,[67] and because all hazard evaluations employ judgmental strategies, some of which are highly questionable,[68] there are no value-free risk assessments. Consequently, hazard analysis, especially risk *evaluation*, is highly politicized and therefore should be accomplished in a political and legal arena, so that all persons affected by a given risk will receive equal consideration.

Only if the naive positivists were correct in their views about risk would it make sense to perform only one hazard evaluation.[69] Since they are not correct, assessors ought to perform alternative evaluations, so as to spell out some of the controversial social and political dimensions of risk policy.[70] In the account that I have been defending, increasing the degree of analytic sophistication is not sufficient for resolving risk conflicts. Policymakers must rely on procedural and democratic, rather than merely scientific, methods of evaluating and managing risk.[71]

Purely scientific methods of risk evaluation are inadequate because there are numerous uncertainties in hazard assessment. Scientists generally are unable to evaluate long-term environmental changes, in part because of the complexity of ecological science.[72] Likewise, epidemiological aspects of risk analysis are often problematic owing to factors such as lack of exposure data, small sample size, recall bias, chance variation, long latency periods, and control selection. Exposure assessments are often uncertain because of synergistic effects, reliance on average doses, and dependence on particular mathematical models that oversimplify the actual situation. Dose-response assessment is uncertain because of the unreliability of particular experimental conditions, the difficulty of estimating whether there is a threshold, incorporation of background hazard rates, and extrapolation from observed doses.[73] Because of these uncertainties, assessors fill gaps in information with inference and judgment. Because they do so, it is important to perform several different analyses of the same risk.[74] Moreover, because the various institutions performing assessments often seize upon whatever data and value judgments aid their cause,[75] it is not wise to rely only on one study. In fact, a variety of government policy groups has already recognized the importance of doing alternative assessments.[76]

Use of Weighted Expert Opinions

Another methodological device for improving hazard evaluation is to weight expert opinions. This procedure amounts to giving more credence to experts whose risk estimates (probabilities) have been vindicated by past predictive success. It is a way to exercise probabilistic control over expert opinions and to make them more objective. Weighting such opinions would reveal whether a hazard assessor (who provides a subjective probability for some accident or failure rate) is "well calibrated." (A subjective probability assessor can be said to be well calibrated if, for every probability value r in the class of all events to which the assessor assigns subjective probability r, the relative frequency with which these events occur is equal to r.[77]) The primary justification for checking the "calibration" of risk assessors is that use of scientific methodology requires testing problem solutions. Not to test them is to reduce science to ideology or metaphysics.[78]

Admittedly, obtaining empirical control of subjective probability assessments is very difficult in the practice of risk analysis. The very reason for resorting to the use of such subjective estimates, based on degrees of belief of experts, is that actual accident frequencies, for example, cannot be determined in any uncontroversially objective way. As was already mentioned, the accidents for which there are no objective probability estimates are typically those involving new technologies. Recognizing this, risk assessors have used subjective probabilities, based on expert opinion, since about 1975. Decision theorists have used them since the 1950s.

It is difficult both to arrive at subjective probabilities and to calibrate them because the numerical values in question are often very small; for example, the per-reactor-year (subjective) probability of a nuclear core melt, as was mentioned earlier in the volume, is 1 in 17,000.[79] For such subjective probabilities, calibration is ruled out; it would take too many years to test the frequency of actual core melts. However, there are many subjective probabilities that go into the calculation of the likelihood of a core melt, and weighting expert opinions in risk assessment may be possible if we are able to use these other, lower-level subjective probabilities. It is also extremely important to do so, because there is a wide divergence of opinion among experts as to their actual values. In the famous WASH-1400 study of nuclear reactor safety, for example, thirty experts were asked to estimate failure probabilities for sixty components. These estimates included, for instance, the rupture probability of a high-quality steel pipe of diameter greater than three inches, per section-hour. The average spread over the sixty components was 167,820. (The spread of these thirty expert opinions, for a given component, is the ratio of the largest to the smallest estimate.) In the same study, another disturbing fact was that the probability estimates of the thirty experts were not independent; if an expert was a pessimist with respect to one component, he tended to be a pessimist with respect to other components as well.[80]

Recently, a group of hazard assessors in the Netherlands used empirical *frequencies* obtained from a study done by Oak Ridge National Laboratories to calibrate some of the more testable subjective *probabilities* used in WASH-1400, one of the best and most renowned risk assessments ever accomplished.[81] Obtained as part of an evaluation of operating experience at nuclear installations, the frequencies were of various types of mishaps involving nuclear reactor subsystems. The Oak Ridge study used operating experience to determine the failure probabilities for seven such subsystems (including loss-of-coolant accidents, auxiliary feedwater-system failures, high-pressure injection failures, long-term core-cooling failures, and automatic depressurization-system failures for both pressurized and boiling water reactors). Amazingly, *all* the values from operating experience fell *outside* the 90 percent confidence bands in the WASH-1400 study. However, there is only a subjective probability of 10 percent that the true value should fall outside these bands. Therefore, if the authors' subjective probabilities were well calibrated, we should expect that approximately 10 percent of the true values would lie outside their respective bands. The fact that all the quantities fall outside these bands means that WASH-1400, allegedly the best risk assessment, is very poorly calibrated. It also exhibits a number of flaws, including an overconfidence bias.[82]

One can calibrate subjective probabilities and thus correct, in part, for these biases in probability estimates.[83] There is extensive psychometric literature on calibrating probability estimates,[84] as well as long-term meteorological experience with calibration techniques. National Weather Service forecasters have been expressing their predictions in probabilistic form since 1965, and numerous analysts have collected and evaluated weather data for predictive accuracy.[85] Nearly all these analyses show excellent calibration. Even more important, calibration has improved weather forecasts since the probabilistic forecasts were introduced.[86]

In response to these arguments for calibrating probability assessors, at least two objections are likely. One is that calibration does not guarantee reliable risk decisions. Admittedly not, but this is not an insurmountable problem, since no process can ensure that it will lead to the right decisions. We cannot command *results* (since that would require having a crystal ball), but we can command *methods*. Hence, our responsiblities in decisionmaking must focus primarily on methods, not on results.[87]

Another objection to calibrating experts is that there is no firm relationship between assessors' performance on the smaller probability estimates, used for checking calibration, and on the larger ones. In probability estimates of a nuclear core melt in particular, there are no good checks or controls for the larger estimates. This objection fails, however, because policymakers ought to try to calibrate expert opinion, in part because it is apparently so often wrong, in part because meteorologists have been successful in doing so, and in part because the consequences of failure to calibrate could be catastropic (e.g., 145,000 people killed in a nuclear core melt).[88]

Given these reasons to calibrate, the key question is how to go about doing it in the best way. The best calibration data we have are the many observed frequencies whose calculated probabilities together comprise larger probabilities (such as those for core melt). Although these lesser figures are not exactly the same as the core-melt probability, they are a *necessary* part of obtaining the larger probabilities and are hence better than no data. To argue against using a second-best check on expert opinion, merely because it is not as good as the best check (knowing the actual frequency), is unrealistic, since knowledge of frequencies is in principle unavailable. If it were available, one would not be relying on expert opinion in the first place.

How Scientific Proceduralism Guarantees Objectivity

All these methodological suggestions (calibration, alternative assessments, ethical weights) for improving risk evaluation and hazard management are predicated on two principles, both defended earlier in this volume. One principle is that assessors ought to give up both the rigid, naive-positivist assumption that experts' risk estimates are completely value free and the erroneous relativist assumption that risk assessment is not objective in any sense. It is objective, in at least the three senses discussed in Chapter Three. The second principle is that contemporary hazard evaluation needs to become more democratic, more open to control by the public, and more responsive to *procedural* accounts of rational risk behavior.

We must now show how to safeguard scientific rationality and objectivity, even though risk-evaluation methods need to take account of democratic, ethical, political, and procedural factors, factors allegedly not capable of being handled in purely rational and narrowly objective ways. The procedural account of hazard evaluation (outlined in Chapter Three) presupposes that rationality and objectivity ultimately require an appeal to particular cases as similar to other cases believed to be correct, just as legal reasoning requires. Aristotle recognized that there are no explicit rules for such judgments, but that inexplicit ones guide moral reasoning. These inexplicit rules or judgments rely on the ability of a group of people, similarly brought up, to see certain cases as like others. This recognition of cases is also what Wittgensteinians are disposed to believe about all instances of human learning. At the final level of risk evaluation, after subjecting the assessment to the tests of predictive and explanatory power and to the rigors of debate over alternative assessments, there can be no specific algorithms to safeguard objectivity, no infinite regress of rules. Ultimately, even rules must give way, not to further appeals to specific (risk-evaluation or risk-assessment) rules, as the naive positivists presuppose, but to a shared appreciation of similarities.[89]

As such, this Popperian and Wittgensteinian account (scientific proceduralism) anchors objectivity to (1) *criticisms* made by the scientific and lay community likely to be affected by risk judgments and (2) *empirical control* over expert opinion (obtained by pursuing the goal of explanatory power, tested by prediction; by calibrating probability assessors; and by performing sensitivity analyses). The criticisms would help to protect the procedural and democratic aspects of risk evaluation, and the empirical control would help to safeguard its predictive and scientific components—that is, its rationality and objectivity.

This account of scientific objectivity is premised on the assumption that open, critical, and methodologically pluralistic approaches to hazard analysis and evaluation (via alternative studies, sensitivity analyses, calibration, and ethical and methodological weighting schemes) can in principle reveal the theoretical, linguistic, and cultural invariants of reality, much as a plurality of experimental perspectives reveals the true invariants of quantum mechanical systems.[90] In the view that I am suggesting, the relevant variance principles applicable to hazard analysis, and especially evaluation, dictate that risk behavior is rational and objective if it survives scrutiny and criticism by different, well-calibrated communities of theory holders, each with different transformations or ethical assessments of the same hazard.[91]

In this view, the risk assessments that we ought to call "rational" are those that have been subjected to systematic critical inquiry regarding explanatory and predictive power, as Popper proposed for science. Risk evaluations that we ought to call "rational" are likewise those that have been subjected to systematic, democratic, and procedural constraints.[92] But systematic, critical inquiry requires a plurality of techniques: sensitivity analyses, calibration, alternative assessments, and so on. According to the epistemology outlined here, what characterizes science-related activities, such as hazard analysis, is that they are susceptible to empirical control. They are evaluated, in part, on the basis of explanatory power and predictive successes. The salient features of science and related activities such as risk assessment are thus empirical and predictive control, criticism of one's own perspectives, and recognition that there are alternative perspectives and methods. Indeed, if objectivity has anything to do with invariance under different theoretical perspectives,[93] then scientists and risk assessors ought to be strongly committed to retaining only those beliefs that survive critical scrutiny. Such a notion of objectivity, however, suggests that the ultimate requirement for improved risk assessment is a whole new theory of rationality, one that is critical, procedural, populist, egalitarian, and democratic, as well as objective, scientific, and controlled in part by prediction and calibration. It requires, in other words, an epistemology in which *what* we ought to *believe* about risk analysis is bootstrapped onto *how* we ought to *act*.[94] For example, we ought to act in ways that recognize due-process rights, give equal consideration to the interests of all persons, and so on.

Objections to Scientific Proceduralism

Scientific proceduralists recognize that the positivists and the cultural relativists are correct in certain respects. The positivists are correct in believing that there are at least general empirical criteria for scientific rationality and objectivity (for example, checking the calibration of risk assessors), and that *reason* ought to alter scientific practice and hazard analysis. The cultural relativists are correct in believing that, for most useful methodological value judgments, scientific rationality is largely a function of specific situations. Hence, scientific practice and actual risk evaluations ought to alter reason.

In Chapter Three, I argued for a multilevel notion of scientific rationality and distinguished among principles or goals, procedures, and actual scientific practice. The explication begun in that chapter rests on the insight that scientific rationality and objectivity are more *universal* than the cultural relativists claim and more *complex* than the naive positivists appear to believe. This very complexity, however, gives scientific proceduralism the ability to answer some of the main charges likely to be directed against either naturalistic accounts of science[95] or against naive positivism.[96]

Against the specific position (scientific proceduralism) outlined here and in Chapter Three, there are at least seven main objections, all of which I believe can be answered: (1) Risk evaluation does not need the alleged improvements (ethical weights, calibration, alternative analyses) mandated by scientific proceduralism, because industry and the market are already accomplishing many of these reforms. (2) To say that there are stable rules or goals of science or risk evaluation and assessment (e.g., "Calibrate expert assessors") presupposes a *realist* view of science. (3) Since this account provides a *normative* view of scientific rationality and objectivity and is committed to some stable, universal goals of hazard analysis (e.g., using accident frequency to check estimated risk probabilities), it appears to be a *positivistic* account. (4) Since I define 'scientific objectivity,' in part, in terms of the criticism and debate of the scientific community, there appears to be no great difference between my view and that of Shapere and Feyerabend. (5) This account of scientific objectivity is "too thin." (6) The proposed goal of science, explanatory power tested by prediction, as achieved through sensitivity analyses and calibration, provides a trivial view of norms in science; as Hempel suggests, goals are "imprecise constraints on scientific theory choice."[97] (7) Alternatively, the goal of science proposed in this account is impossible to meet, because it would require predictive power for probability estimates. The first objection has been expressed by a number of industry risk assessors; the second and third objections have been formulated by Miami philosopher Harvey Siegel, the fourth by Notre Dame philosopher Gary Gutting, and the fifth and seventh by Notre Dame philosopher Phil Quinn. The sixth objection is suggested by one of Hempel's criticisms of Kuhn.[98]

Responses to These Objections

Although space limitations prevent a full answer to these seven objections, I shall briefly sketch the arguments that, if presented in full, would respond to them. First, it is false to say both that risk evaluation does not need the improvements (alternative assessments, ethical and methodological weights, calibration of subjective probabilities) I have suggested, and that industry and the market are already accomplishing these reforms. This objection is the classical industry response: it can keep its own house in order; it does not need government regulations or mandated improvements in risk analysis. Current facts, however, indicate that both these responses are doubtful.

Alternative assessments are necessary, for example, because the public is forced either to accept whatever studies are provided by industry or government or to pay for its own assessments. Since we have already argued that industry risk analyses are often biased,[99] and since no laws or regulations provide for funding alternative assessments, there is a need for obtaining an alternative, nonindustry point of view, a government-funded alternative assessment. As one prominent assessor puts it: Unlike environmental impact assessment, risk assessment "frequently functions as a mere arcane expert process. . . . [It] often lacks procedures for public involvement in the design and critique of an analysis."[100]

There is also an unmet need for placing ethical and evaluative weights on the risk evaluations, so that members of the affected public can choose how to evaluate risks they face. Such weighting is not typically performed, as the discussion earlier in the chapter showed. Because it is not, risk evaluations often exhibit only one type of ethical norms, those of utilitarianism. They ignore considerations of equity and the needs of particular individuals, and they define "acceptable risk" in ways that are unacceptable to numerous potential risk victims, such as workers. All potential risk victims have rights to free, informed consent and to help evaluate risks by means other than utilitarianism and economic efficiency.[101]

Likewise, there is an unmet need to calibrate all probabilistic risk assessments, both because government does not require such calibration and because there is no guarantee that it will be accomplished without such a requirement. If industry and government were eager to calibrate risk assessors and to revise subjective probabilities on the basis of observed frequencies, then existing U.S. risk studies would already have been corrected. Instead, we had to wait for the Dutch to prove the unreliability of the nuclear risk probabilities specified in some U.S. assessments.[102] Industry and government risk assessors have not kept their houses in order; to do so, they need a calibration requirement.

As for the second objection, scientific proceduralism entails no commitment for or against realism. My presupposing that there are general rules of risk assessment (e.g., involving calibration) does not commit me one way or the other regarding realism, since many of the entities (probabilities) having explanatory power may have only hypothetical or heuristic status. Moreover, since I am pursuing an externalist position on scientific rationality, it is reasonable to argue *that* there is some universal, stable goal of science (explanatory and predictive power), without arguing *why* this stability is the case.[103]

Third, there are at least two reasons why this account does not fall victim to any of the flaws of naive positivism. For one thing, it is not committed to purely a priori *rules* of scientific method. The methodological *goals* (e.g., calibration, explanatory and predictive power, sensitivity analyses) defended here underdetermine (fail to prescribe) all *specific* methodological *rules*. This is because the specific rules need to be dictated in part by particular methodological value judgments and the given risk situation.

Fourth, the fact that some rules need to be dictated in part by the particular situation does not mean that my account of scientific objectivity is no different from that of relativists such as Shapere and Feyerabend. Scientific proceduralism is objective in at least the senses outlined in Chapter Three: its ability to withstand criticism, its ability to change on the basis of new facts and probabilities, and its ability to explain and predict both risks and human responses to them.

This notion of scientific objectivity (scientific proceduralism) is not too thin, because it presupposes a notion of scientific rationality dependent in part upon empirical measures, such as calibration and predictive power. Moreover, any stronger definition of scientific objectivity seems likely to fail, either because it might beg the realism question, or because it might presuppose knowledge we do not have. Because every situation in science is different, it is virtually impossible to specify completely, ahead of time, what an *objective* representation of some particular risk-assessment situation might be. Despite this impossibility, the methodological goals outlined in this chapter (e.g., testing explanatory and predictive power, performing alternative assessments, conducting sensitivity analyses) do not provide merely a trivial account of norms in applied science and risk assessment, as the sixth objection suggests. For one thing, they presuppose a rejection of most common versions of naturalism. They also provide an answer to the basic question mentioned in Chapter Three: "Are there *general principles* that account for the rationality of science and risk assessment?"

The goals (like calibration) proposed here likewise are not too strong, in requiring predictive power of risk estimates. Without such goals, one could not *test* a scientific explanation or risk estimate, and one's assessments would be relativistic. Without testing, one could not secure the empirical foundations of science and hazard evaluation or assessment.[104]

Conclusion

Since this chapter, like the rest of the volume, is primarily *philosophical*, it is not meant to provide a precise account of the methodological solutions to problems of risk assessment and evaluation. These details need to be given by statisticians, epidemiologists, psychometricians, economists, and risk assessors. Precise methodological techniques (e.g., for calibration) need to be spelled out, and more examples and more developed arguments need to be provided, in order to support responses to these and òther objections to the position of scientific proceduralism. The argument sketches given thus far, however, suggest some of the ways that we might attempt to improve our methods of risk assessment and evaluation, so as to address the problems outlined earlier in this volume. The argument sketches also show that the notions of scientific rationality and objectivity outlined here deserve further investigation; indeed, much of the epistemological work for this account of hazard evaluation remains to be done. Let's move to the next chapter to examine some of the ways in which we might improve risk management.

Chapter Twelve

Risk Management
Procedural Reforms

During any period in almost any region of the country, one hears reports of local opposition, either to siting unwanted technological facilities or to bearing the environmental risks associated with already existing developments. Names like "Love Canal," "Three Mile Island," "Baltimore Canyon," "Minimata Bay," and "Seabrook" have been etched in our newspapers, our courtrooms, and our fears.

According to some experts, many cases of public opposition to risk are created by self-serving attitudes and unrealistic public expectations, rather than by catastrophic accidents and accelerating cancer rates. These other controversies, they say, represent instances of an "inverse" tragedy of the commons. In Garrett Hardin's "tragedy of the commons," people misuse a "public good," such as clean water, simply because it is free.[1] The "inverse tragedy of the commons," however, occurs when people avoid their share of responsibility for "public bads" that fulfill essential public purposes—for example, when people try to avoid having airports, roads, or toxic waste facilities near them.[2] One of the main tasks of hazard assessment and management is to know when a risk imposition represents a tragedy of the commons, which ought to be avoided, and when it is an inverse tragedy of the commons, which ought to be accepted responsibly.

One reason why it is difficult for the public to determine whether a given risk ought to be accepted or rejected is that evaluators often do not make an adequate case for accepting the risks that are likely to be imposed. They do not do so, in large part, because their hazard analyses often have two main deficiencies. They typically employ a number of questionable evaluative assumptions,[3] epistemological strategies,[4] whose effect on policy is to disenfranchise the public, the potential risk victims.

197

This chapter will provide a brief overview of several procedural ways to improve hazard evaluation and risk management. It will argue that, in order to address some of the problems with equity of risk distribution, compensation, consent, and scientific uncertainty, we need to investigate ways to reform statutes dealing with societal hazards. Moreover, because of the deepening loss of public trust in most institutions, carefully structured citizen participation and negotiation in making risk decisions are the only ways to legitimate them to the public. Policy decisions, especially when they affect health and safety, stand little chance of being accepted, for example, if government and industry continue their current DAD (decide, announce, defend) strategy for siting hazardous facilities and imposing environmental risks. Such a procedure relies on an unstructured, industry-controlled siting process and limited citizen input; the result is that public controversy is virtually guaranteed.[5]

This chapter will not provide specific solutions to problems of managing environmental risks, since these and the arguments for them are best accomplished by specialists in fields such as environmental law and welfare economics. Nevertheless, the general proposals provided in subsequent sections of this chapter should be enough to establish the prima facie plausibility of several proposals: (1) to achieve statutory reform in areas such as toxic torts; (2) to aim at obtaining free, informed consent from all potential risk victims and to include them in decisionmaking about societal hazards; (3) to provide *ex ante* and *ex post* compensation for imposed public risks; (4) to negate all liability limits that protect risky technologies at the expense of the public; and (5) to begin to resolve environmental controversies through negotiation and adversary assessment. Since the distribution of public risks has rarely been fair and has often fallen disproportionately on the powerless and the poor,[6] the proposals aim at a more equitable distribution both of societal hazards and of decisionmaking power regarding them.

Statutory Reform and Risk Management

One of the central ways of reforming risk management is to amend the laws governing environmental or technological hazards, such as the laws governing toxic torts. Statutory improvements in this area are difficult to achieve, as Chapters Four, Five, and Eleven outlined, because there are numerous scientific uncertainties in identifying, estimating, and evaluating societal risks. As a result, litigation related to public safety and health is complex, time consuming, and expensive; toxic tort plaintiffs, for example, must explain how and why a hazard caused a specific condition, even though any of numerous factors could be the real cause. Moreover, the relative contribution of genetic make-up, life-style, and the external environment to human health is difficult to determine. As a consequence, industry and government repeatedly invoke scientific uncertainty as grounds for the failure to reform laws dealing with hazardous substances.[7]

The reason why these legal mechanisms need to be amended is clear if one considers the costs that environmental hazards force on citizens. Public risks typically impose at least three burdens on society: *costs of harm* (e.g., medical bills, pain); *costs of avoiding harm* (e.g., pollution-control mechanisms); and *transaction costs* incurred in allocating harm (e.g., litigation, negotiation, and regulation). If there were no trans-action costs, then society could allocate resources so as to minimize the sum of the costs of harm and avoiding harm. In such a situation, the party imposing risk or damage would have to strike a bargain with the (potential) victims, a bargain leading to an economically efficient out-come.[8] Since our society has transaction costs, however, its laws of lia-bility often lead to economically inefficient outcomes. Also, they favor those who impose risks, rather than those who are their victims, because those who cause risk and harm are not penalized until the damage to victims exceeds their (the victims') transaction costs (e.g., exceeds the costs of the victims' initiating litigation). The net effect is that high transaction costs (often caused by scientific uncertainty) beset attempts to establish liability; trying to prove that someone who imposes a risk (e.g., a toxic dump licensee) is at fault may thus encourage inefficient and unethical allocations of resources.[9] The purpose of this chapter is to examine some efficient and ethical ways of managing societal risks.

To understand the typical difficulties of using the existing legal sys-tem to protect victims of environmental risks, we can consider several characteristics of toxic tort litigation. (1) Often victims do not know how or that they have been put at risk or harmed by toxic substances. (2) The time, effort, and expense of bringing suit often exceed the probable damage award, as is evidenced by the small number of com-pensation awards in cases of occupational cancer. (3) Toxics victims typically have less information than the defendants, usually companies producing hazardous chemicals. These difficulties are illustrated by the fact that, even outside the tort system, workers' compensation boards are typically unable to determine causes of harm. The boards face the same difficulties as plaintiffs within the legal system when they attempt to establish causes of harm despite limited information. In the state of Colorado, for example, less than two plaintiffs per year typically receive workers' compensation awards for occupational cancer, even though epidemiologists estimate that many times this number deserve such benefits.[10]

Private damage actions for victims of environmental hazards are also problematic because many states have statutes of limitations, and most courts require victims to prove that the defendant's behavior *unreasonably* exposed them to a hazardous substance. Most courts also require victims to quantify costs and benefits in attempting to establish fault, to show causation of harm, and to prove that it was "worth" avoiding in a cost-benefit sense. Proving causation is especially difficult, as was noted in Chapter Four, because studies of environmental harm address causality in terms of statistical probabilities, a form of evidence typically not recognized by courts as establishing causation. Even if victims can establish the agent causing their harm, they are still faced with showing which of many exposures or risks are responsible for the actual harm— for example, whether they were exposed to chlorine in the drinking water or in the workplace.[11]

Regulation by administrative agencies, such as the Environmental Protection Agency or the Nuclear Regulatory Commission, likewise often fails to protect victims of environmental hazards, just as do private damage actions. This is in part because, in most such cases, the risk perpetrator is considered innocent until proved guilty. Hence, even though the government possesses resources enabling it to overcome many scientific uncertainties associated with environmental risks and harms, well-financed business interests often dominate regulatory decisions. The Atomic Energy Commission, for example, was so embroiled in lawsuits, because of its catering to vested interests, that it had to be abolished in 1974.[12]

Another difficulty with regulatory agencies is that statutory control is often fragmented among several different commissions. For example, five different federal agencies are responsible for the regulation of toxic chemicals. This duplication of effort creates confusion, inefficiency, and inconsistency. Regulatory agencies also typically have insufficient funds to bring lawsuits in more than 1 or 2 percent of the cases that ought to be tried. Since current regulations do not encourage private-sector research on avoiding unknown environmental dangers, only the government is able to determine the responsibilities of those who impose risks on the public. Moreover, rulemaking is time consuming and cumbersome, so that, even if something is known to cause a risk, it takes more than a century to establish regulatory standards for it.[13]

Statutory Reform, Transaction Costs, and Liability Limits

Given the problems associated with private damage actions and administrative regulations, it is safe to conclude that government and law have not been as effective as they might have been in reducing the societal costs of environmental and technological risks. If we are to manage public hazards more effectively, then we must try to devise ways to reduce the *transaction costs* associated with allocating risks and harms. One way would be to ensure that litigation is not a prerequisite to recovering damages for injury. Compensation could be financed from a fund administered by a government agency. Risk imposers, such as producers of toxic wastes, could contribute to the fund on the basis of the amount and severity of the risk and harm they generate.

A second way to reduce transaction costs would be to ease the *evidentiary burdens* placed on victims in cases where litigation is unavoidable. The Food and Drug Administration, for example, requires pharmaceutical manufacturers to demonstrate that a new drug is safe before it allows sale, instead of presupposing that the manufacturer is innocent until proved guilty. Another example of easing the evidentiary burden on victims occurred in a celebrated case involving the drug diethylstilbestrol (DES). The plaintiff could not identify which of several defendants caused her injury (produced the DES responsible for her cancer), yet one of them did so. Hence, the court eased the victim's evidentiary burden and shifted the burden of proof to the defendants, who were required to show that they were not responsible for the harm. Part of the reason for this shift was that the court determined that defendants are better able to bear the cost of injury caused by a defective product, and that holding manufacturers liable will provide an incentive for product safety.[14]

A third way to reduce transaction costs would be to force people to pay for the risks or harms they impose on society, by internalizing the externalities or social costs of employing hazardous technologies. One way to internalize social costs would be to impose strict liability on those who have caused societal risk or harm. New Jersey's Major Hazardous Waste Facilities Siting Act, for example, contains a provision for strict liability. (I shall argue later for full, but not strict, liability.) The act permits compensation for damage without proof of negligence. By using liability to internalize externalities, the New Jersey law helps the *price* (paid by consumers) of the goods generated by a risky technology to reflect the overall social *costs* (such as injuries or pollution) of producing them. Internalizing social costs or externalities also motivates those in charge of a hazardous technology to avoid causing damages whenever the total social costs of such harm exceed the damage-avoidance costs. This deterrence mechanism is weakened whenever the market price of a commodity does not reflect its total social costs, because the expenses of bringing suit deter many potential victims or plaintiffs. The more the market and the regulatory system reflect true damages and expenses, the greater the incentive to lower the social costs of risk. And the greater this incentive, the better mechanism we have for deterring environmental harm and for allocating risks in an equitable and efficient manner.[15]

A Model Statute for Reform

Deterring harm and distributing risks equitably and efficiently requires that any statutory reform address a fundamental difficulty: inexpensive avoidance of technological and environmental hazards depends largely on liability. Assessing liability individually, however, militates against swift and efficient cost allocations by imposing the transaction costs of litigation. Statutory reform, therefore, must attempt to reduce the transaction costs of liability assignments.

In the model statute he defends, Trauberman provides several ways to avoid some of the high transaction costs. He proposes that anyone suffering from a particular environmentally induced disease, who was exposed to a certain substance (such as asbestos) at a specified level and for a particular duration, should be presumed to have established that the substance caused the disease. Such a presumption, already used in settling black lung cases, would help reduce both the plaintiff's burden of proof and the current problem, for example, of having over 10,000 plaintiffs all filing suit for asbestos-related injuries. It would avoid a situation in which courts, plaintiffs, and defendants spend time and money dealing with identical issues.[16]

A second way to avoid costly and frequent adjudication of similar issues would be to use more class-action suits in cases of pollution- and environment-related injuries and risks. Admittedly, the courts have not welcomed class actions for such cases, reasoning that the issues of exposure, liability, and damages are too diverse for class-action treatment.[17] Nevertheless, it might be possible, with suitable statutory reforms, to certify class actions for environmentally caused risks or harms, and yet to use separate proceedings to determine liability and damages, as happened in the Agent Orange and DES cases.[18] Statutory reforms could also require that those persons whose conduct involves the societal or occupational imposition of environmental risk be held liable without fault for the full damages that they cause. Although their liability could be limited to the extent that other factors are judged to have caused the risk or injury in question, requirements of full liability and liability without fault would invalidate several current statutes concerning environmental and technological hazards. One such statute is the Price-Anderson Act, which reduces most of the liability of commercial nuclear licensees.[19]

The main rationale for negating such liability limits was argued earlier in Chapters Eight and Nine: the necessity to internalize all costs, to ensure the rights of all citizens to compensation for harms or risks imposed on them, to achieve equity, and to provide an incentive for safe management of hazardous technologies. The obvious objection to negating liability limits, however, is that full liability, without fault, might shut down new technologies and discourage inventions and scientific progress.[20]

The response to this objection has already been spelled out earlier in the volume. Economic or technological efficiency does not justify limiting citizens' rights; it does not promote equality; it does not always increase employment; and it places disproportionate environmental risks on the poor. As Thomson puts it, if *A*'s action will cause *B* harm, then *A* must buy this right from *B*, provided the harm is a compensable one.[21] Since the harms associated with liability limits are often incompensable (for example, death from a nuclear core melt), it is even more imperative that the liability not be limited. Apart from these *ethical* considerations, however, there are *practical* reasons for believing that full liability, without fault, need not discourage inventions and scientific progress. In cases where inventions and technologies were essential to the public good, government (taxpayers) could provide the requisite insurance. Insurance pools, financed by individual investors, could also cover possible liabilities associated with innovative and risky technologies. Of course, if no private insurers will take the financial risks associated with a dangerous technology, then this might suggest that such uninsured risks should not be borne by taxpayers either.[22] Even if no one were willing to insure risky technologies, they still could be tested and developed in situations where potential victims gave informed consent and signed releases, much as is done in cases of medical experimentation. Hence, statutory reform, requiring full liability, need not impede technological progress.[23]

Statutory reform also needs to address the problem of apportioning damages for environmental or technology-related injury, especially when there are multiple independent causes of harm. One response to cases with several defendants would be to reject the established causation rule and to substitute a system of joint and several liability for the entire amount of damages, as was done in the landmark case of *Landers v. East Texas Salt Water Disposal Company*.[24] Another possible solution to the problem of determining the responsible defendant, in cases of multiple causation of harm, would be to assign liability based on market share. As was mentioned earlier, the California Supreme Court did exactly this in *Sindell v. Abbott Laboratories*. In this landmark case, the plaintiff was a young woman injured by prenatal exposure to DES. She was unable to identify which of several companies had made the DES taken by her mother, and so she brought suit against the major manufacturers of the drug. Since six or seven companies, out of two to three hundred, were responsible for 90 percent of the market, the court devised a theory of "market share liability." Under this theory, each defendant was held liable for its share of the DES market unless it could show that its product was *not* responsible for the injuries to the plaintiff.[25] In other cases involving multiple defendants, however, any one of a variety of possible rules might be adopted for allocation of liability.[26] My point is not to argue for any particular rules, since their applicability is, in part, situation specific. Rather, the point is that there appear to be grounds for new allocation rules.[27]

The *Sindell* court, for example, in invoking a new rule based on market share, explicitly endorsed apportioning liability based on *risk* (rather than certain *harm*) attributable to each defendant when causation is uncertain. Hence, the *Sindell* case shows that plaintiffs need not prove that the defendants caused the harm.[28] The case therefore provides a foundation for significant reform of tort law, a reform applicable to sophisticated harms that cannot be traced to any particular producer. The rationale for forcing manufacturers who impose such sophisticated harms to bear the costs of injury caused by their products is that these costs "can be insured by the manufacturer and distributed among the public as a cost of doing business."[29]

Assignment of liability on the basis of *risk* (or probability of causing harm), of course, might cause some innocent defendants to be held responsible. On the other hand, such an assignment would avoid a worse consequence of apportioning *full* liability to one defendant merely because that defendant was a substantial factor in the cause of harm. To avoid such a consequence, some situations might require a rule that a plaintiff could obtain proportional recovery based on the risk of harm created by each defendant, if the court determines that it is unreasonable to expect the injured individual to ascertain the precise cause of harm among multiple factors.[30] Another way to reduce transaction costs borne by victims of environmental harm would be to provide that substances posing a reasonable likelihood of causing certain risks or diseases be administratively designated as "hazardous." Such a designation would diminish the burden of proof for the plaintiff or victim and would allow *statistical* evidence (of a causal relationship between exposure to a hazard and some disease) to be admissible in private liability actions.[31]

Statutory reform could also provide for liberal *time* periods for filing claims and actions for recovery. Nonrestrictive statutes of limitations are especially important in reducing transaction costs, because of the long latency periods for diseases such as cancer (thirty years in some instances) and because of the scientific uncertainty often associated with the early stages of harmful, technology-related actions.[32] Likewise, allowing recovery within a liberal *geographical* jurisdiction would also reduce transaction costs. Countries that are exporters of pesticides banned in their own nation, for example, could be held responsible for damages incurred when the chemicals are shipped abroad. Such a law would respond, in part, to some of the criticisms (in Chapter Ten) of the "isolationist strategy." For example, any country accepting international guidelines for production, testing, notification, and labeling of pesticides could be held liable for injuries caused by any product it exports in violation of the guidelines.[33]

To improve the efficiency and equity of market transactions regarding environmental risks and injuries, a new statute could encourage companies, both here and abroad, to provide the public with information about various hazards. For example, the new statute could reduce the aggregate liability of risk imposers if there has been timely notification of potential victims.[34]

Even with such statutory reforms, however, persons exposed to environmentally induced risks and injuries would likely still bear substantial transaction costs. In large part, this is because they would not always be able to identify the substance responsible for their risk or injury, or because the responsible person might not have the financial resources to satisfy claims against him. For these reasons, perhaps litigation should not be a prerequisite to every recovery or risk avoidance. Perhaps a new statute should call for the establishment of an environmental-risk fund that would act as a secondary source of compensation.

Such a fund, mentioned earlier in the chapter, could be financed (1) by industries responsible for environmental and technological hazards (just as Superfund, created to compensate for damages posed by toxic wastes, is financed by a tax on the oil and chemical industries), (2) by "degree-of-hazard taxes," and (3) by public contributions. Those who impose societal risks could be required to make payments to the fund that reflect the magnitude of the compensable harm that they cause. A substantial percentage of the hazard fee, for example, could come from a tax on the manufacturers of tobacco products, asbestos, and other substances that are well-recognized causes of risk and harm. The fund could provide injured individuals, or persons put at risk, with the option of either filing a claim against the fund or bringing a direct action against whoever caused the harm or risk.[35]

Federal statutory precedents for such a fund already exist—for example, under Superfund, the Deepwater Port Act, the Surface Mining Control and Reclamation Act, the Black Lung Benefits Reform Act, and the Outer Continental Shelf Lands Act.[36] However, since the purpose of this chapter is not to provide specific solutions to problems of environmental risk, I shall not discuss further details of this proposed fund. Details about the fund and arguments for it are best presented by specialists in fields such as environmental law and welfare economics. My purpose is merely to establish the prima facie plausibility of several proposals for dealing with the risk problems discussed earlier in this volume. It is also to establish the fact that, if we ignore these problems and fail to modify existing legal mechanisms for dealing with environmental hazards, then society will continue to impose disproportionate costs on those who are most ignorant of, and most vulnerable to, environmental risks.

Informed Consent and Citizen Negotiation

To some extent, protecting those who are most vulnerable to environmental risks (e.g., those who work with toxic chemicals) is a matter of guaranteeing free, informed consent to public and occupational hazards. Statutory reform, as suggested in the previous section, would provide some of these guarantees, since the new statute would include provisions for limiting liability as an incentive for full disclosure of possible hazards.[37] To achieve *explicit* consent, however, we need actual citizen participation in *negotiating* solutions for problems of risk. Moreover, once one realizes that the process of hazard assessment and management is highly value laden and politicized,[38] then negotiation (rather than mere expert decisionmaking) becomes a virtual necessity for ensuring free, informed consent in situations of controversial risk.

If the purpose of negotiation is to defuse highly politicized risk situations, so as to ensure citizens' free, informed consent, such negotiation will need to presuppose that several conditions have been met. First, ideally the bargaining parties ought to be roughly equal in political and economic power, in order to ensure free, procedurally just transactions. This means that both citizens and industry groups need equal funding so as to obtain access to experts, attorneys, and staff assistance. In particular, citizens need to have access to taxpayer monies to fund their negotiations, so that they will not be disadvantaged in any way in bargaining with industry. Second, alternative points of view, different evaluative assumptions, and a variety of risk methodologies ought to be considered. Government would fund the completion of alternative assessments and hazard-management plans,[39] ensuring that all sides to a controversy were represented and well informed. Consideration of alternative positions would be a *requirement* of democratic decisionmaking, rather than a *luxury* accessible only to those who are financially able to participate in administrative hearings or legal appeals. Third, the negotiation process would be controlled not by a regulatory agency with discretionary powers, but by a group of citizens and experts with no conflict of interest in the matter under consideration. Hence, unlike regulatory and administrative decisionmaking, the negotiation would be less likely to be co-opted by unrealistic environmentalists or by unscrupulous industry representives.

On the ethical side, negotiation is often able to equalize the costs and benefits associated with hazards, even though risk imposition usually results in dissociation of costs and benefits. For example, one group of citizens might receive the *benefits* associated with using toxic chemicals, while another set of persons (those who live near the manufacturing plant) might bear the *costs* associated with the hazard. Those affected by risky technologies or environmental actions realize that, without compensation or consent, it is not fair for them to bear the dangers of some activity that benefits the whole society.[40] Economists recognize that such inequities cause a misallocation of resources and a misrepresentation of policy choices.[41] Typically, however, the social costs of this inequitable risk distribution are not taken into account in decisionmaking. Most economists generally consider these social costs or inequities only as "externalities," external to the market processes with which economics is concerned.

As was argued in Chapter Eleven, however, justice demands that we internalize these social costs, perhaps by using risk-cost-benefit analysis that is weighted to reflect considerations of fairness and distributive equity. One way to assess which of a variety of weighting schemes and alternative hazard analyses to employ is to use negotiation among citizens, the relevant industry officials, and policymakers. Since it enables local citizens and potential victims to have a voice in hazard assessment and management, negotiation can be an important means of avoiding antipopulist biases (Chapter Two), reductionist approaches to risk (Chapter Three), as well as the expert-judgment (Chapter Six), probabilistic (Chapter Seven), and producer (Chapter Nine) strategies criticized earlier.

On the *practical* side, negotiation is one way of avoiding costly, time-consuming litigation, as well as local opposition to environmental risks. Many observers are convinced that a hazardous facility, for example, cannot be sited over a community's objections. A local group has many tactics that enable it to get its way: delay, litigation, political pressure, legislative exemption, and gubernatorial override.[42] Individuals and communities have a keen sense of the inequities that result when one group bears the risks and another reaps the benefits. Consequently, they often subscribe to the NIMBY ("not in my backyard") syndrome and, at least in the siting of toxic waste dumps, have usually succeeded in averting the hazard.[43]

One practical way of avoiding the NIMBY syndrome is to negotiate with citizens, in order to determine what actions, if any, might be required to mitigate hazards, to promote safety, or to compensate them for accepting a given societal risk.[44] Project siting generally fails when the government agency attempts to "sell" its premade decision, when it redefines public concerns, when it sponsors no prior public education efforts, and when it merely holds citizen hearings. It is often successful when the agency seeks data on the public's attitudes and needs, when it holds small-group meetings, when it sponsors prior education efforts, and when it exchanges written information with citizens or environmental groups.[45]

Admittedly, proponents of a risky technology might try to avoid negotiation with the public on the grounds that it is costly and time consuming. They might prefer instead to have state governments preempt local decisionmaking. Using legal and regulatory devices to avoid negotiation, impact mitigation, and compensation, however, is ultimately not a *practical* way to move toward siting a hazardous facility or imposing a particular risk on a community. It is impractical because, apart from what the law and the courts say, opponents of an environmental risk (unless they are won over through mitigation and negotiation) can resort to civil disobedience to accomplish their goals. In Michigan, for example, as was already mentioned, local residents put nails and tacks on the highways in order to prevent the state from burying cattle contaminated by polybrominated biphenyls. In other jurisdictions, residents have threatened to dynamite existing risky facilities; they have also taken public officials hostage to vent their anger over policymaking processes. All this suggests that, apart from the ethical and legal questions involved, people will resort to extreme measures to avoid a risk if they believe that their lives or their homes are threatened. In such a situation, only negotiation, and neither law nor force, stands a chance of winning them over.[46]

Since there are a number of different models of risk participation and negotiation within local communities, I shall attempt neither to defend a particular one here nor to answer various questions that might arise in a given model (e.g., who should negotiate and how they should be chosen).[47] Those tasks are better left to policymakers, arbitrators, and sociologists.[48] To illustrate the prima facie plausibility of negotiation, I need only sketch several cases in which it has been used successfully. Environmental sociologist Elizabeth Peelle, a member of the research staff of Oak Ridge National Laboratory, has done much of the pioneer work on successful citizen negotiation in the face of risky technologies and undesirable environmental impacts. (Both she and I count citizen participation as "successful" if it leads to risk decisions acceptable to the informed, affected public.)

By analyzing some of the successful instances of public participation, Peelle was able to determine their common characteristics and hence to suggest criteria for successful negotiation regarding hazards. In one recent essay, she examined a local citizens' task force for a monitored retrievable storage (MRS) facility for nuclear waste in Tennessee; a two-state citizen forum for a Hanford, Washington, nuclear waste project; two local citizens' task forces for toxic waste in North Carolina; and local and state participation in a hazardous waste project in New Mexico. Her conclusion was that, when citizens participate in risk assessment and management and are involved in the decision process, they are more likely to accept the ultimate actions taken in such projects. When decisionmaking includes negotiation, say Peelle and numerous other experts, the possibilities increase for legitimated, stable public policy.[49]

In another essay, Peelle detailed three impact-mitigation plans, two for nuclear power plants in Tennessee and Washington State and one for a coal-burning facility in Wyoming.[50] Faced with opposition from the local county (which refused to rezone the site) and from the Sierra Club and the Farm Bureau (which contested the application for a license to generate electricity), the three utilities (involved in each case) negotiated with citizens on how to promote safety, how to reduce hazards, and how to compensate them for their potential risks and losses.[51] The Wyoming plan, the most comprehensive of the three discussed by Peelle, provided compensation for the risk by guaranteeing the community funds for mental health and social services, recreation, roads, and law enforcement. All three of the risk-abatement plans included some hazard-monitoring provisions.[52] Their annual costs, for each utility, are between $125,000 and $900,000. In each case, the utility gives direct payments to the community, either in the form of prepayments of future taxes or by means of loan guarantees and grants.[53] Because they internalize (through compensation) many of the social costs associated with the imposition of societal risks, and because they are the result of negotiation with the relevant local communities, these impact plans have had at least three desirable effects. They have lessened uncertainties concerning facility siting; they have reduced delays resulting from unresolved issues, such as safety; and, through monitoring impacts, they have provided an urgently needed data base for improving future impact predictions and risk-mitigation plans. The three cases also illustrate a difference in risk-mitigation approaches: the Tennessee and Wyoming plans offer *compensation* for undesirable impacts, such as inequitable risk distributions,[54] whereas the Washington plan provides fiscal *incentives* for acceptance of a risky technology.[55]

Perhaps the best argument for use of incentives and compensation is that offering them to citizens within the context of negotiation is far superior to most existing means of deciding whether to impose environmental risks on communities. Public participation within these existing means of decisionmaking often takes the form of *intervention*; that is, environmentalists and consumer activists appear, speak, and hence "intervene" on behalf of their cause, before the agency (for instance, the Nuclear Regulatory Commission) that has the power to impose a risk on a community. The process is fatally flawed, however, both because intervenor status is hard to obtain and because, once granted, the status does not guarantee adequate funds for representing the point of view of citizens or environmentalists. Moreover, intervenors are typically limited to raising only those issues which the law already requires the agency to take into account, even though other questions may be far more important. In the siting of nuclear power plants, for example, intervenors are not allowed to challenge the adequacy of current standards for radiological protection, but only to question whether a given utility or plant will meet those standards.[56] Consequently, much of the intervenor money that is raised must be used on expensive lawyers who know how to fight highly stylized battles. All this is to little purpose if intervenors cannot challenge the decisionmaking process itself, a procedure that typically disenfranchises the public. Furthermore, decisions to site risky facilities are often a fait accompli by the time an intervenor has his say. Hence, intervenors are often viewed more as obstructionists than as representatives of any reasonable point of view. Use of *incentives* within a framework of negotiation, however, provides a possible opportunity for consensus building rather than mere obstructionism.[57]

For incentives to be successful in increasing public support for risky environmental projects, social scientists have determined that at least three prerequisites must be satisfied: (1) The incentives must guarantee that local criteria for public health and safety will be met; (2) they must provide some measure of local control; and (3) they must legitimate negotiations as a viable mechanism for building consensus and resolving disputes.[58]

Of all three prerequisites, the first is probably the most important. Some of the most successful negotiations have taken place only when developers and manufacturers of risky technologies adopted a comprehensive, integrated program of *risk reduction*. For example, the New Jersey Hazardous Waste Facilities Siting Commission has been successful because it has sought not merely to obtain financial compensation for local citizens but also to reduce the pollutant stream, recycle waste, and detoxify it.[59]

The theory behind such negotiation and risk reduction is that, through the use of neutral or self-interested negotiators, all interested parties can come together, identify areas of common interest, and reach a solution that is fair and mutually acceptable. Besides New Jersey, Massachusetts, Rhode Island, and Wisconsin are also pioneers in negotiating to resolve local risk disputes. All three states preempt local land-use controls, but then throw the owner and operator of the proposed or existing hazardous facility into a procedure that combines methods of mediation, negotiation, and arbitration. (*Mediation* or conciliation, as defined by many policymakers, is a subset of *negotiation*; an approach adapted from labor relations, it uses negotiation to identify the real cooperative actions possible for interdependent parties whose interests and objectives differ. Negotiation typically involves two parties, whereas mediation is handled by a third party seeking to resolve a two-party dispute; neither procedure is ordinarily binding. In *arbitration*, however, two parties sit before a judge, and the outcome is binding.[60]) Some of the elements recognized by social scientists as necessary for successful negotiation include the following: identifying all the relevant parties early in the process, involving affected persons in early information development and evaluation, providing incentives to residents to accept a risk, taking steps to see that all citizens are informed about the proposed action or facility, and ensuring that the benefits exceed the costs for the host communities.[61]

Objections to Negotiation

Admittedly, there are a number of objections to negotiation, both on the part of the affected communities and on the side of the developers or industries seeking to gain risk acceptance from a local group. The *industry* objections typically have to do with the political or economic costs likely to be required because of negotiation. These objections can often be answered by some of the practical considerations advanced in the previous section.[62] A common *citizen* objection to negotiation is that it allows situations in which persons trade health and safety for financial rewards. Citizens claim that negotiation either allows developers and risk imposers to "bribe" local groups, or else it condones communities that want to "extort" compensation from developers.[63]

It is important to put these deficiencies in perspective, however, in order to see why negotiation is needed. Negotiation has all the same flaws that democracy generally has: when citizens are allowed to make choices, they often make mistakes. The only way to guarantee that citizens will never make mistakes is never to allow them to make decisions. Admittedly, neither negotiation nor democracy is a *sufficient condition* for avoiding mistakes such as trading lives for dollars. Negotiation with potential victims is needed, however, because it is a *necessary condition* for avoiding error in hazard evaluation and management; only those affected have the right to consent to the imposition of risk.

The argument throughout this chapter and the preceding ones has *not* been that negotiation has no problems. It has been a much more modest claim: that negotiation (in which citizens have a voice) is preferable to hazard assessment and risk management in which they have no role. The argument here is that negotiation is preferable to the typical current procedure for siting facilities, a strategy that often disenfranchises the public. Negotiation is preferable to preemption of local control, both because citizens have a right to exercise control over activities that threaten their well-being, and because preemption does not silence the risk aversion, civil disobedience, and opposition of persons who believe that their lives are in danger. Only rarely, for example, can states prevent a town from amending the maximum weight limit on a bridge it maintains in order to restrict truck access to a proposed risky facility. Instead, attempted preemption of local control of risks may simply force opponents to turn either to guerrilla tactics of opposition or to costly and time-consuming litigation. Or, as happened in Massachusetts, preemption could force local governments to use their power in state governments to defeat or prevent the operation of a preemption statute.[64]

Another response to criticisms of negotiation is to admit that many hazardous facilities (such as nuclear power plants) probably ought not to be sited, because there are less dangerous ways of providing the same benefits to society, and that any potential risk victims can be bribed if they are somehow disadvantaged in or by society. That they are vulnerable to "bribes," and that they seek to remedy this disadvantage by trading safety for financial rewards, however, is not the fault of negotiation.[65] It is not the fault of negotiation if people in Oregon, for example, vote for a copper smelter because they need the jobs, even though the smelter threatens the lives and safety of all citizens.[66] It is not the fault of negotiation that any humans are so desperate that they feel forced into such choices. As Judith Jarvis Thomson puts it, "It is morally indecent that anyone in a moderately well-off society should be faced with such a choice . . . a choice between starving on the one hand, and running a risk of an incompensable harm on the other."[67] It is the fault of society, not negotiation, if people face such choices. When societal balances of power are inequitable, risk negotiation will reflect those institutional imbalances. It cannot correct injustices already sanctioned by society. Risk negotiation can merely enfranchise those who heretofore had little voice in what hazards were imposed on them. Hence, negotiation does as much as can be expected of it.

Even though negotiation cannot necessarily prevent "bribing" the consumer, there is some evidence that such bribes are unlikely. Environmental sociologists report that noneconomic incentives—such as independent monitoring of risks and hazards, rights to information, and access to decisionmaking—are just as important to most citizens who are negotiating about local environmental risks as are financial incentives.[68] If these findings are correct, then "buying off" citizens, in exchange for lessened safety requirements, may not be very likely.[69]

Moreover, apart from whether negotiation leads to what some might view as "bribes," consumer sovereignty and democracy require that people be allowed to make their own choices.[70] As one philosopher put it, so long as they do not harm others, people ought to be allowed to choose cigarettes and saccharin; they ought to be able to choose nuclear fission and big cars, instead of being forced to accept solar power and small cars.[71] As Mill and many other liberals recognized, people must be allowed to run whatever risks they wish, so long as the consequences affect only them.[72]

To oppose negotiation because it can lead to faulty citizen decisions or to consumers' being co-opted is unrealistic and narrow-minded. It is unrealistic because a technological society cannot avoid all risks. It is narrow-minded because it refuses to recognize that, in a democracy, everyone must make trade-offs. Everyone must have a mutual willingness to share power, make compensatory arrangements, and negotiate regarding risks, whether he is a developer of hazardous technology or a potential citizen victim. Not to negotiate would be to bring society to

a technological standstill. The objection that not everything is negoti-
able, that not everything has its price, is, of course, correct. Not all
harms are compensable. That is why the federal government sets minimum environmental standards. Negotiation, however, is not proposed
as a way to attain less stringent standards. Nothing in this proposal for
negotiation suggests that we should abandon uniform environmental
standards or that we should allow some communities to be victimized
by less stringent risk requirements simply because a given industry has
"bought them off." Rather, negotiation presupposes that a whole system
of uniform environmental standards is in place, that such standards
define what level of risk is minimally acceptable, and that people cannot
"negotiate" their way to less stringent requirements. All that negotiation
does it to compensate potential risk victims, give them more control
over hazards, and reduce their risks.

Negotiation (with concomitant compensation or incentives) is at least
in principle plausible because it is consistent with the legal and philosophical bases of neoclassical economic theory and the compensating
wage differential. According to the theory behind the wage differential,
persons can accept occupational risks provided that they are compensated and give free, informed consent to the risk imposition.[73] Hence,
if negotiation is wrong because it presupposes that compensation can
sometimes be justifiable, then so are the foundations of much of our
law, philosophy, and economics.

Another objection to negotiation is that it involves the unrealistic
presupposition that all persons ought to give free, informed consent
before risks are imposed on them. If society always adhered to this
presupposition, an objector might claim, then many useful programs,
such as public vaccination, could not be implemented.[74] Arguing for
universal vaccination, however, is not a case of attempting to justify
denial of free, informed consent on grounds of expediency. The justification instead is the common good. Presumable, people do not have
the right to refuse vaccination, because, if many do so, they will put
other citizens at risk. Their right to free, informed consent ends where
other persons' rights to bodily security and freedom from injury begin.
Therefore, consent to technological risk is not analogous to consent to
vaccination. Instead, the limits on one's free consent to vaccination are
analogous, for example, to the limits on one's free consent to having
a firearm taken away when it is likely that one will use it wrongly.[75]
And if so, then neither the vaccination nor the firearm case presents
a counterexample to the requirement for consent.

Yet another objection to the negotiation scheme, with its attendant
presuppositions about compensation, is that it would be both impossible

and impractical to compensate persons for all the technological and environmental risks that they face.[76] But even though compensation may be "impractical," to dismiss it as such when there are ethical grounds for requiring it may be unjust, unless the impracticality is so great as to approach impossibility. If rights to compensation were recognized only when it was convenient to do so, there would be no rights. It would not work, for example, to tell a victim of racial discrimination that compensation is impractical, since presumably she has a *right* to compensation. Likewise, it will not do to tell a potential victim of environmental risk that compensation and, therefore, her rights are "impractical."

Compensation is also not impractical, as earlier arguments in this chapter have suggested, if it is the one way of negotiating community acceptance of a societal risk. Moreover, although compensation is difficult, because there are many hazards, we can nevertheless begin negotiating about, and compensating for, the worst environmental risks. Finally, the practicality of compensation and negotiation is established by the fact that our courts and our city councils have already employed them effectively. Compensation has been used to achieve successful community projects, as the Wyoming, Tennessee, New York, and Washington cases (cited earlier in this chapter) illustrate. Hence, it is at least prima facie plausible to argue that we can simply extend the record of these successes by devising federal statutes for risk negotiation and compensation.

Adversary Assessment and Risk Management

Perhaps one of the most disturbing objections to the negotiation and compensation scheme outlined earlier is that it presupposes a benign and cooperative regulatory climate. Yet, if those who disagree about environmental risk will not cooperate, then negotiation will not work. As one legal expert puts it,

[F]irms are not likely to agree voluntarily to ambitious technology-forcing measures involving large capital outlays and substantial risks. Technology-forcing is a major aim of current regulatory statutes, and environmentalists would not abandon that objective willingly in consensus-based negotiations. . . . As long as great interests are at stake and the goals of the major actors are incompatible, which are common characteristics of environmental disputes, there is no reason to doubt that participants would manipulate negotiations and would pursue post-negotiation remedies whenever that behavior is privately advantageous.[77]

If either party to a negotiation sees that more is to be gained from formal legal proceedings or obstructionist tactics than from negotiation, that party will abandon negotiation. The only alternative then would be to use some sort of adversary proceeding. This proceeding would include many of the same guarantees already discussed (earlier in the chapter) in connection with negotiation: (1) It would involve funding citizens' groups, so as to ensure that all parties in the adversary process had equal bargaining power. (2) Consistent with the previous chapter, it would guarantee consideration of different hazard assessments and alternative points of view about risk imposition and management. Finally, (3) the process would be controlled by disinterested parties, not by a regulatory agency.

Since I have written at length elsewhere about adversary proceedings and the "public jury" as vehicles for resolving environmental controversies, I shall not repeat those arguments and objections here.[78] Instead, I shall merely sketch some of the main ideas involved in the notion of adversary assessment. Both scientists and laypeople would take part in adversary proceedings. The procedure would involve scientific experts presenting different technical positions, and social scientists and humanists arguing for alternative evaluative points of view. The final risk decision would be left to some democratic determination, probably a representative process, rather than to experts.

The precedent for adversary assessment of societal risks has been set by a number of citizen panels throughout the country. These are composed almost entirely of laypeople, not scientists, and many of them are responsible, for example, for the formulation and enforcement of scientific research guidelines.[79] City councils in Cambridge (Massachusetts), San Diego, and Ann Arbor, for instance, have taken a number of initiatives in forming such citizen boards. In Cambridge, the city council authorized its city manager to appoint a citizen review board to evaluate the safety procedures required by the U.S. National Institutes of Health (NIH) for recombinant DNA research. Both the city council and the city commissioner unanimously approved the recommendations of the citizen review board.[80]

Need for Procedural Reform of Risk Management

Adversary proceedings would provide several benefits over the current system of decisionmaking regarding societal risk. First, an adversary system would require that funding be given to all sides involved in a controversy. Second, the adversary proceedings would make consideration of alternative positions a requirement of democratic decisionmaking, rather than a luxury accessible only to those financially able to participate in administrative hearings or legal appeals. Third, unlike administrative and regulatory hearings, as well as negotiations, adversary procedures would be decisive. They would also be less likely to be co-opted by environmentalists or developers with vested interests, since they would not be dominated by a regulatory agency capable of exercising discretionary powers. Instead, they would be controlled by a group of citizens chosen because they had no apparent conflict of interest.

Admittedly, a few states and communities have had limited experience in using some of the procedural improvements in risk management suggested in this chapter (e.g., statutes requiring negotiation with, and compensation for, potential victims of societal risk). As a result, industry spokespersons have often alleged that these procedural reforms are not needed, or that they are already being accomplished. Both claims are false, as was argued in Chapter Eleven.

There are no federal statutes guaranteeing negotiation with, and compensation for, potential victims of all forms of societal risk. Currently, negotiation and compensation are not *rights* guaranteed by due process, but *privileges* accessible only to the moderately wealthy. In practice, these privileges are limited to those who are able to bear the transaction costs associated with adjudication through tort law. The whole point of this volume is that public consent to, and control over, risk evaluation and management are not the prerogatives of the rich, but the rights of all. They must therefore be protected by federal statute and administrative law, not subjected to the vagaries of circumstance.

Conclusion

Despite the alleged benefits of negotiation and adversary assessment, both procedures face many obstacles. For one thing, they are expensive (but perhaps not as expensive as the political unrest and loss of lives possibly resulting from erroneous societal decisions about environmental risk). Moreover, people may not be willing to pay the price, either for greater safety or for citizen negotiation. If they are not, they should not be forced to do so, as long as existing protections are equitably distributed.

Even if people would accept both negotiation and adversary assessment as vehicles for mitigating environmental risks, and even if they were willing to pay for them, however, there might still be objections. For one thing, I have not indicated specifically how negotiation and adversary assessment might work—for instance, who would take part in the process. Although I have addressed some of these particulars elsewhere,[81] most of them are better left to policymakers and social scientists. My purpose here has been to sketch some of the reasons why both negotiation and adversary assessment seem to be prima facie plausible.

Another possible objection to mitigating risks via negotiation and adversary assessment might be that reducing hazards is *technically unworkable*, allegedly because there are no economical, safe, feasible alternatives to existing risky technologies. If we decide to avoid use of commercial nuclear fission, for example, less risky energy options must be both developed and workable. Admittedly, all my remarks are predicated on the supposition that less risky technologies are both possible and economical. This supposition needs to be defended, on a case-by-case basis, for each environmental hazard. Obviously, there is no time to do so here, although such a defense conceivably could be given.[82]

Even without a defense of the thesis that less risky technologies are feasible, hazard evaluation could be more rational than it is. If the arguments in this volume are correct, we need to reform our methods, our statutes, our procedures, and (most important) our philosophies for making decisions about risks. On the *ethical* side, we need to recognize that persons have rights to compensation, to informed consent, and to due process; therefore, they have rights to negotiate about, or perhaps even prohibit, the hazards others wish to impose on them.

On the *epistemological* side, we need to recognize that risk evaluation and management are irreducibly political (normative), in much the same way that quantum mechanics is irreducibly statistical (nondeterministic). In physics, we have come to realize that quantum-mechanical measurements "interfere" with the state of the system being measured. In applied science and environmental policy, we have been slower to realize that the human components of societal risk evaluation cannot be removed, even though they "interfere" with positivistic measures of risk.

This book has been a first step in suggesting how we might adopt a more democratic and procedural account of rationality, so as to reflect the human dimensions of hazard assessment and evaluation. It has argued that the public is frequently rational in its risk evaluations and that, even when laypersons are wrong about risk, they often have the right to be wrong. Even, and especially, victims have choices.

Notes

Chapter One

1. L. S. Bacow and J. R. Milkey, "Overcoming Local Opposition to Hazardous Waste Facilities," and D. Morell, "Siting and the Politics of Equity," in *Resolving Locational Conflict*, ed. R. W. Lake (New Bruswick, N.J.: Center for Urban Policy Research, Rutgers University, 1987), pp. 163, 123.

2. Morell, "Siting," p. 119. See also S. Samuels, "The Arrogance of Intellectual Power," in *Phenotypic Variation in Populations*, ed. A. Woodhead, M. Bender, and R. Leonard (New York: Plenum, 1988), pp. 113–120.

3. F. J. Popper, "LP/HC and LULU's [locally unacceptable land uses]: The Political Uses of Risk Analysis in Land-Use Planning," in Lake, *Resolving Locational Conflict*, p. 5.

4. A. D. Tarlock, "State versus Local Control of Hazardous Waste Facility Siting," in Lake, *Resolving Locational Conflict*, p. 138. See D. Cleverly et al., *Municipal Waste Combustion Study* (New York: Taylor and Francis, 1989).

5. T. Gladwin, "Patterns of Environmental Conflict over Industrial Facilities in the United States," in Lake, *Resolving Locational Conflict*, p. 16.

6. J. T. Matthews et al., *World Resources 1986* (New York: Basic Books, 1986), p. 110.

7. P. L. Joskow, "Commercial Impossibility, the Uranium Market, and the Westinghouse Case," *Journal of Legal Studies* 6, no. 1 (January 1977): 165. Information on the 1,000-plant prediction may be found in H. R. Price, "The Current Approach to Licensing Nuclear Power Plants," *Atomic Energy Law Journal* 15, no. 6 (Winter 1974): 230; L. M. Muntzing, "Standardization in Nuclear Power," *Atomic Energy Law Journal* 15, no. 3 (Spring 1973): 22. The later prediction is found in U.S. Department of Energy, *U.S. Commercial Nuclear Power* (Washington, D.C.: Government Printing Office, 1982), p. 37.

8. B. Cohen, "Risk Analyses of Buried Wastes," in *The Risk Assessment of Environmental and Human Health Hazards*, ed. D. J. Paustenbach (New York: Wiley, 1989), p. 575. See, for example, L. Clarke, *Acceptable Risk?* (Berkeley and

Los Angeles: University of California Press, 1989), p. 2. See also A. Weinberg, "Risk Assessment, Regulation, and the Limits," in Woodhead, *Phenotypic Variation*, pp. 121–128; D. Bazelon, "Risk and Responsibility," *Science* 205, no. 4403 (1979): 278; D. Braybrooke and P. Schotch, "Cost-Benefit Analysis under the Constraint of Meeting Needs," working paper, available from Braybrooke at Dalhousie University in Canada; B. Cohen and I. Lee, "A Catalog of Risks," *Health Physics* 36, no. 6 (1979): 707, 720; J. Gardenier, "Panel: Accident Risk Assessment," in Mitre Corporation, *Symposium/Workshop on Nuclear and Nonnuclear Energy Systems: Risk Assessment and Governmental Decision Making* (McLean, Va.: Mitre Corporation, 1979), pp. 399, 467; S. Gibson, "The Use of Quantitative Risk Criteria in Hazard Analysis," in *Risk-Benefit Methodology and Application*, ed. D. Okrent (Los Angeles: School of Engineering and Applied Science, UCLA, 1975), p. 599; W. Hafele, "Energy," in *Science, Technology, and the Human Prospect*, ed. C. Starr and P. Ritterbush (Elmsford, N.Y.: Pergamon Press, 1979), p. 139; L. Lave, "Discussion," in Mitre Corp., *Symposium*, pp. 484, 541; M. Maxey, "Managing Low-Level Radioactive Wastes," in *Low-Level Radioactive Waste Management*, ed. J. Watson (Williamsburg, Va.: Health Physics Society, 1979), pp. 410, 417; D. Okrent, "Panel," in Mitre Corp., *Symposium*, p. 663; C. Starr, "Benefit-Cost Studies in Sociotechnical Systems," in Committee on Public Engineering Policy, *Perspectives on Benefit-Risk Decision Making* (Washington, D.C.: National Academy of Engineering, 1972), pp. 26–27; C. Starr, R. Rudman, and C. Whipple, "Philosophical Basis for Risk Analysis," *Annual Review of Energy* 1 (1976): 636–637; C. Starr and C. Whipple, "Risks of Risk Decisions," *Science* 208, no. 4448 (6 June 1980): 1116; U.S. Nuclear Regulatory Commission, *Reactor Safety Study: An Assessment of Accident Risks in U.S. Commercial Nuclear Power Plants*, NUREG 95/104, WASH-1400 (Washington, D.C.: Government Printing Office, 1975), p. 37.

9. For important social accounts of risk aversion, see note 8 and Samuels, "Arrogance of Intellectual Power"; see also M. Douglas and A. Wildavsky, *Risk and Culture* (Berkeley and Los Angeles: University of California Press, 1982).

10. For discussion of the three stages, see note 16. Some authors place "risk evaluation" in the risk-management category. See J. K. Marquis and G. Siek, "Sensitive Populations and Risk Assessment in Environmental Policymaking," in *Hazard Assessment of Chemicals*, ed. J. Saxena (New York: Taylor and Francis, 1989), p. 21. See also H. M. Seip and A. Heiberg, "Pilot Study of Risk Management of Chemicals in the Environment," in Saxena, *Hazard Assessment*, pp. 5–9.

11. C. Gersuny, *Work Hazards and Industrial Conflicts* (Hanover, N.H.: University Press of New England, 1981), p. 20. S. Levine (see "Panel: Use of Risk Assessment," in Mitre Corp., *Symposium*, p. 634) is one who believes that risk assessment is a science. For a history of risk assessment, see D. Paustenbach, "Introduction," in Paustenbach, *Risk Assessment*, pp. 1–24.

12. R. Carson, *Silent Spring* (Boston: Houghton Mifflin, 1962).

13. D. H. Meadows et al., *The Limits to Growth* (New York: Universe Books, 1972).

14. I. G. Barbour, *Technology, Environment, and Human Values* (New York: Praeger, 1980), p. 188. For more information about NEPA, see P. Wathern, "An Introductory Guide to EIA," in *Environmental Impact Assessment*, ed. P. Wathern (London: Unwin Hyman, 1988), pp. 3–30.

15. E. Eckholm, "Unhealthy Jobs," *Environment* 19, no. 6 (August/September 1977): 29. See Samuels, "Arrogance of Intellectual Power."

16. 1982 Risk Analysis Research and Demonstration Act, H. R. 6159, 97th Cong., 2d sess., sec. 2, lines 19–24.

17. See K. S. Shrader-Frechette, *Risk Analysis and Scientific Method* (Boston: Reidel, 1985), pp. 56–57.

18. For a general overview of risk assessment, see R. N. Andrews, "Environmental Impact Assessment and Risk Assessment," in Wathern, *Environmental Impact Assessment*, pp. 85–97. See also Shrader-Frechette, *Risk Analysis*.

19. P. Feyerabend, "Marxist Fairytales from Australia," *Inquiry* 20, nos. 2–3 (1977): 379. Admittedly, however, it is difficult to characterize this position, since Feyerabend is not always consistent. For example, in " 'Science': The Myth and Its Role in Society" (*Inquiry* 18, no. 2 [1975]: 167–181), Feyerabend distinguishes himself, an epistemological anarchist, from skeptics; skeptics, he says, "regard every view as equally good or equally bad," whereas the anarchist will defend many views, although he has no "everlasting loyalty" to any position (p. 177). Yet, in the same essay, Feyerabend claims that "there is no special [scientific] method that guarantees success or makes it probable" (p. 169). But if one method does not make success more probable than another, then every view is equally good or bad. And if every view is equally good or bad, then Feyerabend is a skeptic, as he has defined skepticism, and he is inconsistent with his own avowed position. For a definition of epistemological anarchism, see Feyerabend, "Science," p. 177. For a discussion of a related position, see R. Ennis, "Research in Philosophy of Science," in *Current Research in Philosophy of Science*, ed. P. Asquith and H. Kyburg (East Lansing, Mich.: Philosophy of Science Association, 1979), pp. 138–170.

20. As Hempel points out, Carnap believed that criteria for theory appraisal are immutable (C. Hempel, "Scientific Rationality," in *Rationality Today*, ed. T. Geraets [Ottawa: University of Ottawa Press, 1979], p. 55). See R. Carnap, *The Logical Structure of the World and Pseudoproblems in Philosophy* (Berkeley and Los Angeles: University of California Press, 1967); *Logical Foundations of Probability* (Chicago: University of Chicago Press, 1950); and *The Continuum of Inductive Methods* (Chicago: University of Chicago Press, 1952). See also M. Schlick, "The Foundations of Knowledge," in *Logical Positivism*, ed. A. J. Ayer (New York: Free Press, 1959), pp. 209–227. Israel Scheffler (in *Science and Subjectivity* [Indianapolis: Hackett, 1982], p. 9), discussing positivism and twentieth-century "scientific philosophies," claims: "Underlying historical changes of theory, there

is, moreover, a constancy of logic and method which unifies each scientific age with that which preceded it and with that which is yet to follow." See also H. Siegel, "What Is the Question concerning the Rationality of Science?" *Philosophy of Science* 52, no. 1 (December 1985): 517–532. Thomas Kuhn claims that "there can be no criterion" for paradigm choice (*The Structure of Scientific Revolutions* [Chicago: University of Chicago Press, 1970], p. 169). As a normative naturalist, Kuhn believes that "values deployed in theory choice are fixed once and for all" (*The Essential Tension* [Chicago: University of Chicago Press, 1977], p. 335). He reaffirms the claim that, although there are no rules that determine theory choice, as the positivists and logical empiricists thought, there are values that influence it (*Essential Tension*, p. 331).

21. We change our goals in response to theories, and vice versa; and we change our goals in response to methods, and vice versa. See D. Shapere, *Reason and the Search for Knowledge* (Dordrecht: Reidel, 1984), pp. xxi–xxx, 207–237, 254, 340, 350–351. See also R. N. Giere, *Explaining Science* (Chicago: University of Chicago Press, 1988).

Paul Feyerabend (in *Against Method* [London: New Left Books, 1975], pp. 205–209), perhaps incorrectly, calls Imre Lakatos a "naturalist." For a good analysis of naturalism, see E. McMullin, "The Shaping of Scientific Rationality," 11 April 1986, unpublished manuscript, p. 9. For a definition of naturalism, see R. Giere, "Philosophy of Science Naturalized," *Philosophy of Science* 52, no. 3 (September 1985): 347. For a longer account of naturalism, see Shapere, *Reason*. McMullin claims that Laudan, in his later work, is also a naturalist. See previous note and L. Laudan, *Science and Values* (Berkeley and Los Angeles: University of California Press, 1984). In *Progress and Its Problems* (Berkeley and Los Angeles: University of California Press, 1977), p. 129, Laudan writes: "such components of rational appraisal as criteria of explanation, . . . scientific testing, . . . inductive inference and the like have undergone enormous transformations." Hence, Laudan claims that rules and criteria of scientific method are not constant (p. 129), although on the next page (130), he suggests that the "*general* nature of rationality" might remain constant, perhaps in the sense of affirming whatever leads to progress or problem-solving ability.

Part of the difficulty with terming various philosophers "naturalists" is that there is often no precise usage of the term. Two senses of naturalism, however, appear to be common. According to one sense, naturalism is the view "according to which methodology is an empirical science in its turn—a study of the behavior of scientists" (K. Popper, *The Logic of Scientific Discovery* [New York: Harper, 1959], p. 52). Popper claims that the early Carnap and the early Wittgenstein were naturalists in this sense (p. 53). According to another sense, naturalism is the view that, although there are no universal, stable, a priori rules in science, norms or goals nonetheless guide science (see Kuhn, *Essential Tension*, p. 331).

22. See note 21 for references to some of these "middle" positions. I defend my own position, midway between naturalism and logical empiricism, in K. S.

Shrader-Frechette, "Scientific Method and the Objectivity of Epistemic Value Judgments," in J. Fenstad et al. (eds.), *Logic, Methodology, and Philosophy of Science* (New York: Elsevier, 1989).

23. See Chapter Three for a discussion of relativism.

24. Douglas and Wildavsky, *Risk and Culture*, pp. 186, 188.

25. Ibid., p. 9.

26. Despite the fact that their explicit claims amount to relativism, Douglas and Wildavsky say that they have conducted their investigations in an objective manner and therefore are not relativists. For an analysis of why their position amounts to relativism, and how they err in denying that they are relativists, see Chapter Three (the section headed "Can Any Risk Evaluation Be Justified?"), later in this volume.

27. For examples of assessors who hold this view, see C. Whipple, "Nonpessimistic Risk Assessment," and R. Golden and N. Karch, "Assessment of a Waste Site Contaminated with Chromium," in Paustenbach, *Risk Assessment*, pp. 1111, 595.

28. See Chapter Three and associated notes for a statement of the naive positivists' view and a criticism of it.

29. See note 30.

30. For a discussion of a number of methodological and ethical problems associated with hazard assessment (especially difficulties related to occupational risk and the alleged compensating wage differential; use of probabilistic risk thresholds; quantification of various hazard parameters; use of benefit-cost analysis; and evaluation of regional equity issues), see Shrader-Frechette, *Risk Analysis*; and *Science Policy, Ethics, and Economic Methodology* (Boston: Reidel, 1985). For discussion of the flawed assessment strategy of ignoring allegedly imperceptible risks, see K. Shrader-Frechette, "Parfit and Mistakes in Moral Mathematics," *Ethics* 96, no. 4 (October 1987): 50–60; and "Parfit, Risk Assessment, and Imperceptible Effects," *Public Affairs Quarterly* 2, no. 4 (October 1988): 75–96. For more about methodological and ethical problems in hazard assessment, see Andrews, "Environmental Impact Assessment."

31. For substantiation of this point, see A. Tversky and D. Kahneman, "Belief in the Law of Small Numbers," and D. Kahneman and A. Tversky, "Subjective Probability," in *Judgment under Uncertainty*, ed. D. Kahneman, P. Slovic, and A. Tversky (Cambridge, England: Cambridge University Press, 1982).

Chapter Two

1. A. M. Brandt, "AIDS in Historical Perspective," in *AIDS: Ethics and Public Policy*, ed. C. Pierce and D. Van De Veer (Belmont, Calif.: Wadsworth, 1988), p. 33.

2. Brandt, "AIDS in Historical Perspective," p. 32.

3. R. C. Johnston, "AIDS and Otherness," in *AIDS*, ed. J. Griggs (New York: United Hospital Fund of New York, 1987), p. 79.

4. C. Pierce and D. Van De Veer, "General Introduction," in Pierce and Van De Veer, *AIDS*, p. 11.

5. C. Holden, "Fear of Nuclear Power: A Phobia?" *Science* 226, no. 4676 (16 November 1984): 814–815.

6. T. Weiss, "Opening Statement," in U.S. Congress, *Federal Response to AIDS*, Hearings before a subcommittee of the Committee on Government Operations, House of Representatives, 98th Cong., 1st sess., 1–3 August 1983 (Washington, D.C.: Government Printing Office, 1983), p. 2.

7. J. Raloff, "Study Upgrades Radiation Risks to Humans," *Science News* 136, nos. 26–27 (23, 30 December 1989): 404.

8. K. Bobo, "Activists Say Chernobyl Can Happen Here," *Not Man Apart* 17, no. 3 (May–June 1987): 10–11. For government estimates of losses resulting from nuclear accidents, see K. S. Shrader-Frechette, *Nuclear Power and Public Policy* (Boston: Reidel, 1983), chap. 4, esp. pp. 78–81. According to Sheldon Novick (in *The Electric War* [San Francisco: Sierra Club, 1976], pp. 152–153), "A million-kilowatt nuclear power plant, after a year of operation, contains ten billion curies of radioactive material, enough (if properly distributed) to kill every one in the U.S." Moreover, much of this radiation remains lethal (capable of ionization causing death, cancer, and genetic damage) for hundreds of thousands of years. In WASH-740, the Brookhaven report, the (pronuclear) government arrived at conservative estimates for effects of a core melt and resultant releases of radioactivity. The report concluded that such an accident could lead to 45,000 immediate deaths, 100,000 injuries, innumerable cancers, contamination of an area the size of Pennsylvania, and up to $17 billion in property damage (see U.S. Atomic Energy Commission, *Theoretical Possibilities and Consequences of Major Accidents in Large Nuclear Power Plants*, WASH-740 [Washington, D.C.: Government Printing Office, 1957], and its update, R. J. Mulvihill et al., *Analysis of United States Power Reactor Accident Probability*, PRC R-695 [Los Angeles: Planning Research Corporation, 1965]). See also J. Elder, "Nuclear Torts: The Price-Anderson Act and the Potential for Uncompensated Injury," *New England Law Review* 11, no. 1 (Fall 1975): 127; T. Black, "Population Criteria of Oregon and the U.S. in the Siting of Nuclear Power Plants," *Environmental Law* 6, no. 3 (Spring 1976): 897; J. J. Berger, *Nuclear Power* (New York: Dell, 1977), p. 45.

9. For information on the latest Price-Anderson liability limit and citizens' arguments against it, see M. Silberman, "Risky Business: Congress Debates Nuclear Insurance," *Not Man Apart* 17, no. 3 (May–June 1987): 1. For the argument that the liability limit would not be needed unless catastrophic accidents were likely, see Shrader-Frechette, *Nuclear Power*, esp. pp. 78–81.

10. For further discussion of nuclear liability, see Chapter Six, section entitled "Removing Liability Limits."

11. D. D. Edwards, "NAS Reports on Pathogens in Poultry . . . and Pesticides in Food," *Science News* 131, no. 23 (6 June 1987): 361.

12. See the following articles by R. Monastersky: "Antarctic Ozone Reaches

Lowest Levels," *Science News* 132, no. 15 (10 October 1987): 230; "More Clues to the Mysterious Ozone Hole," *Science News* 132, no. 12 (19 September 1987): 182; "Flying into an Ozone Hole," *Science News* 132, no. 6 (8 August 1987): 95.

13. E. Efron, "Behind the Cancer Terror," *Reason* 16, no. 1 (May 1984): 23ff.; see also *The News Twisters* (Los Angeles: Nash, 1971) and *The Apocalyptics: Politics, Science, and the Big Cancer Lie* (New York: Simon and Schuster, 1984).

14. See, for example, C. Whipple, "Nonpessimistic Risk Assessment," in *The Risk Assessment of Environmental and Human Health Hazards*, ed. D. J. Paustenbach (New York: Wiley, 1989), p. 1116. Rasmussen is the main author of WASH-1400 (see U.S. Nuclear Regulatory Commission, *Reactor Safety Study: An Assessment of Accident Risks in U.S. Commercial Nuclear Power Plants*, NUREG-75/014, WASH-1400 [Washington, D.C.: Government Printing Office, 1975], p. 37). See also D. Braybrooke and P. Schotch, "Cost-Benefit Analysis under the Constraint of Meeting Needs," working paper, available from Braybrooke at Dalhousie University in Canada.

15. See, for example, A. Weinberg, "Risk Assessment, Regulation, and the Limits," in *Phenotypic Variation in Populations*, ed. A. Woodhead, M. Bender, and R. Leonard (New York: Plenum, 1988), pp. 121–128. See also B. Cohen, "Risk Analyses of Buried Wastes," in Paustenbach, *Risk Assessment*, p. 575; L. Lave, "Discussion," in Mitre Corporation, *Symposium/Workshop on Nuclear and Non-nuclear Energy Systems: Risk Assessment and Governmental Decision Making* (McLean, Va.: Mitre Corporation, 1979), pp. 484, 541; C. Starr and C. Whipple, "Risks of Risk Decisions," *Science* 208, no. 4448 (6 June 1980): 1116; D. Okrent, "Panel: Use of Risk Assessment," in Mitre Corp., *Symposium*, p. 663; D. Bazelon, "Risk and Responsibility," *Science* 205, no. 4403 (1979): 278; B. Cohen and I. Lee,"A Catalog of Risks," *Health Physics* 36, no. 6 (1979): 707; W. Hafele, "Energy," in *Science, Technology, and the Human Prospect*, ed. C. Starr and P. Ritterbush (Elmsford, N.Y.: Pergamon Press, 1979), p. 139; M. Maxey, "Managing Low-Level Radioactive Wastes," in *Low-Level Radioactive Waste Management*, ed. J. Watson (Williamsburg, Va.: Health Physics Society, 1979), pp. 410, 417; C. Starr, "Benefit-Cost Studies in Sociotechnical Systems," in Committee on Public Engineering Policy, *Perspectives on Benefit-Risk Decision Making* (Washington, D.C.: National Academy of Engineering, 1972), pp. 26–27.

For another example of risk assessors in the employ of industry, assessors who charge the public with being irrational, see S. Nealey, "Excessive Fear of Nuclear Technology," unpublished manuscript, Battelle Human Affairs Research Center, Seattle, 1987. For some of the dangers associated with labeling citizens "irrational," see P. M. Sandman, "Getting to Maybe," in *Resolving Locational Conflict*, ed. R. W. Lake (New Brunswick, N.J.: Center for Urban Policy Research, Rutgers University, 1987), p. 327. In this same regard, see B. Wynne, *Risk Management and Hazardous Waste* (New York: Springer-Verlag, 1987), pp. 10ff., 356ff.

16. Mary Douglas, as revealed in her *Risk Acceptability according to the Social Sciences* (New York: Russell Sage Foundation, 1985), pp. 5–18, is much less

critical of populist evaluations of risk that is Aaron Wildavsky, as revealed in his *Searching for Safety* (New Brunswick, N.J.: Transaction Books, 1988), pp. 59–76. See note 45.

17. M. Douglas and A. Wildavsky, *Risk and Culture* (Berkeley and Los Angeles: University of California Press, 1982), pp. 37–39, 80–81; F. Hoyle, *Energy or Extinction* (London: Heinemann, 1977); and J. H. Fremlin, *The Risks of Power Production* (London: Macmillan, 1985) make the same attacks on laypersons as does Weinberg, "Risk Assessment," p. 127. See notes 14, 16, and 19.

18. Douglas and Wildavsky, *Risk and Culture*, pp. 5–7, 167, 182, 198. See note 16. See also Efron, *Apocalyptics*, p. 14.

19. M. Thompson, "To Hell with the Turkeys!" in *Values at Risk*, ed. D. MacLean (Totowa, N.J.: Rowman and Allanheld, 1986), pp. 119–120. See also Efron, *Apocalyptics*, pp. 61, 30; Douglas and Wildavsky, *Risk and Culture*, p. 152; Wildavsky, *Searching for Safety*, pp. 206, 222.

20. Arguments 1, 3, and 5 are formulated by Weinberg, in "Risk Assessment," pp. 126–127. Arguments 3 and 5 are formulated by Whipple, in "Nonpessimistic Risk Assessment," pp. 1111–1117. Arguments 1, 2, and 4 can be found in Thompson, "Turkeys," pp. 119–120, 125, 130. Arguments 3 and 4 are specifically set forth by Wildavsky, in *Searching for Safety*, pp. 19–28. All five of these arguments are given by Efron, in *Apocalyptics*, pp. 25, 61, 129, 179; 42–43; 61; 30; 25, 58; and also by Douglas and Wildavsky, in *Risk and Culture*; Hoyle, in *Energy or Extinction*; Fremlin, in *Risks of Power Production*; Cohen and Lee, in "Catalog of Risks"; Maxey, in "Managing Low-Level Radioactive Wastes"; and L. Rothschild, in "Risk," *Atom* 268 (1979): 30–35.

21. See note 46.

22. See note 16.

23. See note 18.

24. In addition to admitting their prejudice in favor of centrists, Douglas and Wildavsky (in *Risk and Culture*) also accuse sectarians of "cultural bias" (pp. 5–7), of being persons who "can never be satisfied" (p. 184), and of needing to "blame" others (p. 190). These ad hominem charges also suggest the truth of their admission that they are biased against sectarians or laypersons. Some writers likewise claim that Douglas and Wildavsky, for example, may not be *attacking the risk aversion* of sectarians but *explaining the risk-selection strategies* of all three groups (market, hierarchy, sect), just as Thompson (in "Turkeys," p. 132), for example, attempts to explain risk selection in terms of entrepreneurs, autonomists, and sectists. If they were merely explaining, however, they would not need to admit their bias. (See the section headed "Are All Risk Evaluators Biased?" in Chapter Three of this book.) Of course, Douglas and Wildavsky do discuss risk-selection strategies. They say that market groups select loss of economic power as their fear; hierarchical groups select loss of political power as their fear; and sectarians select loss of environmental safety or integrity as their fear. However, if individuals or groups *select* one type of risk as the object of their fear, they they are *averse* to that risk. Particular risk-selection strategies

entail particular risk aversions. Hence, it is false to say that Douglas and Wildavsky are concerned with risk selection but not with risk aversion.

25. Efron, *Apocalyptics*, p. 25. See S. Samuels, "The Arrogance of Intellectual Power," in Woodhead, *Phenotypic Variation*, pp. 115–116. See also Efron, *Apocalyptics*, pp. 129, 179.

26. See note 20. Weinberg, "Risk Assessment," pp. 126–127. See also Douglas and Wildavsky, *Risk and Culture*, pp. 5–7.

27. D. R. Obey, "Export of Hazardous Industries," *Congressional Record*, 95th Cong., 2d sess., 29 June 1978, Vol. 124, part 15, pp. 19763–19764. See H. Shue, "Exporting Hazards," in *Boundaries: National Autonomy and Its Limits*, ed. P. Brown and H. Shue (Totowa, N.J.: Rowman and Littlefield, 1981), p. 107.

28. Douglas and Wildavsky, *Risk and Culture*, pp. 169, 182. See Cohen and Lee, "Catalog of Risks"; Maxey, "Managing Low-Level Radioactive Wastes"; Wildavsky, *Searching for Safety*, pp. 74–75; Weinberg, "Risk Assessment"; Thompson, "Turkeys," pp. 119–120. See also notes 24–27.

29. Efron, *Apocalyptics*, pp. 25, 129; Douglas and Wildavsky, *Risk and Culture*, p. 190. See Wildavsky, *Searching for Safety*, pp. 33–34.

30. Douglas and Wildavsky, *Risk and Culture*, pp. 37, 30.

31. Douglas and Wildavsky, *Risk and Culture*, p. 46. See Wildavsky, *Searching for Safety*, pp. 33–34; Weinberg, "Risk Assessment," pp. 126–127.

32. D. Hume, *An Inquiry concerning Human Understanding*, ed. C. Hendel (Indianapolis: Bobbs-Merrill, 1955), sec. 7, part 2, pp. 84–89.

33. S. Freud, *The Future of an Illusion*, trans. W. D. Robson-Scott (New York: Liveright, 1953), pp. 57, 64–65. Douglas and Wildavsky, like Freud in an analogous case, confuse the alleged psychological or sociological origins of a belief with its justification. This confusion is a fallacy, of course, because justifiable beliefs often have origins that are sociologically suspect, just as erroneous conclusions often have highly persuasive psychological or sociological pedigrees.

34. See H. Kunreuther, J. Linnerooth, and J. Vaupel, "A Decision-Process Perspective on Risk and Policy Analysis," in Lake, *Resolving Locational Conflict*, p. 271.

35. For discussion of the right to know, see Samuels, "Arrogance of Intellectual Power," p. 120. Regarding nuclear fission, citizens are prohibited, by law, from suing the nuclear utility for more than approximately 1 percent of their total losses in the event that the utility causes a catastrophic nuclear accident. See notes 8, 9, and 15, as well as the first section of this chapter; see also Shrader-Frechette, *Nuclear Power*, pp. 73ff.

36. See, for example, C. Flavin, *Electricity for a Developing World*, Worldwatch Paper 70 (Washington, D.C.: Worldwatch Institute, 1986), esp. pp. 45ff.; and A. S. Miller et al., *Growing Power: Bioenergy for Development and Industry*, Study 5 (Washington, D.C.: World Resources Institute, 1986).

37. Efron, *Apocalyptics*, pp. 27, 63; Thompson, "Turkeys," p. 118; Douglas and Wildavsky, *Risk and Culture*, p. 187. See Wildavsky, *Searching for Safety*, pp. 27–31.

38. For example, one might claim that a person directly chose X but indirectly (and *really*) chose Y. But Y could be said to be almost anything, since the evidence for it could be largely intepretational. Douglas and Wildavsky's "indirect" risk choices thus seem uncomfortably like unconscious desires and other events whose existence and meaning are subject both to question and to interpretation. "Indirect" choices are particularly questionable, since one can be said to have made them without having been aware of doing so.

39. K. Popper, "Science: Conjectures and Refutations," in *Conjectures and Refutations: The Growth of Scientific Knowledge* (New York: Harper and Row, 1965), pp. 34–39. Popper noted that astrology, the Marxist theory of history, and the Freudian account of personality are all susceptible to "indirect" verification and therefore to numerous allegedly correct interpretations, simply because they are both vague and lacking in real empirical content.

40. Efron, *Apocalyptics*, pp. 42–44; Douglas and Wildavsky, *Risk and Culture*, pp. 8, 102ff., 174, 187; Thompson, "Turkeys," pp. 126–129.

41. B. Fischhoff, P. Slovic, and S. Lichtenstein, "Facts and Fears," in *Societal Risk Assessment*, ed. R. Schwing and W. Albers (New York: Plenum, 1980), pp. 192, 202; B. Fischhoff et al., "How Safe Is Safe Enough?" *Policy Sciences* 9, no. 2 (1978): 140–142, 148–149; H. Green, "Cost-Benefit Assessment and the Law," *George Washington Law Review* 45, no. 5 (1977): 909–910; R. Kasper, "Perceptions of Risk," in Schwing and Albers, *Societal Risk*, p. 75. Note that a number of social scientists, such as Steve Rayner, would argue (personal communication) that Fischhoff and his associates used samples that were unrepresentative and too small to serve as a basis for their conclusions.

42. R. Weiss, "How Dare We? Scientists Seek the Sources of Risk-Taking Behavior," *Science News* 132, no. 4 (25 July 1987): 57–59.

43. Douglas and Wildavsky, *Risk and Culture*, p. 130. See Wildavsky, *Searching for Safety*, pp. 77–85; Efron, *Apocalyptics*, p. 31; Thompson, "Turkeys."

44. Douglas and Wildavsky, *Risk and Culture*, pp. 132. See Wildavsky, *Searching for Safety*, pp. 77–85; Efron, *Apocalyptics*, pp. 42–44.

45. M. Korchmar, "Radiation Hearings Uncover Dust," *Critical Mass Journal* 3, no. 12 (March 1978): 5. See also J. J. Berger, *Nuclear Power* (New York: Dell, 1977), pp. 65–66, 69, 71; and R. Kraus, "Environmental Carcinogenesis: Regulation on the Frontiers of Science," *Environmental Law* 7, no. 1 (Fall 1976): 83–135. Facts regarding the Orville Kelly case, one of many in which benefits were denied, came from a personal conversation with him in my home on 17 August 1978.

46. Sociologist Steve Rayner made this objection in a personal communication. Rayner's risk research does not appear to have the same flaws as that of Douglas and Wildavsky. See, for example, S. Rayner, "Disagreeing about Risk," in *Risk Analysis, Institutions, and Public Policy*, ed. S. Hadden (New York: Associated Faculty Press, 1984), pp. 150–169; S. Rayner, "Risk and Relativism in Science for Policy," in *The Social and Cultural Construction of Risk*, ed. B.

Johnson and V. Covello (Boston: Reidel, 1987), pp. 5–23; and S. Rayner and R. Cantor, "How Fair Is Safe Enough?" *Risk Analysis* 7, no. 1 (1987): 3–9.

47. Efron, *Apocalyptics*, p. 61. The National Research Council is quoted in R. Kasperson et al., *Social and Economic Aspects of Radioactive Waste Disposal* (Washington, D.C.: National Academy Press, 1984), p. 27.

48. See notes 15–20 for those who make this argument.

49. Douglas and Wildavsky, *Risk and Culture*, p. 22. See notes 15, 17, and 20 for others who make this argument. See also Wildavsky, *Searching for Safety*, pp. 189–203; and L. Maxim, "Problems Associated with the Use of Conservative Assumptions in Exposure and Risk Analysis," in Paustenbach, *Risk Assessment*, pp. 526–560.

50. Douglas and Wildavsky, *Risk and Culture*, pp. 196–198. For others who make this argument, see, for example, Rothschild, "Risk," pp. 30–35; see also notes 15, 17, and 20.

51. See J. Elster, "Introduction," in *Rational Choice*, ed. J. Elster (New York: New York University Press, 1986); A. Tversky and D. Kahneman, "Judgment under Uncertainty," *Science* 185, no. 4157 (1974): 1124–1130; *Judgment under Uncertainty: Heuristics and Biases*, ed. D. Kahneman, P. Slovic, and A. Tversky (Cambridge, England: Cambridge University Press, 1982); and K. Arrow and L. Hurwicz, "An Optimality Criterion for Decision-Making under Uncertainty," in *Uncertainty and Expectation in Economics*, ed. C. F. Carter and J. L. Ford (Clifton, N.J.: Kelley, 1971), pp. 1–11.

52. See the discussion of the Bayesian strategy in Chapter Eight, this volume. See also J. Rawls, *A Theory of Justice* (Cambridge, Mass.: Harvard University Press, 1971), secs. 27–28.

53. Surely one would not counsel "choosing danger" in a potentially catastrophic situation, any more than one would counsel medical doctors to take unnecessary, life-threatening risks with their patients, so as to learn from their mistakes.

54. D. Paustenbach, "A Survey of Health Risk Assessment," in Paustenbach, *Risk Assessment*, p. 36. See also Efron, *Apocalyptics*, pp. 267–270.

55. Efron, *Apocalyptics*, p. 407.

56. Ibid., p. 30; Douglas and Wildavsky, *Risk and Culture*, pp. 13–14. See notes 15, 17, 20, 23–28 for citations to others who make this argument. Wildavsky explicitly makes this argument in *Searching for Safety*, pp. 29–30. See also Paustenbach, "A Survey," p. 36.

57. See W. V. O. Quine and J. S. Ullian, *The Web of Belief*, 2nd ed. (New York: Random House, 1978), pp. 120–121; and H. Putnam, "The 'Innateness Hypothesis' and Explanatory Models in Linguistics," in *Challenges to Empiricism*, ed. H. Morick (Indianapolis: Hackett, 1980), pp. 243–244, 248–249.

58. See Samuels, "Arrogance of Intellectual Power," pp. 113–120. See also Efron, *Apocalyptics*, pp. 42–44; Douglas and Wildavsky, *Risk and Culture*, pp. 8, 102ff., 174, 187; Thompson, "Turkeys," pp. 126–129.

59. See notes 15, 17, 20, 23–28 for citations to others who make this argument. Wildavsky explicitly makes this argument in *Searching for Safety*, pp. 20–21, 125–148. In arguing that the nuclear debate is primarily over nuclear accident probabilities, Starr and Whipple (in "Risks of Risk Decisions") appear to dismiss as unimportant the question of whether the nuclear benefits are worth the risk. In other parts of their work, however, they clearly state that "risks and benefits are not evaluated independently" (p. 1117). I agree. But if risks and benefits are not evaluated independently, how can Starr and Whipple be so sure that the nuclear debate is primarily over the risk probabilities, rather than over whether the benefit is worth the risk? For claims about other studies and the effects of technical knowledge, see Kasperson, *Radioactive Waste Disposal*, pp. 27–28.

60. See notes 14, 15, 20, 49 for others who make this mistake. Many other factors, such as equity of risk distribution (as Douglas recognized in her later work) and benefits gained from the risk, could also explain quite rational risk responses. (For further arguments for this position, see Chapter Six in this volume.) See W. Lowrance, *Of Acceptable Risk: Science and the Determination of Safety* (Los Altos, Calif.: William Kaufmann, 1976); and K. S. Shrader-Frechette, *Risk Analysis and Scientific Method* (Boston: Reidel, 1985), chap. 6. For Douglas's later views, in which she recognizes the importance of equity, see M. Douglas, *Risk Acceptability according to the Social Sciences* (New York: Russell Sage Foundation, 1985), pp. 17–31.

61. Douglas and Wildavsky, *Risk and Culture*, p. 184. See notes 14, 16, 19–24 for others who make this argument. Wildavsky explicitly makes this argument in *Searching for Safety*, pp. 28–29.

62. Efron, *Apocalyptics*, p. 57.

63. Thompson, "Turkeys," pp. 114–130; Efron, *Apocalyptics*, p. 58. Douglas and Wildavsky, *Risk and Culture*, p. 175. See Wildavsky, *Searching for Safety*, pp. 1–2.

64. This criticism suggests that, although social scientists may learn much from discussing Weberian "ideal types," how to specify such types may be a matter of controversy. See, for example, R. Rudner, *Philosophy of Social Science* (Englewood Cliffs, N.J.: Prentice-Hall, 1966), pp. 54–63; and C. Hempel, *Fundamentals of Concept Formation in Empirical Science* (Chicago: University of Chicago Press, 1952).

65. U.S. Congress, Office of Technology Assessment, *Coastal Effects of Offshore Energy Systems*, 2 vols. (Washington, D.C.: Government Printing Office, 1976), 2 (part 1): 11–1; 1:51, 169.

66. Ibid., 1:16, 51–56.

67. Ibid., 1:15–16, 57–59.

68. See notes 8 and 9.

69. Apart from whether Wildavsky, Cohen, Weinberg, Whipple, Douglas, and others are right to dismiss lay opinions on risk, their attitude is questionable from the point of view of social science research. Experts' dismissing public

fears as irrational runs contrary to many contemporary research traditions. Social scientists, in aiming at the ideal of objectivity, are supposed to look at the facts, at people's behavior, and not to impose their own models of rationality on the world. It is paradoxical that, instead of claiming that their risk theories are wrong when they are inconsistent with reasonable public perceptions of risk, some persons typically allege that the public is irrational. (See notes 14, 15, 20, 49.)

70. Although he is a cultural and ethical relativist, Thompson admits that we need a new theory of rationality, a "rationality of truculence," to explain U.S. lay views on societal risk (see "Turkeys," p. 132).

Chapter Three

1. L. Regenstein, "The Toxics Boomerang," in *Environment 85/86*, ed. J. Allen (Guilford, Conn.: Dushkin, 1985), p. 124. For arguments that the government exaggerates the cancer risk, see E. Efron, *The Apocalyptics* (New York: Simon and Schuster, 1984). See also T. Marshall, M. Dubinsky, and S. Boutwell, "A Risk Assessment of a Former Pesticide Production Facility," in *The Risk Assessment of Environmental and Human Health Hazards*, ed. D. J. Paustenbach (New York: Wiley, 1989), pp. 496–497.

2. Regenstein, "Toxics Boomerang," p. 124. S. S. Epstein (in "Cancer, Inflation, and the Failure to Regulate," *Technology Review* 82, no. 3 [December/January 1980]: 42–53) notes that cancer is the only major fatal disease on the increase in the United States; between 1933 and 1970, cancer deaths rose by 11 percent. See J. L. Regens, "Attitudes toward Risk-Benefit Analysis for Managing Effects of Chemical Exposures," in *Risk Management of Chemicals in the Environment*, ed. H. M. Seip and A. B. Heiberg (New York: Plenum, 1989), pp. 75–88. For the 90 percent figure, see J. C. Lashof et al., Health and Life Sciences Division of the U.S. Office of Technology Assessment, *Assessment of Technologies for Determining Cancer Risks from the Environment* (Washington, D.C.: Office of Technology Assessment, 1981), pp. 3, 6ff. Some scientists, however, disagree with the OTA; see J. R. Totter, "Spontaneous Cancer," *Proceedings of the National Academy of Sciences* 77, no. 4 (April 1980): 1763–1767. See also Efron, *Apocalyptics*.

3. Regenstein, "Toxics Boomerang," pp. 122–123. See also J. C. Fine, "A Crisis of Contamination," in Allen, *Environment*, p. 109.

4. U.S. Energy Research and Development Administration, *Final Environmental Impact Statement: Waste Management Operations, Idaho National Engineering Laboratory*, ERDA-1536 (Springfield, Va.: National Technical Information Service, 1977), III-103 and III-104.

5. U.S. Atomic Energy Commission, *Theoretical Possibilities and Consequences of Major Accidents in Large Nuclear Power Plants*, WASH-740 (Washington, D.C.: Government Printing Office, 1957), and its update, R. J. Mulvihill et al., *Analysis*

of United States Power Reactor Accident Probability, PRC R-695 (Los Angeles: Planning Research Corporation, 1965).

6. J. T. Mathews et al., *World Resources 1986* (New York: Basic Books, 1986), p. 2.

7. L. Durrell, *State of the Ark* (New York: Doubleday, 1986), p. 157; Mathews, *World Resources*, p. 8.

8. Durrell, *State of the Ark*, pp. 33, 179; Mathews, *World Resources*, p. 3.

9. E. Eckholm, "Human Wants and Misused Lands," in Allen, *Environment*, p. 11. See also Durrell, *State of the Ark*, p. 34; Mathews, *World Resources*, p. 3.

10. Mathews, *World Resources*, pp. 48–49. See also R. Repetto, *Paying the Price: Pesticide Subsidies in Developing Countries*, Research Report no. 2 (Washington, D.C.: World Resources Institute, 1985), p. 3. For a discussion of third-world environmental risks, see Chapter Ten of this volume.

11. See note 14.

12. See note 85.

13. See R. N. Andrews, "Environmental Impact Assessment and Risk Assessment," in *Environmental Impact Assessment*, ed. P. Wathern (London: Unwin Hyman, 1988), pp. 85–97. See also K. S. Shrader-Frechette, *Science Policy, Ethics, and Economic Methodology* (Boston: Reidel, 1985), chap. 2, pp. 32–66.

14. M. Douglas and A. Wildavsky, *Risk and Culture* (Berkeley and Los Angeles: University of California Press, 1982), p. 186. See also M. Thompson, "To Hell with the Turkeys!" in *Values at Risk*, ed. D. MacLean (Totowa, N.J.: Rowman and Allanheld, 1986), pp. 113–135. In terming Wildavsky, Douglas, and Thompson "cultural relativists," I must add three caveats. First, Wildavsky and Douglas have quite different views on relativism and on risk, with Wildavsky being more relativistic and more biased against the border/environmentalists than Douglas; see Chapter Two of this volume, as well as A. Wildavsky, *Searching for Safety* (New Brunswick, N.J.: Transaction Books, 1988), p. 28. Likewise, see M. Douglas, *Risk Acceptability according to the Social Sciences* (New York: Russell Sage Foundation, 1985), pp. 5–18.

The second caveat is that most social scientists are not cultural relativists in the Wildavsky sense, since they believe neither that comparison among cultures and theories is impossible, nor that reality is a "social construct" (see note 23), nor that "no one is to say that one [judgment] is better or worse" (see note 35). Instead of subscribing to these two positions, most social scientists are *soft relativists*. That is, they believe (as do the naturalists discussed in Chapter One) that, although there are no absolute rules governing theorizing in all situations, nevertheless theorizing can be more or less rational, since it is governed by goals of explanatory and predictive power. Soft relativists also believe that comparison among cultures or theories is possible. One social scientist who exhibits the best characteristics of this dominant position of naturalism or soft relativism is Steve Rayner. See, for example, S. Rayner, "Disagreeing about Risk," in *Risk Analysis, Institutions, and Public Policy*, ed. S. Hadden (New York: Associated Faculty Press, 1984), pp. 150–169; S. Rayner, "Risk and Relativism in Science for Policy," in *The Social and Cultural Construction of Risk*, ed. B. Johnson and V. Covello (Boston: Reidel, 1987), pp. 5–23; and S. Rayner and R. Cantor, "How Fair Is Safe Enough?" *Risk Analysis* 7, no. 1 (1987): 3–9.

A third caveat is that, according to Rayner (a student of Douglas's), Douglas is a soft relativist, not a cultural relativist. If that is so, then it is difficult to explain her claims (above) about "social constructs" and about judgments' not being better or worse. However, see her *Risk Acceptability*.

For an excellent discussion of cultural relativism, see J. Ladd, "Introduction," in *Ethical Relativism*, ed. J. Ladd (New York: University Press of America, 1985), pp. 1–11. See also R. Benedict, *Patterns of Culture* (New York: Pelican, 1946), esp. chap. 7; M. Herskovits, "Cultural Relativism," in Ladd, *Ethical Relativism*, pp. 58–77; Douglas and Wildavsky, *Risk and Culture*, p. 186; and Wildavsky, *Searching for Safety*, pp. 1–3.

15. See C. Whipple, "Nonpessimistic Risk Assessment," and B. Cohen, "Risk Analyses of Buried Wastes," in Paustenbach, *Risk Assessment*, pp. 1111, 575. See also W. Hafele, "Benefit-Risk Tradeoffs in Nuclear Power Generation," in *Energy and the Environment*, ed. H. Ashley, R. Rudman, and C. Whipple (Elmsford, N.Y.: Pergamon Press, 1976), p. 181; D. Okrent and C. Whipple, *Approach to Societal Risk Acceptance Criteria and Risk Management*, Report no. PB-271264 (Washington, D.C.: U.S. Department of Commerce, 1977), pp. 1–9. See also C. Starr and C. Whipple, "Risks of Risk Decisions," *Science* 208, no. 4448 (6 June 1980): 1116; D. Okrent, "Panel: Use of Risk Assessment," in Mitre Corporation, *Symposium/Workshop on Nuclear and Nonnuclear Energy Systems: Risk Assessment and Governmental Decision Making* (McLean, Va.: Mitre Corporation, 1979), p. 663; D. Bazelon, "Risk and Responsibility," *Science* 205, no. 4403 (1979): 278; B. Cohen and I. Lee, "A Catalog of Risks," *Health Physics* 36, no. 6 (1979): 707; W. Hafele, "Energy," in *Science, Technology, and the Human Prospect*, ed. C. Starr and P. Ritterbush (Elmsford, N.Y.: Pergamon Press, 1979), p. 139; M. Maxey, "Managing Low-Level Radioactive Wastes," in *Low-Level Radioactive Waste Management*, ed. J. Watson (Williamsburg, Va.: Health Physics Society, 1979), pp. 410, 417; C. Starr, "Benefit-Cost Studies in Sociotechnical Systems," in Committee on Public Engineering Policy, *Perspectives on Benefit-Risk Decision Making* (Washington, D.C.: National Academy of Engineering, 1972), pp. 26–27. Finally, see L. Lave, "Discussion," in Mitre Corp., *Symposium*, p. 484; F. Hoyle, *Energy or Extinction* (London: Heinemann, 1977); and J. H. Fremlin, *The Risks of Power Production* (London: Macmillan, 1985).

Other writers who charge that real risks can be objectively measured and hence distinguished from merely "perceived" risks are L. Rothschild, "Risk," *Atom* 268 (1979): 30–35; M. Morgan, "Probing the Question," *IEEE Spectrum* (November 1981): 58–64, and "Choosing and Managing Risk," *IEEE Spectrum* (December 1981): 53–60; and M. Jones-Lee, "The Value of Life . . . ," *Geneva Papers on Risk* 10 (1985): 141–173. For a discussion of actual/perceived risk and positivism, see B. Wynne, *Risk Management and Hazardous Waste* (New York: Springer-Verlag, 1987), esp. pp. 357–396. See also D. Paris and J. Reynolds,

The Logic of Policy Inquiry (New York: Longman, 1983), pp. 6ff., 14–78; Chapter Four, this volume (esp. the section headed "Role of Values in Risk Evaluation and Science"); and K. S. Shrader-Frechette, *Risk Analysis and Scientific Method* (Boston: Reidel, 1985), chap. 2.

16. For a discussion of values and objectivity in science, see L. Laudan, *Science and Values* (Berkeley and Los Angeles: University of California Press, 1984); and M. Scriven, "The Exact Role of Value Judgments in Science," in *Proceedings of the 1972 Biennial Meeting of the Philosophy of Science Association*, ed. R. S. Cohen and K. Schaffner (Boston: Reidel, 1974), pp. 219–247. Reprinted in *Introductory Readings in the Philosophy of Science*, ed. E. D. Klemke, R. Hollinger, and A. Kline (Buffalo, N.Y.: Prometheus Books, 1980).

By "naive positivism" I mean the belief that there is a fact-value dichotomy and that the only objects of knowledge are facts. Since naive positivists claim that facts are the only objects of knowledge, it follows that they believe all knowledge claims must be empirically confirmed and that one can have no knowledge of values. Both of these tenets correspond to early or naive positivism, as defined by Abbagnano (see below); later positivists, such as Hempel, rejected the belief that facts are the only objects of knowledge; hence, they are not naive positivists.

According to N. Abbagnano ("Positivism," in *The Encyclopedia of Philosophy*, ed. P. Edwards [New York: Macmillan, 1967], 6:414), "the characteristic theses of positivism are that science is the only valid knowledge and facts the only possible objects of knowledge; that philosophy does not possess a method different from science.... Positivism, consequently,... opposes any... procedure of investigation that is not reducible to scientific method." As Laudan points out, because they have disallowed talk about developments in "metaphysics, logic, [and] ethics ... 'positivist' [sociologists,] philosophers, and historians of science who see the progress of science entirely in empirical terms have completely missed the huge significance of these developments for science as well as for philosophy" (L. Laudan, *Progress and Its Problems* [Berkeley and Los Angeles: University of California Press, 1977], pp. 61–62).

17. See Chapter Eight of this volume.

18. For an account of this problem, see K. S. Shrader-Frechette, "Values and Hydrogeological Method: How Not to Site the World's Largest Nuclear Dump," in *Planning for Changing Energy Conditions*, Energy Policy Studies 4, ed. J. Byrne and D. Rich (New Brunswick, N.J.: Transaction Books, 1988), pp. 101–138.

19. See H. F. Kraybill, "Pesticide Toxicity and the Potential for Cancer," *Pest Control* 43, no. 12 (December 1975): 10–16.

20. See note 85.

21. Douglas and Wildavsky, *Risk and Culture*, p. 188. See Wildavsky, *Searching for Safety*, pp. 1–14, and Thompson, "Turkeys," pp. 122ff.

22. See note 18.

23. Douglas and Wildavsky, *Risk and Culture*, p. 186. See Wildavsky, *Searching for Safety*, pp. 1–14.

24. Douglas and Wildavsky, *Risk and Culture*, p. 198. See Wildavsky, *Searching for Safety*, pp. 1–14, and Thompson, "Turkeys," p. 118.

25. See note 35.

26. See note 24. Note that not all social scientists attack laypersons. Indeed, most—including Steve Rayner (see note 14)—do not.

27. See notes 29 through 33.

28. See note 33.

29. Like Douglas and Wildavsky (in *Risk and Culture*, pp. 187, 191), M. Herskovits (in *Cultural Anthropology* [New York: Knopf, 1955], chap. 19, sec. 2) compares ethical and aesthetic judgments.

30. Douglas and Wildavsky, *Risk and Culture*, pp. 187–188. Cultural relativists maintain that anything can be justified, given a particular culture. See, for example, Herskovits, *Cultural Anthropology*, chap. 19, secs. 2 and 4; and W. G. Sumner, "Folkways," in Ladd, *Ethical Relativism*, pp. 28, 31–32, 35. See also Thompson, "Turkeys," pp. 122ff., and note 35.

31. Cultural relativists often note the similarities between primitives and members of other societies; see, for example, Herskovits, *Cultural Anthropology*, chap. 19, sec. 4. See Douglas and Wildavsky, *Risk and Culture*, pp. 39, 80–81. Thompson (in "Turkeys," pp. 116–119) compares risk taking in the Himalayas and in Europe, whereas Weinberg compares medieval witch hunting and contemporary risk aversion (see A. Weinberg, "Risk Assessment, Regulation, and the Limits," in *Phenotypic Variation in Populations*, ed. A. Woodhead, M. Bender, and R. Leonard [New York: Plenum, 1988], p. 127). Thompson and Weinberg allege that the same structures dictate risk behavior in this variety of contexts.

32. Just as Douglas and Wildavsky (in *Risk and Culture*, pp. 54–63, 83–152) attribute the "problems" of sectarians to their membership in sectarian environmentalist groups, so also cultural relativists emphasize the problems created by dominating membership in a certain group (see, for example, Sumner, "Folkways," pp. 27ff.; Herskovits, *Cultural Anthropology*, chap. 19, sec. 3; and Thompson, "Turkeys," pp. 119–120).

33. Douglas and Wildavsky, *Risk and Culture*, pp. 63–64, 71, 73, 194; Efron, *Apocalyptics*, p. 62. See Wildavsky, *Searching for Safety*, pp. 4–12. Rothschild ("Risk," pp. 30–35) argues that more knowledge does not make laypersons more rational about risk. Cultural relativists W. G. Sumner ("Folkways," p. 39) and F. Engels ("Ethics and Law: Eternal Truths," in Ladd, *Ethical Relativism*, pp. 15–21) argue that knowledge provides no help in overcoming cultural and ethical relativism. See also Thompson, "Turkeys," pp. 118–119.

34. N. Harley, "Environmental Lung Cancer Risk from Radon Daughter Exposure," in Paustenbach, *Risk Assessment*, pp. 612ff.

35. Douglas and Wildavsky, *Risk and Culture*, pp. 187, 191. See also Efron, *Apocalyptics*, p. 67; Wildavsky, *Searching for Safety*, pp. 4–12. See note 32.

36. Although the variety of arguments against cultural and ethical relativism (see note 14) cannot be presented here, see Ladd's "Introduction" and the following articles in *Ethical Relativism*: W. D. Ross, "The Meaning of Right," pp. 40ff.; P. T. Taylor, "Social Science and Ethical Relativism," pp. 95ff.; Ladd, "The Issue of Relativism," pp. 107ff.

37. See note 85 and later sections of this chapter.

38. See note 34.

39. Douglas and Wildavsky, *Risk and Culture*, pp. 187–188. See Wildavsky, *Searching for Safety*, p. 3. See also Herkovits, *Cultural Anthropology*, chap. 19, sec. 3; Sumner, "Folkways," pp. 27ff.

40. D. Turnbull and J. Rodricks, "A Comparative Risk Assessment of DEHP as a Component of Baby Pacifiers, Teethers, and Toys," in Paustenbach, *Risk Assessment*, pp. 868ff.

41. See note 36.

42. For discussion of the compensating wage differential, see K. S. Shrader-Frechette, *Risk Analysis and Scientific Method* (Boston: Reidel, 1985), chap. 4, pp. 97–124.

43. See Chapter Ten for a discussion of cases in which environmental risks have been imposed on innocent persons for exactly this reason.

44. Douglas and Wildavsky, *Risk and Culture*, p. 198. See Wildavsky, *Searching for Safety*, pp. 2–3.

45. See note 36.

46. Douglas and Wildavsky, *Risk and Culture*, p. 187. See Wildavsky, *Searching for Safety*, pp. 2–3.

47. Their own words commit them to an ethical and epistemological relativism, to the thesis that no one "view of risk . . . is better or worse" than another (*Risk and Culture*, p. 187). Their response to the charge of second-level, or meta-level, relativism is to claim that their first-order accounts of social organization have been done with impartial care. However, the charge of relativism is not directed against their first-order social descriptions (of hierarchy, market, and sect) but against their second-order judgments about criteria for comparing and evaluating all social descriptions. See note 36.

48. Thompson, "Turkeys," p. 120; Douglas and Wildavsky, *Risk and Culture*, pp. 80–81, 187. See also Wildavsky, *Searching for Safety*, pp. 69–72; Herskovits, *Cultural Anthropology*, chap. 19, sec. 3.

49. Douglas and Wildavsky, *Risk and Culture*, p. 39. See also Wildavsky, *Searching for Safety*, pp. 69–72.

50. Douglas and Wildavsky, *Risk and Culture*, pp. 37–38. See also Wildavsky, *Searching for Safety*, pp. 69–72. See Efron, *Apocalyptics*, pp. 25, 30, 58; and Weinberg, "Risk Assessment," p. 127.

51. See Sumner, "Folkways," p. 37, for example. See also Efron, *Apocalyptics*, pp. 27, 58; and Weinberg, "Risk Assessment," p. 127.

52. Douglas and Wildavsky, *Risk and Culture*, pp. 186–187, 198. See also

Thompson, "Turkeys," p. 120; Wildavsky, *Searching for Safety*, pp. 69–72; Efron, *Apocalyptics*, pp. 62, 67.

53. See notes 29–33: "The selection of risk is a matter of social organization."

54. B. Fischhoff et al., "How Safe Is Safe Enough?" *Policy Sciences* 9, no. 2 (1978): 140–142, 150; B. Fischhoff, P. Slovic, and S. Lichtenstein, "Facts and Fears," in *Societal Risk Assessment*, ed. R. Schwing and W. Albers (New York: Plenum, 1980), p. 202. See also R. Kasper, "Perceptions of Risk," in Schwing and Albers, *Societal Risk*, p. 75. For a psychological response to cultural relativism, see, for example, K. Duncker, "Ethical Relativity," in Ladd, *Ethical Relativism*, pp. 43ff.

55. Fischhoff, "How Safe Is Safe Enough?" pp. 148–149; see also H. Green, "Cost-Benefit Assessment and the Law," *George Washington Law Review* 45, no. 5 (1977): 909–910.

56. Efron, *Apocalyptics*, pp. 27, 62.

57. Douglas and Wildavsky, *Risk and Culture*, p. 132. The membership is also composed primarily of white-collar, middle-class, and professional workers, not blue-collar, lower-class, and hourly-wage workers (p. 130).

58. Douglas and Wildavsky, *Risk and Culture*, pp. 122–123, 130. See also Wildavsky, *Searching for Safety*, pp. 35–36.

59. See R. Nash, *Wilderness and the American Mind*, rev. ed. (New Haven, Conn.: Yale University Press, 1973).

60. See Chapter Eight in this volume.

61. Efron, *Apocalyptics*, p. 43; Douglas and Wildavsky, *Risk and Culture*, pp. 122–124, 102–174; Thompson, "Turkeys," pp. 120–121. See also Wildavsky, *Searching for Safety*, p. 34; Herskovits, *Cultural Anthropology*, chap. 19, sec. 3; Sumner, "Folkways," pp. 27ff.

62. Douglas and Wildavsky, *Risk and Culture*, p. 125; Thompson, "Turkeys," pp. 120–122. See also Wildavsky, *Searching for Safety*, pp. 34ff.

63. See note 2.

64. Douglas and Wildavsky, *Risk and Culture*, pp. 13–14.

65. Douglas and Wildavsky, *Risk and Culture*, p. 186. See also Wildavsky, *Searching for Safety*, pp. 59–60; Thompson, "Turkeys," p. 120.

66. Douglas and Wildavsky, *Risk and Culture*, p. 184. See also Wildavsky, *Searching for Safety*, pp. 60ff.

67. Douglas and Wildavsky, *Risk and Culture*, p. 188. See also Wildavsky, *Searching for Safety*, pp. 60ff.

68. See note 51.

69. See notes 12 and 14.

70. See notes 15 and 85.

71. See notes 15 and 16.

72. See note 15.

73. See Whipple, "Nonpessimistic Risk Assessment," pp. 1111, 1116. The

"principle of neutrality" is quoted by C. V. Kidd, "Technology Assessment in the Executive Office of the President," in *Technology Assessment: Understanding the Social Consequences of Technological Applications*, ed. R. G. Kasper (New York: Praeger, 1972), p. 131. See Starr and Whipple, "Risks of Risk Decisions," pp. 1115–1117. See also J. Burnham, "Panel: Use of Risk Assessment," in Mitre Corp., *Symposium*, p. 678; W. Hafele, "Benefit-Risk Tradeoffs in Nuclear Power Generation," in *Energy and the Environment*, ed. H. Ashley, R. Rudman, and C. Whipple (Elmsford, N.Y.: Pergamon Press, 1976), p. 181; D. Okrent and C. Whipple, *Approach to Societal Risk Acceptance Criteria and Risk Management*, Report no. PB-271264 (Washington, D.C.: U.S. Department of Commerce, 1977), pp. 1–9; W. Lowrance, *Of Acceptable Risk: Science and the Determination of Safety* (Los Altos, Calif.: William Kaufmann, 1976), p. xx; W. Rowe, *An Anatomy of Risk* (New York: Wiley, 1977), pp. 3, 5; Kasper, "Perceptions of Risk," p. 72.

74. U.S. Congress, Office of Technology Assessment, *Annual Report to the Congress for 1976* (Washington, D.C.: Government Printing Office, 1976), p. 63; and *Technology Assessment in Business and Government* (Washington, D.C.: Government Printing Office, 1977), p. 9. See Cohen, "Risk Analyses," p. 575.

75. D. Nelkin, "Wisdom, Expertise, and the Application of Ethics," *Science, Technology, and Human Values* 6, no. 34 (Spring 1981): 16–17. Inasmuch as Nelkin condemns philosophical discussion of the "rights and wrongs" of science policy, she disallows talk about the ethics of science policy. Hence, her disallowing this talk about ethics is tantamount to subscribing to positivism.

76. R. A. Carpenter, "Technology Assessment and the Congress," in Kasper, *Technology Assessment*, p. 42.

77. See H. Longino, "Beyond 'Bad Science': Skeptical Reflections on the Value-Freedom of Scientific Inquiry," unpublished essay, March 1982, done with the assistance of National Science Foundation Grant OSS 8018095.

78. Ibid., pp. 6–9.

79. Ibid., pp. 10–12.

80. For discussion of relevant examples from the history of science, see H. I. Brown, *Perception, Theory and Commitment* (Chicago: University of Chicago Press, 1977), pp. 97–100, 147; and K. S. Shrader-Frechette, "Recent Changes in the Concept of Matter: How Does 'Elementary Particle' Mean?" in *Philosophy of Science Association 1980*, ed. P. D. Asquith and R. N. Giere (East Lansing, Mich.: Philosophy of Science Association, 1980), 1:302ff.

81. Scriven, "Role of Value Judgments in Science" (see note 16); E. McMullin, "Values in Science," in *Philosophy of Science Association 1982*, ed. P. D. Asquith (East Lansing, Mich.: Philosophy of Science Association, 1983), vol. 2.

82. Scriven, "Role of Value Judgments in Science"; McMullin, "Values in Science." See also the following works by C. Hempel: *Aspects of Scientific Explanation* (New York: Free Press, 1965); "Scientific Rationality," in *Rationality Today*, ed. T. Geraets (Ottawa: University of Ottawa Press, 1979); "Science and Human Values," in Klemke et al., *Introductory Readings*; and "Valuation and Objectivity

in Science," in *Physics, Philosophy, and Psychoanalysis*, ed. R. Cohen and L. Laudan (Dordrecht: Reidel, 1983).

83. Scriven, "Role of Value Judgments in Science"; E. Nagel, *The Structure of Science* (New York: Harcourt, Brace, 1961), p. 492. See Hempel, *Aspects of Scientific Explanation*.

84. Hempel, "Science and Human Values," p. 263; "Scientific Rationality," pp. 45–66; "Valuation and Objectivity," pp. 73–100. See note 15.

85. For excellent philosophical accounts of how risk assessment can be objectively tested, see the essays by D. Hattis and D. Smith, P. Humphreys, and J. Humber and R. Almeder in *Quantitative Risk Assessment*, ed. J. Humber and R. Almeder (Clifton, N.J.: Humana Press, 1987), pp. 57–106, 205–224, 239–262, respectively. For examples of value-laden risk assessments, see Shrader-Frechette, *Science Policy*, pp. 74–80. See notes 13 and 14 in the next chapter for references about values and objectivity.

86. See notes 15 and 19 of this chapter.

87. See N. Hanson, *Patterns of Discovery* (Cambridge, England: Cambridge University Press, 1958); T. S. Kuhn, *The Structure of Scientific Revolutions*, 2nd ed. (Chicago: University of Chicago Press, 1969); M. Polanyi, *Personal Knowledge*, 2nd ed. (New York: Harper and Row, 1964); and S. Toulmin, *Foresight and Understanding* (New York: Harper and Row, 1961). See notes 15 and 16.

88. W. K. Foell, "Assessment of Energy/Environment Systems," in *Environment Assessment of Socioeconomic Systems*, ed. D. F. Burkhardt and W. H. Ittelson (New York: Plenum, 1978), p. 196; U.S. Congress, *Technology Assessment Activities in the Industrial, Academic, and Governmental Communities*, Hearings before the Technology Assessment Board of the Office of Technology Assessment, 94th Cong., 2d sess., 8–10 and 14 June 1976 (Washington, D.C.: Government Printing Office, 1976), pp. 66, 200, 220. See A. B. Lovins, "Cost-Risk-Benefit Assessments in Energy Policy," *George Washington Law Review* 5, no. 45 (August 1977): 940.

89. See M. C. Tool, *The Discretionary Economy: A Normative Theory of Political Economy* (Santa Monica, Calif.: Goodyear, 1979), p. 279. See also R. M. Hare, "Contrasting Methods of Environmental Planning," in *Ethics and Problems of the 21st Century*, ed. K. E. Goodpaster and K. M. Sayre (Notre Dame, Ind.: University of Notre Dame Press, 1979), p. 65.

90. See Tool, *Discretionary Economy*, p. 280.

91. Perception is structured by the world outside us and yet is susceptible to the imprint of our own presuppositions, values, and theories. Therefore, although observations or facts may be seen in *different* ways, they may not be seen in *any* way.

92. See notes 15, 75, and 85.

93. J. W. Falco and R. Moraski, "Methods Used in the United States for the Assessment and Management of Health Risk Due to Chemicals," in Seip and Heiberg, *Risk Management of Chemicals*, pp. 37–60. See Shrader-Frechette, *Science Policy*, chap. 9, pp. 286–315.

94. See Andrews, "Environmental Impact Assessment." For another discussion of these same points, see E. S. Quade, *Analysis for Public Decisions* (New York: American Elsevier, 1975), pp. 269ff.; and C. H. Weiss and M. J. Bucuvalas, *Social Science Research and Decision Making* (New York: Columbia University Press, 1980), p. 26.

95. This same point is also made by C. E. Lindblom and D. K. Cohen, *Usable Knowledge: Social Science and Social Problem Solving* (New Haven, Conn.: Yale University Press, 1979), p. 64.

96. See note 15.

97. See notes 14 and 36.

98. For an account of this episode, see A. Einstein, *Ideas and Opinions*, trans. S. Bergmann (New York: Crown, 1954), pp. 205–210; A. Einstein, *The World as I See It*, trans. A. Harris (New York: Philosophical Library, 1949), pp. 81–89; and P. Frank, *Einstein: His Life and Times*, trans. G. Rosen (New York: Knopf, 1974), pp. 234–235.

99. A. Camus, *Notebooks*, trans. J. O'Brien (New York: Knopf, 1974). See S. Samuels, "The Arrogance of Intellectual Power," in Woodhead, *Phenotypic Variation*, pp. 113–120.

100. Quoted by J. Primack and F. von Hippel, *Advice and Dissent: Scientists in the Political Arena* (New York: Basic Books, 1974). When one is dealing with a policy that has the potential to cause great harm, it could be argued that one has a moral obligation not to be neutral. See W. D. Ross, *The Right and the Good* (Oxford: Clarendon Press, 1930), chap. 2.

101. For arguments to support this claim, see B. Wynne, *Risk Management and Hazardous Waste* (New York: Springer-Verlag, 1987), pp. 13–15; note 54 in this chapter; and K. S. Shrader-Frechette, "Economics, Risk-Cost-Benefit Analysis, and the Linearity Assumption," in *Philosophy of Science Association 1982*, ed. P. D. Asquith and T. Nickles (Ann Arbor, Mich.: Philosophy of Science Association, 1982), 1:219–223.

102. See note 85.

103. Note 14 explains this claim.

104. See note 15.

105. See Chapter Eleven in this volume. See also Andrews, "Environmental Impact Assessment," and Samuels, "Arrogance of Intellectual Power." See also note 85.

106. For a defense of this thesis (1), see Hempel, "Scientific Rationality," esp. pp. 55–56, and "Valuation and Objectivity," p. 91. See also W. Sellars, *Philosophical Perspectives* (Springfield, Ill.: Thomas, 1967), p. 410; and J. W. Cornman, *Skepticism, Justification, and Explanation* (Boston: Reidel, 1980), pp. 8–9, 15, 26, 67–88, 93. See note 81.

107. See the section headed "Are Environmentalists Distrustful?" in Chapter Two.

108. See note 57. Likewise, to the degree that existing risk assessments alleged that the Chernobyl accident was "impossible," then to that same extent

have the analyses failed both to explain and to predict the actual occurrence of the Russian accident.

109. Although I believe that there is at least one general, universal criterion for theory choice, my account of scientific rationality and objectivity does not fall victim to the naive-positivist account (as does that of Carnap, for example) for at least four reasons: (1) I am not committed to a priori rules of scientific method, although I am committed to a normative account of it. (2) I am not committed to specific rules of method that are universal, but only to *general goals* of method that are universal. (3) I am committed to the belief that, just as observation and experiment often underdetermine theory, so also this universal methodological goal (explanatory power as tested by prediction) underdetermines (or fails to dictate) specific methodological rules; hence, the rules must be dictated largely by practice, largely by the particular situation. (4) I make a naturalistic appeal to the criticism of the scientific community, and ultimately an appeal to cases, rather than to specific rules, in order to help define "scientific objectivity."

110. It will not do to say that a risk judgment is objective if it fits the situation or the "facts," because (1) we don't want to beg the realism question regarding the status of any alleged facts; (2) we might not have all the facts; and (3) since every risk situation will be different, it is virtually impossible to specify, ahead of time, what an evenhanded representation of a particular situation might be.

111. See Hempel, "Scientific Rationality," p. 56, and "Valuation and Objectivity," p. 91; McMullin, "Values in Science"; and Sellars, *Philosophical Perspectives*, p. 410 (see note 106). All these writers hold this view.

112. The position is procedural because it relies on democratic procedures—namely, criticism by laypeople likely to be affected by the risk judgments, as well as criticism by scientists.

113. See note 85.

114. Scriven, "Role of Value Judgments in Science," and T. Nagel, *The View from Nowhere* (New York: Oxford University Press, 1986), pp. 143–153. For a related account of rationality and objectivity within the risk-assessment context, see A. Rip, "Experts in Public Arenas," in *Regulating Industrial Risks*, ed. H. Otway and M. Peltu (London: Butterworths, 1985), pp. 94–110.

115. See Scriven, "Role of Value Judgments in Science," p. 286.

116. K. Popper, *The Open Society and Its Enemies* (Princeton, N.J.: Princeton University Press, 1950), pp. 403–406; *Conjectures and Refutations* (New York: Basic Books, 1962), p. 63; and *The Logic of Scientific Discovery* (New York: Harper and Row, 1965), p. 56.

117. See note 15.

118. Douglas and Wildavsky, *Risk and Culture*, p. 188. See also Wildavsky, *Searching for Safety*, p. 3; Thompson, "Turkeys."

119. See note 14.

120. P. Feyerabend, "Changing Patterns of Reconstruction," *British Journal for the Philosophy of Science* 28, no. 4 (1977): 368.

121. See T. Kulka, "How Far Does Anything Go? Comments on Feyerabend's Epistemological Anarchism," *Philosophy of the Social Sciences* 7, no. 3 (1977): 279–280.

122. See G. Hellman, "Against Bad Method," *Metaphilosophy* 10, no. 2 (April 1979): 194; W. V. O. Quine and J. Ullian, *Web of Belief*, 2nd ed. (New York: Random House, 1978); Hempel, *Aspects of Scientific Explanation*, p. 463. See also Scriven, "Role of Value Judgments in Science," p. 277.

123. See H. Siegel, "What Is the Question concerning the Rationality of Science?" *Philosophy of Science* 52, no. 4 (1985): 524–526; R. Rudner, *Philosophy of Social Science* (Englewood Cliffs, N.J.: Prentice-Hall, 1966), pp. 4–5.

124. See R. M. Hare, *Moral Thinking: Its Levels, Methods, and Point* (Oxford: Oxford University Press, 1981).

125. See R. Newell, *Objectivity, Empiricism, and Truth* (New York: Routledge and Kegan Paul, 1986).

126. See note 85.

127. Hellman (in "Against Bad Method," pp. 200–201) makes a similar point.

128. I. Scheffler, "Discussion: Vision and Revolution: A Postscript on Kuhn," *Philosophy of Science* 39, no. 3 (1972): 369.

Chapter Four

1. J. Raloff, "Fallout over Nevada's Nuclear Destiny," *Science News* 137, no. 1 (16 January 1990): 11–12.

2. J. Neel, "Statement," in U.S. Congress, *Low-Level Radioactive Waste Disposal*, Hearings before a Subcommittee of the Committee on Government Operations, House of Representatives, 94th Cong., 2d sess., 23 February, 12 March, and 6 April 1976 (Washington, D.C.: Government Printing Office, 1976), p. 258. See also U.S. Geological Survey, vertical file, *Maxey Flats: Publicity* (Louisville, Ky.: Water Resources Division, U.S. Department of the Interior, n.d.). (The Louisville office of the U.S. Geological Survey is responsible for monitoring the Maxey Flats radioactive facility.) Finally, see A. Weiss and P. Columbo, *Evaluation of Isotope Migration: Land Burial*, NUREG/CR-1289, BNL-NUREG-51143 (Washington, D.C.: U.S. Nuclear Regulatory Commission, 1980), p. 5.

3. See, for example, D. Paustenbach, "A Comprehensive Methodology for Assessing the Risks . . . [of] Dioxin," in *The Risk Assessment of Environmental and Human Health Hazards*, ed. D. J. Paustenbach (New York: Wiley, 1989), pp. 296–328.

4. G. Meyer, "Maxey Flats Radioactive Waste Burial Site: Status Report," Advanced Science and Technology Branch, U.S. Environmental Protection Agency, 19 February 1975, p. 9.

5. P. S. Zurer, "U.S. Charts Plans for Nuclear Waste Disposal," *Chemical and Engineering News* 61, no. 27 (18 July 1983): 20–38.

6. For information on the hazards of plutonium, see J. I. Fabrikant et al., Committee on the Biological Effects of Ionizing Radiation, *Health Risks of Radon and Other Internally Deposited Alpha-Emitters: BEIR IV* (Washington, D.C.: National Academy Press, 1988), pp. 303–347. See also J. M. Deutsch and the Interagency Review Group on Nuclear Waste Management, *Report to the President*, TID-2817 (Springfield, Va.: National Technical Information Service, October 1978); U.S. Environmental Protection Agency, *Considerations of Environmental Protection Criteria for Radioactive Waste* (Washington, D.C.: Environmental Protection Agency, 1978). For information on the Kentucky site, see B. Kiernan et al., Legislative Research Commission, *Report of the Special Advisory Committee on Nuclear Waste Disposal*, no. 142 (Frankfort, Ky.: Legislative Research Commission, October 1977). Transuranics such as plutonium are no longer considered part of low-level radioactive waste by government regulators; so current low-level burial does not include them.

7. W. F. Naedele, "Nuclear Grave Is Haunting Kentucky," *Philadelphia Bulletin*, 17 May 1979, pp. 1–3. F. Browning, "The Nuclear Wasteland," *New Times* 7, no. 1 (July 1976): 43. D. Zettwock, Project Director for U.S. Geological Survey monitoring of the Maxey Flats site, interview with K. Shrader-Frechette, 2 August 1986 (unpublished, 4 pages).

8. L. Cox and P. Ricci, "Legal and Philosophical Aspects of Risk Analysis," in Paustenbach, *Risk Assessment*, p. 1026.

9. H. Kunreuther, J. Linnerooth, and J. Vaupel, "A Decision-Process Perspective on Risk and Policy Analysis," in *Resolving Locational Conflict*, ed. R. W. Lake (New Brunswick, N.J.: Center for Urban Policy Research, Rutgers University, 1987), p. 261. (Liquefied natural gas is a potential source of energy requiring a fairly complicated technological process for its utilization. It also has a low probability of creating severe losses because it becomes explosive in its gaseous state. During transport, it can be converted to its liquid state at about 1/600 of its gaseous volume. After being shipped in special tankers, it is regasified at a terminal and distributed.)

10. N. C. Rasmussen, "Methods of Hazard Analysis and Nuclear Safety Engineering," in *The Three Mile Island Nuclear Accident*, ed. T. Moss and D. Sills (New York: New York Academy of Sciences, 1981).

11. See, for example, D. Cleverly et al., *Municipal Waste Combustion Study* (New York: Taylor and Francis, 1989), pp. 2.6–2.12. See also S. Frishman, Director, Texas Nuclear Waste Programs Office, "Response to Post Hearing Questions from the U.S. Senate Committee on Environment and Public Works, Subcommittee on Nuclear Regulation," Nuclear Waste Repository Program Oversight Hearing, Washington, D.C., 2 June 1987 (unpublished statement, 7 pages). Finally, see J. K. Marquis and G. Siek, "Sensitive Populations and Risk Assessment in Environmental Policymaking," in *Hazard Assessment of Chemicals*, ed. J. Saxena (New York: Taylor and Francis, 1989), pp. 22–25.

12. W. V. O. Quine and J. Ullian, *The Web of Belief*, 2nd ed. (New York: Random House, 1978), chap. 1.

13. R. Rudner, "The Scientist *qua* Scientist Makes Value Judgments," in *Introductory Readings in the Philosophy of Science*, ed. E. D. Klemke, R. Hollinger, and A. Kline (Buffalo, N.Y.: Prometheus Books, 1980), p. 236.

14. See note 10, Chapter One.

15. H. M. Seip and A. B. Heiberg, "Pilot Study of Risk Management of Chemicals in the Environment," in *Risk Management of Chemicals in the Environment*, ed. H. M. Seip and A. B. Heiberg (New York: Plenum, 1989), pp. 6–7. See also W. Hafele, "Benefit-Risk Tradeoffs in Nuclear Power Generation," in *Energy and the Environment*, ed. H. Ashley, R. Rudman, and C. Whipple (Elmsford, N.Y.: Pergamon Press, 1976), p. 181; D. Okrent and C. Whipple, *Approach to Societal Risk Acceptance Criteria and Risk Management*, Report no. PB-271264 (Washington, D.C.: U.S. Department of Commerce, 1977), pp. 1–9. See the previous chapter for a discussion of the naive-positivist views.

16. See note 13 and B. Allen and K. Crump, "Aspects of Quantitative Risk Assessment as Applied to Cancer," in *Quantitative Risk Assessment*, ed. J. M. Humber and R. F. Almeder (Clifton, N.J.: Humana Press, 1987), pp. 129–146. For an account of the method of hypothesis deduction, see C. Hempel, *Philosophy of Natural Science* (Englewood Cliffs, N.J.: Prentice-Hall, 1966).

17. See C. Whipple, "Nonpessimistic Risk Assessment," in Paustenbach, *Risk Assessment*, pp 1105–1120. See also U.S. Nuclear Regulatory Commission, *Reactor Safety Study: An Assessment of Accident Risks in U.S. Commercial Nuclear Power Plants*, NUREG-75/104, WASH-1400 (Washington, D.C.: Government Printing Office, 1975), p. 37; C. Starr and C. Whipple, "Risks of Risk Decisions," *Science* 208, No. 4448 (6 June 1980): 1116; B. Cohen and I. Lee, "A Catalog of Risks," *Health Physics* 36, No. 6 (1979): 707; W. Hafele, "Energy," in *Science, Technology, and the Human Prospect*, ed. C. Starr and P. Ritterbush (Elmsford, N.Y.: Pergamon Press, 1979), p. 139; and M. Maxey, "Managing Low-Level Radioactive Wastes," in *Low-Level Radioactive Waste Management*, ed. J. Watson (Williamsburg, Va.: Health Physics Society, 1979), pp. 410, 417. See also B. Cohen, "Risk Analyses of Buried Wastes," in Paustenbach, *Risk Assessment*, p. 575.

18. See R. N. Andrews, "Environmental Impact Assessment and Risk Assessment," in *Environmental Impact Assessment*, ed. P. Wathern (London: Unwin Hyman, 1988), pp. 85–97. See also S. E. Dreyfus, "Formal Models vs. Human Situational Understanding . . . ," *Technology and People* 1 (1982): 61; D. MacLean, "Understanding the Nuclear Power Controversy," in *Scientific Controversies*, ed. A. Caplan and H. Engelhardt (Cambridge, England: Cambridge University Press, 1987), part V; and D. MacLean, "Quantified Risk Assessment and the Quality of Life," in *Uncertain Power*, ed. D. Zinberg (Elmsford, N.Y.: Pergamon Press, 1983), part V. Finally, see L. Clarke, *Acceptable Risk? Making Decisions in a Toxic Environment* (Berkeley and Los Angeles: University of California Press, 1989).

19. Allen and Crump, "Aspects of Quantitative Risk Assessment," p. 14. See also D. Hattis and J. Smith, "What's Wrong with Quantitative Risk Assessment?" in Humber and Almeder, *Quantitative Risk Assessment*, pp. 23, 57–105.

20. See the last chapter for arguments on this point. See also note 11.

21. S. Levine, "Panel: Use of Risk Assessment," in Mitre Corporation, *Symposium/Workshop on Nuclear and Nonnuclear Energy Systems: Risk Assessment and Governmental Decision Making* (McLean, Va.: Mitre Corporation, 1979), p. 634. See Paustenbach, "A Comprehensive Methodology," pp. 296–328.

22. F. Hapgood, "Risk-Benefit Analysis: Putting a Price on Life," *Atlantic Monthly* 243, no. 1 (January 1979): 38. Assessors determine the amount of money necessary to save a life by dividing the increment in dollars spent yearly for risk abatement in a particular area by the additional lives saved annually in that area. For a recent discussion of value-of-life problems, see J. L. Regens, "Attitudes toward Risk-Benefit Analysis for Managing Effects of Chemical Exposures," in Seip and Heiberg, *Risk Management of Chemicals*, pp. 75–88.

23. For other examples of how it is evaluative, see Allen and Crump, "Aspects of Quantitative Risk Assessment"; Hattis and Smith, "What's Wrong with Quantitative Risk Assessment?"; and P. Ricci and A. Henderson, "Fear, Fiat, and Fiasco," in *Phenotypic Variation in Populations*, ed. A. Woodhead, M. Bender, and R. Leonard (New York: Plenum, 1988), pp. 285–293. See also R. Setlow, "Relevance of Phenotypic Variation in Risk," in Woodhead, *Phenotypic Variation*, pp. 1–5.

24. M. Schneiderman, "Risk Assessment: Where Do We Want It to Go? What Do We Do to Make It Go There?" in Humber and Almeder, *Quantitative Risk Assessment*, pp. 107–128. See E. Foulkes, "Factors Determining Target Doses," in Saxena, *Hazard Assessment of Chemicals*, pp. 31–47.

25. K. A. Busch, "Statistical Approach to Quantitative Risk Assessment," in Humber and Almeder, *Quantitative Risk Assessment*, pp. 9–55. See also Setlow, "Phenotypic Variation in Risk."

26. Rudner, "Scientist *qua* Scientist," pp. 130ff.

27. See E. McMullin, "Values in Science," in *Philosophy of Science Association 1982*, ed. P. Asquith (East Lansing, Mich.: Philosophy of Science Association, 1983), vol. 2, sec. 1. See also sections headed "The Principle of Neutrality" and "The Case against Neutrality " in Chapter Three of this volume.

28. See McMullin, "Values in Science," vol. 2, secs. 1, 2, 4. See also E. Nagel, *The Structure of Science* (New York: Harcourt, Brace, 1961), p. 492.

29. Some of the major epistemic values that are part of scientific evaluation are predictive accuracy, internal coherence, external consistency, unifying power, fertility, and simplicity.

30. See McMullin, "Values in Science," vol. 2, secs. 4, 5, 6. See the section headed "A Path between Naive Positivism and Cultural Relativism" in Chapter Three of this volume.

31. This objection was made by University of Virginia philosopher Paul Humphreys in response to an oral presentation of this chapter in Atlanta.

32. Moreover, if a postulate that is adopted because of a list of methodological *preferences*, rather than hard data, is not a value, then a highly stipulative and restrictive sense of the term 'value' must underlie this claim. But if so, then

there are strong reasons for believing that value judgments in the sense already explained are indeed part of science.

33. The annual risk of death from air pollution in the eastern United States is 2×10^{-4}, as compared to 3.6×10^{-3} from smoking a pack a day (Seip and Heiberg, "Pilot Study," in *Risk Management of Chemicals*, p. 4). See K. S. Shrader-Frechette, *Nuclear Power and Public Policy* (Boston: Reidel, 1983), esp. chaps. 1 and 4.

34. For studies of carcinogen risk assessment, see Paustenbach, *Risk Assessment*. For discussion of the methodological problems arising at each of the three stages of risk assessment, see Cox and Ricci, "Legal and Philosophical Aspects," pp. 1033–1036. See also D. J. Paustenbach, "Introduction" and "A Survey of Health Risk Assessment," in *Risk Assessment*, pp. 1–24, 27–124; K. S. Shrader-Frechette, *Risk Analysis and Scientific Method* (Boston: Reidel, 1985), pp. 15–51; F. Press, *Risk Assessment in the Federal Government* (Washington, D.C.: National Academy Press, 1983); and *Quantitative Risk Assessment in Regulation*, ed. L. Lave (Washington, D.C.: Brookings Institution, 1982).

35. G. Bakale, "Detection of Mutagens and Carcinogens by Physicochemical Techniques," in Saxena, *Hazard Assessment of Chemicals*, p. 86. See also Shrader-Frechette, *Risk Analysis*, p. 20. For more information on risk identification and epidemiological methods, see Woodhead, *Phenotypic Variation*, and Paustenbach, *Risk Assessment*.

36. D. D. Edwards, "Food Science," *Science News* 131, no. 23 (6 June 1987): 361.

37. H. E. Longino, "Comments on 'What's Wrong with Quantitative Risk Assessment?' " presented at the Philosophy of Science Association meeting, Pittsburgh, 24 October 1986, pp. 3–11. See also Fabrikant, *Health Risks of Radon*, Shrader-Frechette, *Nuclear Power*, pp. 25–27. For some of the difficulties associated with formulating dose-response curves, see Paustenbach, *Risk Assessment*; Saxena, *Hazard Assessment of Chemicals*; and Woodhead, *Phenotypic Variation*.

38. Longino,"Comments," p. 3. See also J. Purdham, "Whose Life Is It Anyway?" *At the Centre: The Canadian Centre for Occupational Health and Safety* 10, no. 1 (March 1987): 9; and Foulkes, "Target Doses," pp. 43ff. For one study that does take account of some synergistic effects, see Fabrikant, *Health Risks of Radon*, pp. 442ff. For problems with dose because of phenotypic variation, see Woodhead, *Phenotypic Variation*.

39. For problems associated with the pathways of toxic chemicals, see Foulkes, "Target Doses"; and G. Zapponi and C. Lupi, "Environmental and Health Impact Assessment of Soil Pollutants: The Seveso Accident as a Typical Example," in Seip and Heiberg, *Risk Management of Chemicals*, pp. 111–126.

40. See F. von Hippel and T. Cochran, "Chernobyl, the Emerging Story: Estimating Long-Term Health Effects," *Bulletin of the Atomic Scientists* 42, no. 7 (August/September 1986): 18–24, esp. 21. (*Note:* Because of a misprint, this volume was originally misnumbered as vol. 43, no. 1.) See also, for example,

E. Marshall, "Reactor Explodes Amid Soviet Silence," *Science* 232, no. 4752 (16 May 1986): 814–815.

41. D. Nebert, "Genes Encoding Drug-Metabolizing Enzymes," in Woodhead, *Phenotypic Variation*, p. 59.

42. See E. Mishan, *Cost-Benefit Analysis* (New York: Praeger, 1976). See also Regens, "Risk-Benefit Analysis," pp. 75–88.

43. See Cox and Ricci, "Legal and Philosophical Aspects," pp. 1038ff.; S. Samuels, "The Arrogance of Intellectual Power," in Woodhead, *Phenotypic Variation*, pp. 113–120. See also Shrader-Frechette, *Risk Analysis*, esp. chaps. 2, 5, 6, and 7.

44. See C. Starr, "General Philosophy of Risk-Benefit Analysis," in *Energy and the Environment*, ed. H. Ashley, R. Rudman, and C. Whipple (Elmsford, N.Y.: Pergamon Press, 1976), pp. 6ff. For discussion of revealed preferences, see Clarke, *Acceptable Risk?* pp. 148ff., and Shrader-Frechette, *Risk Analysis*, pp. 34ff., 169ff.

45. See B. Fischhoff et al., *Acceptable Risk* (New York: Cambridge University Press, 1981). For further discussion of expressed preferences, see Shrader-Frechette, *Risk Analysis*, pp. 41ff. and 167ff., as well as L. Cox, "Comparative Risk Measures," in Woodhead, *Phenotypic Variation*, pp. 236ff.

46. Fischhoff, *Acceptable Risk*, pp. 87–88. See also Cox and Ricci, "Legal and Philosophical Aspects," pp. 128–141; Shrader-Frechette, *Risk Analysis*, pp. 44ff.

47. For discussion of the Dow, Monsanto, and Agent Orange studies, see H. Leung and D. Paustenbach, "Assessing Health Risks in the Workplace," in Paustenbach, *Risk Assessment*, pp. 699–705. For discussion of weapons tests involving people in the U.S. military service, see the section headed "Are Environmentalists Distrustful?" in Chapter Two. See also Shrader-Frechette, *Nuclear Power*, pp. 99–100, and V. P. Bond, "Causality of a Given Cancer after Known Radiation Exposure," in *Hazards: Technology and Fairness*, ed. R. W. Kates et al. (Washington, D.C.: National Academy Press, 1986), pp. 24–43. See the last two chapters of this volume for proposed reforms.

48. H. Inhaber, "Risk with Energy from Conventional and Nonconventional Sources," *Science* 203, no. 4382 (23 February 1979): 718–723. See also H. Inhaber, *Risk of Energy Production*, Report no. AECB-1119 (Ottawa: Atomic Energy Control Board, 1978).

49. Inhaber, "Risk with Energy," p. 718. For an excellent methodological critique of Inhaber's energy studies, see P. Gleick and J. Holdren, "Assessing Environmental Risks of Energy," *American Journal of Public Health* 71, no. 9 (September 1981): 1046–1050.

50. According to L. S. Johns and associates, of the OTA Solar Energy Staff (in *Application of Solar Technology to Today's Energy Needs*, 2 vols. [Washington, D.C.: U.S. Office of Technology Assessment, 1978], 1:3), "Onsite solar devices could be made competitive in markets representing over 40 percent of U.S. energy demand by the mid-1980's." The OTA staff goes on to say that low-

temperature solar uses, which comprise 40 percent of total U.S. energy needs, are currently competitive economically with existing alternatives (pp. 13–14), even in cities such as Boston, Albuquerque, and Omaha, where heating needs are often significant (pp. 31ff.).

51. Inhaber, "Risk with Energy," p. 721. See Gleick and Holdren, "Assessing Environmental Risks."

52. Ibid.

53. Inhaber, "Risk with Energy," pp. 721–722. See Gleick and Holdren, "Assessing Environmental Risks."

54. Inhaber, "Risk with Energy," pp. 721–722. For further criticism of the Inhaber report, see J. Herbert, C. Swanson, and P. Reddy, "A Risky Business," *Environment* 21, no. 6 (July/August 1979): 28–33; and J. Holdren, K. Smith, and G. Morris, "Energy: Calculating the Risks," *Science* 204, no. 4393 (11 May 1979): 564–568; and Gleick and Holdren, "Assessing Environmental Risks."

55. A. J. Van Horn and R. Wilson, "The Status of Risk-Benefit Analysis," discussion paper, Energy and Environmental Policy Center, Harvard University, Cambridge, Mass., 1976, p. 18; P. D. Pahner, "The Psychological Displacement of Anxiety," in *Risk-Benefit Methodology and Applications*, ed. D. Okrent (Los Angeles: School of Engineering and Applied Science, UCLA, 1975), p. 574. See also R. Zeckhauser, "Procedures for Valuing Lives," *Public Policy* 23, no. 4 (1975): 442.

56. See note 54.

Chapter Five

1. J. M. Mann, Director, Special Program on AIDS, World Health Organization, in U.S. Congress, *Hearing before the Committee on Labor and Human Resources*, U.S. Senate, 16 January 1987 (Washington, D.C.: Government Printing Office, 1987), p. 96.

2. R. Bayer, *Private Acts, Social Consequences* (New York: Macmillan, 1989), p. 236. There are a number of ways, in the West, in which AIDS victims' chances of survival can be increased. See D. D. Edwards, "Boosting Cell Numbers in AIDS," *Science News* 132, no. 11 (12 September 1987): 165. Volunteers in the United States can also be injected with an experimental AIDS vaccine; see D. D. Edwards, "Human Test of AIDS Vaccine Approved," *Science News* 132, no. 8 (22 August 1987): 116, and "Enzyme Blockers Slay AIDS 'Giants,'" *Science News* 132, no. 19 (7 November 1987).

3. See A. Wildavsky, "No Risk Is the Highest Risk of All," *American Scientist* 67, no. 1 (1979).

4. See D. Hattis and J. Smith, "What's Wrong with Quantitative Risk Assessment?" in *Quantitative Risk Assessment*, ed. J. Humber and R. Almeder (Clifton, N.J.: Humana Press, 1987), pp. 57–105.

5. S. Novick, *The Electric War* (San Francisco: Sierra Club, 1976), pp. 318–319. See E. D. Muchnicki, "The Proper Role of the Public in Nuclear Power

Plant Licensing Decisions," *Atomic Energy Law Journal* 15, no. 1 (Spring 1973): 55, 59. See also S. Samuels, "The Arrogance of Intellectual Power," in *Phenotypic Variation in Populations*, ed. A. Woodhead, M. Bender, and R. Leonard (New York: Plenum, 1988), pp. 113–120.

6. See R. N. Andrews, "Environmental Impact Assessment and Risk Assessment," in *Environmental Impact Assessment*, ed. P. Wathern (London: Unwin Hyman, 1988), pp. 85–97. See also K. S. Shrader-Frechette, *Science Policy, Ethics, and Economic Methodology* (Boston: Reidel, 1985), pp. 68–71.

7. C. Whipple, "Nonpessimistic Risk Assessment," in *The Risk Assessment of Environmental and Human Health Hazards*, ed. D. J. Paustenbach (New York: Wiley, 1989), pp. 1105–1120. See also the previous chapter; Hattis and Smith, "What's Wrong with Quantitative Risk Assessment?"; and B. Allen and K. Crump, "Aspects of Quantitative Risk Assessment as Applied to Cancer," in Humber and Almeder, *Quantitative Risk Assessment*, pp. 129–146.

8. For an example of assessors who hold this belief, see L. Lave and B. Leonard, "Regulating Coke Oven Emissions," in Paustenbach, *Risk Assessment*, p. 1069. For ethical problems associated with valuing lives, see J. L. Regens, "Attitudes toward Risk-Benefit Analysis for Managing Effects of Chemical Exposures," in *Risk Management of Chemicals in the Environment*, ed. H. M. Seip and A. B. Heiberg (New York: Plenum, 1989), pp. 84–85. See also Seip and Heiberg, "Pilot Study of Risk Management of Chemicals in the Environment," in *Risk Management of Chemicals*, p. 7. See also C. Starr and C. Whipple, "Risks of Risk Decisions," *Science* 208, no. 4448 (6 June 1980): 1118; D. Okrent, "Comment on Societal Risk," *Science* 208, no. 4442 (1980): 374; M. Maxey, "Managing Low-Level Radioactive Wastes," in *Low-Level Radioactive Waste Management*, ed. J. Watson (Williamsburg, Va.: Health Physics Society, 1979), p. 401; C. Comar, "Risk: A Pragmatic *De Minimus* Approach," *Science* 203, no. 4378 (1979): 319; and B. Cohen and I. Lee, "A Catalog of Risks," *Health Physics* 36, no. 6 (1979): 707.

9. One important reason why different persons have different needs is phenotypic variations in populations; see J. K. Marquis and G. Siek, "Sensitive Populations and Risk Assessment in Environmental Policymaking," in *Hazard Assessment of Chemicals*, ed. J. Saxena (New York: Taylor and Francis, 1989), pp. 1–30. See also Woodhead, *Phenotypic Variation*. Some persons also oppose standardization in risk assessment or management because, they claim, different lives, costs, and benefits are incommensurable; see Samuels, "Arrogance of Intellectual Power," and K. S. Shrader-Frechette, *Risk Analysis and Scientific Method* (Boston: Reidel, 1985), pp. 61–87.

10. R. Dworkin, *Taking Rights Seriously* (Cambridge, Mass.: Harvard University Press, 1977), pp. 267–279. For phenotypic reasons why it is impossible to accord the same risk treatment to everyone, see Woodhead, *Phenotypic Variation*.

11. This situation reveals that one never serves merely one goal or value. Rather, every decision has its opportunity costs.

12. Cancer "strikes one out of four Americans," and the number is increasing; "60 to 90 percent of cancer is associated with the environment and therefore is theoretically preventable" (J. C. Lashof et al., *Assessment of Technologies for Determining Cancer Risks from the Environment* [Washington, D.C.: U.S. Office of Technology Assessment, Health and Life Sciences Division, June 1981], p. 3). Admittedly, as S. H. Unger (private communication) points out, many of these cancers are not *in practice* preventable, because they are caused by factors such as natural background radiation. Also, industry spokespersons vehemently deny that this cancer rate is associated with industrial activities (see D. Paustenbach, "A Survey of Health Risk Assessment," in Paustenbach, *Risk Assessment*, p. 36).

13. Quoted by D. Parfit, *Reasons and Persons* (Oxford: Clarendon Press, 1984), p. 511.

14. Comar, "Risk: A Pragmatic *De Minimis* Approach," p. 319. For discussion of *de minimis* risk, see L. Cox and P. Ricci, "Legal and Philosophical Aspects of Risk Analysis," in Paustenbach, *Risk Assessment*, pp. 1028–1041. See also R. Golden and N. Karch, "Assessment of a Waste Site Contaminated with Chromium," in Paustenbach, *Risk Assessment*, p. 595.

15. See the previous note; see also, for example, Starr and Whipple, "Risks of Risk Decisions," p. 1119; and U.S. Nuclear Regulatory Commission, *Reactor Safety Study: An Assessment of Accident Risks in U.S. Commercial Nuclear Power Plants*, NUREG-75/014, WASH-1400 (Washington, D.C.: Government Printing Office, 1975), pp. 38–39.

16. The figure of 10^{-6} is sometimes accepted by risk assessors as the average annual death rate from disease (see, for example, Nuclear Regulatory Commission, *Reactor Safety Study*, p. 39), and it is typically taken as a cutoff point below which risks are assumed to be negligible. More often, assessors claim that the death rate from disease is 10^{-4} and that the natural-hazards mortality rate is 10^{-6} (see, for example, C. Starr, *Current Issues in Energy* [Elmsford, N.Y.: Pergamon Press, 1979], pp. 14ff.). See L. Cox and P. Ricci, "Risk, Uncertainty, and Causation," in Paustenbach, *Risk Assessment*, pp. 134–135.

17. For arguments against average protection and a *de minimis* standard, see Samuels, "Arrogance of Intellectual Power," pp. 116–120. See also A. M. Freeman, "Income Distribution and Environmental Quality," in *Pollution, Resources, and the Environment*, ed. A. Enthoven and A. M. Freeman (New York: Norton, 1973), p. 101. See also, for example, W. Rowe, *An Anatomy of Risk* (New York: Wiley, 1977), p. 290; and B. Fischhoff, P. Slovic, and S. Lichtenstein, "Facts and Fears," in *Societal Risk Assessment*, ed. R. Schwing and W. Albers (New York: Plenum, 1980), p. 208. Moreover, as S. H. Unger (private communication) pointed out, even though the average number of deaths may be the same, for two different risks to which the same population is subjected, it is not clear that both risks are equally desirable or undesirable. See Shrader-Frechette, *Risk Analysis*, chap. 6, esp. pp. 170–171; see also chaps. 3 and 5 in the same volume

for discussion of problems with determination of harms from average numbers of fatalities.

18. See A. Baier, "Poisoning the Wells," in *Values at Risk*, ed. D. MacLean (Totowa, N.J.: Rowman and Allanheld, 1986), esp. pp. 66–67. See also W. Viscusi, *Risk by Choice* (Cambridge, Mass.: Harvard University Press, 1983), pp. 38ff; C. Brown, "Equalizing Differences in the Labor Market," *Quarterly Journal of Economics* 94, no. 1 (February 1980): 113–134; A. E. Dillingham, "The Injury Risk Structure of Occupations and Wages," Ph.D. diss., Cornell University, 1979; R. A. McLean et al., "Compensating Wage Differentials for Hazardous Work: An Empirical Analysis," *Quarterly Review of Economics and Business* 18, no. 3 (1978): 97–107; C. Olson, "Trade Unions, Wages, Occupational Injuries, and Public Policy," Ph.D. diss., University of Wisconsin, Madison, 1979; R. S. Smith, *Compensating Wage Differentials and Hazardous Work*, Technical Analysis Paper no. 5 (Washington, D.C.: Office of Evaluation, Office of the Assistant Secretary for Policy Evaluation and Research, U.S. Department of Labor, 1973); R. Thaler and S. Rosen, "The Value of Saving a Life," in *Household Production and Consumption*, ed. N. E. Terleckyi (New York: National Bureau of Economic Research, 1976), pp. 265–298; and W. K. Viscusi, *Employment Hazards* (Cambridge, Mass.: Harvard University Press, 1979).

For a classic study on the compensating wage differential, see J. Graham and D. Shakow, "Risk and Reward," *Environment* 23, no. 8 (October 1981): 14–20, 44–45; and J. Graham et al., "Risk Compensation," *Environment* 25, no. 1 (January/February 1983): 14–27. Graham and Shakow showed that, when all workers were lumped together according to salary, from lowest paid to highest paid, the average annual probability of fatality increased as the average worker salary increased, much as the theory of the compensating wage differential predicts; each increment in risk of death was associated with an increment in pay. When Graham and his associates followed labor market segmentation theory, however, and disaggregated the workers into two separate groups, they were able to show that, despite higher risk, compensation did not exist for many subgroups in the labor force, particularly unskilled workers, females and members of minorities, workers in small firms, nonunionized workers, workers without seniority benefits, and workers with unstable jobs and low wages. Hence, any argument that the market, through such a differential, compensates persons for their risks cannot in general be substantiated.

19. E. Eckholm, "Unhealthy Jobs," *Environment* 19, no. 6 (August/September 1977): 31–33; see also D. Berman, *Death on the Job* (London: Monthly Review Press, 1978). See Paustenbach, "A Survey," pp. 34–35; and Samuels, "Arrogance of Intellectual Power," pp. 113–120.

20. See, for example, M. W. Jones-Lee, *The Value of Life: An Economic Analysis* (Chicago: University of Chicago Press, 1976), p. 39; Eckholm, "Unhealthy Jobs," pp. 33–34. See C. Starr, "General Philosophy of Risk-Benefit Analysis," in *Energy and the Environment*, ed. H. Ashley, R. Rudman, and C. Whipple

(Elmsford, N.Y.: Pergamon Press, 1976), pp. 15ff.; and Viscusi, *Risk by Choice*, p. 46. See also R. Bayer, "Occupational Exposure and the Lead Standard," in MacLean, *Values at Risk*, pp. 60–76.

21. J. Egerton, "Appalachia's Absentee Landlords," *The Progressive* 45, no. 6 (June 1981): 43–45; and J. Gaventa and W. Horton, Appalachia Land Ownership Task Force, *Land Ownership Patterns and Their Impacts on Appalachian Communities* (Washington, D.C.: Appalachian Regional Commission, 1981), 1:25–59, 210–211. See K. S. Shrader-Frechette, "Agriculture, Ethics, and Restrictions on Property Rights," *Journal of Agricultural Ethics* 1, no. 1 (1988): 21–40.

22. For third-world examples, see Chapter Ten.

23. See A. M. Capron, "Medical Research in Prisons," *Hastings Center Report* 3 (June 1976): 4–6; E. Pattulo, "Who Risks What in Social Research?" *Hastings Center Report* 10 (April 1980): 15–18. See also Shrader-Frechette, *Risk Analysis*, p. 119; and H. Jonas, "Philosophical Reflections on Experimenting with Human Subjects," in *Ethics in Perspective*, ed. K. J. Struhl and P. R. Struhl (New York: Random House, 1975), pp. 342–353. See also D. MacLean, "Risk and Consent," in MacLean, *Values at Risk*, pp. 17–30.

24. A. Brandt, "Racism and Research: The Case of the Tuskegee Syphilis Study," *Hastings Center Report* 8 (December 1978): 21–29.

25. Bayer, "Occupational Exposure," p. 72.

Chapter Six

1. R. Weiss, "How Dare We? Scientists Seek the Sources of Risk-Taking Behavior," *Science News* 132, no. 4 (25 July 1987): 58.

2. Ibid., p. 59.

3. Many risk assessors (such as Cohen, Hafele, Okrent, Whipple, Jones-Lee, Rothschild, and Morgan) employ this strategy. See, for example, C. Whipple, "Nonpessimistic Risk Assessment," in *The Risk Assessment of Environmental and Human Health Hazards*, ed. D. J. Paustenbach (New York: Wiley, 1989), pp. 1112–1113; B. Cohen, "Risk Analyses of Buried Wastes," in Paustenbach, *Risk Assessment*, p. 575. See Chapter Three of this volume for citations to these risk assessors' claims about the distinction between actual and perceived risks.

4. E. Liebow and J. Fawcett, "Socioeconomic Aspects of Repository-Related Risk Perceptions: A Preliminary Literature Review," Battelle Human Affairs Research Center, Seattle, 16 July 1987, pp. 4, 6; see also J. Short, "The Social Fabric at Risk: Toward the Social Transformation of Risk-Analysis," *American Sociological Review* 49, no. 6 (December 1984): 711–725; and C. Perrow, *Normal Accidents: Living with High-Risk Technologies* (New York: Basic Books, 1984).

5. See note 3.

6. For example, see Whipple, "Nonpessimistic Risk Assessment," p. 1113; and E. Liebow (Battelle Human Affairs Research Center, Seattle), letter to author, 17 July 1987; Liebow and Fawcett, "Socioeconomic Aspects"; E. Liebow

and D. Herborn, "Assessing the Economic and Social Effects of Perceiving the Repository as 'Risky': A Preliminary Approach," Battelle Human Affairs Research Center, Seattle, 28 May 1987. On 6 August 1987, the Battelle researchers assembled experts from all over the United States to discuss the problems associated with mitigating the impacts of risk *perceptions*; see *Assessing Social and Economic Effects of Perceived Risk*, ed. S. M. Nealey and E. Liebow (Richland, Wash.: Pacific Northwest Laboratory, March 1988), PNL-6515, BHARC-800/88/005 UC-70.

7. See R. E. Kasperson et al., "Radioactive Wastes and the Social Amplification of Risk," in *Waste Management '87: Proceedings of the Symposium on Waste Management at Tucson, Arizona* (Tucson: University of Arizona Press, 1987), p. 2; Liebow and Fawcett, "Socioeconomic Aspects," p. 4; Liebow and Herborn, "Assessing Economic and Social Effects," p. 3.

8. Liebow, letter to author, 17 July 1987, p. 1; Liebow and Fawcett, "Socioeconomic Aspects," p. 1. For an excellent discussion of the risk perceptions of the public, see B. Wynne, *Risk Management and Hazardous Waste* (New York: Springer-Verlag, 1987), pp. 10ff.

9. See Chapter Four.

10. See Chapter Two.

11. See *Values at Risk*, ed. D. MacLean (Totowa, N.J.: Rowman and Allanheld, 1986). See also K. S. Shrader-Frechette, *Risk Analysis and Scientific Method* (Boston: Reidel, 1985), pp. 176ff. Finally, see R. N. Andrews, "Environmental Impact Assessment and Risk Assessment," in *Environmental Impact Assessment*, ed. P. Wathern (London: Unwin Hyman, 1988), pp. 85–97; and L. Cox and P. Ricci, "Legal and Philosophical Aspects of Risk Analysis," in Paustenbach, *Risk Assessment*, pp. 1017–1046.

12. See Chapter Eight.

13. For discussion of the formaldehyde case, see P. Ricci and A. Henderson, "Fear, Fiat, and Fiasco," in *Phenotypic Variation in Populations*, ed. A. Woodhead, M. Bender, and R. Leonard (New York: Plenum, 1988), pp. 288–293. See also D. Paustenbach, "A Survey of Health Risk Assessment," and R. Gammage and C. Travis, "Formaldehyde Exposure and Risk," in Paustenbach, *Risk Assessment*, pp. 38–39, 601–611.

14. See the next chapter for discussion of this point.

15. A. Tversky and D. Kahneman, "Belief in the Law of Small Numbers," in *Judgment under Uncertainty: Heuristics and Biases*, ed. D. Kahneman, P. Slovic, and A. Tversky (Cambridge, England: Cambridge University Press, 1982), pp. 23–31; D. Kahneman and A. Tversky, "Subjective Probability," in Kahneman, *Judgment under Uncertainty*, pp. 46–47. See also note 13.

16. See the previous note. See also S. Oskamp, "Overconfidence in Case-Study Judgments," in Kahneman, *Judgment under Uncertainty*, pp. 287–293.

17. See Whipple, "Nonpessimistic Risk Assessment," and Cohen, "Risk Analyses."

18. For various definitions of risk, see, for example, L. Cox, "Comparative

Risk Measures," in Woodhead, *Phenotypic Variation*, pp. 233–243. See also earlier chapters in this volume. For discussion of "relative risk," for example, see the following items in Paustenbach's *Risk Assessment*: B. Ames, R. Magaw, and L. Gold, "Ranking Possible Carcinogens," pp. 1083ff.; M. Layard and A. Silvers, "Epidemiology in Environmental Risk Assessment," p. 159; N. Harley, "Environmental Lung Cancer Risk from Radon Daughter Exposure," p. 620; and Cohen, "Risk Analyses," p. 574.

19. Liebow and Herborn, "Assessing Economic and Social Effects," p. 4.

20. L. W. Barnthouse et al., "Population Biology in the Courtroom: The Hudson River Controversy," *BioScience* 34, no. 1 (January 1984): 17–18.

21. E. Peelle (Oak Ridge National Laboratory), "The MRS Task Force: Economic and Non-economic Incentives . . . ," unpublished manuscript based on lecture given at Waste Management '87 Conference, University of Arizona, 4 March 1987; see also note 18 and Andrews, "Environmental Impact Assessment."

22. Examples of important essays on risk and consent are included in MacLean, *Values at Risk*, and in *Hazards: Technology and Fairness*, ed. R. W. Kates et al. (Washington, D.C.: National Academy Press, 1986); see also Cox and Ricci, "Legal and Philosophical Aspects." Examples of classic essays on informed consent and medical experimentation include H. Jonas, "Philosophical Reflections on Experimenting with Human Subjects," W. Curran, "The Tuskegee Syphilis Study," and B. Barber, "The Ethics of Experimentation," in *Moral Choices*, ed. P. Rieff and I. Finkle (Del Mar, Calif.: Publishers Inc., 1977), pp. 254ff. See also P. Freund, "Ethical Problems in Human Experimentation," H. Beecher, "Ethics and Clinical Research," and C. Havighurst, "Compensating Persons Injured in Human Experimentation," in *Readings on Ethical and Social Issues in Biomedical Engineering*, ed. R. Wertz (Englewood Cliffs, N.J.: Prentice-Hall, 1973), pp. 16–54.

23. See Chapters Eleven and Twelve. See also note 16. See E. Peelle, "Hazardous Waste Management Outlook," unpublished manuscript, research published by TVA and U.S. Department of Energy, contract no. DE-AC05–840R21400; E. Peelle et al., "Incentives and Nuclear Waste Siting," *Energy Systems and Policy* 7, no. 4 (1983): 323ff.

24. For arguments to this effect, see Chapters Eight, Ten, Eleven, and Twelve of this volume, as well as J. J. Thomson, *Rights, Restitution, and Risk* (Cambridge, Mass.: Harvard University Press, 1986). See also S. A. Carnes et al., "Incentives in Nuclear Waste Siting," in *Resolving Locational Conflict*, ed. R. W. Lake (New Brunswick, N.J.: Center for Urban Policy Research, Rutgers University, 1987), pp. 354ff. See also M. O'Hare, "Not on My Block You Don't," *Public Policy* 25, no. 4 (1977): 407–458.

25. For discussion of compensation for risks, see part 2 of Kates, *Hazards*. See Shrader-Frechette, *Risk Analysis*, chap. 4, for a discussion of the compensating wage differential. See also Shrader-Frechette, *Science Policy, Ethics, and Economic Methodology* (Boston: Reidel, 1985).

26. See L. S. Bacow and J. R. Milkey, "Overcoming Local Opposition to Hazardous Waste Facilities," in Lake, *Resolving Locational Conflict*, pp. 164ff.

27. Ibid., p. 164.

28. For discussion of "necessary risks," see S. Samuels, "The Arrogance of Intellectual Power," in Woodhead, *Phenotypic Variation*, pp. 118ff.

29. For further discussion of risk compensation, see Cox and Ricci, "Legal and Philosophical Aspects," pp. 1017–1046; S. Carnes et al., *Incentives and the Siting of Radioactive Waste Facilities*, ORNL/5880 (Oak Ridge, Tenn.: Oak Ridge National Laboratories, 1982); H. Kunreuther, J. Linerooth, and J. Vaupel, "A Decision-Process Perspective on Risk and Policy Analysis," in Lake, *Resolving Locational Conflict*, pp. 260–274, esp. pp. 270ff.; R. McMahon et al., *Using Compensation and Incentives When Siting Hazardous Waste Management Facilities*, SW 942 (Washington, D.C.: U.S. Environmental Protection Agency, 1981); M. O'Hare and D. R. Sanderson, "Fair Compensation and the Boomtown Problem," in Lake, *Resolving Locational Conflict*, pp. 376ff.; H. Raiffa, *The Art of Science and Negotiation* (Cambridge, Mass.: Harvard University Press, 1982); G. Rochlin, *The Role of Participatory Impact Assessment in Radioactive Waste Management Program Activities*, Report no. IGS/RW-002 (Berkeley: Institute of Governmental Studies, University of California, 1980); P. M. Sandman, "Getting to Maybe," in Lake, *Resolving Locational Conflict*, pp. 333ff.

30. K. S. Shrader-Frechette, *Nuclear Power and Public Policy* (Boston: Reidel, 1983), p. 78.

31. M. Silberman, "Risky Business: Congress Debates Nuclear Insurance," *Not Man Apart*, May–June 1987, p. 1.

32. Shrader-Frechette, *Nuclear Power*, chap. 4, pp. 73–101.

Chapter Seven

1. A. Weinberg, "Risk Assessment, Regulation, and the Limits," in *Phenotypic Variation in Populations*, ed. A. Woodhead, M. Bender, and R. Leonard (New York: Plenum, 1988), pp. 121–128.

2. M. Maxey, "Managing Low-Level Radioactive Wastes," in *Low-Level Radioactive Waste Management*, ed. J. Watson (Williamsburg, Va.: Health Physics Society, 1979), pp. 400–409.

3. See, for example, B. Cohen, "Risk Analyses of Buried Wastes," in *The Risk of Environmental and Human Health Hazards*, ed. D. J. Paustenbach (New York: Wiley, 1989), p. 575. See also C. Whipple, "Nonpessimistic Risk Assessment," in Paustenbach, *Risk Assessment*, pp. 1112–1113. Finally, see B. Cohen and I. Lee, "A Catalog of Risks," *Health Physics* 36, no. 6 (1979): 707; W. Hafele, "Energy," in *Science, Technology, and the Human Prospect*, ed. C. Starr and P. Ritterbush (Elmsford, N.Y.: Pergamon Press, 1979), p. 139; C. Starr, "Benefit-Cost Studies in Sociotechnical Systems," in Committee on Public Engineering Policy, *Perspectives on Benefit-Risk Decision Making* (Washington, D.C.: National Academy of Engineering, 1972), pp. 26–27; L. Lave, "Discussion," in Mitre

Corporation, *Symposium/Workshop on Nuclear and Nonnuclear Energy Systems: Risk Assessment and Governmental Decision Making* (McLean, Va.: Mitre Corporation, 1979), p. 484.

4. See, for example, Cohen, "Risk Analyses," p. 575; and Whipple, "Nonpessimistic Risk Assessment," pp. 1112–1113. See also K. S. Shrader-Frechette, "Economics, Risk-Cost-Benefit Analysis, and the Linearity Assumption," in *Philosophy of Science Association 1982*, ed. P. Asquith and T. Nickles (East Lansing, Mich.: Philosophy of Science Association, 1982), vol. 1.

5. L. Cox and P. Ricci, "Legal and Philosophical Aspects of Risk Analysis," in Paustenbach, *Risk Assessment*, pp. 1017–1046. See also W. Rowe, *An Anatomy of Risk* (New York: Wiley, 1977), p. 926.

6. B. Fischhoff, P. Slovic, and S. Lichtenstein, "Facts and Fears," in *Societal Risk Assessment*, ed. R. Schwing and W. Albers (New York: Plenum, 1980), p. 207. See also R. W. Kates et al., *Hazards: Technology and Fairness* (Washington, D.C.: National Academy Press, 1986), part 2.

7. S. Samuels, "The Arrogance of Intellectual Power," in Woodhead, *Phenotypic Variation*, pp. 113–120. See also P. D. Pahner, "The Psychological Displacement of Anxiety: An Application to Nuclear Energy," in *Risk-Benefit Methodology and Application*, ed. D. Okrent (Los Angeles: School of Engineering and Applied Science, UCLA, 1975), p. 575.

8. P. Gleick and J. Holdren, "Assessing the Environmental Risks of Energy," *American Journal of Public Health* 71, no. 9 (September 1981): 1046. See also A. J. Van Horn and R. Wilson, "The Status of Risk-Benefit Analysis," discussion paper, Energy and Environmental Policy Center, Harvard University, 1976, p. 19.

9. C. Starr and C. Whipple, "Risks of Risk Decisions," *Science* 208, no. 4448 (6 June 1980): 1116; Cohen, "Risk Analyses," pp. 575–576.

10. Starr, "Benefit-Cost Studies," pp. 26–27.

11. Ibid., pp. 27–29.

12. Cohen, "Risk Analyses," p. 575; Starr and Whipple, "Risks of Risk Decisions," p. 1116; C. Starr, *Current Issues in Energy* (Elmsford, N.Y.: Pergamon Press, 1979), pp. 16–17.

13. See note 9.

14. H. Otway, "Risk Assessment and the Social Response to Nuclear Power," *Journal of the British Nuclear Engineering Society* 16, no. 4 (1977): 331.

15. Ibid.

16. Ibid., p. 332.

17. Ibid.

18. E. Lawless, *Technology and Social Shock* (New Brunswick, N.J.: Rutgers University Press, 1977), pp. 497–498, 512.

19. J. W. Falco and R. Moraski, "Methods Used in the United States for the Assessment and Management of Health Risk Due to Chemicals," in *Risk Management of Chemicals in the Environment*, ed. H. M. Seip and A. B. Heiberg (New York: Plenum, 1989), pp. 37–60.

20. R. Reitz et al., "Use of Physiological Pharmacokinetics in Cancer Risk Assessments," in Paustenbach, *Risk Assessment*, pp. 238–265, esp. p. 258.

21. Falco and Moraski, "Methods," p. 55.

22. Lawless, *Technology*, pp. 349–357, 434–435, 490.

23. Fischhoff, "Facts and Fears"; Kates, *Hazards*; B. Fischhoff et al., "How Safe Is Safe Enough?" *Policy Sciences* 9, no. 2 (1978): 150. See also Cox and Ricci, "Legal and Philosophical Aspects," pp. 1017–1046.

24. See note 51.

25. Fischhoff, "Facts and Fears," p. 192.

26. Ibid.

27. Fischhoff, "How Safe Is Safe Enough?" pp. 140–142, and "Facts and Fears," p. 202. See also R. Kasper, "Perceptions of Risk and Their Effects on Decision Making," in Schwing and Albers, *Societal Risk*, p. 75.

28. Fischhoff, "How Safe Is Safe Enough?" pp. 148–149; and H. Green, "Cost-Benefit Assessment and the Law," *George Washington Law Review* 45, no. 5 (1977): 909–910. See also L. Clarke, *Acceptable Risk? Making Decisions in a Toxic Environment* (Berkeley and Los Angeles: University of California Press, 1989), pp. 178–182.

29. Fischhoff, "Facts and Fears," p. 208; and Rowe, *Anatomy of Risk*, p. 290. See Cox and Ricci, "Legal and Philosophical Aspects," pp. 1036–1037.

30. J. Yellin, "Judicial Review and Nuclear Power," *George Washington Law Review* 45, no. 5 (1977): 992.

31. Ibid., p. 987. See Whipple, "Nonpessimistic Risk Assessment," p. 1111.

32. Yellin, "Judicial Review," pp. 983–984.

33. Ibid., pp. 987–988. See P. Huber, "The Bhopalization of American Tort Law," in Kates, *Hazards*, pp. 89–110.

34. Clarke, *Acceptable Risk?* p. 181.

35. R. N. Andrews, "Environmental Impact Assessment and Risk Assessment," in *Environmental Impact Assessment*, ed. P. Wathern (London: Unwin Hyman, 1988), pp. 85–97.

36. Starr and Whipple, "Risks of Risk Decisions," p. 1116.

37. U.S. Nuclear Regulatory Commission, *Reactor Safety Study: An Assessment of Accident Risks in U.S. Commercial Nuclear Power Plants*, NUREG-75/014, WASH-1400 (Washington, D.C.: Government Printing Office, 1975), pp. 15, 40, 96–97, 224.

38. Cox and Ricci, "Legal and Philosophical Aspects," p. 1027.

39. D. Okrent and C. Whipple, *Approach to Societal Risk Acceptance Criteria and Risk Management*, PB-271264 (Washington, D.C.: U.S. Department of Commerce, 1975), p. 10. For information on the risk posed by methylene chloride, see Falco and Moraski, "Methods," and Reitz, "Physiological Pharmacokinetics."

40. W. Lowrance, "The Nature of Risk," in Schwing and Albers, *Societal Risk*, p. 6. See Rowe, *Anatomy of Risk*, p. 264.

41. W. Fairley, "Criteria for Evaluating the 'Small' Probability," in Okrent, *Risk-Benefit Methodology*, p. 425.

42. See Falco and Moraski, "Methods"; Reitz, "Physiological Pharmacokinetics." See also Nuclear Regulatory Commission, *Reactor Safety Study*, Appendix XI, 2-1—2-14; W. Hafele, "Benefit-Risk Tradeoffs in Nuclear Power Generation," in *Energy and the Environment: A Risk-Benefit Approach*, ed. H. Ashley et al. (Elmsford, N.Y.: Pergamon Press, 1976), pp. 159–169. See Whipple, "Nonpessimistic Risk Assessment," and Cohen, "Risk Analyses."

43. Gleick and Holdren, "Assessing Environmental Risks," p. 1046.

44. Ibid., pp. 1046, 1049. See R. Zeckhauser, "Procedures for Valuing Lives," *Public Policy* 23, no. 4 (1975): 445; Committee on Public Engineering Policy, *Perspectives on Benefit-Risk Decision Making* (Washington, D.C.: National Academy of Engineering, 1972), p. 10. See also Lowrance, "Nature of Risk," p. 11.

45. N. C. Rasmussen, "Methods of Hazard Analysis and Nuclear Safety Engineering," in *The Three Mile Island Nuclear Accident*, ed. T. Moss and D. Sill (New York: New York Academy of Sciences, 1981), p. 29.

46. Fairley, "Criteria," pp. 406–407.

47. L. Philipson, "Panel," in Mitre Corp., *Symposium*, p. 246.

48. Fischhoff, "How Safe Is Safe Enough?" pp. 144–149, 215. See Cox and Ricci, "Legal and Philosophical Aspects."

49. Kasper, "Perceptions of Risk," p. 73. For examples of these uncertainties, see D. Cleverly et al., *Municipal Waste Combustion Study* (New York: Taylor and Francis, 1989), pp. A-10, 2-6, 2-12, and 3-18.

50. L. Cox and P. Ricci, "Risk, Uncertainty, and Causation," in Paustenbach, *Risk Assessment*, p. 151. See also L. Maxim, "Problems Associated with the Use of Conservative Assumptions in Exposure and Risk Analysis," in Paustenbach, *Risk Assessment*, pp. 526ff.

51. A. Lovins, "Cost-Risk-Benefit Assessment in Energy Policy," *George Washington Law Review* 45, no. 5 (1977): 926. Similar problems are expressed, for example, by J. Harkins, E. Scott, and W. Walsh, "A Legal Viewpoint," in Woodhead, *Phenotypic Variation*, pp. 218ff.; see also R. Cortesi, "Variation in Individual Response," in Woodhead, *Phenotypic Variation*, pp. 288–289.

52. Nuclear Regulatory Commission, *Reactor Safety Study*, pp. 108–109, 118, 186, 239, 245–246.

53. See Cohen, "Risk Analyses," p. 575; and Whipple, "Nonpessimistic Risk Assessment," pp. 1111–1113.

54. See Chapter Three in this volume.

55. H. Stretton, *Capitalism, Socialism, and the Environment* (Cambridge, England: Cambridge University Press, 1976), p. 51. See Andrews, "Environmental Impact Assessment," pp. 85–97.

56. D. Dickson, *The Politics of Alternative Technology* (New York: Universe Books, 1975), p. 189. See Chapters Two and Five for further discussion of the views of Okrent, Starr, Whipple, Maxey, Cohen, and Lee.

57. Ibid. See also Stretton, *Capitalism*, p. 189.

58. Samuels, "Arrogance of Intellectual Power," p. 118.

59. Cited in D. Bazelon, "Risk and Responsibility," *Science* 205, no. 4403 (1979): 277–280.

Chapter Eight

1. B. Ames, R. Magaw, and L. Gold, "Ranking Possible Carcinogens," in *The Risk Assessment of Environmental and Human Health Hazards*, ed. D. J. Paustenbach (New York: Wiley, 1989), pp. 1090, 1093. For discussion of saccharin and cyclamates, see C. Whipple, "Nonpessimistic Risk Assessment," in Paustenbach, *Risk Assessment*, pp. 1109–1110. Finally, see D. MacLean, "Introduction," in MacLean, *Values at Risk* (Totowa, N.J.: Rowman and Allanheld, 1986), p. 1.

2. The controversial U.S. government report WASH-1400 calculated the per-year, per-reactor probability of a nuclear core melt as 1 in 17,000; for the 151 existing and planned U.S. reactors, the probability of a core melt during their lifetime is 1 in 4. See U.S. Nuclear Regulatory Commission, *Reactor Safety Study: An Assessment of Accident Risks in U.S. Commercial Nuclear Power Plants*, NUREG-75/014, WASH 1400 (Washington, D.C.: Government Printing Office, 1975); K. S. Shrader-Frechette, *Nuclear Power and Public Policy* (Boston: Reidel, 1983), pp. 84–85.

3. Union of Concerned Scientists, *The Risks of Nuclear Power Reactors: A Review of the NRC Reactor Safety Study, WASH 1400* (Cambridge, Mass.: Union of Concerned Scientists, 1977); Nuclear Energy Policy Study Group, *Nuclear Power: Issues and Choices* (Cambridge, Mass.: Ballinger, 1977) (this report was funded by the Ford Foundation and carried out by the Mitre Corporation); R. M. Cooke, "Risk Assessment and Rational Decision Theory," *Dialectica* 36, no. 4 (1982): 334.

4. See Cooke, "Risk Assessment."

5. For a defense of a risk-evaluation strategy that is cautious and conservative, see S. Samuels, "The Arrogance of Intellectual Power," in *Phenotypic Variation in Populations*, ed. A. Woodhead, M. Bender, and R. Leonard (New York: Plenum, 1988), pp. 113–120.

6. J. Harsanyi, "Can the Maximin Principle Serve as a Basis for Morality? A Critique of John Rawls's Theory," *American Political Science Review* 69, no. 2 (1975): 594. For this and other decision rules, such as minimax regret, see M. Resnick, *Choices* (Minneapolis: University of Minnesota Press, 1987), pp. 26–37.

7. As he puts it: "In the case of risk, acceptance of Bayesian theory is now virtually unanimous. In the case of uncertainty, the Bayesian approach is still somewhat controversial, though the last two decades have produced a clear trend toward its growing acceptance by expert opinion" (J. Harsanyi, "Advances in Understanding Rational Behavior," in *Rational Choice*, ed. J. Elster [New York: New York University Press, 1986], p. 88). See also J. Harsanyi, "Understanding Rational Behavior," in *Foundational Problems in the Special Sci-*

ences, ed. R. E. Butts and J. Hintikka (Boston: Reidel, 1977), 2:322; A. Tversky and D. Kahneman, "The Framing of Decisions and the Psychology of Choice," in Elster, *Rational Choice,* p. 125.

8. See Resnick, *Choices,* p. 32.

9. Harsanyi, "Maximin Principle," p. 594; Harsanyi, "Understanding Rational Behavior," pp. 320–321. For a treatment of individual decisions under uncertainty, see R. D. Luce and H. Raiffa, *Games and Decisions* (New York: Wiley, 1957), pp. 275–326.

10. Quoted in H. Otway and M. Peltu, *Regulating Industrial Risks* (London: Butterworths, 1985), p. 4. Hacking also points out that risk assessors rarely have the knowledge of probabilities that they need (see I. Hacking, "Culpable Ignorance of Interference Effects," in MacLean, *Values at Risk,* pp. 136–154). See also L. Cox and P. Ricci, "Risk, Uncertainty, and Causation," in Paustenbach, *Risk Assessment,* pp. 125–156.

11. Harsanyi, "Understanding Rational Behavior," p. 320; Otway and Peltu, *Regulating Industrial Risks,* p. 115; Resnick, *Choices,* p. 36. For the Von Neumann–Morgenstern approach to expected utility, see Resnick, *Choices,* pp. 88–91.

12. Harsanyi, "Maximin Principle," p. 594. See also R. C. Jeffrey, *The Logic of Decision* (Chicago: University of Chicago Press, 1983); J. Marschak, "Towards an Economic Theory of Organization and Information," in *Decision Processes,* ed. R. Thrall, C. Coombs, and R. Davis (London: Wiley, 1954), pp. 187ff.; L. Ellsworth, "Decision-Theoretic Analysis of Rawls' Original Position," in *Foundations and Applications of Decision Theory,* ed. C. A. Hooker, J. J. Leach, and E. F. McClennen (Dordrecht: Reidel, 1978), 2:29ff. For the view that choice situations involving uncertainty should be analyzed according to their utility, see R. Davis, "Introduction," and C. Coombs and D. Beardslee, "On Decision-Making under Uncertainty," in Thrall, *Decision Processes,* p. 14 and pp. 255ff. For an opposed point of view, see E. F. McClennen, "The Minimax Theory and Expected Utility Reasoning," in Hooker, *Decision Theory,* 2:337ff. See also J. Milnor, "Games against Nature," in Thrall, *Decision Processes,* pp. 49ff.

13. Harsanyi, "Understanding Rational Behavior," p. 323; see also J. Harsanyi, "On the Rationale of the Bayesian Approach," in Butts and Hintikka, *Foundational Problems,* vol. 2. See Resnick, *Choices,* p. 36; for a definition, discussion, and proof of the Von Neumann–Morgenstern expected-utility theorem, see Resnick, *Choices,* pp. 88ff. See Harsanyi, "Understanding Rational Behavior," pp. 320–322, for a brief discussion of Bayesian decision theory and its associated axioms. For criticism of *averaging* in risk evaluation, see Samuels, "Arrogance of Intellectual Power," pp. 113–114. See also D. MacLean, "Social Values and the Distribution of Risk," in MacLean, *Values at Risk.*

14. Harsanyi, "Maximin Principle," p. 595. For a discussion of the maximin rule, see Resnick, *Choices,* pp. 26ff. For a discussion of individual decisionmaking under uncertainty, including maximin, see R. D. Luce and H. Raiffa, *Games and Decisions* (New York: Wiley, 1958), chap. 13.

15. J. Rawls, *A Theory of Justice* (Cambridge, Mass.: Harvard University Press, 1971), pp. 75–83.

16. This example is based on Resnick, *Choices*, p. 41. See Luce and Raiffa, *Games and Decisions*, pp. 275–326.

17. Obviously, the more general question of using Bayesian versus maximin decision rules, in all cases, is too broad to be settled here—partly because it mirrors a larger controversy in postmedieval moral philosophy between the utilitarians and the contractarians. The utilitarian tradition is represented by Hume, Adam Smith, Bentham, Mill, and many contemporary social scientists and moral philosophers, such as Harsanyi and Smart. The contractarian (or social-contract) tradition is represented by Locke, Rousseau, Kant, and contemporary moral philosophers such as Rawls. The analysis in this chapter is not directed at the larger question of whether a Bayesian/utilitarian or a maximin/contractarian analysis is better for all situations. My own opinion is (1) that Bayesian rules are better in many cases of $risk_B$ or certainty and in many situations of *individual* (not *societal*) risk taking, and (2) that both Bayesian and maximin strategies are needed in moral philosophy. However, I shall not take the time here to argue these points in detail. As Sen points out, utilitarianism and contractarianism capture two different aspects of welfare considerations. Both provide necessary conditions for ethical judgments, but neither alone is sufficient. Utilitarians are unable to explain how to evaluate different *levels* of welfare, and contractarians are unable to explain how to evaluate gains and losses of welfare. See A. K. Sen, "Rawls versus Bentham: An Axiomatic Examination of the Pure Distribution Problem," in *Reading Rawls*, ed. N. Daniels (New York: Basic Books, 1981), pp. 283–292.

18. See note 144.

19. Harsanyi, "Maximin Principle," p. 595. For a similar argument, see Whipple, "Nonpessimistic Risk Assessment," p. 1111.

20. See C. Starr and C. Whipple, "Risks of Risk Decisions," *Science* 208, no. 4448 (1980): 1118. See also J. Hushon, "Plenary Session Report," in Mitre Corporation, *Symposium/Workshop on Nuclear and Nonnuclear Energy Systems: Risk Assessment and Governmental Decision Making* (McLean, Va.: Mitre Corporation, 1979), p. 748. See also D. Okrent, "Comment on Societal Risk," *Science* 208, no. 4442 (1980): 374; M. Maxey, "Managing Low-Level Radioactive Wastes," in *Low-Level Radioactive Waste Management*, ed. J. Watson (Williamsburg, Va.: Health Physics Society, 1979), p. 401; J. D. Graham, "Some Explanations for Disparities in Lifesaving Investments," *Policy Studies Review* 1, no. 4 (May 1982): 692–704; C. Comar, "Risk: A Pragmatic *De Minimus* Approach," *Science* 203, no. 4378 (1979): 319; and B. Cohen and I. Lee, "A Catalog of Risks," *Health Physics* 36, no. 6 (1979): 707.

21. J. Rawls, "Some Reasons for the Maximin Criterion," *American Economic Review* 64, no. 1, papers and proceedings (May 1974): 141–146, esp. 142. See MacLean, "Introduction" (to *Values at Risk*), p. 12.

22. Harsanyi, "Maximin Principle," p. 605.

23. For an excellent essay on the centrality of *consent* to risk assessment and evaluation, see D. MacLean, "Risk and Consent," in MacLean, *Values at Risk*, pp. 17–30.

24. P. Diamond, "Cardinal Welfare, Individualistic Ethics, and Interpersonal Comparisons of Utility," *Journal of Political Economy* 75, no. 5 (October 1967): 765–766; A. Sen, "Welfare Inequalities and Rawlsian Axiomatics," in Butts and Hintikka, *Foundational Problems*, 2:276.

25. Harsanyi, "Bayesian Approach," p. 384, and "Understanding Rational Behavior," p. 321.

26. As Harsanyi (in "Bayesian Approach," p. 382) puts it, "the Bayesian approach stands or falls with the validity or invalidity of its *rationality axioms*."

27. For a discussion of "process rationality," see J. G. March, "Bounded Rationality," in Elster, *Rational Choice*, p. 148. For a discussion of procedural reforms in risk assessment, see R. N. Andrews, "Environmental Impact Assessment and Risk Assessment," in *Environmental Impact Assessment*, ed. P. Wathern (London: Unwin Hyman, 1988), pp. 85–97.

28. If people attempting to make rational societal decisions are bound by ethical obligations, then what Clifford and Michalos have called an "ethics of belief" might exist (see W. K. Clifford, *Lectures and Essays* [London: Macmillan, 1986]; and A. C. Michalos, *Foundations of Decisionmaking* [Ottowa: Canadian Library of Philosophy, 1987], pp. 204–218). Even Harsanyi divides the "general theory of rational behavior" into three branches: utility theory, game theory, and ethics (see "Maximin Principle"; "Understanding Rational Behavior," p. 323; and "Bayesian Approach").

29. Harsanyi, "Maximin Principle," pp. 594–595.

30. Ibid., p. 595.

31. For example, why should one choose to avoid an airplane delay (a benefit) at the risk or cost of facing a 10^{-6} probability that an essential mechanism on the plane will break down? A perfectly rational response, in such a situation, might be that one does not gamble with one's life except to obtain a comparably great benefit (see J. W. N. Watkins, "Towards a Unified Decision Theory: A Non-Bayesian Approach," in Butts and Hintikka, *Foundational Problems*, 2:351).

32. Watkins ("Unified Decision Theory," p. 375) gives an interesting example to illustrate this point:

Consider a certain result r and a family of gambles $G_p{}'$ defined as getting r with probability p and nothing otherwise. Classical utility theory evaluates the utility of G_p as $p.u(r)$. Since $u(r)$ is constant this means that $u(G_p)$ is a linear function of p. In particular, equal increases in p mean equal increases in $u(G_p)$. But do we not evaluate the step from $G_{0.99}$ to $G_{1.00}$ higher than e.g. from $G_{0.5}$ to $G_{0.51}$?

Watkins's example shows that sometimes a result—such as the avoidance of a nuclear core melt—is not a linear function of p; that is, the result does not become more desirable in direct proportion as the probability of avoidance increases. Instead, says Watkins, the jump from a probability of 0.99 to 1.00 is worth more than the jump from, say, 0.50 to 0.51, since the first jump represents the value attached to complete avoidance of the risk. This example suggests that rational decisionmakers are not necessarily Bayesian. This same point is made in L. Cox and P. Ricci, "Legal and Philosophical Aspects of Risk Analysis," in Paustenbach, *Risk Assessment*, p. 1025.

33. B. Ames, R. Magaw, and L. Gold, "Ranking Possible Carcinogenic Hazards," *Science* 236, no. 4799 (17 April 1987): 271–280. For other criticisms of relative risk and the linearity assumption, see K. S. Shrader-Frechette, *Risk Analysis and Scientific Method* (Boston: Reidel, 1985), pp. 157ff.

34. See Hacking, "Culpable Ignorance"; and D. Kahneman and A. Tversky, "Subjective Probability," in *Judgment under Uncertainty: Heuristics and Biases*, ed. D. Kahneman, P. Slovic, and A. Tversky (Cambridge, England: Cambridge University Press, 1982), p. 46. See also D. Kahneman and A. Tversky, "On the Psychology of Prediction," in Kahneman, *Judgment under Uncertainty*, p. 68.

35. Harsanyi, "Maximin Principle," p. 595. See Whipple, "Nonpessimistic Risk Assessment," p. 1111.

36. Harsanyi, "Maximin Principle," p. 595.

37. Resnick, *Choices*, pp. 35–37.

38. Harsanyi, "Maximin Principle," p. 598.

39. See MacLean, "Introduction" and "Risk and Consent" (in *Values at Risk*).

40. Harsanyi, "Maximin Principle," p. 595; see K. J. Arrow, "Some Ordinalist-Utilitarian Notes on Rawls's Theory of Justice," *Journal of Philosophy* 70, no. 9 (10 May 1983): 255.

41. Someone might claim that the disutility of failing to notify the sheriff immediately, in the state where the leak is not fixed within thirty minutes, should be greater than − 16. See note 40 and the text for a response to this objection.

42. For a defense of the claim that societal well-being requires that there be a right to impose some risks on others, see A. Sen, "The Right to Take Personal Risks," in MacLean, *Values at Risk*, pp. 155–170; for an opposite point of view, see MacLean, "Risk and Consent." Also, one might argue, informing the sheriff of the leak would be like yelling "fire" in a dark and crowded auditorium. This was the excuse given in the Brown's Ferry nuclear accident; for an account, see Shrader-Frechette, *Nuclear Power*, pp. 88ff.

43. See Resnick, *Choices*, pp. 43, 205–212, for discussion of interpersonal comparisons of utility. If Bayesianism requires these interpersonal comparisons, one might argue, so much the worse for it, especially since Rawls's minimax strategy requires only that agents in situations of uncertainty be able to generate an ordinal ranking of the worst-off individuals.

44. Harsanyi, "Maximin Principle," p. 596.

45. Ibid., p. 597.

46. A third problem with Harsanyi's examples in his third argument is that

he presupposes that the maximin criterion is used outside the context of normal societal institutions and ethics. However, if there is an ethical and a legal obligation to guarantee equal opportunity to all citizens, then society must try to give equal consideration to the interests of the mathematician and the retarded person. See Rawls, *Theory of Justice*, pp. 54–83, and "Distributive Justice," in *Philosophy, Politics, and Society*, 3rd series, ed. P. Laslett and W. G. Runciman (Oxford: Blackwell, 1967), pp. 58–82, esp. sec. 2; see also R. D. Rosenkrantz, "Distributive Justice," in Hooker, *Decision Theory*, 2:111. Compare Rawls, *Theory of Justice*, p. 302.

47. Harsanyi, "Maximin Principle."

48. Ibid., p. 599. For a discussion of equity in risk assessment, see Cox and Ricci, "Legal and Philosophical Aspects," pp. 1017–1022; and D. MacLean, "Philosophical Issues for Centralized Decisions," in MacLean, *Values at Risk*, pp. 17–30.

49. Harsanyi, "Maximin Principle," p. 598; see also p. 600. For a criticism of the use of average values in risk assessment, see Samuels, "Arrogance of Intellectual Power," pp. 113–114, and MacLean, "Distribution of Risk."

50. See, for example, S. M. Stigler, "Thomas Bayes's Bayesian Inference," *Journal of the Royal Statistical Society* A 145 (1982): 250–258; and J. O. Berger, "The Robust Bayesian Viewpoint," in *Robustness of Bayesian Analyses*, ed. J. B. Kadane (New York: Elsevier, 1984), pp. 63–124.

51. See Luce and Raiffa, *Games and Decisions*, pp. 284ff.; see also K. Arrow, "Alternative Approaches to the Theory of Choice in Risk-Taking Situations," *Econometrica* 19, no. 4 (October 1951): 404–437; E. Nagel, "Principles of the Theory of Probability," *International Encyclopedia of Unified Science* (Chicago: University of Chicago Press, 1939); and L. J. Savage, *The Foundations of Statistics* (New York: Wiley, 1954).

52. See, for example, V. Kerry Smith, "Benefit Analysis for Natural Hazards," *Risk Analysis* 6, no. 3 (1986): 325ff.; and I. Levi, "Newcomb's Many Problems," in Hooker, *Decision Theory*, 1:382. See also S. Vail, "Alternative Calculi of Subjective Probabilities," in Thrall, *Decision Processes*, pp. 87ff.

53. See A. Tversky and D. Kahneman, "Judgment under Uncertainty" and "Subjective Probability," in Kahneman, *Judgment under Uncertainty*, pp. 3ff., 32ff. See also J. Elster, "Introduction," in Elster, *Rational Choice*, pp. 6, 18–19.

54. See H. L. Dreyfus and S. E. Dreyfus, "Decision Analysis Model of Rationality," in Butts and Hintikka, *Foundational Problems*, 2:121ff. For criticisms of the use of subjective probabilities in risk assessment, see Hacking, "Culpable Ignorance."

55. Resnick, *Choices*, p. 37.

56. If such a list cannot be specified, it would be impossible to meet the conditions necessary for assigning equal probabilities to states. This point was noted in Luce and Raiffa, *Games and Decisions*, pp. 284–285.

57. This point was also made in Luce and Raiffa, *Games and Decisions*, pp. 284–285.

58. To avoid this problem, statisticians use the *median*, rather than the *average*, as an indicator for the value of a group of numbers (such as utilities) when the dispersion is unclear. See D. Gauthier, "The Social Contract," in Hooker, *Decision Theory*, 2:52. See also MacLean, "Distribution of Risk," and Samuels, "Arrogance of Intellectual Power."

59. He says: "The equiprobability assumption can be justified by the principle of indifference, and also by the moral principle of assigning the same *a priori* weight to every individual's interests" (Harsanyi, "Maximin Principle," p. 599). See the previous note.

60. D. Cleverly et al., *Municipal Waste Combustion Study* (New York: Taylor and Francis, 1989), pp. 2–9.

61. D. Nebert, "Genes Encoding Drug-Metabolizing Enzymes," in Woodhead, *Phenotypic Variation*, p. 59.

62. See K. Borch, "Ethics, Institutions, and Optimality," in *Decision Theory and Social Ethics*, ed. H. W. Gottinger and W. Leinfellner (Dordrecht: Reidel, 1978), p. 242; C. Gersuny, *Work Hazards and Industrial Conflict* (Hanover, N.H.: University Press of New England, 1981), p. 1. For a discussion of risk and equity, see MacLean, "Distribution of Risk."

63. Luce and Raiffa, *Games and Decisions*, p. 299.

64. Ibid., chap. 13, esp. p. 293.

65. Ibid., chap. 13. If use of the equiprobability assumption is questionable in situations of *societal* decisionmaking, then why does Harsanyi insist on it? The answer to this question brings us to Harsanyi's fifth argument (in "Maximin Principle," p. 599): Since "a rational decision maker simply cannot help using subjective probabilities" in making risk decisions, following a maximin rule amounts to doing something irrational; it "will really amount to assigning probability one (or nearly one) to the worst possibility in any given case." To see the problems with this fifth argument, recall the earlier discussion of Harsanyi's first argument and the discussion of organically grown vegetables.

66. Rawls, *Theory of Justice*, pp. 75–78. See Samuels, "Arrogance of Intellectual Power," pp. 113–120.

67. Rawls, *Theory of Justice*, pp. 12–17.

68. For Rawls, given the choice of two distributions, one is more fair if the person who is worst off under it is better off than the worst-off person under the other distribution. For a defense of the maximin principle, see Gauthier, "Social Contract," pp. 47ff. See also P. Gardenfors, "Fairness without Interpersonal Comparisons," *Theoria* 44, part 2 (1978): 57ff. Finally, see F. Zagare, *Game Theory* (Beverly Hills, Calif.: Sage, 1984), pp. 21–23.

69. Rawls, *Theory of Justice*, p. 94.

70. Rawls, "Distributive Justice," pp. 58–82, esp. sec. 4; see Rosenkrantz, "Distributive Justice," pp. 91ff., for a discussion of Rawls's difference principle. See also Ellsworth, "Analysis of Rawls' Position," pp. 29ff.; and C. R. Plott, "Rawls's Theory of Justice," in Gottinger and Leinfellner, *Decision Theory*, pp. 201–214.

71. This is Harsanyi's position, as defended in "Maximin Principle." For a similar argument, made by risk assessors, see L. Lave and B. Leonard, "Regulating Coke Oven Emissions," in Paustenbach, *Risk Assessment*, pp. 1068–1069.

72. W. T. Blackstone, "On the Meaning and Justification of the Equality Principle," in *The Concept of Equality*, ed. W. T. Blackstone (Minneapolis: Burgess, 1969), p. 121.

73. J. Rawls, "Justice as Fairness," in *Philosophy of Law*, ed. J. Feinberg and H. Gross (Encino, Calif.: Dickenson, 1975), p. 284. For a discussion of rights theories in the context of risk assessments, see A. Baier, "Poisoning the Wells," in MacLean, *Values at Risk*, pp. 49–74.

74. For arguments to this effect, see M. C. Beardsley, "Equality and Obedience to Law," in *Law and Philosophy*, ed. S. Hook (New York: New York University Press, 1964), pp. 35–36. See also I. Berlin, "Equality," in Hook, *Law and Philosophy*, p. 33; W. K. Frankena, "Some Beliefs about Justice," in Feinberg and Gross, *Philosophy of Law*, pp. 250–251; M. Markovic, "The Relationship between Equality and Local Autonomy," in *Equality and Social Policy*, ed. W. Feinberg (Urbana: University of Illinois Press, 1978), p. 93; Rawls, "Justice as Fairness," pp. 277, 280, 282; G. Vlastos, "Justice and Equality," in *Social Justice*, ed. R. B. Brandt (Englewood Cliffs, N.J.: Prentice-Hall, 1962), pp. 50, 56.

75. J. R. Pennock, "Introduction," in *The Limits of the Law*, Nomos 15, Yearbook of the American Society for Political and Legal Philosophy, ed. J. R. Pennock and J. W. Chapman (New York: Lieber-Atherton, 1974), pp. 2, 6.

76. See J. Rawls, "Justice as Fairness," *Journal of Philosophy* 54, no. 22 (October 1957): 653–662; J. Rawls, "Justice as Fairness," *Philosophical Review* 67 (April 1958): 164–194. See also Rawls, *Theory of Justice*, pp. 3–53. For discussion of compensation regarding risks, see *Hazards: Technology and Fairness*, ed. R. W. Kates et al., (Washington, D.C.: National Academy Press, 1986), part 2.

77. See K. S. Shrader-Frechette, *Science Policy, Ethics, and Economic Methodology* (Boston: Reidel, 1985), pp. 221–222.

78. See Rawls, *Theory of Justice*, p. 586; and A. Sen, "Welfare Inequalities and Rawlsian Axiomatics," in Butts and Hintikka, *Foundational Problems*, 2:288.

79. See note 82. Although treating people differently can be justified despite a framework of equal rights, there have to be morally relevant reasons for doing so—for example, discrimination as a reward for merit or virtue, as a recompense for past deeds, as compensation for past wrongs, as an incentive for future actions that are desirable, or as a provision for special needs (such as those of the handicapped).

80. See Shrader-Frechette, *Science Policy*, pp. 220–221.

81. See Cox and Ricci, "Legal and Philosophical Aspects," pp. 1026–1027. See also Shrader-Frechette, *Science Policy*, pp. 222ff.; Frankena, "Beliefs about Justice," pp. 252–257. The position described here as "prima facie political egalitarianism" appears to be close to what Frankena defends as "procedural egalitarianism." For Frankena, procedural egalitarians are to be distinguished from substantive egalitarians, who believe that there is some factual respect in

which all human beings are equal. Procedural egalitarians deny that there is some such factual respect.

82. Morally relevant grounds for discrimination are grounds for saying that there are differences between cases, even when we apply the principle that similar cases ought to be treated similarly. We have come to believe that skin color, for example, is not a morally relevant basis, but that ability to do a certain job might be. For analysis of this question, see W. K. Frankena, "The Concept of Social Justice," in Brandt, *Social Justice*, pp. 10, 14. See R. Taylor, "Justice and the Common Good," in Blackstone, *Concept of Equality*, pp. 94–97. See note 78.

83. For discussion on this point, see J. Rees, *Equality* (New York: Praeger, 1971), pp. 116–117, 120; R. B. Stewart, "Paradoxes of Liberty, Integrity, and Fraternity: The Collective Nature of Environmental Quality and Judicial Review of Administrative Action," *Environmental Law* 7, no. 3 (Spring 1977): 474–476; J. R. Pennock, *Democratic Political Theory* (Princeton, N.J.: Princeton University Press, 1979), pp. 16–58, esp. p. 38; and O. Patterson, "Inequality, Freedom, and the Equal Opportunity Doctrine," in Feinberg, *Equality and Social Policy*, p. 31. See Rawls, *Theory of Justice*. See also note 74 and S. I. Benn, "Egalitarianism and the Equal Consideration of Interests," in *Equality*, Nomos 9, Yearbook of the American Society for Political and Legal Philosophy, ed. J. R. Pennock and J. W. Chapman (New York: Lieber-Atherton, 1968), pp. 75–76.

84. Lave and Leonard (in "Coke Oven Emissions," pp. 1068–1069) make such an argument. See H. Bethe, "The Necessity of Fission Power," *Scientific American* 234, no. 1 (January 1976): 26ff., who also makes such an argument. For a brief defense of the thesis that we can define rationality in terms of efficiency, see Michalos, "Foundations of Decisionmaking," pp. 135–142.

85. This argument is made, for example, by assessors such as Lave and Leonard (in "Coke Oven Emissions," pp. 1068–1069). See Shrader-Frechette, *Nuclear Power*, p. 29; J. Maddox, *The Doomsday Syndrome* (London: Macmillan, 1972), p. 213; P. Drucker, "Saving the Crusade," in *Environmental Ethics*, ed. K. S. Shrader-Frechette (Pacific Grove, Calif.: Boxwood Press, 1981), pp. 102, 103, 200; M. M. Maxey, "Radwastes and Public Ethics," *Health Physics* 34, no. 2 (February 1978): 129–135, esp. 132. See also Cox and Ricci, "Legal and Philosophical Aspects," p. 1038.

86. Frankena (in "Concept of Social Justice," p. 15) uses this argument. He offers it as a sound (and apparently the only) basis for justifying inequalities and differences in treatment among persons.

87. See Markovic, "Equality and Local Autonomy," pp. 85, 87–88; Patterson, "Inequality," pp. 33–34; H. Laski, "Liberty and Equality," in Blackstone, *Concept of Equality*, pp. 170, 173; Rees, *Equality*, pp. 61–79; and H. J. Gans, "The Costs of Inequality," in *Small Comforts for Hard Times*, ed. M. Mooney and F. Stuber (New York: Columbia University Press, 1977), pp. 50–51.

88. For a discussion of distributive equity related to risk assessment, see

MacLean, "Distribution of Risk." These Census Bureau statistics are cited by A. Larkin, "The Ethical Problem of Economic Growth vs. Environmental Degradation," in Shrader-Frechette, *Environmental Ethics*, p. 212. See also D. C. North and R. L. Miller, *The Economics of Public Issues* (New York: Harper and Row, 1971), p. 151, who substantiate this same point. Similar statistics for England are cited by Rees, *Equality*, pp. 30–32. See Patterson, "Inequality," p. 36.

89. See Shrader-Frechette, *Science Policy*, chap. 7, sec. 3.2; note 88 above; Patterson, "Inequality," pp. 21–30; B. Williams, "The Idea of Equality," in Blackstone, *Concept of Equality*, pp. 49–53; and J. H. Scharr, "Equality of Opportunity and Beyond," in Pennock and Chapman, *Equality*, pp. 231–240. See also Pennock, *Democratic Political Theory*, pp. 36–37; and J. P. Plamenatz, "Equality of Opportunity," in Blackstone, *Concept of Equality*.

90. See A. Gibbard, "Risk and Value," in MacLean, *Values at Risk*, pp. 97–99. See also E. J. Mishan, *21 Popular Economic Fallacies* (New York: Praeger, 1969), p. 236; Shrader-Frechette, *Nuclear Power*, pp. 123ff.

91. See Mishan, *Economic Fallacies*, pp. 232–233, 245ff.; Rees, *Equality*, p. 36. See also Plamenatz, "Equality of Opportunity," and Larkin, "Ethical Problems."

92. R. Grossman and G. Daneker, *Jobs and Energy* (Washington, D.C.: Environmentalists for Full Employment, 1977), pp. 1–2.

93. Between 1947 and 1977, for example, employment in the service sector increased 95 percent, more than in any other sector. See note 92.

94. See Gibbard, "Risk and Value"; Shrader-Frechette, *Science Policy*, pp. 227–228.

95. Mishan, *Economic Fallacies*, p. 237.

96. R. B. Stewart, "Pyramids of Sacrifice? Problems of Federalism in Mandating State Implementation of Natural Environmental Policy," in *Land Use and Environment Law Review, 1978*, ed. F. A. Strom (New York: Clark Boardman, 1978), p. 172. Numerous detailed economic analyses support this point. See, for example, A. M. Freeman, "Distribution of Environmental Quality," in *Environmental Quality Analysis*, ed. A. V. Kneese and B. T. Bower (Baltimore: Johns Hopkins University Press, 1972), pp. 271–275. See also A. V. Kneese and C. L. Schultze, *Pollution, Prices, and Public Policy* (Washington, D.C.: Brookings Institution, 1975), p. 28.

97. See V. Brodine, "A Special Burden," *Environment* 13, no. 2 (March 1971): 24. See D. N. Dane, "Bad Air for Children," *Environment* 18, no. 9 (November 1976): 26–34. See also A. M. Freeman, "Income Distribution and Environmental Quality," in *Pollution, Resources, and the Environment*, ed. A. C. Enthoven and A. M. Freeman (New York: Norton, 1973), p. 101. Enthoven and Freeman make the same point, regarding air pollution, that Kneese and Haveman make (A. V. Kneese, "Economics and the Quality of the Environment," in Enthoven and Freeman, *Pollution*, pp. 74–79; A. M. Freeman, R. H. Haveman, and A. V. Kneese, *The Economics of Environmental Policy* [New York: Wiley, 1973], p.

143). See also P. Asch and J. J. Seneca, "Some Evidence on the Distribution of Air Quality," *Land Economics* 54, no. 3 (August 1978): 278–297; and D. D. Ramsey, "A Note on Air Pollution, Property Values, and Fiscal Variables," *Land Economics* 52, no. 2 (May 1976): 230–234.

98. See Gibbard, "Risk and Value," p. 96. See also Samuels, "Arrogance of Intellectual Power"; and, for example, J. Stein, "Water for the Wealthy," *Environment* 19, no. 4 (May 1977): 6–14. The point is documented well by Freeman (in "Distribution of Environmental Quality," p. 275), who argues that pollution is not "the great leveler," since the wealthy have "the means to protect themselves" from environmental insults. Even the issue of who benefits most from pollution controls is complex (see Freeman, "Distribution of Environmental Quality," pp. 271–273; "Income Distribution," pp. 101–104; *Economics of Environmental Policy*, pp. 144–145; and Kneese, "Economics and Quality of Environment," pp. 78–80). Freeman, Haveman, Kneese, and other economists conclude: "on balance, . . . the improvement would be pro poor" (Freeman, *Economics of Environmental Policy*, pp. 143–144). In any case, there are several means whereby the costs of pollution control can be shifted from the poor and middle class to members of higher-income groups (see Freeman, "Income Distribution," pp. 104–105, and *Economics of Environmental Policy*, pp. 145–148).

99. For a similar argument, see Samuels, "Arrogance of Intellectual Power," pp. 113–120. See also Shrader-Frechette, *Science Policy*, pp. 228–229.

100. See J. L. Regens, "Attitudes toward Risk-Benefit Analysis for Managing Effects of Chemical Exposures," in *Risk Management of Chemicals in the Environment*, ed. H. M. Seip and A. B. Heiberg (New York: Plenum, 1989), pp. 75–88. Those who are disproportionately burdened with environmental and technological hazards have a further claim against those who favor Bayesian strategies for risk decisions under uncertainty. As Hans Jonas expressed it, one has a moral obligation to protect the utterly helpless. Absolute helplessness demands absolute protection ("Philosophical Reflections on Experimenting with Human Subjects," in *Ethics in Perspective*, ed. K. J. Struhl and P. R. Struhl [New York: Random House, 1975], pp. 242–353).

101. R. B. Brandt, *Ethical Theory* (Englewood Cliffs, N.J.: Prentice-Hall, 1959), pp. 415–420. For arguments supporting this point, see R. Taylor, "Justice and the Common Good," in Hook, *Law and Philosophy*; M. C. Beardsley, "Equality and Obedience to Law," in Hook, *Law and Philosophy*, p. 193; and Pennock, *Democratic Political Theory*, p. 143.

102. J. Harsanyi, "Nonlinear Social Welfare Functions," *Theory and Decision* 7 (1975): 61–82, esp. 74–77. For discussions of Harsanyi's ability to deal with equity and distributional issues, see R. Nunan, "Harsanyi vs. Sen: Does Social Welfare Weigh Subjective Preferences?" and E. F. McClennen, "Utility and Equity: Sen vs. Harsanyi," *Journal of Philosophy* 78, no. 10 (October 1981): 586–600, 600–601.

103. Without an in-principle guarantee of equity, such as a law or a decision

rule, there is no assurance that people's preferences will reflect values such as fairness or equity (see Kates, *Hazards*, part 2; see also Cox and Ricci, "Legal and Philosophical Aspects").

104. Harsanyi himself admits that one "cannot determine what is 'good' for different persons, with reference to any pre-existing moral standard, but only with reference to the preferences of these persons themselves" ("Ethics in Terms of Hypothetical Imperatives," *Mind* 67, no. 267 [July 1958]: 311–313). See also Nunan, "Harsanyi vs. Sen," p. 594.

105. See Nunan, "Harsanyi vs. Sen," p. 596.

106. J. Harsanyi, "Cardinal Welfare, Individualistic Ethics, and Interpersonal Comparisons of Utility," *Journal of Political Economy* 63, no. 4 (August 1955): 434–435; and "Bayesian Decision Theory and Utilitarian Ethics," *American Economic Review* 67, no. 2 (March 1977): 223–228.

107. See Nunan, "Harsanyi vs. Sen," pp. 596–599. If Harsanyi assumes that utilities are based on personal consumption, he can only have a utilitarian result, which he claims he has (a result in which social welfare is a linear function of individual utilities).

108. What about a second argument in favor of the maximin strategy: that it would avoid the Bayesian problem of using subjective probabilities in a situation of uncertainty? Although Bayesian decision theorists have argued for the need to use subjective probabilities, since the expected-utility and average-utility measures require probabilities (see, for example, L. Savage, *The Foundations of Statistics* [New York: Wiley, 1954]), Rawls (among others) argues that it makes no sense, in the absence of compelling empirical facts, to use subjective probabilities (Rawls, *Theory of Justice*, secs. 27–28).

109. See Samuels, "Arrogance of Intellectual Power," p. 119, and Rawls, *Theory of Justice*, pp. 172, 323; see also March, "Bounded Rationality," p. 153.

110. This same point is made by R. Coburn, "Technology Assessment, Human Good, and Freedom," in *Ethics and Problems of the 21st Century*, ed. K. E. Goodpaster and K. M. Sayre (Notre Dame, Ind.: University of Notre Dame Press, 1979), pp. 109–110.

111. See Cox and Ricci, "Legal and Philosophical Aspects," pp. 1038ff., who make a similar argument. See G. Kennedy, "Social Choice and Policy Formation," in *Human Values and Economic Policy*, ed. S. Hook (New York: New York University Press, 1967), p. 142. See also J. Ladd, "The Use of Mechanical Models for the Solution of Ethical Problems," in Hook, *Human Values*, pp. 167–168.

112. See Tversky and Kahneman, "Framing of Decisions," pp. 123ff.

113. March, "Bounded Rationality," p. 153.

114. This point also is made by R. B. Brandt, "Personal Values and the Justification of Institutions," and by Ladd, "Mechanical Models," in Hook, *Human Values*, pp. 37, 159, 166.

115. See Samuels, "Arrogance of Intellectual Power," pp. 113–120.

116. See Cox and Ricci, "Risk, Uncertainty, and Causation," p. 153, for a discussion of Bayesian risk.

117. A similar observation is made by Kennedy in "Social Choice," p. 148.

118. Harsanyi, "Maximin Principle," p. 600.

119. Ibid., p. 602. For a treatment of comparisons of interpersonal utility, see Luce and Raiffa, *Games and Decisions*, pp. 33–34.

120. See previous note.

121. Harsanyi, "Maximin Principle," p. 601.

122. See note 119 above.

123. See note 119 above.

124. In my view, although I shall not take the time to argue the point here, utility functions provide excellent measures of welfare, but only after one takes account of certain guarantees consistent with basic psychological laws—for example, that people wish to be treated fairly. See note 119 above.

125. For criticisms of the use of *average* utility in risk assessment, see MacLean, "Distribution of Risk." For a related argument, see Gauthier, "Social Contract," pp. 52–53.

126. See Rawls, *Theory of Justice*, pp. 321–324.

127. As discussed earlier in the text, Harsanyi can have linearity and a consumption-based notion of welfare, or he can deny linearity and have no vehicle for determining welfare. If a risk itself has utility or disutility for a particular person, the Von Neumann–Morgenstern utility function cannot represent the situation. See H. L. Dreyfus and S. E. Dreyfus, "Decision Analysis Model of Rationality," in Hooker, *Decision Theory*, 1:115–117; Resnick, *Choices*, pp. 43, 207–212.

128. A related point is made by Coburn in "Technology Assessment," p. 111.

129. A. Sen ("Welfare Inequalities and Rawlsian Axiomatics," in Butts and Hintikka, *Foundational Problems*, 2:271–279) argues for the same point.

130. Rawls, *Theory of Justice*, p. 117.

131. Related points regarding risk assessment are made by Cox and Ricci, "Legal and Philosophical Aspects," pp. 1038ff. See, for example, Rawls, *Theory of Justice*, pp. 117, 191–192; D. Lyons, "Introduction" and "Human Rights and the General Welfare," in *Rights*, ed. D. Lyons (Belmont, Calif.: Wadsworth, 1979), pp. 11, 181–184.

132. See Chapter Eleven in this volume; see also notes 54–55 of Chapter Eleven.

133. See Chapter Eleven, this volume.

134. Harsanyi, "Maximin Principle," pp. 601–602.

135. See the section "Harsanyi versus Rawls," earlier in this chapter.

136. A Bayesian utilitarian could deal with this case only by claiming that, in such situations (analogous to the earlier cases of supererogatory acts), utility would not be served if parents could not fulfill parental duties, ahead of maximizing expected utility. But this response leads to the same difficulty, an inconsistent utilitarianism.

137. Hacking (in "Culpable Ignorance") makes similar points about risk

evaluation. Another source of difficulties is that the utility concept itself is structured in ambiguous ways (see H. G. Bohnert, "The Logical Structure of the Utility Concept," in Thrall, *Decision Processes*, pp. 221ff.). Because of this ambiguity, how to make the requisite utilitarian calculations is controversial (Harsanyi, "Maximin Principle," p. 602; see Rawls, *Theory of Justice*, p. 320).

138. Some of these unknown variables are a result of phenotypic variation in populations. See, for example, Woodhead, *Phenotypic Variation*; see also Rawls, *Theory of Justice*, pp. 158–161, 191.

139. If the earlier sections of this chapter were correct in arguing that those who are economically deprived bear a disproportionate share of technological and environmental risks, then it might be easier to predict who is least advantaged.

140. Harsanyi, "Maximin Principle," p. 602.

141. Although it does not have the status of a second-order rule, Rawls's first principle, to be interpreted along with the difference principle, requires that "each person engaged in an institution or affected by it has an equal right to the most extensive liberty compatible with a like liberty for all" (Rawls, "Distributive Justice"). See also Rosenkrantz, "Distributive Justice," p. 11. Compare Rawls, *Theory of Justice*, p. 302. For a discussion of rights relevant to risk assessment and management, see Baier, "Poisoning the Wells."

142. Harsanyi, "Maximin Principle," p. 602.

143. See, for example, Lyons, "Human Rights and General Welfare," pp. 176–181; and J. C. Smart, "Utilitarianism," *Encyclopedia of Philosophy*, ed. P. Edwards (New York: Collier-Macmillan, 1967), 8:206–212.

144. Harsanyi, "Maximin Principle," p. 602. See Baier, "Poisoning the Wells."

145. See Rawls, *Theory of Justice*, p. 586; and A. Sen, "Welfare Inequalities and Rawlsian Axiomatics," in Butts and Hintikka, *Foundational Problems*, 2:288.

146. Public Law 91–190, *United States Statutes at Large*, 91st Cong., 1st sess., 1969, 83:852–856; see esp. part I, secs. 101(b)2 and 101(c).

147. Such maximin rules might help protect potential victims of catastrophe from the vagaries of bureaucratic decisionmaking. See Samuels, "Arrogance of Intellectual Power," pp. 113–120.

148. The Pearl Harbor example is cited by M. Douglas and A. Wildavsky, *Risk and Culture* (Berkeley and Los Angeles: University of California Press, 1982), p. 94.

149. P. Slovic, B. Fischhoff, and S. Lichtenstein, "Facts vs. Fears," in Kahneman, *Judgment under Uncertainty*, p. 485.

150. J. Raloff and J. Silberner, "Chernobyl: Emerging Data on Accident," *Science News* 129, no. 19 (1986): 292.

151. For the worst-case estimate, see R. Mulvihill et al., *Analysis of United States Power Reactor Accident Probability*, PRC R-695 (Los Angeles: Planning Research Corporation, 1965). This is an update of the 1957 U.S. Atomic Energy Commission report, WASH-740.

152. A. Tversky and D. Kahneman, "Belief in the Law of Small Numbers," and "Judgment under Uncertainty," in Kahneman, *Judgment under Uncertainty,* pp. 23–31, 4–11.

153. Tversky and Kahneman, "Judgment under Uncertainty," pp. 11–14.

154. Ibid., pp. 14–20.

155. Slovic, "Facts vs. Fears," p. 463.

156. Kahneman and Tversky, "Subjective Probability," p. 32. See Hacking, "Culpable Ignorance."

157. Kahneman and Tversky, "Subjective Probability," p. 46.

158. Kahneman, Tversky, and other researchers found that psychologists themselves, who should know better, used their feelings of confidence in their understanding of cases as a basis for predicting behavior and diagnosing ailments, even though there was no correlation between their feelings of confidence and the correctness of the judgments (S. Oskamp, "Overconfidence in Case-Study Judgments," in Kahneman, *Judgment under Uncertainty,* pp. 287–293).

159. See Shrader-Frechette, *Nuclear Power,* pp. 98–100.

160. Slovic, "Facts vs. Fears," pp. 475–478.

161. "In particular, we have seen that sample size has no effect on subjective sampling distributions, that posterior binomial estimates are determined (in the aggregate case, at least) by sample proportion rather than by sample difference, and that they do not depend on the population proportion. In his evaluation of evidence, man is apparently not a conservative Bayesian: he is not Bayesian at all" (Kahneman and Tversky, "Subjective Probability," p. 46).

162. As Harsanyi (in "Bayesian Approach," p. 382) puts it, "the Bayesian approach stands or falls with the validity or invalidity of its *rationality axioms.*"

163. Likewise, when discounted future earnings are rejected as a measure of the value of life, legitimate use of benefit-cost analysis is strengthened.

164. This objection is made, for example, by Lave and Leonard, in "Coke Oven Emissions," pp. 1064–1081.

165. Oberlin College mathematician Dr. Jeff Witmer formulated this objection in a private conservation with the author.

Chapter Nine

1. H. Otway, "Regulation and Risk Analysis," in *Regulating Industrial Risks,* ed. H. Otway and M. Peltu (London: Butterworths, 1985), pp. 10–11.

2. This point is made, for example, by L. Lave and B. Leonard, "Regulating Coke Oven Emissions," in *The Risk Assessment of Environmental and Human Health Hazards,* ed. D. J. Paustenbach (New York: Wiley, 1989), pp. 1064–1081. See also C. Starr, R. Rudman, and C. Whipple, "Philosophical Basis for Risk Analysis," *Annual Review of Energy* 1 (1976): 629–662.

3. C. W. Churchman, *Theory of Experimental Inference* (New York: Macmil-

lan, 1947). See S. Axinn, "The Fallacy of the Single Risk," *Philosophy of Science* 33, nos. 1–2 (1966): 154–162.

4. J. Harsanyi, "Can the Maximin Principle Serve as a Basis for Morality? A Critique of John Rawls's Theory," *American Political Science Review* 69, no. 2 (1975): 594. See Chapter Eight of this volume. Admittedly, some risk decisions minimize both industry and public risk, and some maximize both industry and public risk. The dilemma arises when only one can be minimized, so that a choice must be made between the two.

5. A. Kaplan, *The Conduct of Inquiry* (San Francisco: Chandler, 1964), p. 253.

6. J. J. Thomson, *Rights, Restitution, and Risk* (Cambridge, Mass.: Harvard University Press, 1986).

7. Grave harms, for both plaintiffs and defendants, are also likely to be greater in the criminal case; hence the tougher standard of proof. There likewise appears to be a greater potential for abuse in the criminal law than in civil or tort law, since all crimes are potentially political crimes, especially in a tyrannical society. This may arise from the fact that criminal law enforces the power of the *state*, whereas civil-tort law merely enforces the power of the legal *individual*.

8. Two industry risk assessors concluded, for example, that the risk of cancer to the public because of a waste site contaminated with chromium was "insignificant" (see R. Golden and N. Karch, "Assessment of a Waste Site Contaminated with Chromium," in Paustenbach, *Risk Assessment*, pp. 577–598). Likewise, two risk assessors employed by Procter and Gamble analyzed the danger posed by a chemical widely used in laundry detergents made by their company. Assessing the chemical, nitrilotriacetic acid, they said that, although it is highly toxic, the chemical "causes no environmental problems" and "no risk to humans" because the average dose received by humans is below the level required to initiate cancer (see R. Anderson and C. Alden, "Risk Assessment for Nitrilotriacetic Acid," in Paustenbach, *Risk Assessment*, pp. 390–426). See also note 2, Chapter Eight, this volume.

9. For an example of a risk assessment performed by industry analysts, who likely underestimated the risks, see H. Leung and D. Paustenbach, "Assessing Health Risks in the Workplace," in Paustenbach, *Risk Assessment*, pp. 689–710. In their study, Leung (who works for Syntex Corporation) and Paustenbach (who works for McLaren Company) claimed that, despite their exposure to dioxin and despite their having residual chloracne for twenty-six years, Dow Chemical workers and Monsanto workers showed "no significant differences in a variety of clinical parameters." However, the assessors did not mention (1) for how long a period the exposed workers were studied, (2) how many workers were studied, or (3) which "clinical parameters" were examined for the exposed workers. Failure to detect harms to the exposed workers hence could be a result of (1) too short a time for the study, (2) too few workers being studied, and (3) inappropriate or incomplete clinical parameters being investigated. For all these reasons, the industry risk assessors likely underestimated

the hazard from dioxin. See R. M. Cooke, "Risk Assessment and Rational Decision Theory," *Dialectica* 36 (no. 4), 334. See also note 8 above.

10. See Harsanyi, "Maximin Principle"; M. Resnick, *Choices* (Minneapolis: University of Minnesota Press, 1987), pp. 26–37.

11. See Cooke, "Risk Assessment," pp. 341–342.

12. Regarding the difficulty of proving causality, see, for example, P. Ricci and A. Henderson, "Fear, Fiat, and Fiasco," in *Phenotypic Variation in Populations*, ed. A. Woodhead, M. Bender, and R. Leonard (New York: Plenum, 1988), pp. 285–293. See also J. W. Falco and R. Moraski, "Methods Used in the United States for the Assessment and Management of Health Risk Due to Chemicals," in *Risk Management of Chemicals in the Environment*, ed. H. M. Seip and A. B. Heiberg (New York: Plenum, 1989), pp. 37–60; and L. Cox and P. Ricci, "Risk, Uncertainty, and Causation," in Paustenbach, *Risk Assessment*, pp. 125–156.

13. See, for example, H. Shue, "Exporting Hazards," in *Boundaries: National Autonomy and Its Limits*, ed. P. Brown and H. Shue (Totowa, N.J.: Rowman and Littlefield, 1981), pp. 107–145; J. Lichtenberg, "National Boundaries and Moral Boundaries," in Brown and Shue, *Boundaries*, pp. 79–100.

14. J. Bentham, *Principles of the Civil Code*, in *The Works of Jeremy Bentham*, ed. J. Bowring (New York: Russell and Russell, 1962), 1:301.

15. See, for example, L. Becker, "Rights," in *Property*, ed. L. Becker and K. Kipnis (Englewood Cliffs, N.J.: Prentice-Hall, 1984), p. 76. For a discussion of the flaws in this view of rights, see A. Baier, "Poisoning the Wells," in *Values at Risk*, ed. D. MacLean (Totowa, N.J.: Rowman and Allanheld, 1986), pp. 49–74.

16. See, for example, J. Bentham, *Principles of Morals and Legislation*, in Bowring, *Works*, 1:36; J. Feinberg, *Social Philosophy* (Englewood Cliffs, N.J.: Prentice-Hall, 1973), pp. 29, 59; J. Rachels, "Euthanasia," in *Matters of Life and Death*, ed. T. Regan (New York: Random House, 1980), p. 38.

17. See L. Cox and P. Ricci, "Legal and Philosophical Aspects of Risk Analysis," in Paustenbach, *Risk Analysis*, pp. 22–26. See also W. Hoffman and J. Fisher, "Corporate Responsibility," in Becker and Kipnis, *Property*, pp. 211–220.

18. See M. Peltu, "The Role of Communications Media," in Otway and Peltu, *Regulating Industrial Risks*, p. 132.

19. Ibid., pp. 132–136.

20. See A. C. Michalos, *Foundations of Decisionmaking* (Ottowa: Canadian Library of Philosophy, 1987), pp. 202ff.; and H. S. Denenberg et al., *Risk and Insurance* (Englewood Cliffs, N.J.: Prentice-Hall, 1964). See also Cox and Ricci, "Legal and Philosophical Aspects," p. 1035.

21. Thomson, *Rights*, p. 158.

22. For the centrality and importance of consent in risk evaluation, see D. MacLean, "Introduction" and "Risk and Consent," in MacLean, *Values at Risk*, pp. 1–16, 17–30.

23. See K. S. Shrader-Frechette, *Nuclear Power and Public Policy* (Boston: Reidel, 1983), pp. 74–78.

24. Harsanyi, in "Maximin Principle," uses this argument, as does L. Maxim,

"Problems Associated with the Use of Conservative Assumptions in Exposure and Risk Analysis," in Paustenbach, *Risk Assessment,* pp. 539–555. Other risk assessors who use this argument include, for example, Lave and Leonard, "Coke Oven Emissions," pp. 1068–1069.

    25. See Shrader-Frechette, *Nuclear Power,* pp. 33–35.

    26. See W. Frankena, "The Concept of Social Justice," in *Social Justice,* ed. R. Brandt (Englewood Cliffs, N.J.: Prentice-Hall, 1962), pp. 10, 14; Shue, "Exporting Hazards"; and Lichtenberg, "National Boundaries." See also Cox and Ricci, "Legal and Philosophical Aspects."

    27. D. Eddy, "Probabilistic Reasoning in Clinical Medicine," in *Judgment under Uncertainty: Heuristics and Biases,* ed. D. Kahneman, P. Slovic, and A. Tversky (Cambridge, England: Cambridge University Press, 1982), p. 267. See also the following articles in this collection: S. Oskamp, "Overconfidence in Case-Study Judgments," p. 292; P. Slovic, B. Fischhoff, and S. Lichtenstein, "Facts vs. Fears," p. 475.

    28. Shrader-Frechette, *Nuclear Power,* chap. 1.

    29. See P. Huber, "The Bhopalization of American Tort Law," in *Hazards: Technology and Fairness,* ed. R. Kates et al. (Washington, D.C.: National Academy Press, 1986), pp. 94–95, 106–107. See also Shrader-Frechette, *Nuclear Power,* chap. 4.

    30. See, for example, A. B. Lovins and J. H. Price, *Non-Nuclear Futures* (New York: Harper and Row, 1975). See also C. Flavin, *Nuclear Power: The Market Test* (Washington, D.C.: Worldwatch Institute, 1983).

    31. See Cooke, "Risk Assessment," pp. 345–347.

    32. Thomson, *Rights,* p. 172.

    33. For discussion of this argument, see Frankena, "Concept of Social Justice," p. 15, and Chapter Eight of this volume.

    34. For discussion of procedural rationality, see Chapters Two and Three of this volume. For analyses of collective strategies whereby consumers might exercise their sovereignty, see K. S. Shrader-Frechette, *Science Policy, Ethics, and Economic Methodology* (Boston: Reidel, 1985), pp. 286–312. See T. Schelling, *Choice and Consequence* (Cambridge, Mass.: Harvard University Press, 1984), pp. 145–146.

    35. Schelling, *Choice and Consequences,* pp. 145–146.

    36. See, for example, J. S. Mill, *On Liberty* (Buffalo, N.Y.: Prometheus Books, 1986), esp. p. 16.

    37. See Chapter Ten of this volume.

    38. Lave and Leonard, "Coke Oven Emissions," pp. 1068–1069.

    39. Ibid., pp. 1071–1078.

    40. See Chapter Five and the discussion of the *de minimis* dilemma.

    41. B. Emmet et al., "The Distribution of Environmental Quality," in *Environmental Assessment,* ed. D. Burkhardt and W. Ittelson (New York: Plenum, 1978), pp. 367–374; J. Egerton, "Appalachia's Absentee Landlords," *The Progressive* 45, no. 6 (June 1981): 43ff.; and K. S. Shrader-Frechette, *Risk Analysis*

and Scientific Method (Boston: Reidel, 1985), pp. 97–122. See also MacLean, "Risk and Consent."

42. C. Starr, "General Philosophy of Risk-Benefit Analysis," in *Energy and the Environment*, ed. H. Ashley, R. Rudman, and C. Whipple (Elmsford, N.Y.: Pergamon Press, 1976), p. 16. See Cox and Ricci, "Legal and Philosophical Aspects."

43. Slovic, "Facts vs. Fears," p. 488. See Chapters Eleven and Twelve, this volume.

Chapter Ten

1. D. R. Obey, "Export of Hazardous Industries," *Congressional Record*, 95th Cong., 2d sess., 29 June 1978, Vol. 124, part 15, pp. 19763–19764. For an excellent discussion of international risk problems, see G. Majone, "The International Dimension," in *Regulating Industrial Risks*, ed. H. Otway and M. Peltu (London: Butterworths, 1985), pp. 40–56. For mathematical models of the risk of lung cancer posed by asbestos, see H. Leung and D. J. Paustenbach, "Assessing Health Risks in the Workplace," in *The Risk Assessment of Environmental and Human Health Hazards*, ed. D. J. Paustenbach (New York: Wiley, 1989), p. 695.

2. H. Shue, "Exporting Hazards," in *Boundaries: National Autonomy and Its Limits*, ed. P. Brown and H. Shue (Totowa, N.J.: Rowman and Littlefield, 1981), p. 107.

3. D. Weir and M. Schapiro, "The Circle of Poison," in *Environment 85/86*, ed. J. Allen (Guilford, Conn.: Dushkin, 1985), p. 188.

4. J. T. Mathews et al., *World Resources 1986* (New York: Basic Books, 1986), pp. 48–49. See also R. Repetto, *Paying the Price: Pesticide Subsidies in Developing Countries*, Research Report no. 2 (Washington, D.C.: World Resources Institute, 1985), p. 3.

5. D. Lyons, "Review of Fishkin's *The Limits of Obligation*," *Ethics* 94, no. 2 (January 1983): 329.

6. Regarding act utilitarians and rule utilitarians, see D. Lyons, *Forms and Limits of Utilitarianism* (Oxford: Clarendon Press, 1967); Lyons also argues for equivalence between the two positions. See also *Contemporary Utilitarianism*, ed. M. Bayles (New York: Doubleday, 1968). For more discussion of utilitarianism, see Chapter Eight of this volume. For a critique of a utilitarian account of risk evaluation and management, see S. Samuels, "The Arrogance of Intellectual Power," in *Phenotypic Variation in Populations*, ed. A. Woodhead, M. Bender, and R. Leonard (New York: Plenum, 1988), pp. 113–120.

7. J. Smart, "An Outline of a System of Utilitarian Ethics," in *Utilitarianism*, ed. J. Smart and B. Williams (Cambridge, England: Cambridge University Press, 1973), p. 72. See also J. S. Mill, *"Utilitarianism," "On Liberty," and "Representative Government"* (New York: Dutton, 1910), pp. 58–59. For risk assessors who pro-

mote this argument, see L. Lave and B. Leonard, "Regulating Coke Oven Emissions," in Paustenbach, *Risk Assessment,* pp. 1064–1081.

8. C. Gersuny, *Work Hazards and Industrial Conflicts* (Hanover, N.H.: University Press of New England, 1981), p. 20.

9. See Chapter Five of this volume, esp. the discussion of the *de minimis* dilemma. See also K. S. Shrader-Frechette, *Risk Analysis and Scientific Method* (Boston: Reidel, 1985), chap. 5.

10. Smart, "Utilitarian Ethics," p. 69.

11. J. Rawls, *A Theory of Justice* (Cambridge, Mass.: Harvard University Press, 1971); C. Fried, *Right and Wrong* (Cambridge, Mass.: Harvard University Press, 1978); A. Donagan, *The Theory of Morality* (Chicago: University of Chicago Press, 1977). See also S. I. Benn, "Egalitarianism and the Equal Consideration of Interests," in *Equality,* Nomos 9, Yearbook of the American Society for Political and Legal Philosophy, ed. J. R. Pennock and J. W. Chapman (New York: Lieber-Atherton, 1968), pp. 75–76; and W. Frankena, *Ethics* (Englewood Cliffs, N.J.: Prentice-Hall, 1963), pp. 41–42. Finally, see W. Frankena, "The Concept of Social Justice," in *Social Justice,* ed. R. Brandt (Englewood Cliffs, N.J.: Prentice-Hall, 1962), pp. 10, 14.

12. For one version of the countervailing-benefits argument, see J. Harsanyi, "Can the Maximin Principle Serve as a Basis for Morality? A Critique of John Rawls's Theory," *American Political Science Review* 69, no. 2 (June 1975): 602. For the damaging effects of the countervailing-benefits argument in second- and third-world countries, see A. Hittle, "Eastern Europe Confronts the Ecological Barrier," *Not Man Apart* 18, no. 4 (August/September 1988): 8–11.

13. See Shue, "Exporting Hazards," pp. 117ff.

14. See note 6.

15. Mill, *On Liberty,* chaps. 1, 3, 4, 5. See Chapter Nine of this volume.

16. See A. Gewirth, *Human Rights* (Chicago: University of Chicago Press, 1982), p. 157; and D. Lyons, "Human Rights and the General Welfare," in *Rights,* ed. D. Lyons (Belmont, Calif.: Wadsworth, 1979), p. 182.

17. Mill, *Utilitarianism,* chap. 5. See Lyons, "Human Rights and General Welfare," pp. 176ff.

18. Mill, *Utilitarianism,* chap. 5, par. 33.

19. Ibid., chap. 5.

20. Ibid., chap. 5, par. 25. For discussion of this point, see A. Baier, "Poisoning the Wells," in *Values at Risk,* ed. D. MacLean (Totowa, N.J.: Rowman and Allanheld, 1986), pp. 49–74.

21. See Gewirth, *Human Rights,* p. 157, who makes a similar point.

22. Shue, "Exporting Hazards," p. 122. For criticism of the position that Shue rejects, see Samuels, "Arrogance of Intellectual Power."

23. J. Lichtenberg, "National Boundaries and Moral Boundaries," in Brown and Shue, *Boundaries,* p. 87.

24. See C. Beitz, *Political Theory and International Relations* (Princeton, N.J.: Princeton University Press, 1979), and "Cosmopolitan Ideals and National Sentiment," *Journal of Philosophy* 80, no. 30 (October 1983): 591–600. See also Rawls,

Theory of Justice. Finally, see H. Shue, "The Burdens of Justice," *Journal of Philosophy* 80, no. 30 (October 1983): 600–608.

25. J. Rawls, "Kantian Constructivism in Moral Theory," *Journal of Philosophy* 77, no. 9 (September 1980): 515–572. See also Beitz, "Cosmopolitan Ideals," p. 595.

26. Beitz, *Political Theory*, pp. 129–136, 143–153; and Lichtenberg, "National Boundaries." See Baier, "Poisoning the Wells," pp. 58–59, who makes this same point.

27. W. Blackstone, "On the Meaning and Justification of the Equality Principle," in *The Concept of Equality*, ed. W. Blackstone (Minneapolis: Burgess, 1969).

28. J. Rawls, "Justice as Fairness," in *Philosophy of Law*, ed. J. Feinberg and H. Gross (Encino, Calif.: Dickenson, 1975), p. 284. See also H. Shue, "The Geography of Justice," *Ethics* 92, no. 4 (July 1982): 714, 718.

29. M. Beardsley, "Equality and Obedience to Law," in *Law and Philosophy*, ed. S. Hook (New York: New York University Press, 1964), pp. 35–36. See also I. Berlin, "Equality," in Blackstone, *Concept of Equality*, p. 33; W. Frankena, "Some Beliefs about Justice," in Feinberg and Gross, *Philosophy of Law*, pp. 250–251; M. Markovic, "The Relationship between Equality and Local Autonomy," in *Equality and Social Policy*, ed. W. Feinberg (Urbana: University of Illinois Press, 1978), p. 83; and Rawls, "Justice as Fairness," pp. 277, 280, 282. Finally, see G. Vlastos, "Justice and Equality," in Brandt, *Social Justice*, pp. 50, 56.

30. J. R. Pennock, "Introduction," in *The Limits of the Law*, Nomos 15, Yearbook of the American Society for Political and Legal Philosophy, ed. J. R. Pennock and J. W. Chapman (New York: Lieber-Atherton, 1974), pp. 2, 6.

31. P. Singer, "Famine, Affluence, and Morality," in *Philosophy Now*, ed. K. Struhl and P. Struhl (New York: Random House, 1980), pp. 485–488.

32. Shue, "Exporting Hazards," pp. 119–123. See also Baier, "Poisoning the Wells," pp. 84ff.

33. Quoted by Weir and Schapiro in "Circle of Poison," p. 119.

34. Weir and Schapiro, "Circle of Poison," p. 119.

35. Ibid.

36. See the discussion of consumer sovereignty in the previous chapter.

37. W. Viscusi, *Risk by Choice* (Cambridge, Mass.: Harvard University Press, 1983), pp. 37–38; and Shrader-Frechette, *Risk Analysis*, chap. 4.

38. See B. Wynne, *Risk Management and Hazardous Waste* (New York: Springer-Verlag, 1987), pp. 286–287.

39. Ibid., pp. 287–288.

40. Ibid., p. 288.

41. See Rawls, *Theory of Justice*, p. 87.

42. See M. Jones-Lee, *The Value of Life* (Chicago: University of Chicago Press, 1976), p. 39. See also E. Eckholm, "Unhealthy Jobs," *Environment* 19, no. 6 (August/September 1977): pp. 33–34. Finally, see Viscusi, *Risk by Choice*, p. 46. The Mexico statistic is from Shue, "Exporting Hazards," p. 129.

43. E. Eckholm, "Human Wants and Misused Lands," in Allen, *Environment*,

p. 5. See A. Kuflick, "Review of Henry Shue, *Basic Rights*," *Ethics* 94, no. 2 (January 1984): 320, for an account of the difficulties of describing "coercion" and "free consent."

44. L. Clarke, *Acceptable Risk? Making Decisions in a Toxic Environment* (Berkeley and Los Angeles: University of California Press, 1989).

45. See Shue, "Exporting Hazards," pp. 130ff., for a similar argument. See Lave and Leonard, "Coke Oven Emissions," pp. 1068–1069, for an industry perspective.

46. Gewirth, *Human Rights*, p. 186.

47. See K. S. Shrader-Frechette, *Environmental Ethics* (Pacific Grove, Calif.: Boxwood Press, 1981), chap. 6. See also D. Paustenbach, "A Survey of Environmental Risk Assessment," in Paustenbach, *Risk Assessment*, pp. 103ff.

48. See Shue, "Exporting Hazards," pp. 131–133.

49. In connection with the countervailing-benefits argument, I argued that individuals' bodily security was threatened by technologically induced damage having a *high probability of occurrence*. Presumably, our security is not threatened by improbable harms, but what level of risk is acceptable?

50. L. Cox and P. Ricci, "Legal and Philosophical Aspects of Risk Analysis," in Paustenbach, *Risk Assessment*, pp. 1038ff. See Shrader-Frechette, *Risk Analysis*, chaps. 4–5.

51. 10 *Code of Federal Regulations* sec. 20 (Washington, D.C.: Government Printing Office, 1978), p. 182; 10 C.F.R. sec. 50, Appendix I, p. 372; and U.S. Nuclear Regulatory Commission, *Issuances* 5, book 2 (Washington, D.C.: Government Printing Office, 30 June 1977), pp. 928, 980. See Shrader-Frechette, *Risk Analysis*, pp. 125–127.

52. See notes 8 and 9 in Chapter Nine. See, especially, Leung and Paustenbach, "Assessing Health Risks," pp. 689–710. See also Wynne, *Risk Management*, pp. 286–288.

53. Shue, "Exporting Hazards," pp. 135ff.

54. Lichtenberg, "National Boundaries," pp. 80ff.

55. H. Shue, *Basic Rights* (Princeton, N.J.: Princeton University Press, 1980), p. 139; and Kuflick, "Review of Shue," p. 322.

56. See J. A. Horberry, "Fitting USAID to the Environmental Assessment Provisions of NEPA," in *Environmental Impact Assessment*, ed. P. Wathern (London: Unwin Hyman, 1988), pp. 286–299.

57. T. Nagel, "Ruthlessness in Public Life," in *Mortal Questions* (New York: Cambridge University Press, 1979), p. 84.

58. J. Fishkin, *The Limits of Obligation* (New Haven, Conn.: Yale University Press, 1982). See also D. Lyons, "Review of Fishkin's *The Limits of Obligation*," *Ethics* 94, no. 2 (January 1984): 328–329; and Kuflick, "Review of Shue," pp. 321–322.

59. See Singer, "Famine," pp. 485–488.

60. Shue, "Burdens of Justice," pp. 602ff.

61. Ibid., p. 607. For arguments espousing the rights of distant persons, see

J. Sterba, *The Demands of Justice* (Notre Dame, Ind.: University of Notre Dame Press, 1980), chaps. 2 and 6.

62. Shue, "Exporting Hazards," p. 135.

63. Ibid., p. 136.

64. Lichtenberg, "National Boundaries," p. 91.

65. See G. Hardin, "Living on a Lifeboat," *BioScience* 24, no. 10 (October 1974): 561–568. See Shrader-Frechette, *Environmental Ethics*, pp. 37ff. For the data on GNP, see Sterba, *Demands of Justice*, pp. 127ff.

66. See D. Callahan, "Doing Well by Doing Good: Garrett Hardin's 'Lifeboat Ethics,' " *Hastings Center Report* 4, no. 6 (December 1974): 3.

67. Weir and Schapiro, "Circle of Poison," p. 120.

68. Ibid., p. 119.

69. F. Sartor and D. Rondia, "Mathematical and Biological Uncertainties in the Assessment of a Permissible Blood Lead Concentration," in *Risk Management of Chemicals in the Environment*, ed. H. Seip and A. Heiberg (New York: Plenum, 1989), p. 127.

70. R. Monastersky, "Depleted Ring around Ozone Hole," *Science News* 136, no. 21 (18 November 1989): 324.

71. See K. Goldberg, "Efforts to Prevent Misuse of Pesticides Exported to Developing Countries: Progressing beyond Regulation and Notification," *Ecology Law Quarterly* 12, no. 4 (1985): 1025–1051.

72. See Shue, *Basic Rights*, part 3; see also Kuflick, "Review of Shue," pp. 322–323.

73. Obey, "Export of Hazardous Industries," pp. 19763, 19765. See also Shue, "Exporting Hazards," pp. 137–138, 144.

74. J. Seiberling and C. Schneider, "How Congress Can Help Developing Countries Help Themselves," in *Journal '86: Annual Report of the World Resources Institute* (Washington, D.C.: World Resources Institute, 1986), pp. 57, 59.

75. See G. Webb, "Global Effort Kills World Bank Loan to Brazil," *Not Man Apart* 19, no. 1 (February–May 1989): 16. See also L. Brown and E. Wolf, "Reversing Africa's Decline," in *State of the World 1986*, ed. L. Brown (New York: Norton, 1986), p. 182.

76. Thucydides, *The History of the Peloponnesian War*, book I, sec. 141.

Chapter Eleven

1. J. I. Fabrikant et al., Committee on the Biological Effects of Ionizing Radiation, *Health Risks of Radon and Other Internally Deposited Alpha-Emitters: BEIR IV* (Washington, D.C.: National Academy Press, 1988), pp. 24–29.

2. Ibid., p. 30.

3. Ibid., p. 76. WLM stands for "working level month," a unit of radon exposure. The WL is defined as any combination of the short-lived radon daughters in 1 liter of air that results in the ultimate release of 1.3×10^5 megaelectron volts of potential alpha energy. Exposure of a miner to this con-

centration for a working month of 170 hours is a WLM. (See Fabrikant, *Health Risks of Radon*, p. 27.)

4. Fabrikant, *Health Risks of Radon*, p. 155.

5. L. Cox and P. Ricci, "Legal and Philosophical Aspects of Risk Analysis," in *The Risk Assessment of Environmental and Human Health Hazards*, ed. D. J. Paustenbach (New York: Wiley, 1989), p. 1027.

6. See Chapters One and Three.

7. See, for example, H. Latin, "Ideal versus Real Regulatory Efficiency: Implementation of Uniform Standards and 'Fine-Tuning' Regulatory Reform," *Stanford Law Review* 37 (May 1985): 1267–1332; and "The Feasibility of Occupational Health Standards: An Essay on Legal Decisionmaking under Uncertainty," *Northwestern University Law Review* 78, no. 3 (1983): 583–617. See S. Samuels, "The Arrogance of Intellectual Power," in *Phenotypic Variation in Populations*, ed. A. Woodhead, M. Bender, and R. Leonard (New York: Plenum, 1988), pp. 113–120.

8. See, for example, L. Maxim, "Problems Associated with the Use of Conservative Assumptions in Exposure and Risk Analysis," in Paustenbach, *Risk Assessment*, p. 526–560. See B. Cohen, "Risk Analyses of Buried Wastes," in Paustenbach, *Risk Assessment*, pp. 561–576. See also B. A. Ackerman and R. B. Stewart, "Reforming Environmental Law," *Stanford Law Review* 37 (May 1985): 1333–1365; and B. Ackerman et al., *The Uncertain Search for Environmental Quality* (New York: Free Press, 1974). Finally, see R. Reitz et al., "Use of Physiological Pharmacokinetics in Cancer Risk Assessments," in Paustenbach, *Risk Assessment*, pp. 238–264; L. Lave and B. Leonard, "Regulating Coke Oven Emissions," in Paustenbach, *Risk Assessment*, pp. 1064–1080; C. Whipple, "Nonpessimistic Risk Assessment," in Paustenbach, *Risk Assessment*, pp. 1105–1120; A. Weinberg, "Risk Assessment, Regulation, and the Limits," in Woodhead, *Phenotypic Variation*, pp. 121–128.

9. See Chapters Five through Ten in this volume.

10. See H. B. Leonard and R. Zeckhauser, "Cost-Benefit Analysis Applied to Risks: Its Philosophy and Legitimacy," and A. Gibbard, "Risk and Value," in *Values at Risk*, ed. D. MacLean (Totowa, N.J.: Rowman and Allanheld, 1986), pp. 31–48, 94–112. See also chap. 5 of K. S. Shrader-Frechette, *Science Policy, Ethics, and Economic Methodology* (Boston: Reidel, 1985).

11. L. J. Carter, "Dispute over Cancer Risk Quantification," *Science* 203, no. 4387 (30 March 1979): 1324–1325. See C. Starr and C. Whipple, "Risks of Risk Decisions," *Science* 208, no. 4448 (6 June 1980): 1118; I. Barbour, *Technology, Environment, and Human Values* (New York: Praeger, 1980), pp. 163–164; and Cox and Ricci, "Legal and Philosophical Aspects," pp. 1038ff.

12. A. B. Lovins, "Cost-Risk-Benefit Assessments in Energy Policy," *George Washington Law Review* 45, no. 5 (August 1977): 912.

13. For discussion of these objections, see Cox and Ricci, "Legal and Philosophical Aspects," pp. 1038ff.; Samuels, "Arrogance of Intellectual Power," pp. 113–120. See also R. N. Andrews, "Environmental Impact Assessment and Risk

Assessment," in *Environmental Impact Assessment*, ed. P. Wathern (London: Unwin Hyman, 1988), pp. 85–97. See J. L. Regens, "Attitudes toward Risk-Benefit Analysis for Managing Effects of Chemical Exposures," in *Risk Management of Chemicals in the Environment*, ed. H. M. Seip and A. B. Heiberg (New York: Plenum, 1989), pp. 75–88; and S. Gage, "Risk Assessment in Governmental Decisionmaking," in Mitre Corporation, *Symposium/Workshop on Nuclear and Nonnuclear Energy Systems: Risk Assessment and Governmental Decision Making* (McLean, Va.: Mitre Corporation, 1979), p. 13. See also F. Farmer, "Panel: Accident Risk Assessment," W. Lowrance, "Discussion," and L. Lave, "Discussion," in Mitre Corp., *Symposium*, pp. 426, 152, 190. For problems with benefit-cost analysis, see K. J. Arrow, *Social Choice and Individual Values* (New York: Wiley, 1951); E. Stokey and R. Zeckhauser, *A Primer for Policy Analysis* (New York: Norton, 1978); H. F. McKay, *Arrow's Theorem: The Paradox of Social Choice* (New Haven, Conn.: Yale University Press, 1980); P. K. Pattanaik, *Voting and Collective Choice* (Cambridge, England: Cambridge University Press, 1971); A. K. Sen, *Collective Choice and Social Welfare* (San Francisco: Holden-Day, 1970); W. Gaertner, "An Analysis of Several Necessary and Sufficient Conditions for Transitivity under the Majority Decision Rule," in *Aggregation and Revelation of Preferences*, ed. J. J. Laffont (New York: Elsevier, 1979), pp. 91–112. See also E. A. Pozner, "Equity, Nonfeasible Alternatives and Social Choice: A Reconsideration of the Concept of Social Welfare," in Laffont, *Aggregation*, pp. 161–173; C. W. Churchman, "On the Intercomparison of Utilities," in *The Structure of Economic Science*, ed. S. R. Krupp (Englewood Cliffs, N.J.: Prentice-Hall, 1966), p. 255; G. Tullock, "Public Choice in America," in *Collective Decision Making*, ed. C. S. Russell (Baltimore: Johns Hopkins University Press, 1979), pp. 27–45; and E. F. McClennen, "Constitutional Choice: Rawls *versus* Harsanyi," in *Philosophy in Economics*, ed. J. C. Pitt (Boston: Reidel, 1981). For a discussion of alleged incommensurability, see, for example, S. Jellinek, "Risk Assessment at the EPA," and S. Samuels, "Panel: Accident Risk Assessment," in Mitre Corp., *Symposium*, pp. 63–64, 391–392. See also K. S. Shrader-Frechette, "Technology Assessment as Applied Philosophy of Science," *Science, Technology, and Human Values* 6, no. 33 (1980): 33–50. For problems with attempting to reduce a variety of cost, benefit, and risk parameters to some common denominator, such as money, see Samuels, "Accident Risk Assessment," p. 391; and the following items in Mitre Corp., *Symposium*: M. Baram, "Panel: Use of Risk Assessment," p. 622; A. Hull, "Panel: Public Perception of Risk," p. 579; C. Whipple, "Panel: Public Perception of Risk," p. 576; and J. O'Neill, "Discussion," p. 31. See also O'Neill, "Discussion," pp. 23–24, and A. Brown, "Plenary Session Report," pp. 693–694.

14. S. E. Dreyfus, "Formal Models vs. Human Situational Understanding: Inherent Limitations on the Modeling of Business Expertise," *Technology and People* 1 (1982): 133–165. See also S. Dreyfus, "The Risks! and Benefits? of Risk-Benefit Analysis," paper presented at the Western Division meeting of the American Philosophical Association, 24 March 1983, Berkeley, Calif. (Stuart

Dreyfus, a professor of operations research at the University of California, Berkeley, is the brother of Hubert Dreyfus, a professor of philosophy at the same institution. They share the beliefs attributed to Stuart in this paper and often coauthor essays defending this point of view. See, for example, S. Dreyfus and H. Dreyfus, "The Scope, Limits, and Training Implications of Three Models of . . . Behavior," ORC 79–2, Operations Research Center, University of California, Berkeley, February 1979.) For a similar argument, see Samuels, "Arrogance of Intellectual Power," p. 119.

15. A. MacIntyre, "Utilitarianism and Cost-Benefit Analysis," in *Ethics and the Environment*, ed. D. Scherer and T. Attig (Englewood Cliffs, N.J.: Prentice-Hall, 1983), pp. 139–151. See D. MacLean, "Social Values and the Distribution of Risk," in MacLean, *Values at Risk*, pp. 75–93.

16. See R. N. Giere, "Technological Decisionmaking," in *Reason and Decision*, ed. M. Bradie and K. Sayre (Bowling Green, Ohio: Bowling Green State University Press, 1981), part III.

17. P. Self, *Econocrats and the Policy Process: The Politics and Philosophy of Cost-Benefit Analysis* (London: Macmillan, 1975), pp. 70–75.

18. Dreyfus, "Formal Models," p. 161; L. H. Tribe, "Technology Assessment and the Fourth Discontinuity," *Southern California Law Review* 46, no. 3 (June 1973): 659; R. H. Socolow, "Failures of Discourse," in Scherer and Attig, *Ethics and the Environment*, p. 169; D. MacLean, "Understanding the Nuclear Power Controversy," in *Scientific Controversies*, ed. A. L. Caplan and H. T. Engelhardt (Cambridge, England: Cambridge University Press, 1983), part V.

19. See Samuels, "Arrogance of Intellectual Power," pp. 118–119; see also MacLean, "Nuclear Power Controversy," part V; Socolow, "Failures of Discourse," pp. 152–166; and Dreyfus, "Formal Models," p. 163.

20. Dreyfus, "The Risks!" p. 2.

21. See Cox and Ricci, "Legal and Philosophical Aspects," p. 1040; Self, *Econocrats*, p. 70; MacIntyre, "Utilitarianism," pp. 143–145; Lovins, "Cost-Risk-Benefit Assessments," pp. 913–916. See also R. Coburn, "Technology Assessment, Human Good, and Freedom," in *Ethics and Problems of the 21st Century*, ed. K. E. Goodpaster and K. M. Sayre (Notre Dame, Ind.: University of Notre Dame Press, 1979), p. 108; E. Mishan, *Cost-Benefit Analysis* (New York: Praeger, 1976), pp. 160–161; G. Myrdal, *The Political Element in the Development of Economic Theory*, trans. P. Steeten (Cambridge, Mass.: Harvard University Press, 1955), p. 89; and S. S. Stevens, "Measurement, Psychophysics, and Utility," in *Measurement: Definitions and Theories*, ed. C. W. Churchman and P. Ratoosh (New York: Wiley, 1959), pp. 36–52.

22. MacLean, "Nuclear Power Controversy," part V.

23. Lovins, "Cost-Risk-Benefit Assessments," pp. 929–930. See D. MacLean, "Quantified Risk Assessment and the Quality of Life," in *Uncertain Power*, ed. D. Zinberg (Elmsford, N.Y.: Pergamon Press, 1983), part V.

24. MacLean, "Distribution of Risk," pp. 75–93; Tribe, "Technology As-

sessment," pp. 628–629; MacLean, "Quantitative Risk Assessment," parts V and VI; MacIntyre, "Utilitarianism," pp. 139–142; and A. Gewirth, "Human Rights and the Prevention of Cancer," in Scherer and Attig, *Ethics and the Environment*, p. 177.

25. MacLean, "Distribution of Risk," pp. 75–93; Gewirth, "Human Rights," p. 175. See also N. Ashford, "The Limits of Cost-Benefit Analysis in Regulatory Decisions," in *Resolving Locational Conflict*, ed. R. W. Lake (New Brunswick, N.J.: Center for Urban Policy Research, Rutgers University, 1987), pp. 427–432.

26. See D. W. Pearce, "Introduction," in *The Valuation of Social Cost*, ed. D. W. Pearce (New York: Allen and Unwin, 1978). See also Self, *Econocrats*, p. 78.

27. Mishan, *Cost-Benefit Analysis*, p. 383, makes this same point.

28. See Self, *Econocrats*; and R. M. Hare, "Contrasting Methods of Environmental Planning," in Goodpaster and Sayre, *Ethics*, pp. 64–68.

29. Dreyfus, "The Risks!" p. 1.

30. MacIntyre, "Utilitarianism," p. 151.

31. See note 21.

32. See notes 17 and 18.

33. See Coburn, "Technology Assessment."

34. A. K. Sen, "Rawls versus Bentham: An Axiomatic Examination of the Pure Distribution Problem," in *Reading Rawls*, ed. N. Daniels (New York: Basic Books, 1981), pp. 283–292.

35. MacLean, "Quantified Risk Assessment," part IV.

36. Similar points are made by D. M. Hausman, "Are General Equilibrium Theories Explanatory?" and by E. J. Green, "On the Role of Fundamental Theory in Positive Economics," in *Philosophy in Economics*, ed. J. C. Pitt (Boston: Reidel, 1981), pp. 26–28 and p. 14. See Ashford, "Limits of Cost-Benefit Analysis."

37. N. S. Care, "Participation and Policy," *Ethics* 88, no. 1 (July 1978): 316–337.

38. Since considering the various risks, costs, and benefits of a project, and assigning numerical values to them, is one way of being rational about policymaking, the use of RCBA would seem to enhance fulfillment of the rationality condition mentioned by Care.

39. See C. W. Churchman, "On the Intercomparison of Utilities," in *The Structure of Economic Science*, ed. S. R. Krupp (Englewood Cliffs, N.J.: Prentice-Hall, 1966), p. 256.

40. For a similar example, see Mishan, *Cost-Benefit Analysis*, p. 161.

41. Although the $20-per-family scheme is only an arbitrary "thought experiment," it illustrates well that estimating consequent gains and losses often can provide a useful framework for thinking realistically about technological risk.

42. MacIntyre, "Utilitarianism," pp. 140–141. See Samuels, "Arrogance of Intellectual Power," pp. 118–119, for a similar claim.

43. Giere, in "Technological Decisionmaking," part III, employs a similar argument. This point is also clear in Cox and Ricci, "Legal and Philosophical Aspects," pp. 1027–1030.

44. Ralph Keeney, a student of Howard Raiffa's, made this point in a private conversation at Berkeley in January 1983.

45. See Gewirth, "Human Rights." See Cox and Ricci, "Legal and Philosophical Aspects," pp. 1038–1039 and the discussion of rights.

46. P. Suppes, "Decision Theory," in *Encyclopedia of Philosophy*, ed. P. Edwards (New York: Macmillan, 1967), 2:311. P. S. Dasgupta and G. M. Heal, *Economic Theory and Exhaustible Resources* (Cambridge, England: Cambridge University Press, 1979), pp. 269–281.

47. See note 65. This suggestion is analogous to requiring more than one data set for the evaluation of a particular risk. See, for example, D. Paustenbach, "A Survey of Health Risk Assessment," in Paustenbach, *Risk Assessment*, p. 104.

48. Pearce, *Valuation of Social Cost*, p. 132. This point is defended in great detail in Shrader-Frechette, "Technology Assessment," pp. 34–41.

49. Pearce, *Valuation of Social Cost*, p. 134.

50. This same point is made by A. M. Freeman, "Distribution and Environmental Quality," in *Environmental Quality Analysis*, ed. A. V. Kneese and B. T. Bower (Baltimore: Johns Hopkins University Press, 1972), pp. 247–248; and by Shrader-Frechette, "Technology Assessment," pp. 35–37.

51. The economist B. A. Weisbrod maintained that *all* public projects that are adopted, despite their failure to be vindicated by classical (not ethically weighted) RCBA, are implemented because of an implicit set of utility *weights* attached by the political process. If this is true, then it makes sense to inform the political process by supplying it with a number of alternative, explicitly weighted RCBAs among which the public can decide. See K. Basu, *Revealed Preferences of Government* (Cambridge, England: Cambridge University Press, 1980), p. 23.

52. See D. MacLean, "Risk and Consent," in MacLean, *Values at Risk*, pp. 22–23. See the discussion of revealed preferences, along with other RCBA methods, in Chapter Four.

53. See Basu, *Revealed Preferences*, esp. chap. 9. See previous note.

54. J. S. Mill, *Utilitarianism*, in *John Stuart Mill*, ed. M. Warnock (New York: Meridian, 1962), p. 310; see also p. 321.

55. B. A. Weisbrod, "Income Redistribution Effects and Benefit-Cost Analysis," in *Problems in Public Expenditure Analysis*, ed. S. B. Chase (Washington, D.C.: Brookings Institution, 1967), pp. 177–208. See also P. Dasgupta, S. Marglin, and A. K. Sen, *Guidelines for Project Evaluation*, Project Formulation and Evaluation Series, no. 2 (New York: United Nations Industrial Development Organization, 1972). See R. Haveman, "Comment on the Weisbrod Model," in Chase, *Public Expenditure*, pp. 209–222; Basu, *Revealed Preferences*, pp. 23–24; A. M. Freeman, "Income Redistribution and Social Choice: A Pragmatic Approach," *Public Choice* 7 (Fall 1969): 3–22; E. J. Mishan, "Flexibility and Consistency in

Project Evaluation," *Economica* 41, no. 161 (1974): 81–96; and R. A. Musgrave, "Cost-Benefit Analysis and the Theory of Public Finance," in *Cost-Benefit Analysis*, ed. R. Layard (Baltimore: Penguin, 1972), pp. 101–116. See also Cox and Ricci, "Legal and Philosophical Aspects," pp. 1038–1039.

56. Kneese and his associates stipulate that the general criteria representing alternative ethical systems be *transitive*, so as to avoid the consequences of Arrow's famous Impossibility Theorem.

57. A. V. Kneese, S. Ben-David, and W. D. Schulze, "The Ethical Foundations of Benefit-Cost Analysis," in *Energy and the Future*, ed. D. MacLean and P. G. Brown (Totowa, N.J.: Rowman and Littlefield, 1982), pp. 59–74. See also "A Study of the Ethical Foundations of Benefit-Cost Analysis Techniques," unpublished report, done with funding from the National Science Foundation, Program in Ethics and Values in Science and Technology, August 1979.

58. Kneese, "Ethical Foundations," pp. 63–65; "Study of Ethical Foundations," pp. 13–23.

59. Kneese, "Study of Ethical Foundations," pp. 83–119.

60. See the next note for citations to my work on ethical weights, as proposed here. A lexicographic ordering is one in which the attributes of alternatives are ordered by importance, and the alternative is chosen with the best value on the most important attribute. If there are two alternatives of equal value, then this procedure is repeated for those alternatives in terms of the next attribute, and so on until a unique alternative emerges or until all alternatives have been considered. The lexicographic ordering on a set of tuples $(x_1, \ldots, x_n)$, where x_1 is an element of X_1 and X_1 is simply ordered by $=$, is defined as follows. $(a_1, \ldots, a_n) = (b_1, \ldots, b_n)$ if and only if

(i) $a_1 = b_1$, or

(ii) $(a_1 = b_1$ and $a_2 = b_2)$, or

$\ldots$

(n) $a_1 = b_1$ and $\ldots$ and $a_{n-1} = b_{n-1}$ and $a_n = b_n$.

A simple ordering on a set X is a relation (which may be denoted $=$) having the properties

(i) for every a and b in X,
either $a = b$ or $b = a$ (comparability);

(ii) for every a, b, and c in X,
if $a = b$ and $b = c$,
then $a = c$ (transitivity).

As Kneese recognizes, a list of transitive, lexicographically ordered rules would have to be treated as a set of mathematically specified constraints on the outcomes of a particular RCBA. The big advantage of such a system is that it would allow one to order social situations on the basis of the relative priority of ethical claims, without requiring that all the different types of considerations relevant to a choice be collapsed into one dimension, such as utility, equity, or merit. See K. R. MacCrimmon and D. A. Wehrung, "Trade-off Analysis," in *Conflicting Objectives in Decisions*, ed. D. Bell, R. Keeney, and H. Raiffa (New York: Wiley, 1977), p. 143. See Kneese, "Ethical Foundations," pp. 62–63.

61. See K. S. Shrader-Frechette, *Science Policy, Ethics, and Economic Methodology* (Boston: Reidel, 1985), chaps. 8–9. See also S. Stasnick, "Neo-Utilitarian Ethics and the Ordinal Representation Assumption," in Pitt, *Philosophy in Economics*.

62. E. Mishan, *Economics for Social Decisions* (New York: Praeger, 1972), p. 23. See also Mishan, *Cost-Benefit Analysis*, pp. 403–415.

63. A. J. Culyer, "The Quality of Life and the Limits of Cost-Benefit Analysis," in *Public Economics and the Quality of Life*, ed. L. Wingo and A. Evans (Baltimore: Johns Hopkins University Press, 1977), pp. 143, 150, 151. See Andrews, "Environmental Impact Assessment."

64. See note 60.

65. See R. F. Mikesell, *The Rate of Discount for Evaluating Public Projects* (Washington, D.C.: American Enterprise Institute for Public Policy Research, 1977). See also Mishan, *Cost-Benefit Analysis*, pp. 175–219, 408–410.

66. See, for example, Chapter Eight. See also L. Cox, "Comparative Risk Measures," in Woodhead, *Phenotypic Variation*, pp. 233–243.

67. See Chapters Three through Five.

68. See Chapters Six through Ten.

69. See Chapter Three.

70. Ackerman (see *Search for Environmental Quality*, pp. 9–78) is one environmental writer who makes such an assumption; see Latin, "Ideal versus Real Regulatory Efficiency," pp. 1276ff. See Andrews, "Environmental Impact Assessment."

71. Latin, "Ideal versus Real Regulatory Efficiency," pp. 1274–1283.

72. Ibid., p. 1274.

73. L. Cox and P. Ricci, "Risk, Uncertainty, and Causation," in Paustenbach, *Risk Assessment*, pp. 125–156. See also R. Cortesi, "Variation in Individual Response," in Woodhead, *Phenotypic Variation*, pp. 281–284. See R. Setlow, "Relevance of Phenotypic Variation in Risk," in Woodhead, *Phenotypic Variation*, pp. 1–5. Finally, see V. N. Houk et al., Executive Committee, Department of Health and Human Services (DHHS) Committee to Coordinate Environmental and Related Programs (CCERP), *Risk Assessment and Risk Management of Toxic Substances: A Report to the Secretary* (Washington, D.C.: Department of Health and Human Services, April 1985), pp. 22–28.

74. See Latin, "Ideal versus Real Regulatory Efficiency," pp. 1308–1309. See the previous note.

75. For examples of this point, see H. Leung and D. Paustenbach, "Assessing Health Risks in the Workplace," and R. Golden and N. Karch, "Assessment of a Waste Site Contaminated with Chromium," in Paustenbach, *Risk Assessment*, pp. 689–710, 577–598. See also H. Kunreuther et al., "A Decision-Process Perspective on Risk and Policy Analysis," in Lake, *Resolving Locational Conflict*, pp. 267ff.

76. The U.S. Department of Health and Human Services (DHHS), for example, has recommended that "the available options and their drawbacks should be made public knowledge" and that doing different hazard evaluations of the same chemical, for example, is very important (Houk, *Risk Assessment*, p. 32). See Cox and Ricci, "Risk Measures," p. 153.

77. See R. Cooke, *Subjective Probability and Expert Opinion* (New York: Oxford University Press, 1991), chap. 9.

78. See Houk, *Risk Assessment*, p. 33.

79. For discussion of problems with subjective probabilities, see Chapter Eight and I. Hacking, "Culpable Ignorance of Interference Effects," in MacLean, *Values at Risk*. For the nuclear risk probability, see K. S. Shrader-Frechette, *Nuclear Power and Public Policy* (Boston: Reidel, 1983), pp. 84–85.

80. Cooke, *Subjective Probability*, chap. 2.

81. U.S. Nuclear Regulatory Commission, *Reactor Safety Study: An Assessment of Accident Risks in U.S. Commercial Nuclear Power Plants*, NUREG-75/014, WASH-1400 (Washington, D.C.: Government Printing Office, 1975), pp. 157ff. This figure is also a per-year, per-reactor probability.

82. Cooke, *Subjective Probability*, chap. 9.

83. See Pickard, Lowe, and Garrick, Inc., *Methodology for Probabilistic Risk Assessment of Nuclear Power Plants* (Irvine, Calif.: University of California Press, 1981); G. Apostolakis, "The Broadening of Failure Rate Distributions in Risk Analysis: How Good Are the Experts?" *Risk Analysis* 5, no. 2 (1985); J. Van Steen, "Expert Opinion Use for Probability Assessment in Safety Studies," *European Journal of Operational Research* (1986). Finally, see R. Cooke, M. Mendel, and W. Thijs, "Calibration and Information in Expert Resolution," unpublished manuscript, available from R. Cooke, Technical University of Delft, Netherlands.

84. See, for example, Morgan et al., *Technological Uncertainty in Policy Analysis* (Pittsburgh: Carnegie-Mellon University Press, 1982).

85. See, for example, Murphy and Winkler, "Can Weather Forecasters Formulate Reliable Probability Forecasts of Precipitation and Temperature?" *National Weather Digest* 2, no. 1 (1977): 2–9.

86. Cooke, *Subjective Probability*, chap. 9.

87. See A. C. Michalos, *Foundations of Decisionmaking* (Ottawa: Canadian Library of Philosophy, 1978), p. 160; see also pp. 156ff.

88. See note 79.

89. See B. Williams, *Ethics and the Limits of Philosophy* (Cambridge, Mass.: Harvard University Press, 1985), pp. 97–98.

90. The view that objective features of reality are those that are invariant under certain kinds of transformations goes back at least to Leibniz and remains central to science. Variance principles are central to both special and general relativity and to the work of many algebraists in this century.

91. For a similar view, see D. G. Holdsworth, Ontario Hydroelectric, "Objectivity, Scientific Theories, and the Perception of Risk," paper presented to the Philosophy of Science Colloquium, University of Toronto, March 1983, pp. 3–9.

92. See Williams, *Ethics*, pp. 199–200. For suggestions in this regard, see Andrews, "Environmental Impact Assessment," and Cox and Ricci, "Legal and Philosophical Assumptions."

93. See D. G. Holdsworth, Ontario Hydroelectric, "Objectivity and Control," paper presented to the Philosophy Forum, University of Toronto, February 1985, pp. 7–11.

94. I am indebted to D. G. Holdsworth, Ontario Hydroelectric, for many insights that we share. See his "Rational Risk Assessment and the Illusion of Technique," paper presented at the University of Waterloo, 12 November 1986, pp. 7–10.

95. See Giere, "Technological Decisionmaking."

96. See H. Siegel, "What Is the Question concerning the Rationality of Science?" *Philosophy of Science* 52, no. 1 (December 1985): 525–528.

97. Except for the Hempel objection, all of them were made in private communication by the persons named.

98. C. Hempel, "Valuation and Objectivity in Science," in *Physics, Philosophy, and Psychoanalysis*, ed. R. Cohen and L. Lauden (Dordrecht: Reidel, 1983), p. 87.

99. Industry risk assessments of coke-oven emissions appeared to be biased, as were industry risk assessments of chromium, nitrilotriacetic acid, and dioxin. See, for example, Lave and Leonard, "Coke Oven Emissions"; Leung and Paustenbach, "Assessing Health Risks"; Golden and Karch, "Assessment of a Waste Site."

100. Andrews, "Environmental Impact Assessment," p. 94.

101. See Samuels, "Arrogance of Intellectual Power," pp. 116–119. See note 51.

102. See Cooke, *Subjective Probability*; Houk, *Risk Assessment*, p. 33; Nuclear Regulatory Commission, *Reactor Safety Study*, pp. 157ff.; and sources cited in notes 73 and 77–79.

103. T. Nagel, *The View from Nowhere* (New York: Oxford University Press, 1986), p. 81; R. Chisholm, *The Foundations of Knowing* (Minneapolis: University of Minnesota Press, 1982), pp. 61ff.

104. Someone might also object that this account of scientific proceduralism is Popperian and hence circular, in that it presupposes that the relevant criticism is rational, even though there is no non-question-begging criterion for determining when a criticism is rational. If it is not rational, then using it to test a

risk theory is also not rational. This additional objection fails because it ignores the argument (given in Chapter Three) that there is at least one *general*, universal goal or criterion of theory choice in science and risk assessment: explanatory power as tested by prediction. This means that criticisms of theories must be evaluated in terms of this criterion or goal, and that there is a basis for evaluating the rationality of theories and of criticisms of them.

Chapter Twelve

1. G. Hardin, "The Tragedy of the Commons," *Science* 162, no. 3859 (13 December 1968): 1243–1248.

2. See A. D. Tarlock, "State vs. Local Control of Hazardous Waste Facility Siting," in *Resolving Locational Conflict*, ed. R. W. Lake (New Brunswick, N.J.: Center for Urban Policy Research, Rutgers University, 1987), pp. 140–141. For discussion of the inverse tragedy of the commons, see E. Peelle, "Social Impact Mitigation and Nuclear Waste," statement to the Subcommittee on Rural Development, Senate Committee on Agriculture, Nutrition, and Forestry (Social Impact Assessment Group, Energy Division, Oak Ridge National Laboratory), 26 August 1980, p. 3.

3. See Chapters Two through Five in this volume.

4. See Chapters Six through Ten in this volume.

5. E. Peelle, "Risk-Benefit Perception," paper presented at the Battelle Human Affairs Research Center, Seattle, 6 August 1987; Peelle points out that the "DAD" strategy was used as recently as 1985, in connection with the siting of the Monitored Retrievable Storage facility in Tennessee.

6. For discussion of the disproportional distribution of public risks, see, for example, J. F. Short, "The Social Fabric at Risk," *American Sociological Review* 49, no. 6 (December 1984): 718.

7. See H. Latin, "Ideal versus Real Regulatory Efficiency: Implementation of Uniform Standards and 'Fine-Tuning' Regulatory Reforms," *Stanford Law Review* 37 (May 1985): 1267–1332, esp. 1309, 1329–1330. See also J. Trauberman, "Statutory Reform of Toxic Torts: Relieving Legal, Scientific, and Economic Burdens on the Chemical Victim," *Harvard Environmental Law Review* 7, no. 2 (1983): 177–296, esp. 183. For philosophical analyses of some of the problems associated with establishing causality in cases of environmental risk and harm, see J. J. Thomson, *Rights, Restitution, and Risk* (Cambridge, Mass.: Harvard University Press, 1986), pp. 154–251. See also P. Ricci and A. Henderson, "Fear, Fiat, and Fiasco," and R. Setlow, "Relevance of Phenotypic Variation in Risk," in *Phenotypic Variation in Populations*, ed. A. Woodhead, M. Bender, and R. Leonard (New York: Plenum, 1988), pp. 285–293 and pp. 1–5.

8. See Trauberman, "Statutory Reform," p. 187; and Thomson, *Rights*, pp. 157–158.

9. See Senate Committee on Environment and Public Works, 97th Cong., 2d sess., *Injuries and Damages from Hazardous Wastes* (Washington, D.C.: Gov-

ernment Printing Office, 1982), pp. 115–117; Latin, "Ideal versus Real Regulatory Efficiency," pp. 1309, 1329–1330; and Trauberman, "Statutory Reform," p. 187.

10. See P. Sandman, "Getting to Maybe," in Lake, *Resolving Locational Conflict*, pp. 338–339; see also Trauberman, "Statutory Reform," pp. 189–191, and Thomson, *Rights*, pp. 166ff.

11. See Latin, "Ideal versus Real Regulatory Efficiency," p. 1309; and Trauberman, "Statutory Reform," pp. 191–202. See also Thomson, *Rights*, pp. 66–77; and H. L. A. Hart and A. M. Honore, *Causation in the Law* (Oxford: Oxford University Press, 1959).

12. L. Cox and P. Ricci, "Legal and Philosophical Aspects of Risk Analysis," in *The Risk Assessment of Environmental and Human Health Hazards*, ed. D. J. Paustenbach (New York: Wiley, 1989), pp. 1017–1046. For AEC information, see K. S. Shrader-Frechette, *Nuclear Power and Public Policy* (Boston: Reidel, 1983), p. 12.

13. N. Abrams and J. Primack, "Helping the Public Decide," in Lake, *Resolving Locational Conflict*, pp. 77–79. See also Latin, "Ideal versus Real Regulatory Efficiency," pp. 1267, 1277, 1281–1287, 1298ff.; and Trauberman, "Statutory Reform," pp. 203–206. See Ricci and Henderson, "Fear, Fiat, and Fiasco," pp. 290–291, for examples of conflicts among advisory and regulatory agencies.

14. See *Sindell v. Abbott Laboratories*, 607 P.2d 924, 26 Cal. 3d 588, 163 Cal. Rptr. 132, esp. 136, 144 (1980). For a discussion of the DES (*Sindell*) case, see Trauberman, "Statutory Reform," pp. 210–211; and Thomson, *Rights*, pp. 192–224. For the FDA example, see Cox and Ricci, "Legal and Philosophical Aspects," pp. 1026–1027.

15. For information about the New Jersey siting act, see Sandman, "Getting to Maybe," pp. 325–337. For information on nuclear liability, see Shrader-Frechette, *Nuclear Power*, chaps. 4–5, pp. 73–135. See also Trauberman, "Statutory Reform," pp. 211–212, and Thomson, *Rights*, p. 172.

16. See Trauberman, "Statutory Reform," pp. 235–236; see also Thomson, *Rights*, pp. 194, 211–212, for arguments about how and when to shift the burden of proof.

17. See, for example, *Mervak v. City of Niagara Falls*, 101 Misc. 2d 68, 420 N.Y.S. 2d 687 (Supreme Court 1979); *Yandle v. P.P.G. Industries*, 65 F.R.D. 566 (E.D. Tex. 1974); *Morrissy v. Eli Lilly and Co.*, 76 Ill. App. 3d 753, 394 N.E. 2d 830, 413 N.Y.S. 2d (New York App. Div. 1979).

18. See *Sindell v. Abbott Laboratories* (cited in note 12). See also Trauberman, "Statutory Reform," p. 236.

19. See Shrader-Frechette, *Nuclear Power*, chap. 4.

20. Bill Pease, of the Energy and Resources Group at the University of California, Berkeley, made this objection on 26 February 1988, at my lecture on risk reform.

21. Thomson, *Rights*, pp. 157, 206.

22. See Shrader-Frechette, *Nuclear Power*, chaps. 2, 4, 5.

23. Reckless or wanton misconduct by the plaintiff, however, could limit the defendant's liability, under the statute proposed by Trauberman. Admittedly, several problems would arise in applying any type of apportionment rule to large numbers of defendants. See Thomson, *Rights*, p. 209; and Trauberman, "Statutory Reform," pp. 213–216, 230–232.

24. For discussion of such cases of joint and several liability, see Thomson, *Rights*, pp. 209, 216–217; see also E. P. Jorgensen, "Joint and Several Liability for Hazardous Waste Releases under Superfund," *Virginia Law Review* 68, no. 5 (May 1982): 1168–1170.

25. See notes 14, 28, 29 for information about the *Sindell* case.

26. See, for example, Jorgensen, "Joint and Several Liability," pp. 1173–1185, esp. pp. 1184–1185.

27. In this regard, see P. Huber, "The Bhopalization of American Tort Law," in *Hazards: Technology and Fairness*, ed. R. W. Kates et al. (Washington, D.C.: National Academy Press, 1986), pp. 89–110.

28. See *Sindell* case as reported in 163 Cal. Rptr. 132–152; see also Trauberman, "Statutory Reform," pp. 232–233. For a philosophical discussion of the *Sindell* case, see Thomson, *Rights*, pp. 192–224.

29. See *Sindell* case in 163 Cal. Rptr., p. 144; see also 24 Cal. 2d 462, 150 P.2d 441; Restatement of Torts 2d, sec. 402A, comment c, pp. 349–350.

30. See Trauberman, "Statutory Reform," pp. 230–232.

31. See Thomson, *Rights*, pp. 192ff., 211ff., for discussion of burden of proof in such cases; see also Trauberman, "Statutory Reform," pp. 218–220. For problems regarding "statistical lives," see Cox and Ricci, "Legal and Philosophical Aspects," p. 1038.

32. See Shrader-Frechette, *Nuclear Power*, pp. 99ff.; Trauberman, "Statutory Reform," pp. 216–218.

33. See K. Goldberg, "Efforts to Prevent Misuse of Pesticides Exported to Developing Countries: Progressing beyond Regulation and Notification," *Ecology Law Quarterly* 12, no. 4 (1985): 1048ff.

34. See M. O'Hare, "Improving the Use of Information in Environmental Decision Making," in Lake, *Resolving Locational Conflict*, pp. 209–231; see also Trauberman, "Statutory Reform," pp. 191–192, 216–225.

35. See Jorgensen, "Joint and Several Liability," pp. 1157–1195, esp. pp. 1159–1162, for discussion of how the Superfund operates. See also Trauberman, "Statutory Reform," pp. 237–238. Finally, see C. Zamuda, "Superfund Risk Assessments," in Paustenbach, *Risk Assessment*, pp. 266–295.

36. See Trauberman, "Statutory Reform," p. 237.

37. See S. Raynor, "Risk and Relativism in Science for Policy," in *The Social and Cultural Construction of Risk*, ed. B. Johnson and V. Covello (Boston: Reidel, 1987), pp. 17–18.

38. See Chapter Six in this volume.

39. See Chapter Eleven in this volume.

40. See Tarlock, "State vs. Local Control," pp. 120–121. See also D. Morell, "Siting and Politics of Equity," in Lake, *Resolving Locational Conflict*, pp. 126–129. For discussion of issues of risk and consent, see D. MacLean, "Risk and Consent," in *Values at Risk*, ed. D. MacLean (Totowa, N.J.: Rowman and Allanheld, 1986), pp. 17–30.

41. See E. Mishan, *Technology and Growth* (New York: Praeger, 1969), pp. 38–39, and *The Costs of Economic Growth* (New York: Praeger, 1967), pp. 55, 128–129; see also Shrader-Frechette, *Nuclear Power*, pp. 120–129.

42. See Sandman, "Getting to Maybe," p. 325.

43. F. J. Popper, "Siting LULU's [locally unacceptable land uses]," *Planning* 47, no. 4 (1981): 12–15; E. Peelle and R. Ellis, "Hazardous Waste Management Outlook," *Forum for Applied Research and Public Policy* 2, no. 3 (September 1987): 68–77.

44. See H. Kunreuther, J. Linnerooth, and J. Vaupel, "A Decision-Process Perspective on Risk and Policy Analysis," in Lake, *Resolving Locational Conflict*, pp. 269–270. For discussion of negotiation, see Ricci and Henderson, "Fear, Fiat, and Fiasco," pp. 281–293; and Cox and Ricci, "Legal and Philosophical Aspects," pp. 1023–1026.

45. Peelle and Ellis, "Hazardous Waste Management." See G. Bingham, "Resolving Environmental Disputes," in Lake, *Resolving Locational Conflict*, pp. 319–321.

46. See L. S. Bacow and J. R. Milkey, "Overcoming Local Opposition to Hazardous Waste Facilities," in Lake, *Resolving Locational Conflict*, p. 163. See also E. Peelle, "Innovative Process and Inventive Solutions," p. 6, unpublished manuscript, 1986, available from Peelle at the Energy Division, Oak Ridge National Laboratory, Oak Ridge, Tenn. 37831. See E. Peelle, "Mitigating Community Impacts of Energy Development," *Nuclear Technology* 44 (June 1979): 132–140, esp. 133–134. See Peelle and Ellis, "Hazardous Waste Management."

47. See, for example, Tarlock, "State vs. Local Control," pp. 151–153.

48. For discussion of these issues, see, for example, Abrams and Primack, "Helping the Public Decide," pp. 79–84; S. Gusman, "Selecting Participants for a Regulatory Negotiation," *Environmental Impact Assessment Review* 4, no. 2 (1983): 195–202; M. O'Hare and D. Sanderson, "Fair Compensation and the Boomtown Problem," *Urban Law Annual* 14 (1977): 101–133; and A. C. Michalos, *Foundations of Decisionmaking* (Ottawa: Canadian Library of Philosophy, 1978), pp. 219–253.

49. E. Peelle, "Beyond the NIMBY Impasse II: Public Participation in an Age of Distrust," unpublished manuscript; abstract available from E. Peelle, Energy Division, Oak Ridge National Laboratory, Oak Ridge, Tenn. 37831. See D. Ducsik, "Citizen Participation in Power Plant Siting," in Lake, *Resolving Locational Conflict*, pp. 92ff., 103ff. See also Abrams and Primack, "Helping the Public Decide," pp. 89–90.

50. See Peelle, "Mitigating Community Impacts," pp. 134–135. For further case studies of successful negotiation at the community level, see Morell, "Siting," pp. 129–133.

51. In the Tennessee and Wyoming projects, for example, the utilities agreed to a number of safety measures recommended by the local community. In addition, they agreed to provide assistance or financial help for education, water and sewage systems, health and medical services, local government budgets, planning and coordination, and housing.

52. Peelle, "Mitigating Community Impacts," pp. 135–136. Local participation in the three risk-mitigation plans has been accomplished primarily through elected officials. For the importance of citizen control of hazard monitoring, see Sandman, "Getting to Maybe," p. 329.

53. Peelle, "Mitigating Community Impacts," pp. 136–138.

54. Ibid., p. 138. Compensating local communities for bearing some environmental or technological risk can take the form of either *ex ante* compensation or *ex post* compensation. Through *ex ante* compensation, risk imposers make payments in money or in kind at the time a hazardous facility, for example, is approved. Through *ex post* compensation, risk imposers reimburse particular individuals or groups who suffer losses from an injury or accident in the future. See Kunreuther, "Decision-Process Perspective," pp. 270–271. See also S. A. Carnes et al., "Incentives and Nuclear Waste Siting," *Energy Systems and Policy* 7, no. 4 (1983): 323–351; and Bacow and Milkey, "Overcoming Local Opposition," p. 166.

55. *Incentives* provide a benefit or reward apart from actual compensation for costs; they may include financial or in-kind payments, as well as political, environmental, or other benefits, such as local tax payments (Peelle, "Social Impact Mitigation," p. 10). See Bacow and Milkey, "Overcoming Local Opposition," pp. 164ff., for discussion of incentives.

56. See, for example, Shrader-Frechette, *Nuclear Power*, pp. 92–93.

57. For a discussion of intervention and alternatives to it, see Abrams and Primack, "Helping the Public Decide," pp. 88–89; and Ducsik, "Citizen Participation," pp. 94–95.

58. Carnes, "Incentives." Different people and different populations are likely to prefer different incentive packages. See Raynor, "Risk and Relativism," pp. 19–20. See also Bingham, "Resolving Environmental Disputes," pp. 319–321.

59. See Peelle and Ellis, "Hazardous Waste Management," pp. 76–77.

60. For a discussion of some of the particulars of arbitration and negotiation, see Tarlock, "State vs. Local Control," pp. 157–158; and Bacow and Milkey, "Overcoming Local Opposition," pp. 172–174. For a discussion of various mediation processes, their efficiency, and their success, see G. W. Cormick, "The Myth, the Reality, and the Future of Environmental Mediation," and G. Bingham, "Resolving Environmental Disputes," in Lake, *Resolving Locational Conflict*, pp. 302–313, 314–323.

61. See Peelle and Ellis, "Hazardous Waste Management," pp. 76–77; E.

Peelle, "The MRS Task Force: Economic and Non-Economic Incentives for Local Public Acceptance of a Proposed Nuclear Waste Packaging and Storage Facility," paper presented at the 1987 Waste Management Conference, Tucson, Ariz., 4 March 1987; available from E. Peelle, Oak Ridge National Laboratory, Oak Ridge, Tenn. 37831.

62. See also Ducsik, "Citizen Participation," pp. 96–113, for further consideration of some of these objections and evaluations of them.

63. This objection is formulated by Bacow and Milkey, "Overcoming Local Opposition," p. 165, among others. Regarding "trading lives for dollars," see D. MacLean, "Social Values and the Distribution of Risk," in MacLean, *Values at Risk*, pp. 85–88.

64. See Morell, "Siting," pp. 122–125; Bacow and Milkey, "Overcoming Local Opposition," pp. 161–163, 183; and L. Susskind and S. Cassella, "The Dangers of Preemptive Legislation," *Environmental Impact Assessment Review* 1, no. 1 (1980): 9–26. For a general account of various models for preemption, see Tarlock, "State vs. Local Control," pp. 141–146.

65. See Shrader-Frechette, *Nuclear Power*, for a defense of this point of view. For similar arguments, see Thomson, *Rights*, p. 172.

66. This objection was made by Bill Pease of the Energy and Resources Group (ERG) at the University of California, Berkeley, on 26 February 1988, in response to a lecture that I gave there.

67. Thomson, *Rights*, p. 172.

68. Those with years of experience in community dispute resolution maintain that health risk is the greatest concern of citizens discussing the location of a hazardous facility or the acceptance of some environmental danger. Citizens view safety as a precondition for discussion and are unwilling to make any trade-offs where their lives are concerned. (Sandman, "Getting to Maybe," pp. 333–334.)

69. See Peelle and Ellis, "Hazardous Waste Management," esp. its note 28; W. A. O'Connor, "Incentives for the Construction of Low-Level Nuclear Waste Facilities," in *Low Level Waste*, Final Report of the National Governors' Association Task Force on Low-Level Radioactive Waste Disposal (Washington, D.C.: Government Printing Office, 1980); E. Peelle, "Siting Strategies for an Age of Distrust," paper presented at the U.S. Department of Energy, Argonne National Laboratory, 30 June 1987, available from Peelle at the Energy Division, Oak Ridge National Laboratory, Oak Ridge, Tenn. 37831. See also Carnes, "Incentives," pp. 323–351; and E. Peelle, "Innovative Process and Inventive Solutions," p. 6, unpublished manuscript, 1986, available from Peelle at Oak Ridge.

70. See Chapter Nine in this volume.

71. See Thomson, *Rights*, pp. 157, 170–171.

72. Admittedly, however, the consequences of most societal risks rarely affect only a few people.

73. See MacLean, "Risk and Consent," pp. 17–30; see also K. S. Shrader-Frechette, *Risk Analysis and Scientific Method* (Boston: Reidel, 1985), chap. 4; Bacow and Milkey, "Overcoming Local Opposition," p. 165.

74. This response was made by Bill Pease of ERG at the University of California, Berkeley, on 26 February 1988, in a response to a lecture that I gave there.

75. In this latter case, one does not say that she has denied a gunman's right to free, informed consent when she takes away the gun that he wants to use to commit murder. The gunman's right to free, informed consent (to having his gun taken away) is limited by the equal rights of others to protection. Even in cases of environmental risk, one's rights to free, informed consent are balanced by the basic rights of other people to goods such as bodily security and equal treatment.

76. This objection was made by Bill Pease of ERG at the University of California, Berkeley, on 26 February 1988, in response to a lecture that I gave there.

77. Latin, "Ideal versus Real Regulatory Efficiency," pp. 1293–1295.

78. See K. S. Shrader-Frechette, *Science Policy, Ethics, and Economic Methodology* (Boston: Reidel, 1985), chap. 9.

79. K. G. Nichols and the OECD for Science, Technology, and Industry, *Technology on Trial* (Paris: Organization for Economic Cooperation and Development, 1979), p. 99.

80. Nichols, *Technology on Trial*, p. 100. In spite of these successes, citizen review panels have at least three deficiencies: (1) They ordinarily have no operating budget and hence are unable both to reimburse expert witnesses and to work toward a long-range plan for developing a cumulative base of information. (2) Without a required system of adversary proceedings, complete with cross-examination of expert witnesses from opposing sides, members of citizen review panels have been required to try to educate themselves with respect to the issues under consideration. (3) Like recourse to the legal system, use of citizen panels in major technology- or environment-related controversies is purely optional.

81. See note 78.

82. Although the feasibility of a variety of "soft" technologies needs to be substantiated on a case-by-case basis, it is possible to outline some of the arguments for feasibility. See, for example, C. Flavin and S. Postel, "Developing Renewable Energy," in *State of the World 1984*, ed. L. R. Brown et al. (New York: Norton, 1984), pp. 137ff.; C. Flavin, "Reforming the Electric Power Industry," in *State of the World 1986*, ed. L. R. Brown et al. (New York: Norton, 1986), pp. 105–116; C. Flavin and C. Polluck, "Harnessing Renewable Energy," in *State of the World 1985*, ed. L. R. Brown et al. (New York: Norton, 1985), pp. 180ff.; L. R. Brown, "The Coming Solar Age," in *Environment*, ed. J. Allen (Guilford, Conn.: Dushkin, 1985), pp. 61ff.; W. U. Chandler, "Increasing Energy Efficiency," in Brown, *State of the World 1985*, pp. 151–164. See *Energy Future*, ed. R. Stobaugh and D. Yergin (New York: Random House, 1979); and C. Flavin, "Reassessing the Economics of Nuclear Power," in Brown, *State of the World 1984*, esp. pp. 118–132.

Index of Names

Index of Subjects

Compositor: J. Jarrett Engineering, Inc.
Text: 10/12 Baskerville
Display: Baskerville
Printer and Binder: Maple-Vail Book Manufacturing Group